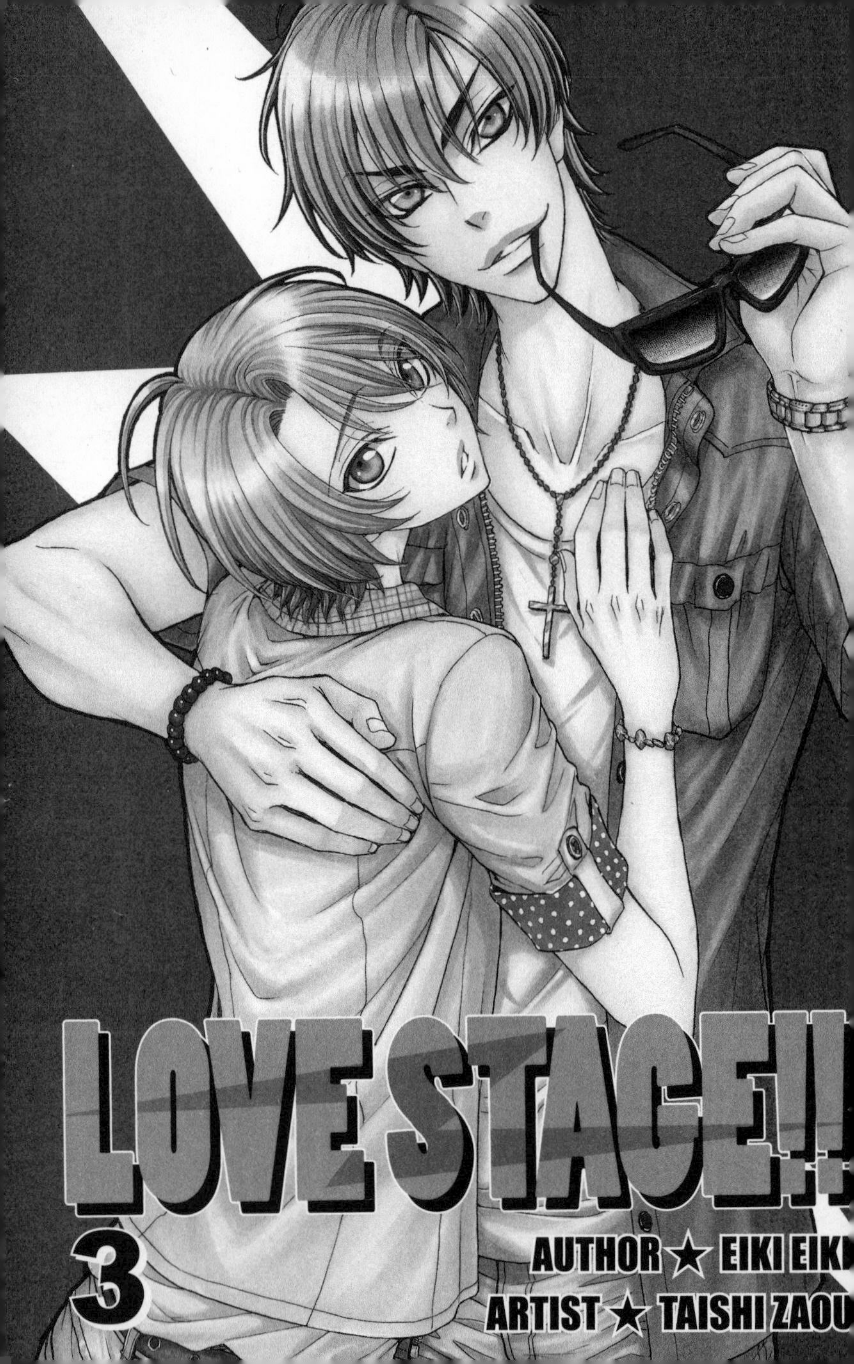
LOVE STAGE!!
3
AUTHOR ★ EIKI EIKI
ARTIST ★ TAISHI ZAOU

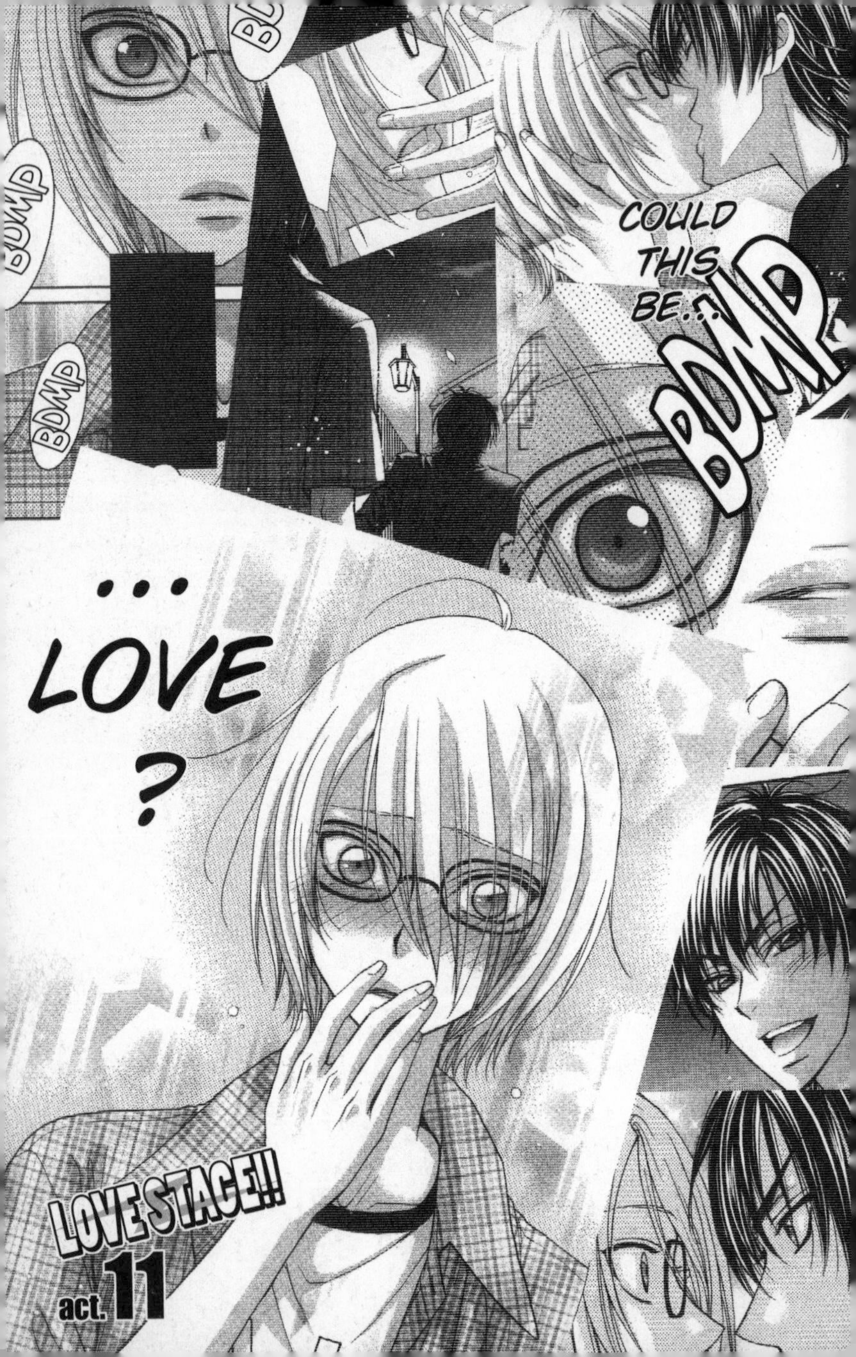
COULD THIS BE...
BDMP
BDMP
BDMP
BDMP
... LOVE ?
LOVE STAGE!!
act. 11

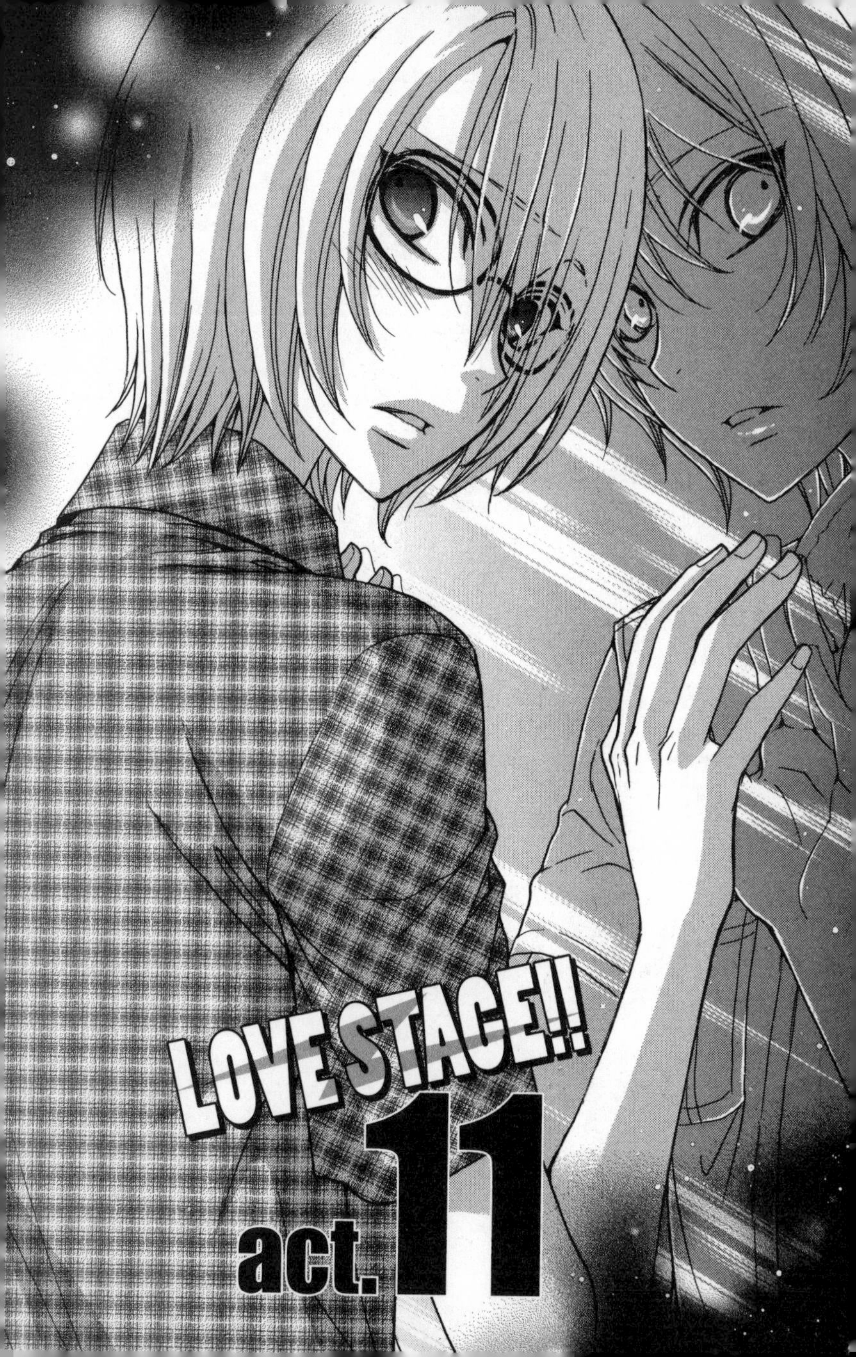
LOVE STAGE!!
act. 11

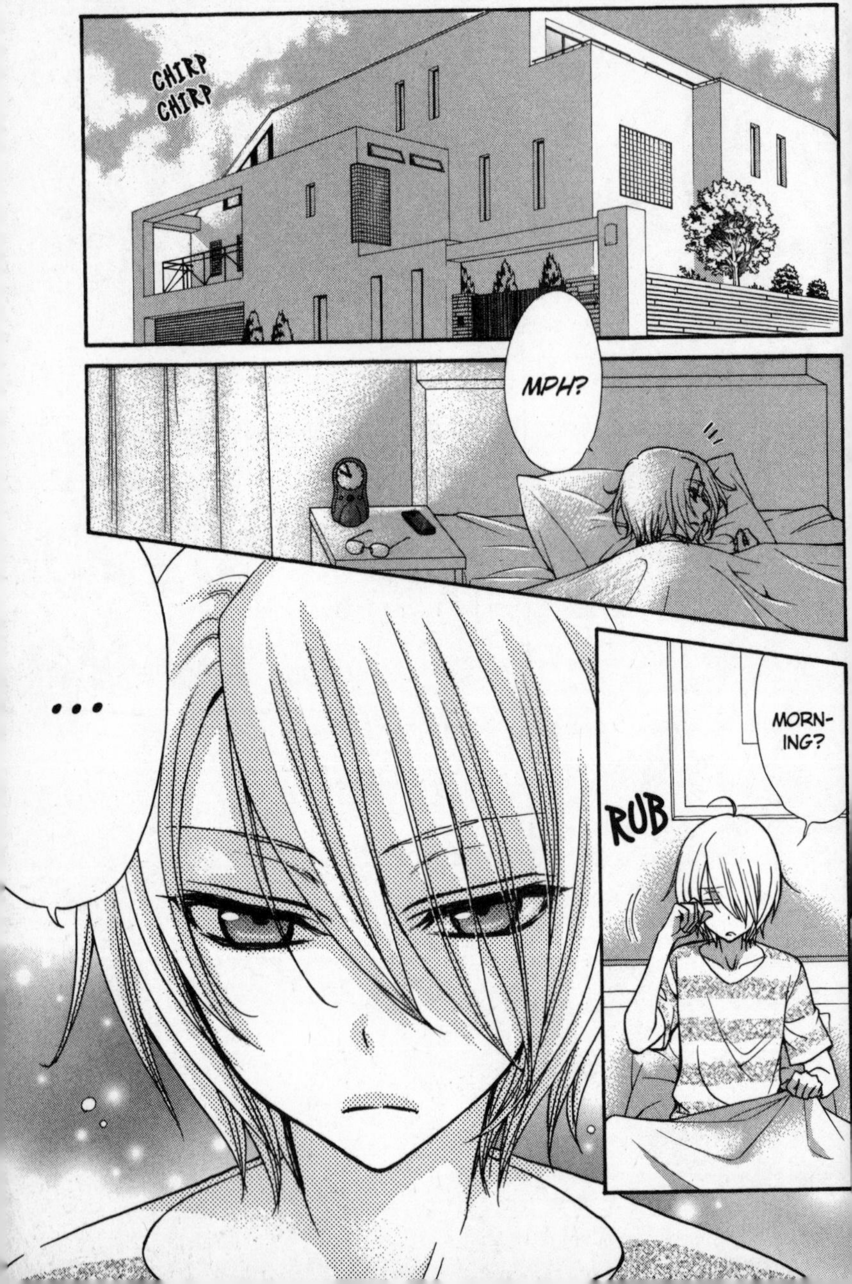
CHIRP
CHIRP
MPH?
MORN-
ING?
RUB
...

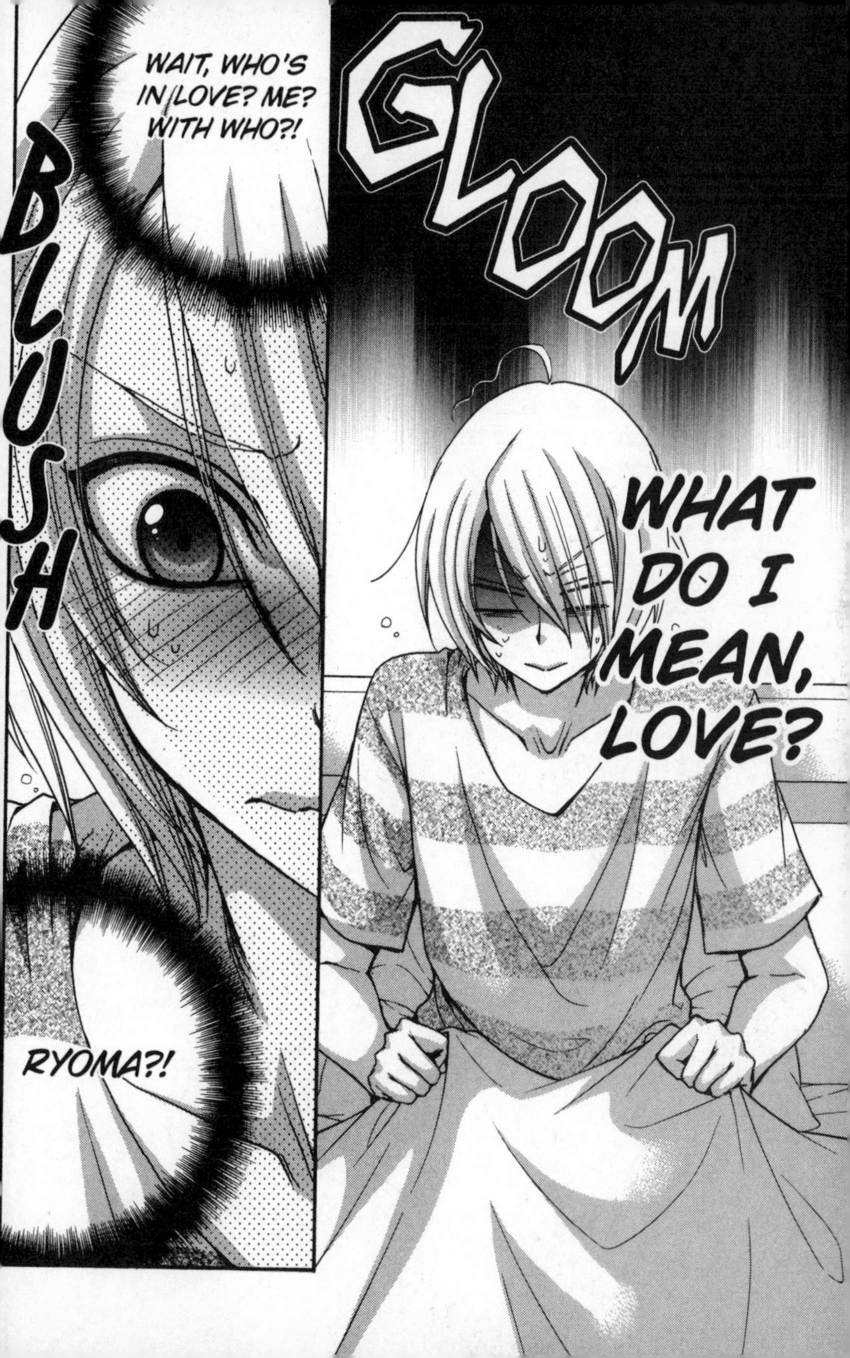
GLOOM
WHAT DO I MEAN, LOVE?
WAIT, WHO'S IN LOVE? ME? WITH WHO?!
BLUSH
RYOMA?!

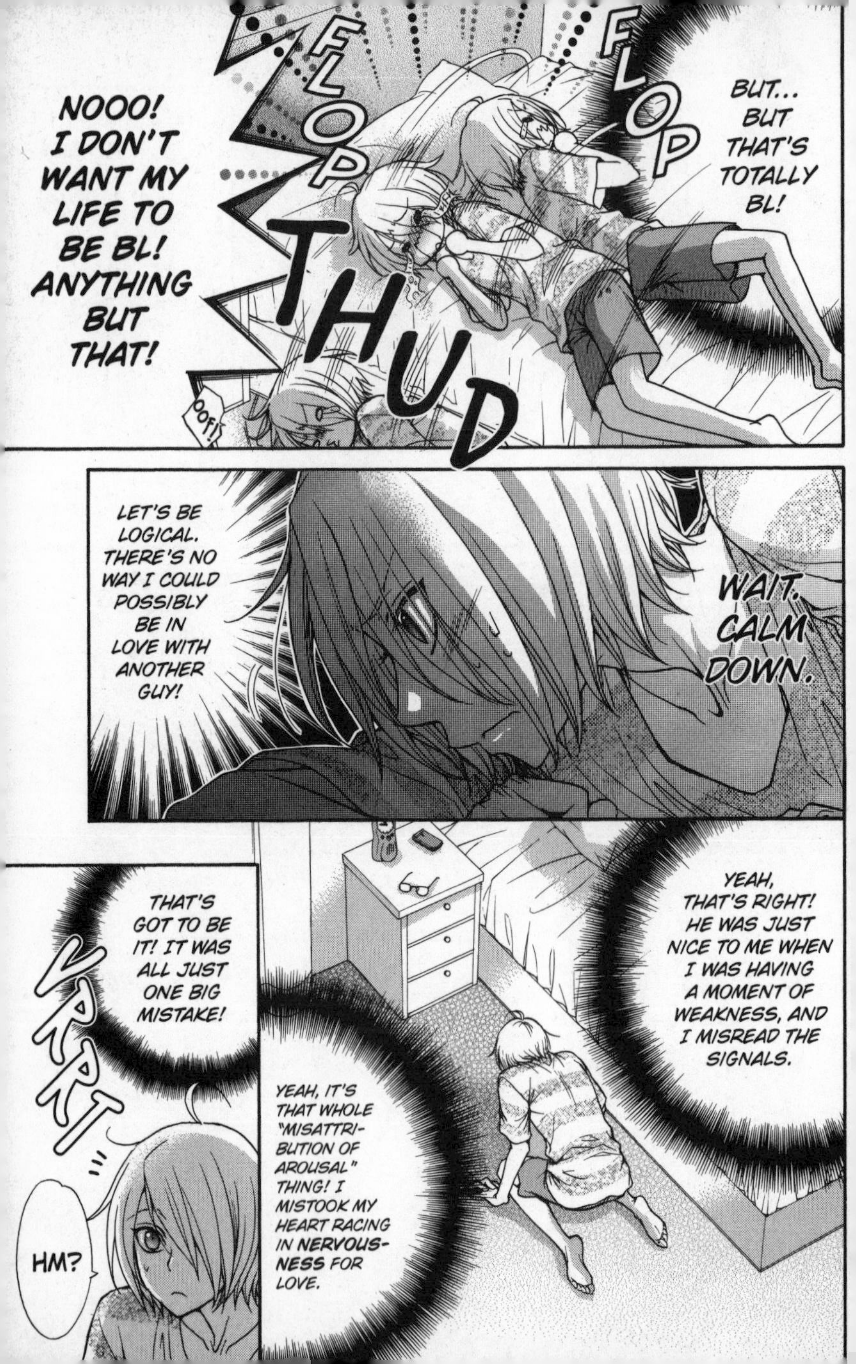
FLOP
BUT... BUT THAT'S TOTALLY BL!
FLOP
NOOO! I DON'T WANT MY LIFE TO BE BL! ANYTHING BUT THAT!
THUD
OOF!
WAIT. CALM DOWN.
LET'S BE LOGICAL. THERE'S NO WAY I COULD POSSIBLY BE IN LOVE WITH ANOTHER GUY!
YEAH, THAT'S RIGHT! HE WAS JUST NICE TO ME WHEN I WAS HAVING A MOMENT OF WEAKNESS, AND I MISREAD THE SIGNALS.
YEAH, IT'S THAT WHOLE "MISATTRIBUTION OF AROUSAL" THING! I MISTOOK MY HEART RACING IN NERVOUSNESS FOR LOVE.
THAT'S GOT TO BE IT! IT WAS ALL JUST ONE BIG MISTAKE!
VRRT
HM?

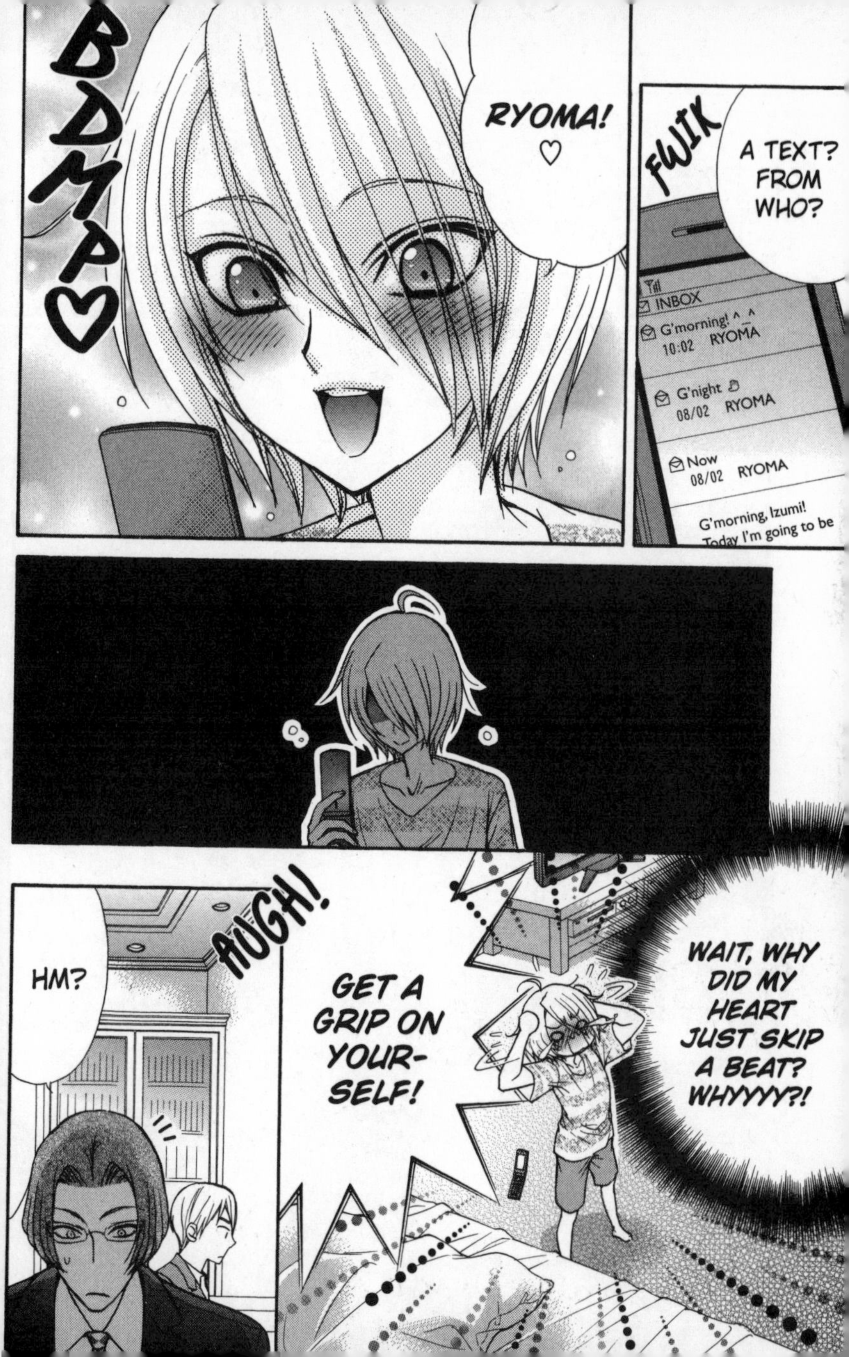
FWIK
A TEXT? FROM WHO?
INBOX
G'morning! ^_^
10:02 RYOMA
G'night
08/02 RYOMA
Now
08/02 RYOMA
G'morning, Izumi!
Today I'm going to be
BDMP♡
RYOMA! ♡
WAIT, WHY DID MY HEART JUST SKIP A BEAT? WHYYYY?!
AUGH!
GET A GRIP ON YOUR-SELF!
HM?

HE'S PROBABLY HAVING TROUBLE DEALING WITH HIS NERVES RIGHT NOW.

AH, WELL. I CAN'T SAY I DON'T UNDERSTAND IT.

YES, SIR. HE'S BEEN LIKE THAT EVERY MORNING SINCE HE CAME HOME.

WAS THAT SHOUT FROM IZUMI?

8 20×× AUGUST

SATURDAY MAGAZINE ON SALE!

水 WED	木 THU	金 FRI	土 SAT
1	2	3	4
8	9	10	11
	17	18	

AFTER ALL, TOMORROW IS HIS PRESS CONFERENCE FOR HIS DEBUT.

And so...

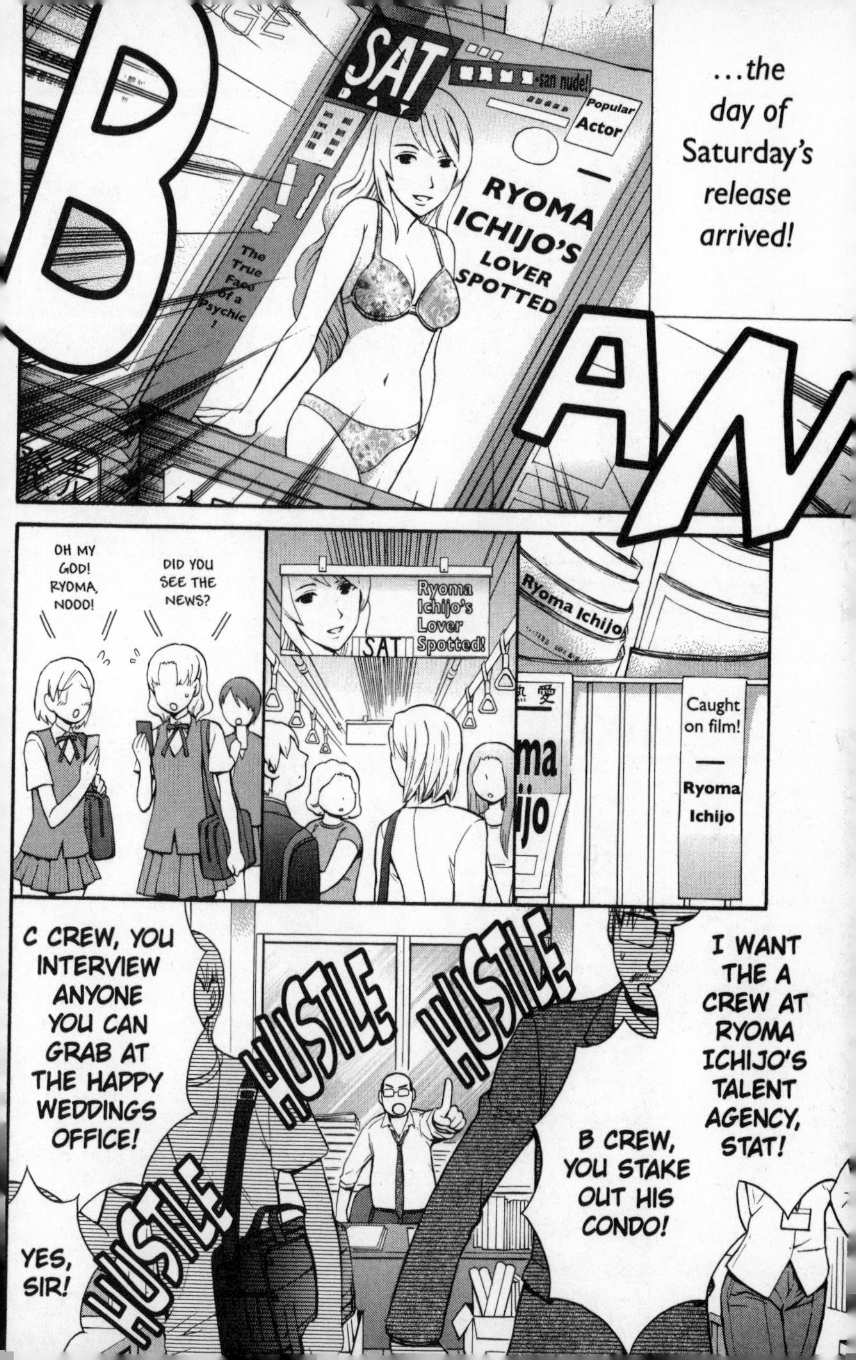
...the day of Saturday's release arrived!
SAT
-san nude!
Popular Actor
RYOMA ICHIJO'S LOVER SPOTTED
The True Face of a Psychic!
BAN
Ryoma Ichijo
Caught on film!
— Ryoma Ichijo
Ryoma Ichijo's Lover Spotted!
SAT
DID YOU SEE THE NEWS?
OH MY GOD! RYOMA, NOOO!
I WANT THE A CREW AT RYOMA ICHIJO'S TALENT AGENCY, STAT!
B CREW, YOU STAKE OUT HIS CONDO!
C CREW, YOU INTERVIEW ANYONE YOU CAN GRAB AT THE HAPPY WEDDINGS OFFICE!
HUSTLE HUSTLE HUSTLE
YES, SIR!

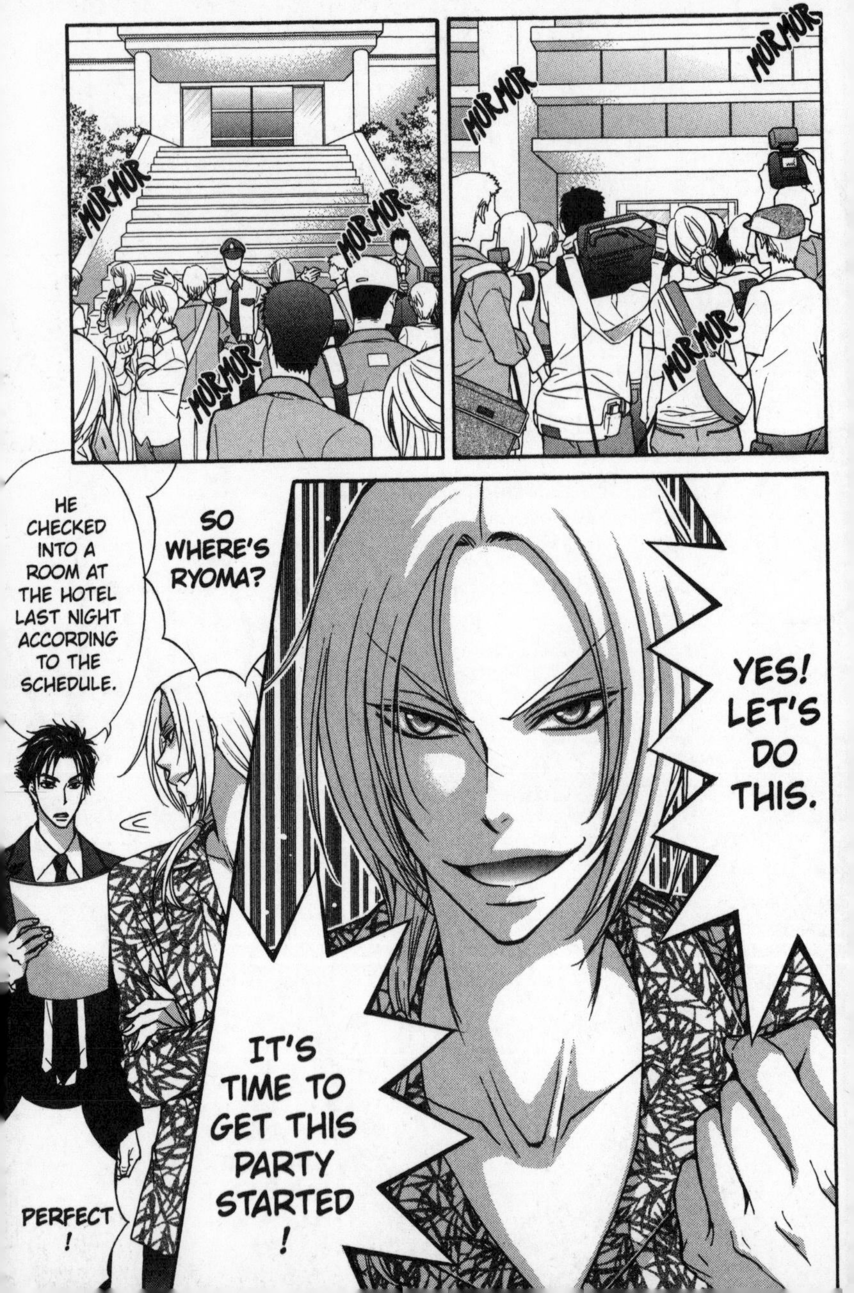
MURMUR
MURMUR
MURMUR
MURMUR
MURMUR
MURMUR
SO WHERE'S RYOMA?
HE CHECKED INTO A ROOM AT THE HOTEL LAST NIGHT ACCORDING TO THE SCHEDULE.
PERFECT!
YES! LET'S DO THIS.
IT'S TIME TO GET THIS PARTY STARTED!

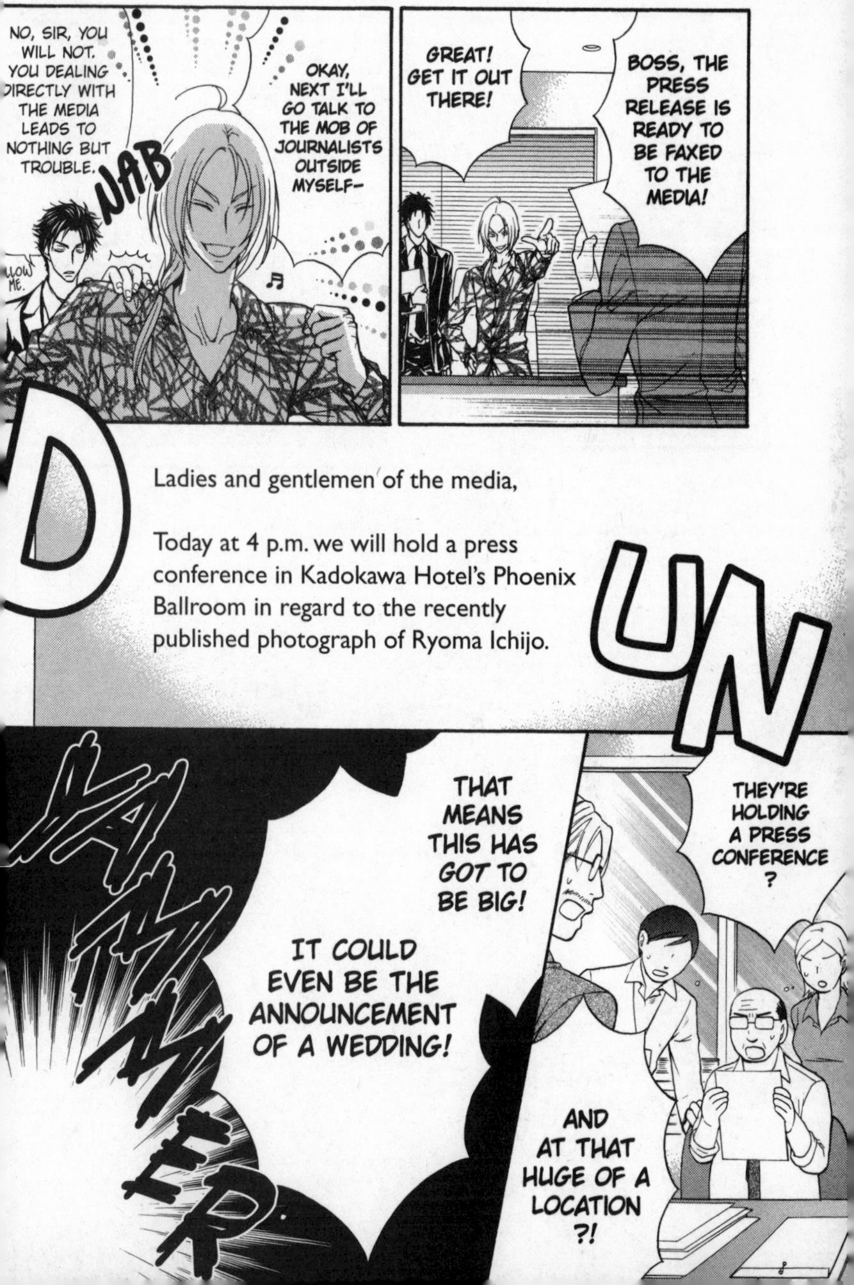
BOSS, THE PRESS RELEASE IS READY TO BE FAXED TO THE MEDIA!
GREAT! GET IT OUT THERE!
OKAY, NEXT I'LL GO TALK TO THE MOB OF JOURNALISTS OUTSIDE MYSELF–
NAB
NO, SIR, YOU WILL NOT. YOU DEALING DIRECTLY WITH THE MEDIA LEADS TO NOTHING BUT TROUBLE.
LLOW ME.
DUN
Ladies and gentlemen of the media,
Today at 4 p.m. we will hold a press conference in Kadokawa Hotel's Phoenix Ballroom in regard to the recently published photograph of Ryoma Ichijo.
THEY'RE HOLDING A PRESS CONFERENCE?
THAT MEANS THIS HAS GOT TO BE BIG!
AND AT THAT HUGE OF A LOCATION?!
IT COULD EVEN BE THE ANNOUNCEMENT OF A WEDDING!
YAMMER

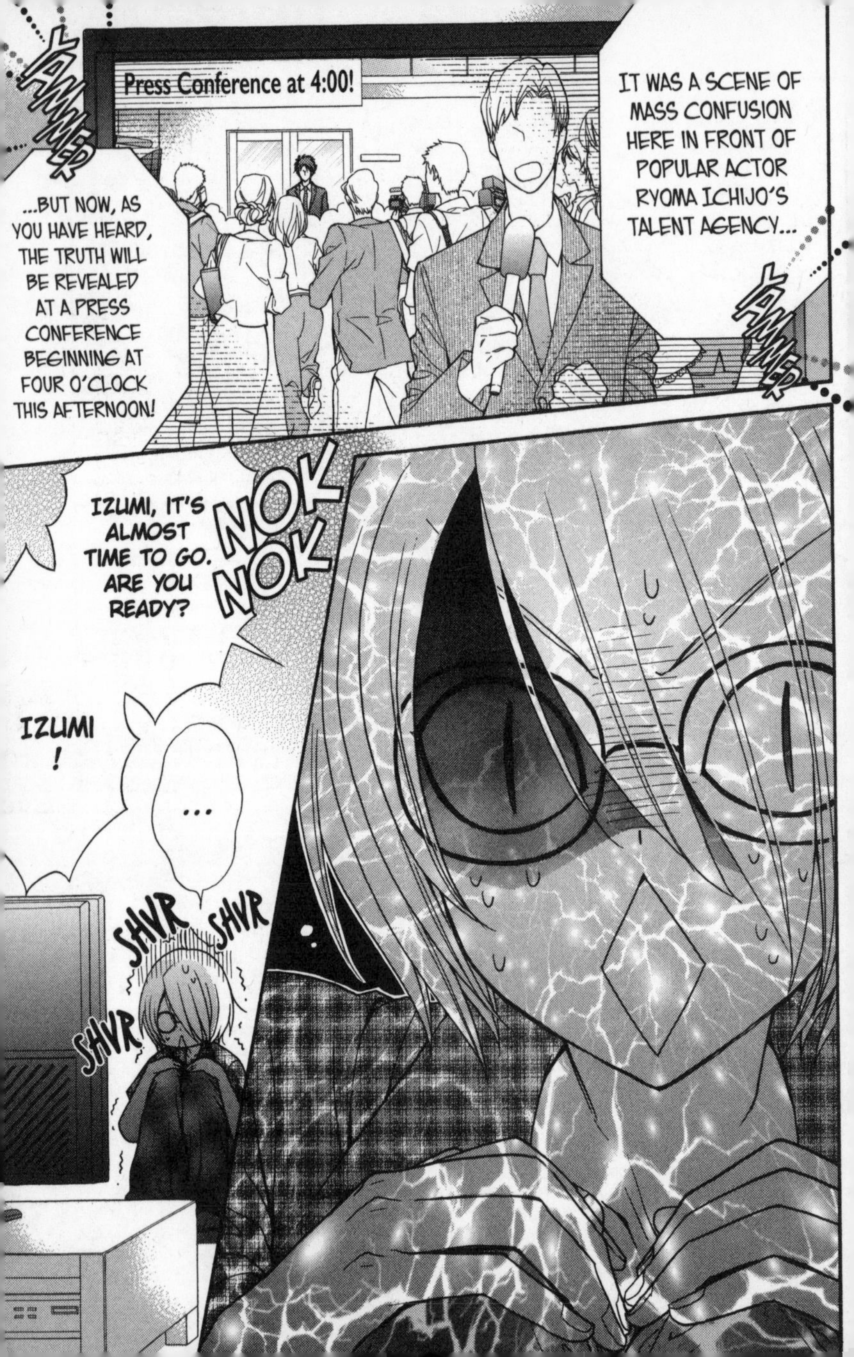
YAMMER
IT WAS A SCENE OF MASS CONFUSION HERE IN FRONT OF POPULAR ACTOR RYOMA ICHIJO'S TALENT AGENCY...
Press Conference at 4:00!
YAMMER
...BUT NOW, AS YOU HAVE HEARD, THE TRUTH WILL BE REVEALED AT A PRESS CONFERENCE BEGINNING AT FOUR O'CLOCK THIS AFTERNOON!
NOK NOK
IZUMI, IT'S ALMOST TIME TO GO. ARE YOU READY?
IZUMI!
...
SHVR SHVR SHVR

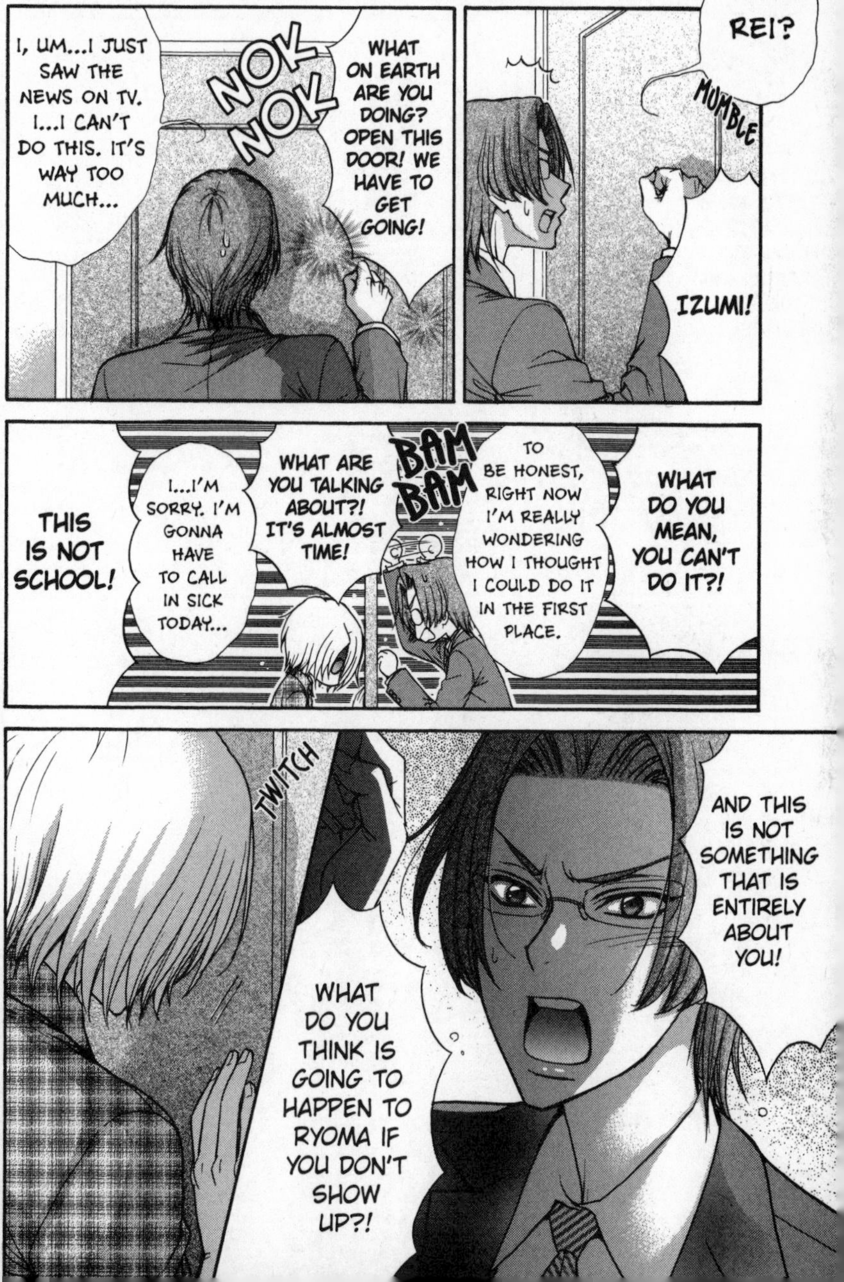
REI?
MUMBLE
IZUMI!
WHAT ON EARTH ARE YOU DOING? OPEN THIS DOOR! WE HAVE TO GET GOING!
NOK NOK
I, UM...I JUST SAW THE NEWS ON TV. I...I CAN'T DO THIS. IT'S WAY TOO MUCH...
WHAT DO YOU MEAN, YOU CAN'T DO IT?!
TO BE HONEST, RIGHT NOW I'M REALLY WONDERING HOW I THOUGHT I COULD DO IT IN THE FIRST PLACE.
BAM BAM
WHAT ARE YOU TALKING ABOUT?! IT'S ALMOST TIME!
I...I'M SORRY. I'M GONNA HAVE TO CALL IN SICK TODAY...
THIS IS NOT SCHOOL!
AND THIS IS NOT SOMETHING THAT IS ENTIRELY ABOUT YOU!
TWITCH
WHAT DO YOU THINK IS GOING TO HAPPEN TO RYOMA IF YOU DON'T SHOW UP?!

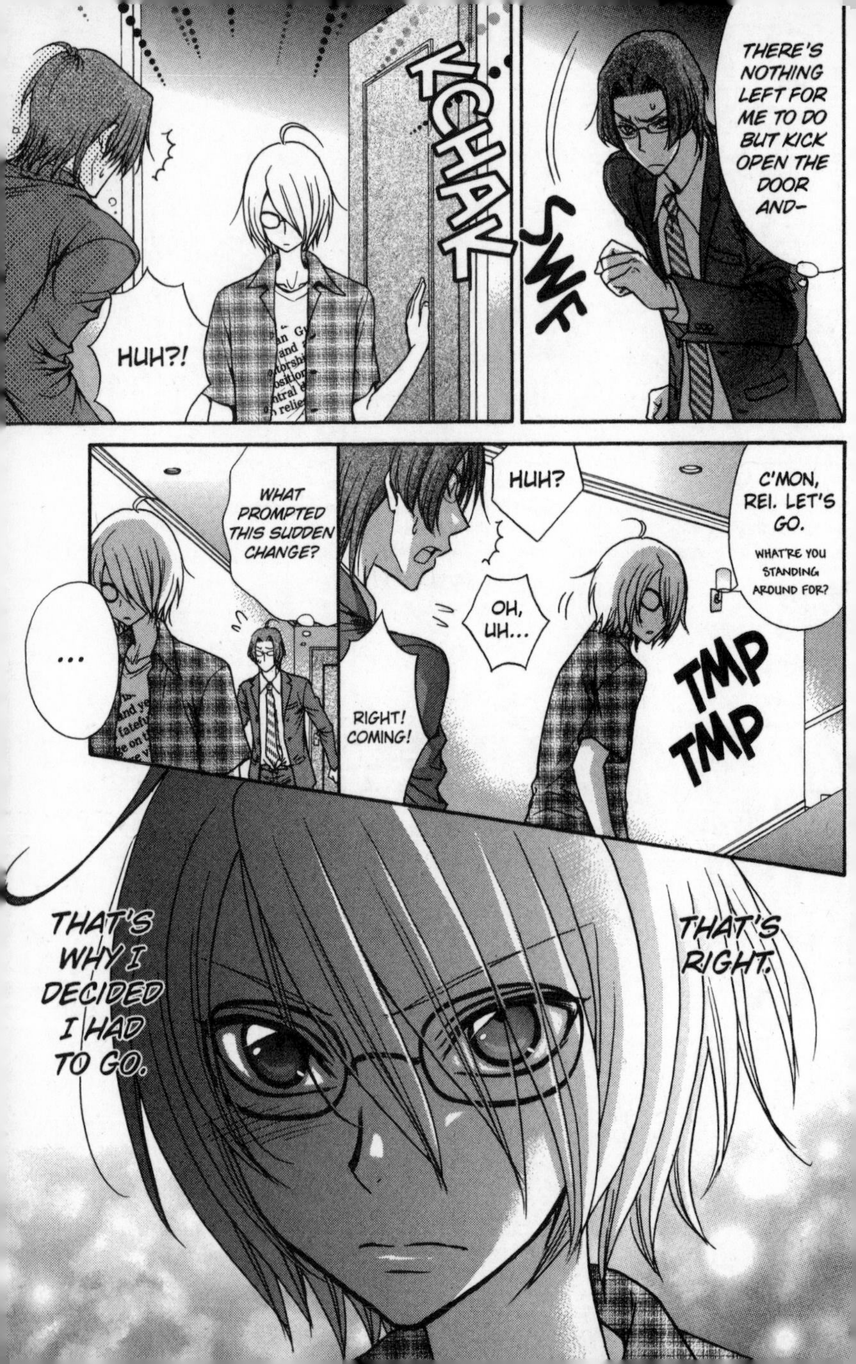
THERE'S NOTHING LEFT FOR ME TO DO BUT KICK OPEN THE DOOR AND-
SWF
KCHAK
HUH?!
C'MON, REI. LET'S GO.
WHAT'RE YOU STANDING AROUND FOR?
TMP TMP
HUH?
OH, UH...
RIGHT! COMING!
WHAT PROMPTED THIS SUDDEN CHANGE?
...
THAT'S RIGHT.
THAT'S WHY I DECIDED I HAD TO GO.

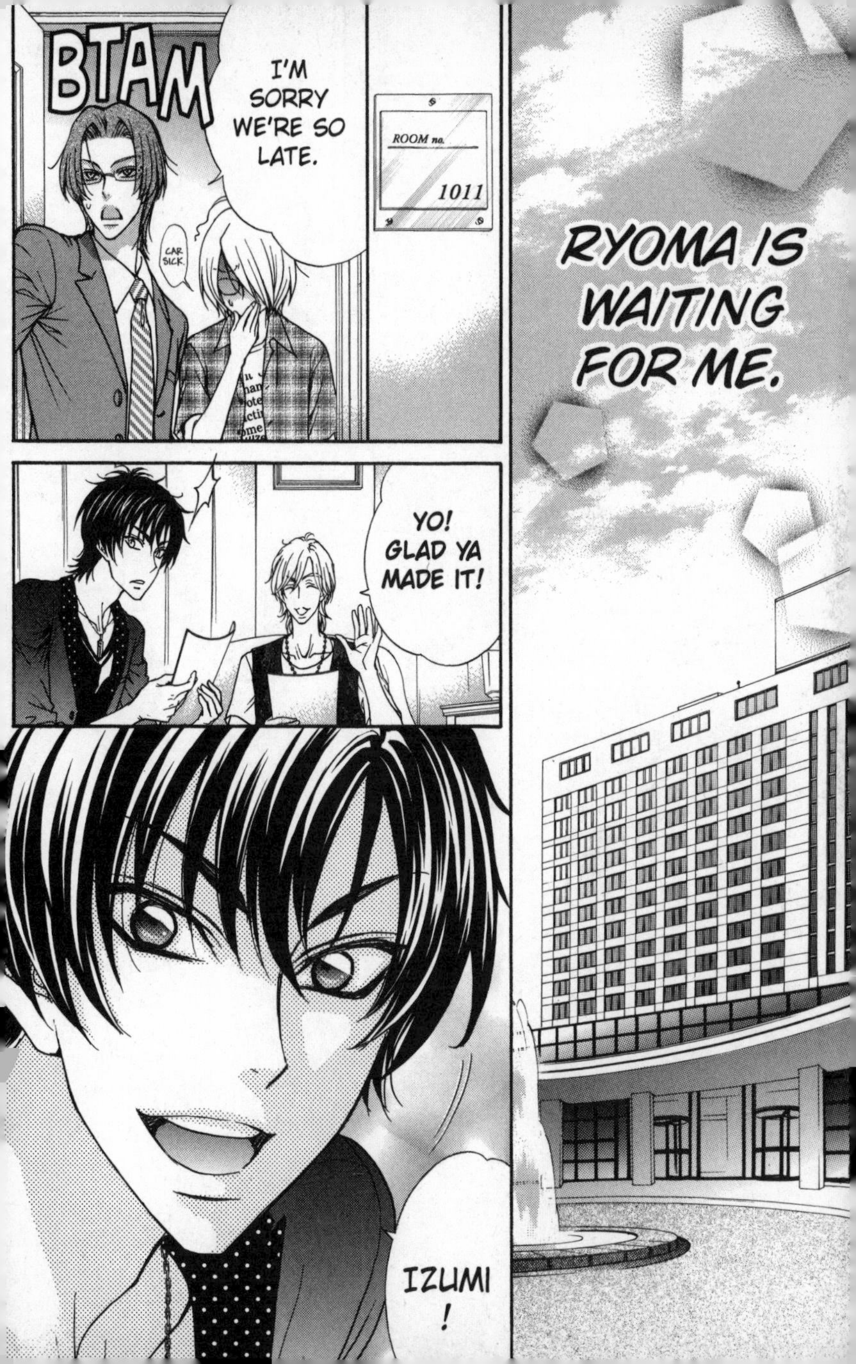
RYOMA IS WAITING FOR ME.
BTAM
I'M SORRY WE'RE SO LATE.
ROOM no.
1011
CAR SICK.
YO! GLAD YA MADE IT!
IZUMI!

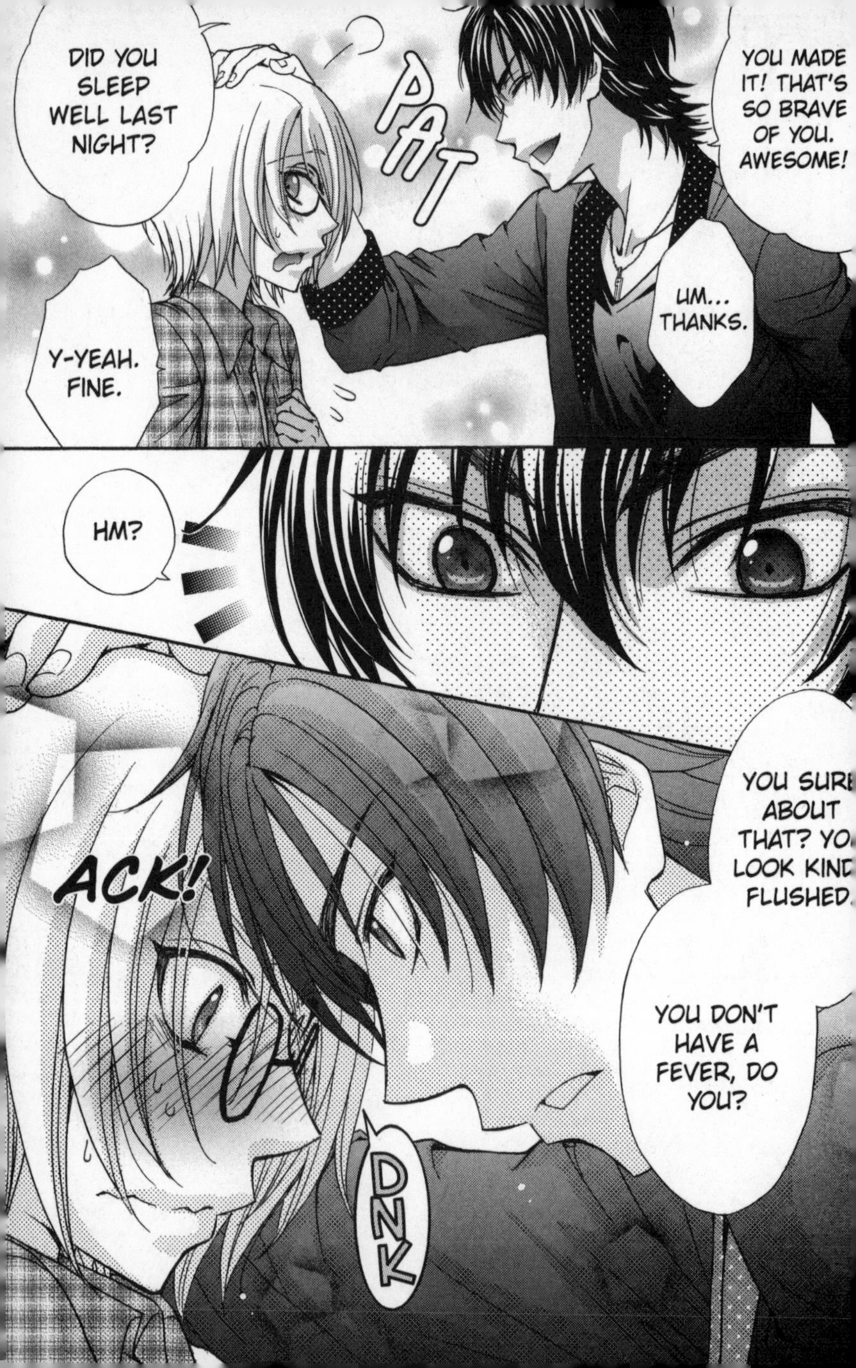
YOU MADE IT! THAT'S SO BRAVE OF YOU. AWESOME!
PAT
UM... THANKS.
DID YOU SLEEP WELL LAST NIGHT?
Y-YEAH. FINE.
HM?
YOU SURE ABOUT THAT? YO LOOK KIND FLUSHED.
YOU DON'T HAVE A FEVER, DO YOU?
ACK!
DNK

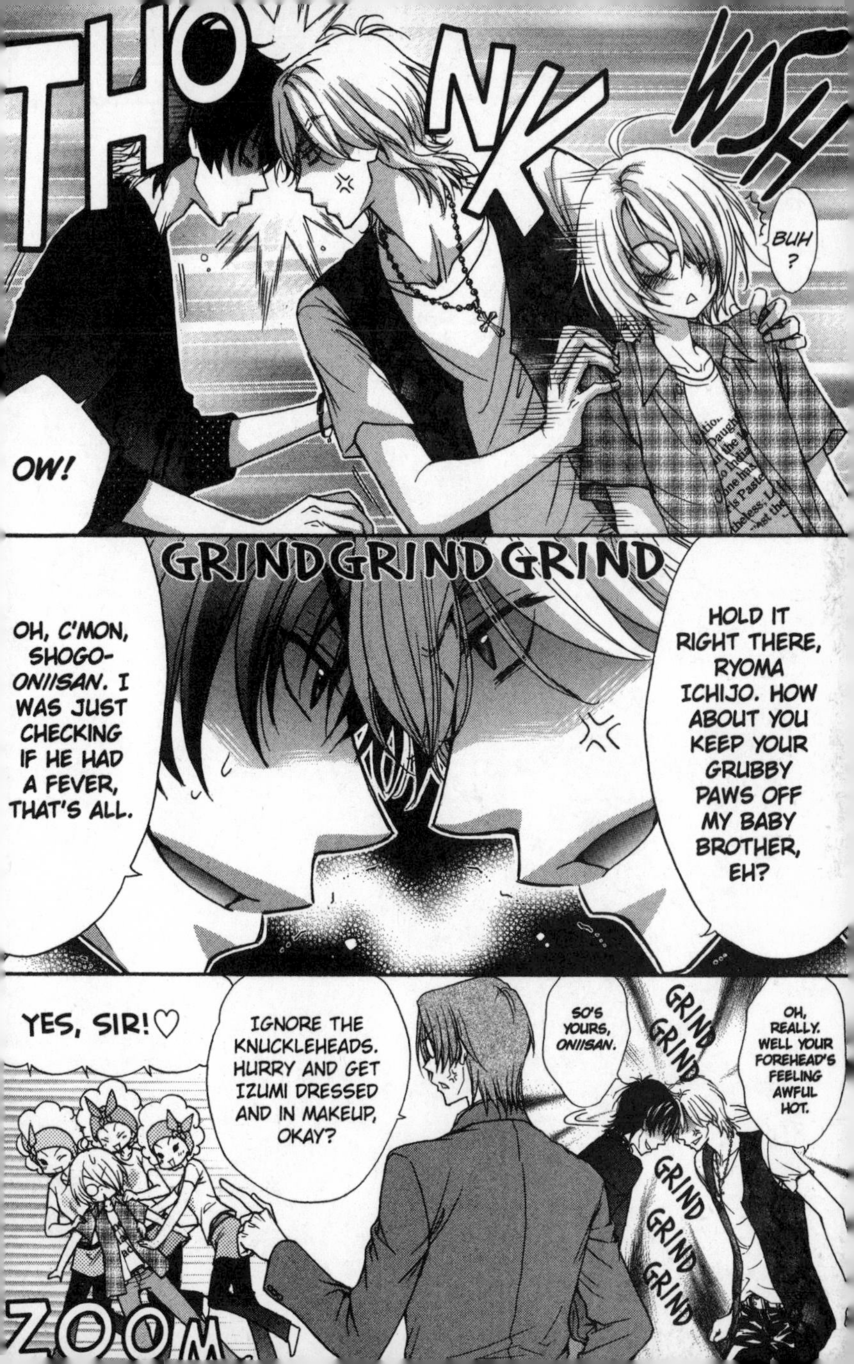
WSH
BUH?
THONK
OW!
GRINDGRINDGRIND
HOLD IT RIGHT THERE, RYOMA ICHIJO. HOW ABOUT YOU KEEP YOUR GRUBBY PAWS OFF MY BABY BROTHER, EH?
OH, C'MON, SHOGO-ONIISAN. I WAS JUST CHECKING IF HE HAD A FEVER, THAT'S ALL.
OH, REALLY. WELL YOUR FOREHEAD'S FEELING AWFUL HOT.
SO'S YOURS, ONIISAN.
GRIND GRIND GRIND
GRIND GRIND GRIND
IGNORE THE KNUCKLEHEADS. HURRY AND GET IZUMI DRESSED AND IN MAKEUP, OKAY?
YES, SIR!♡
ZOOM

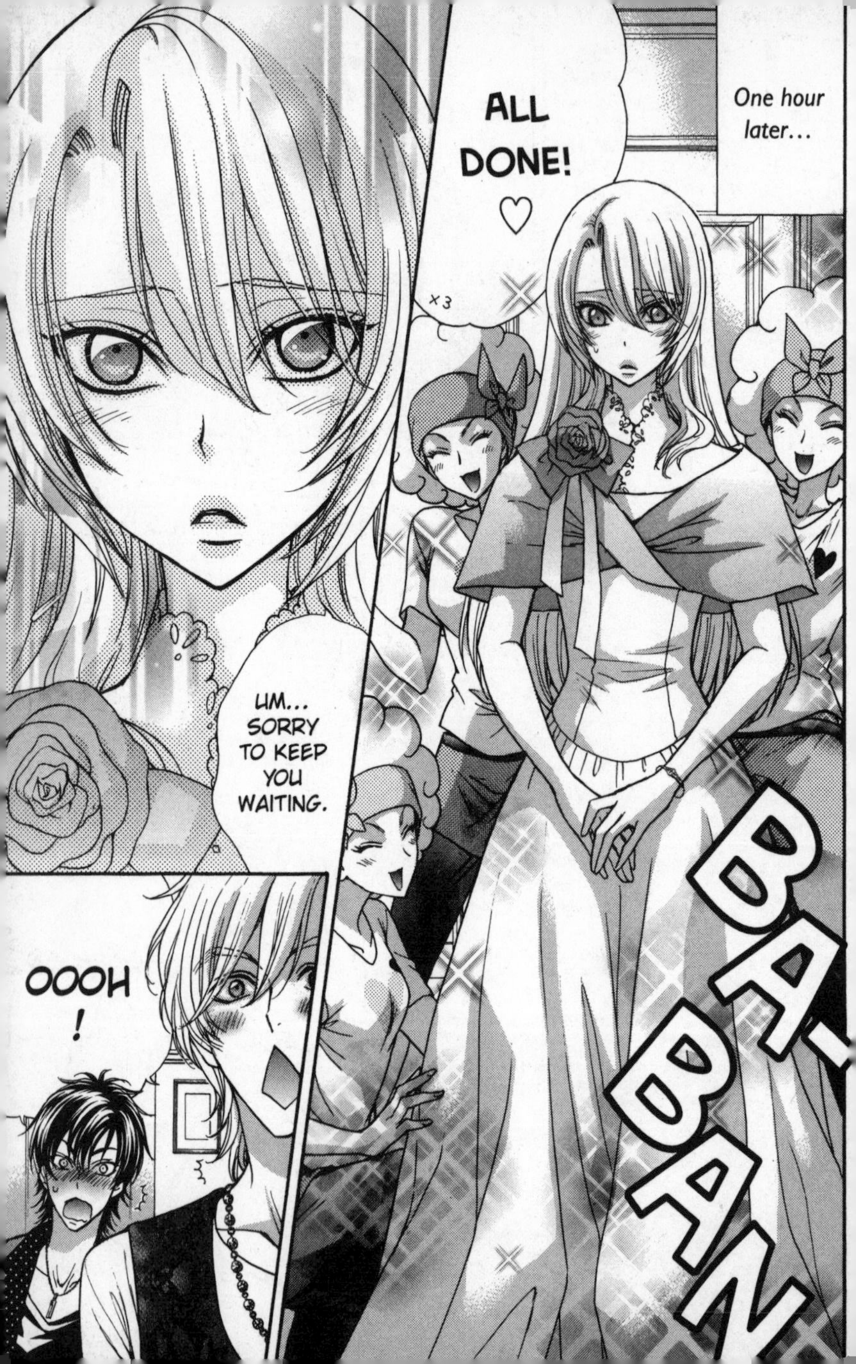
One hour later…
ALL DONE! ♡
×3
BA-BAN
UM... SORRY TO KEEP YOU WAITING.
OOOH!

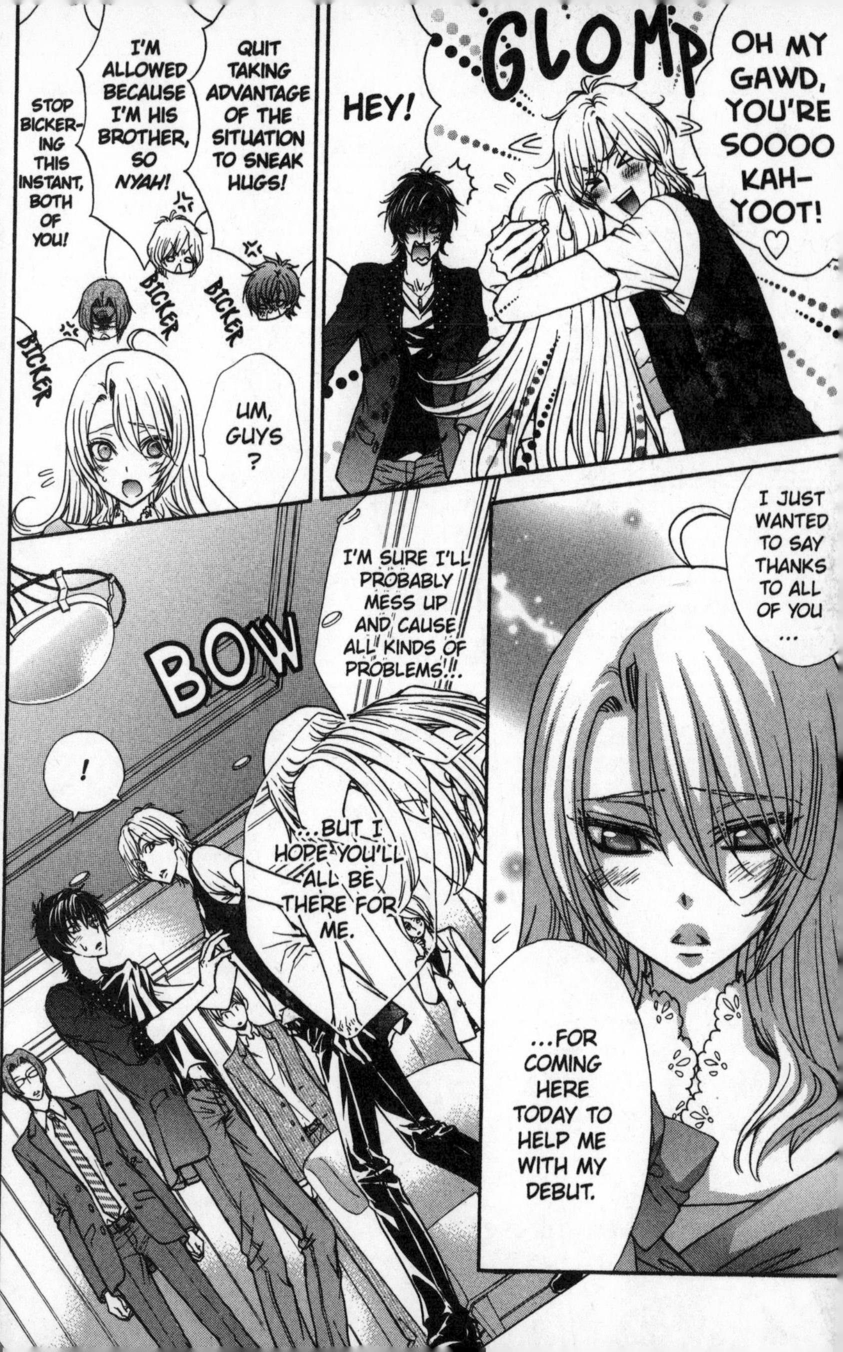

OH MY GAWD, YOU'RE SOOOO KAH-YOOT! ♥
GLOMP
HEY!
QUIT TAKING ADVANTAGE OF THE SITUATION TO SNEAK HUGS!
I'M ALLOWED BECAUSE I'M HIS BROTHER, SO *NYAH!*
STOP BICKERING THIS INSTANT, BOTH OF YOU!
BICKER
BICKER
BICKER
UM, GUYS?
I JUST WANTED TO SAY THANKS TO ALL OF YOU ...
...FOR COMING HERE TODAY TO HELP ME WITH MY DEBUT.
I'M SURE I'LL PROBABLY MESS UP AND CAUSE ALL KINDS OF PROBLEMS...
BOW
...BUT I HOPE YOU'LL ALL BE THERE FOR ME.
!

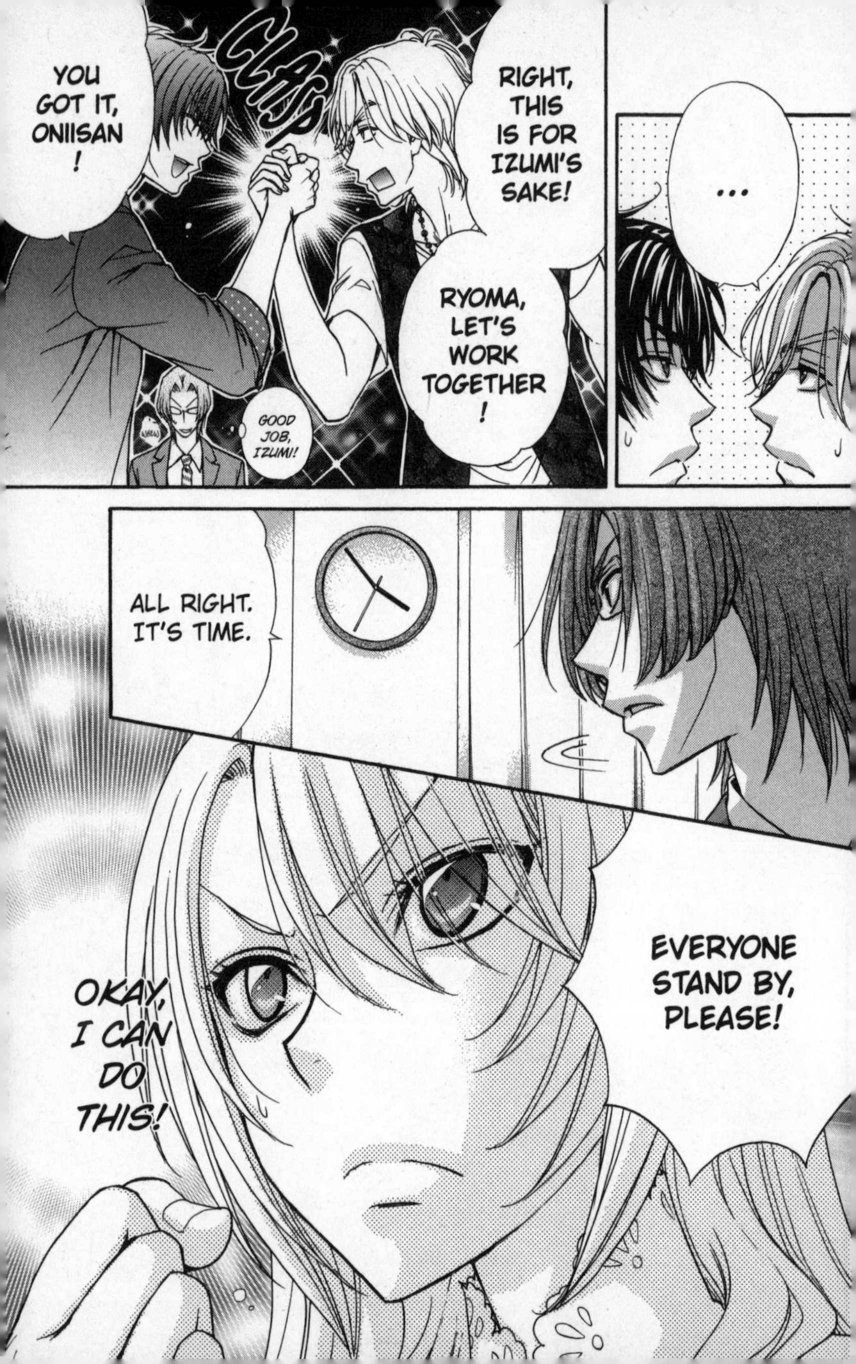
...
RIGHT, THIS IS FOR IZUMI'S SAKE!
CLASP
YOU GOT IT, ONIISAN!
RYOMA, LET'S WORK TOGETHER!
GOOD JOB, IZUMI!
ALL RIGHT. IT'S TIME.
EVERYONE STAND BY, PLEASE!
OKAY, I CAN DO THIS!

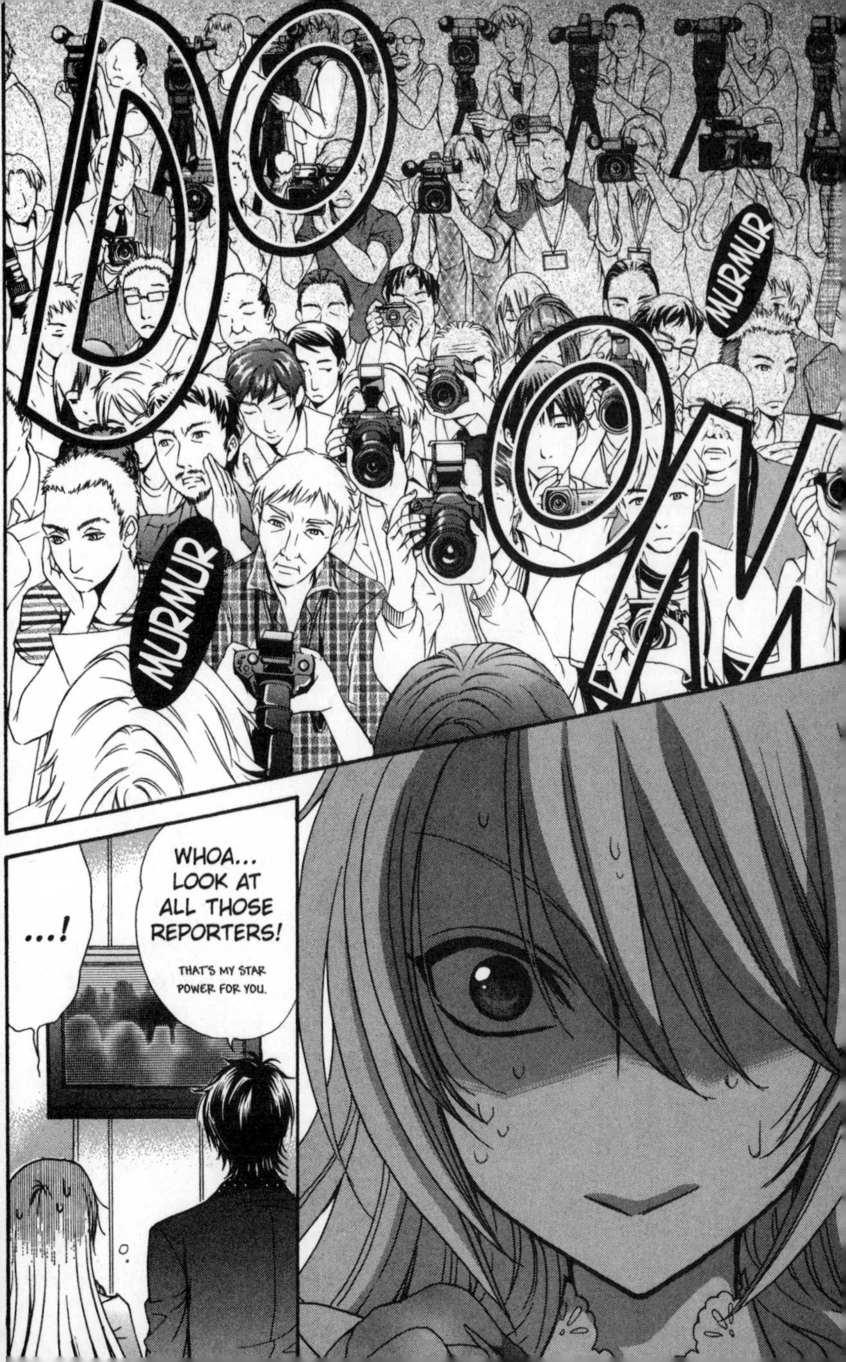
DOOM
MURMUR
MURMUR
WHOA... LOOK AT ALL THOSE REPORTERS!
THAT'S MY STAR POWER FOR YOU.
...!

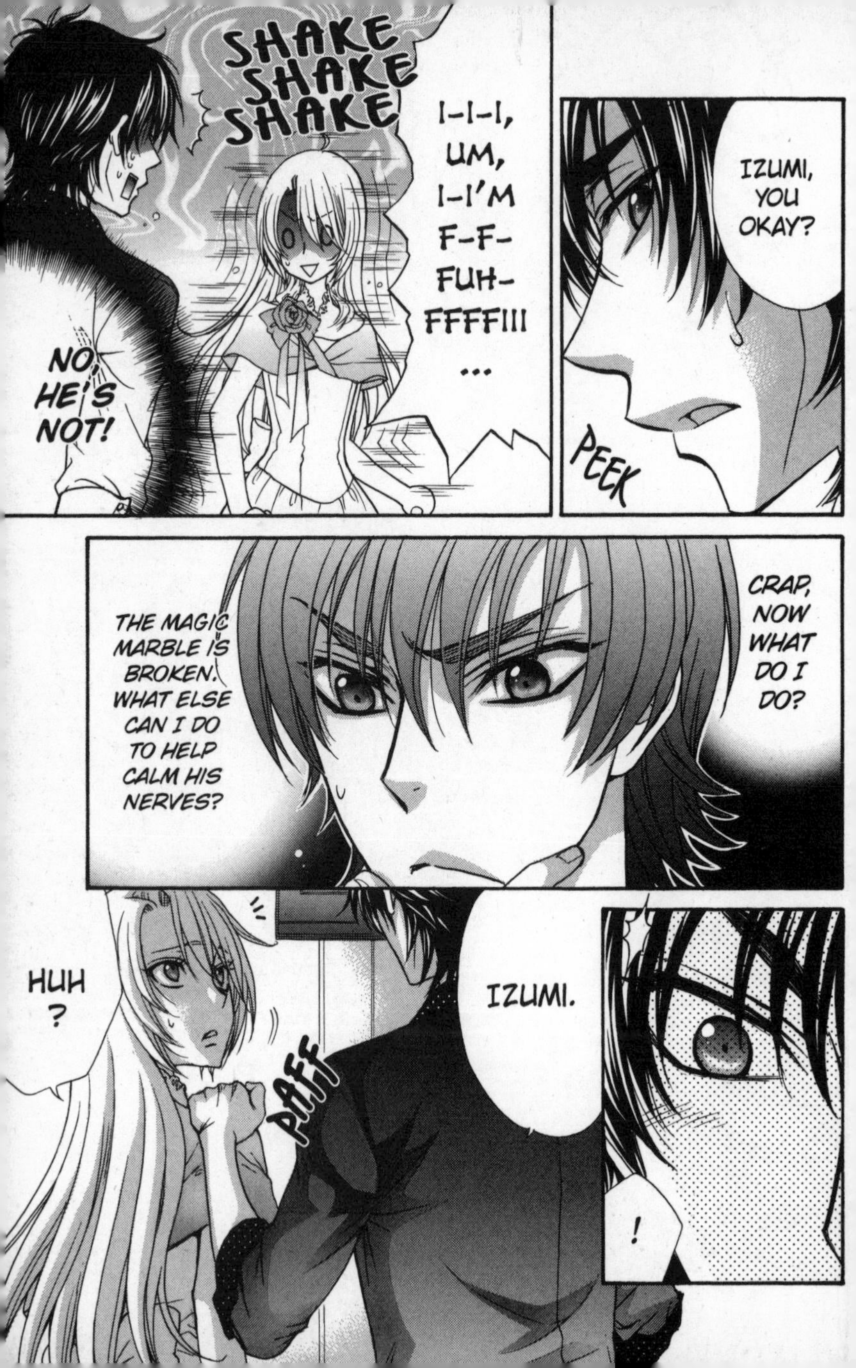
IZUMI, YOU OKAY?
PEEK
SHAKE SHAKE SHAKE
I-I-I, UM, I-I'M F-F-FUH-FFFF!!! ...
NO, HE'S NOT!
CRAP, NOW WHAT DO I DO?
THE MAGIC MARBLE IS BROKEN. WHAT ELSE CAN I DO TO HELP CALM HIS NERVES?
!
IZUMI.
PAFF
HUH?

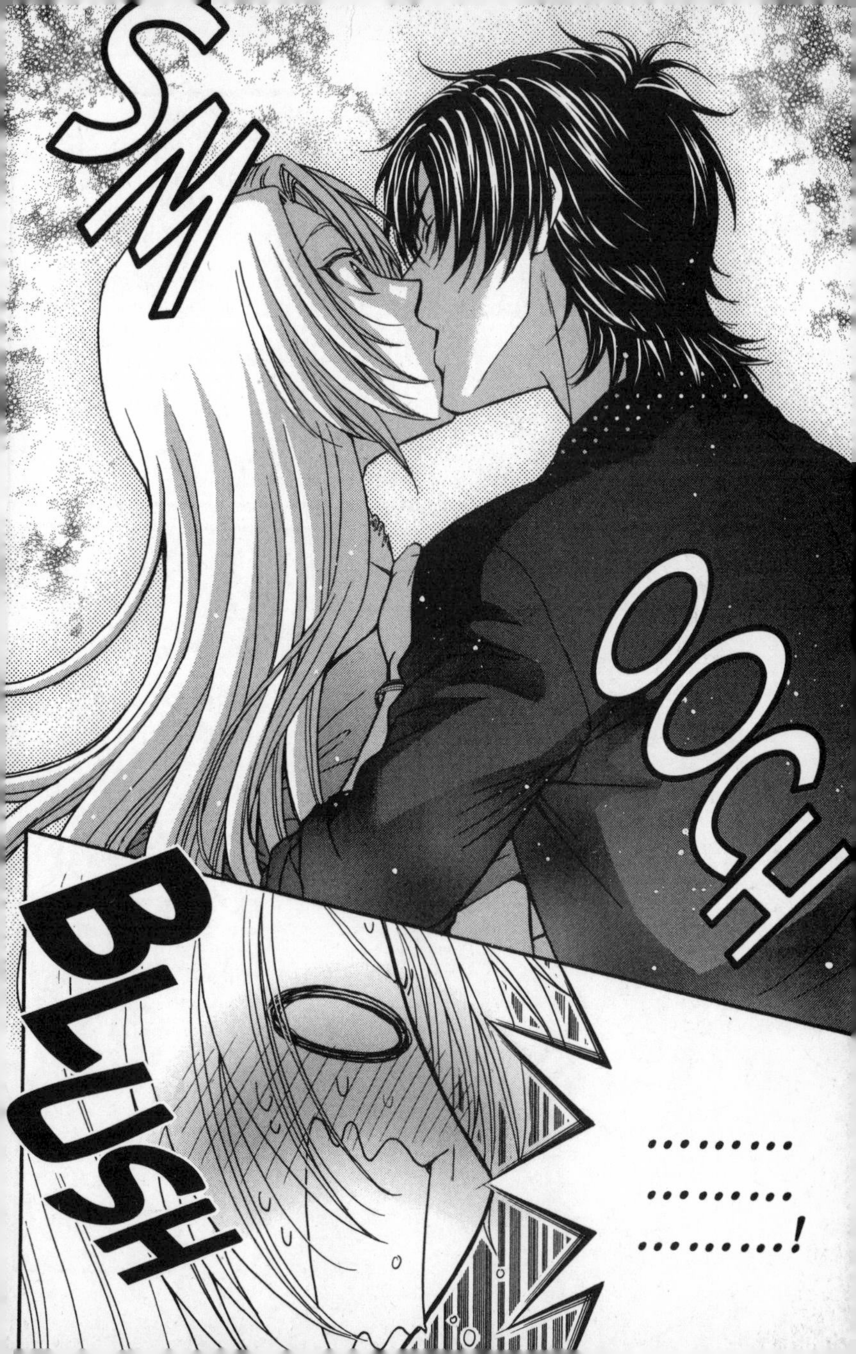
SMOOCH
....
....
.........!
BLUSH

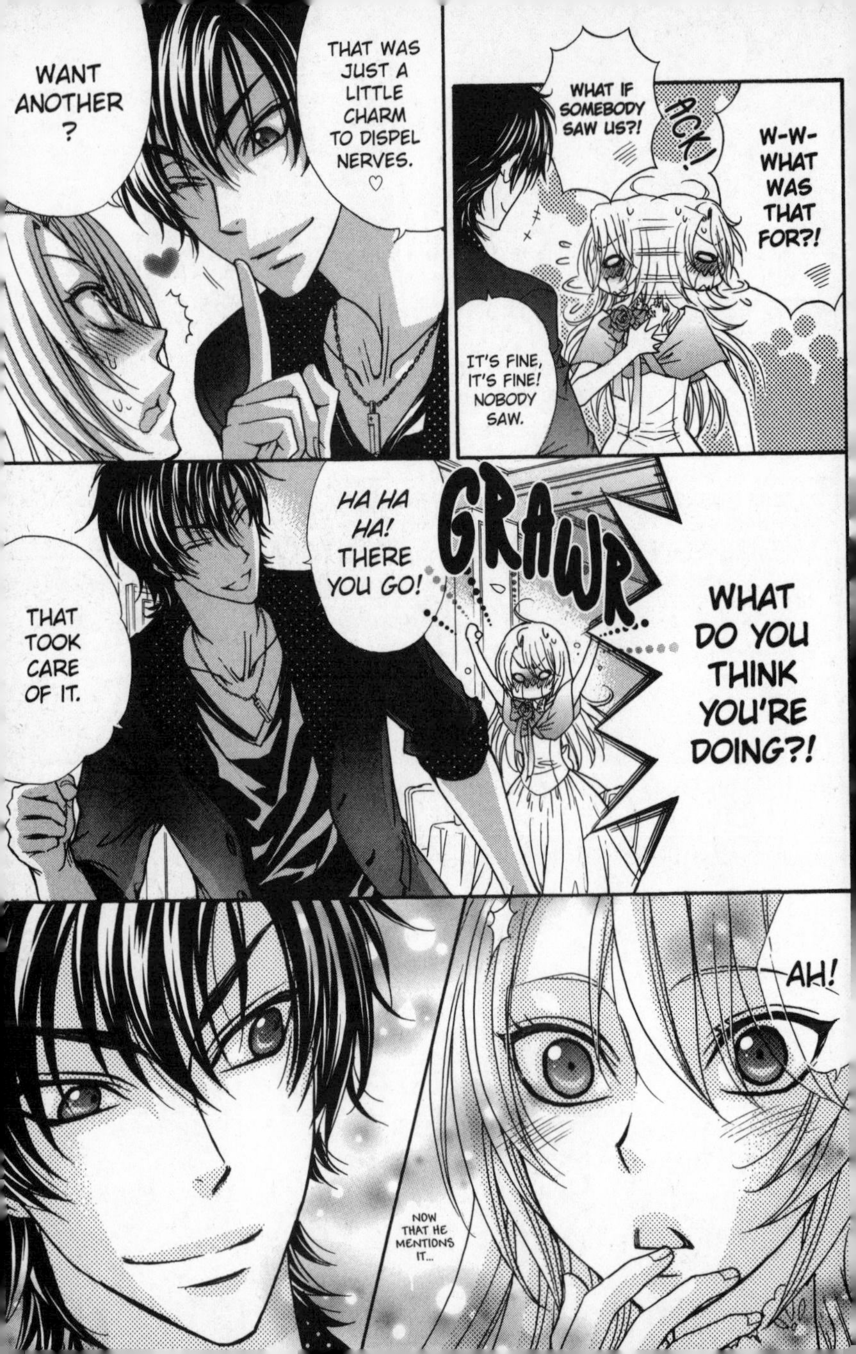
THAT WAS JUST A LITTLE CHARM TO DISPEL NERVES. ♡
WANT ANOTHER?
W-W-WHAT WAS THAT FOR?!
ACK!
WHAT IF SOMEBODY SAW US?!
IT'S FINE, IT'S FINE! NOBODY SAW.
WHAT DO YOU THINK YOU'RE DOING?!
GRAWR
HA HA HA! THERE YOU GO!
THAT TOOK CARE OF IT.
AH!
NOW THAT HE MENTIONS IT...

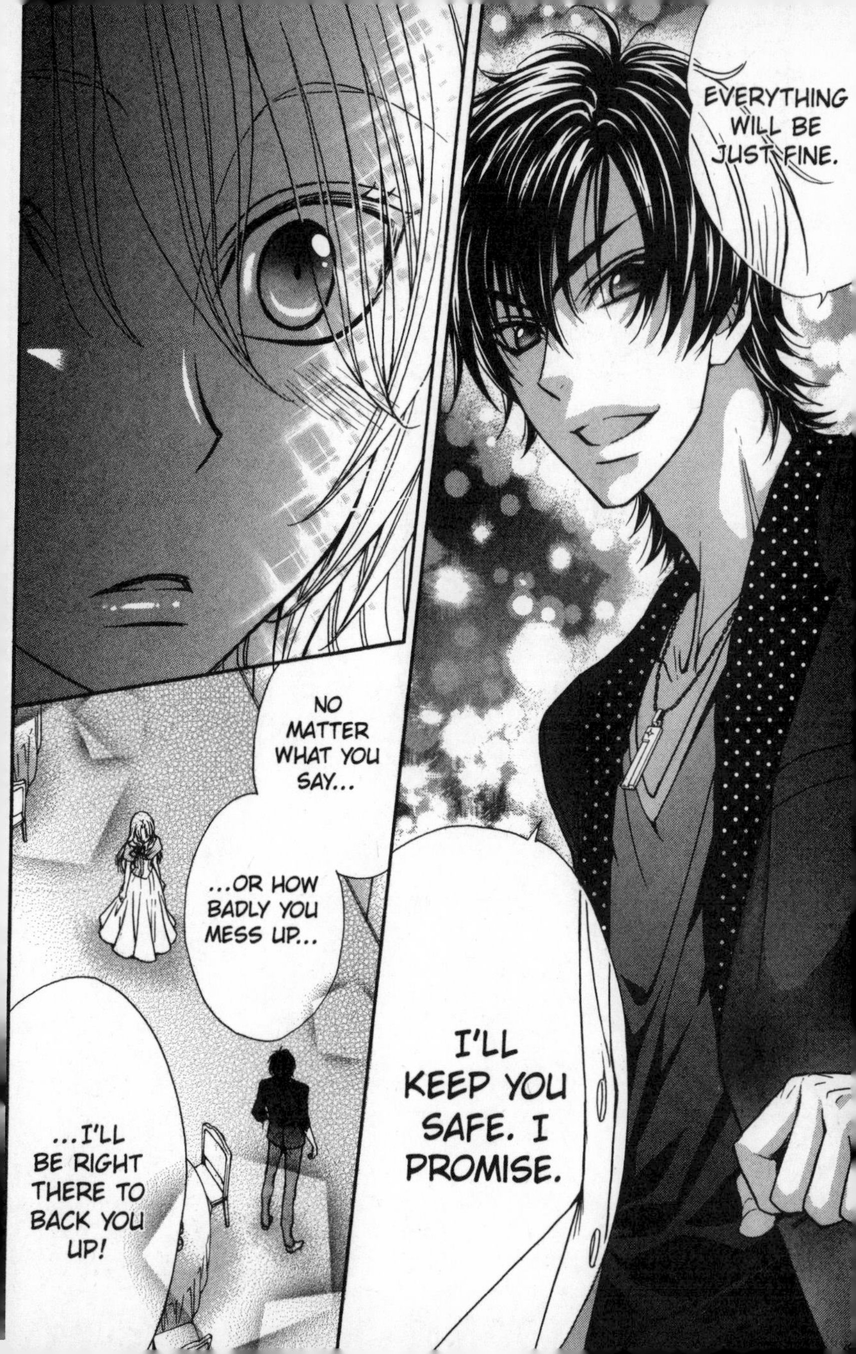
EVERYTHING WILL BE JUST FINE.
NO MATTER WHAT YOU SAY...
...OR HOW BADLY YOU MESS UP...
...I'LL BE RIGHT THERE TO BACK YOU UP!
I'LL KEEP YOU SAFE. I PROMISE.

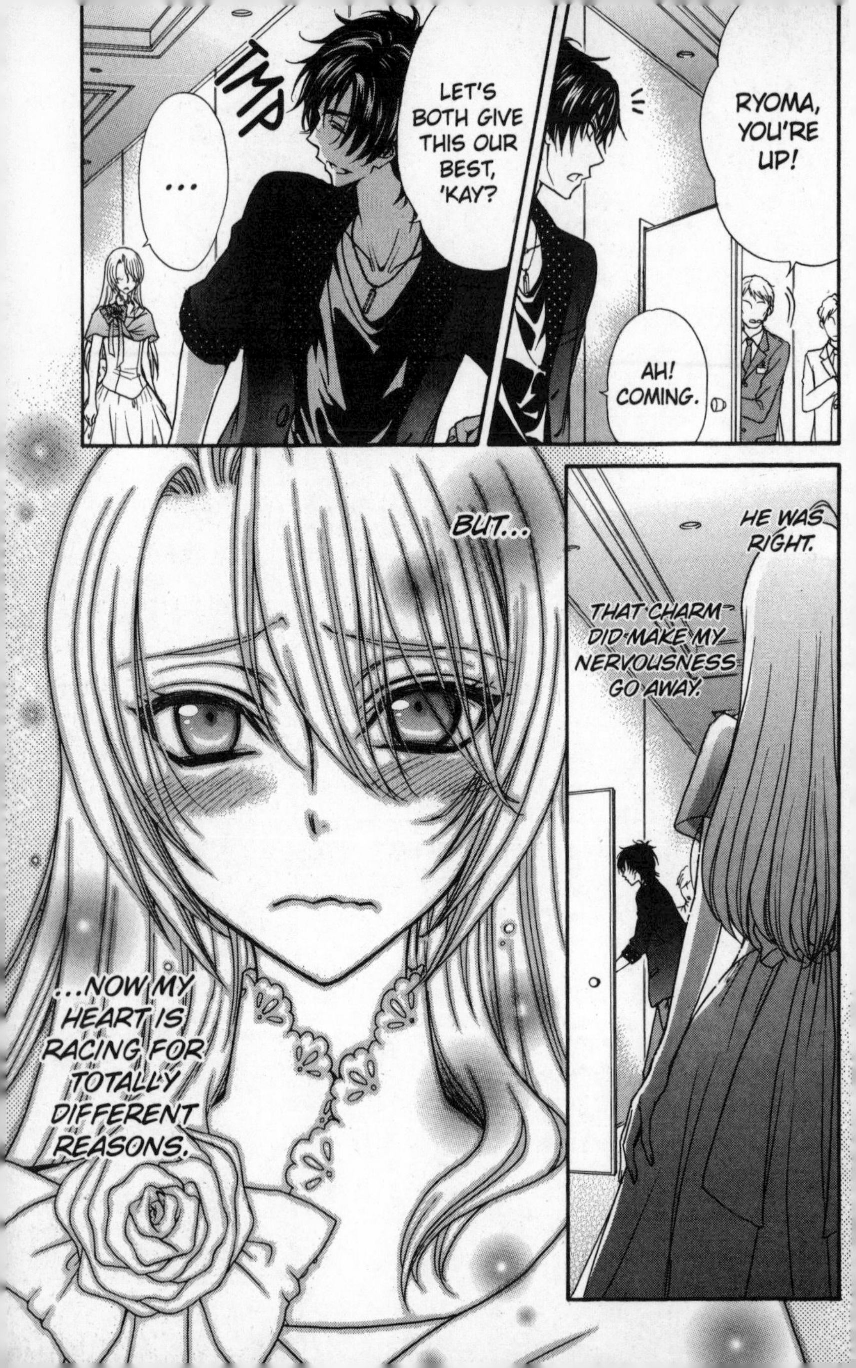
RYOMA, YOU'RE UP!
AH! COMING.
LET'S BOTH GIVE THIS OUR BEST, 'KAY?
TMP
...
HE WAS RIGHT.
THAT CHARM DID MAKE MY NERVOUSNESS GO AWAY.
BUT...
...NOW MY HEART IS RACING FOR TOTALLY DIFFERENT REASONS.

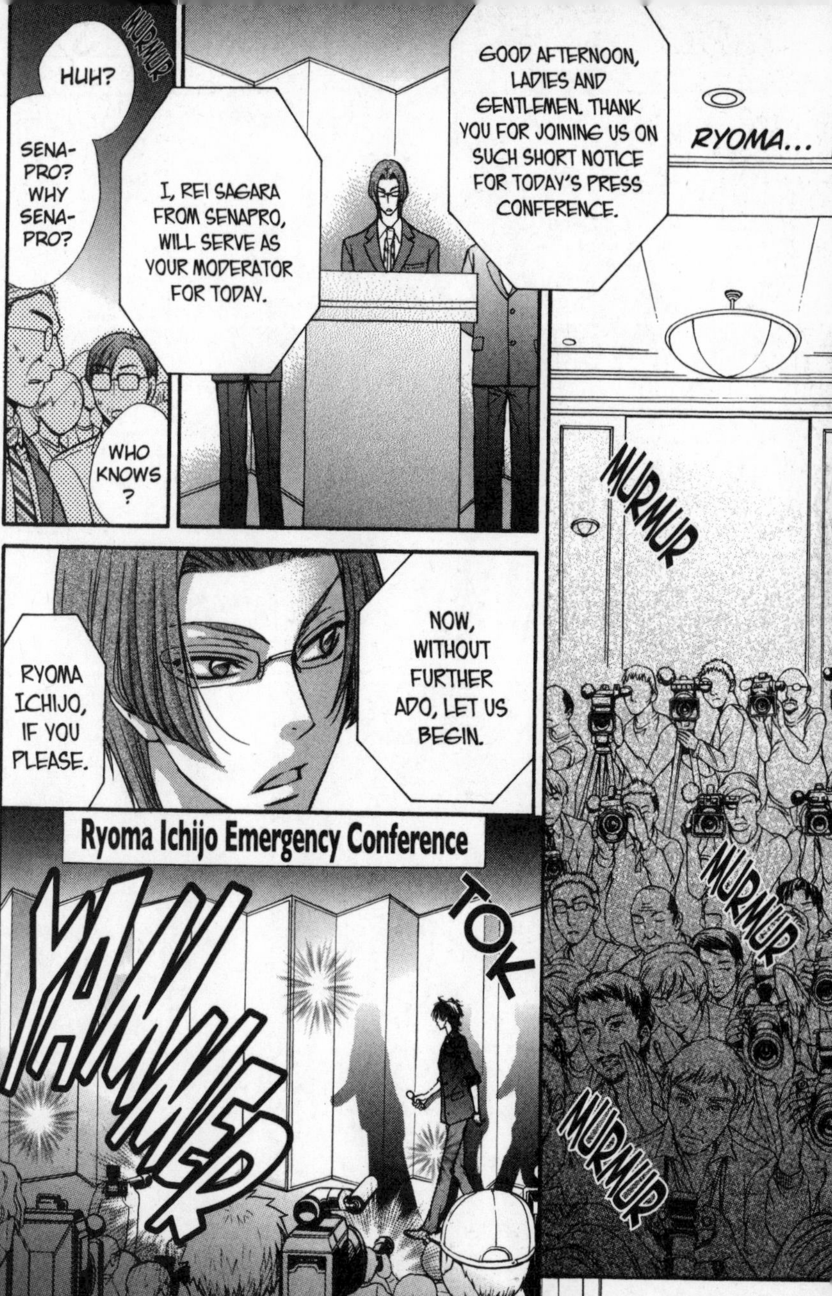
RYOMA...
GOOD AFTERNOON, LADIES AND GENTLEMEN. THANK YOU FOR JOINING US ON SUCH SHORT NOTICE FOR TODAY'S PRESS CONFERENCE.
I, REI SAGARA FROM SENAPRO, WILL SERVE AS YOUR MODERATOR FOR TODAY.
MURMUR
HUH?
SENA-PRO? WHY SENA-PRO?
WHO KNOWS?
MURMUR
NOW, WITHOUT FURTHER ADO, LET US BEGIN.
RYOMA ICHIJO, IF YOU PLEASE.
Ryoma Ichijo Emergency Conference
YAMMER
TOK
MURMUR
MURMUR

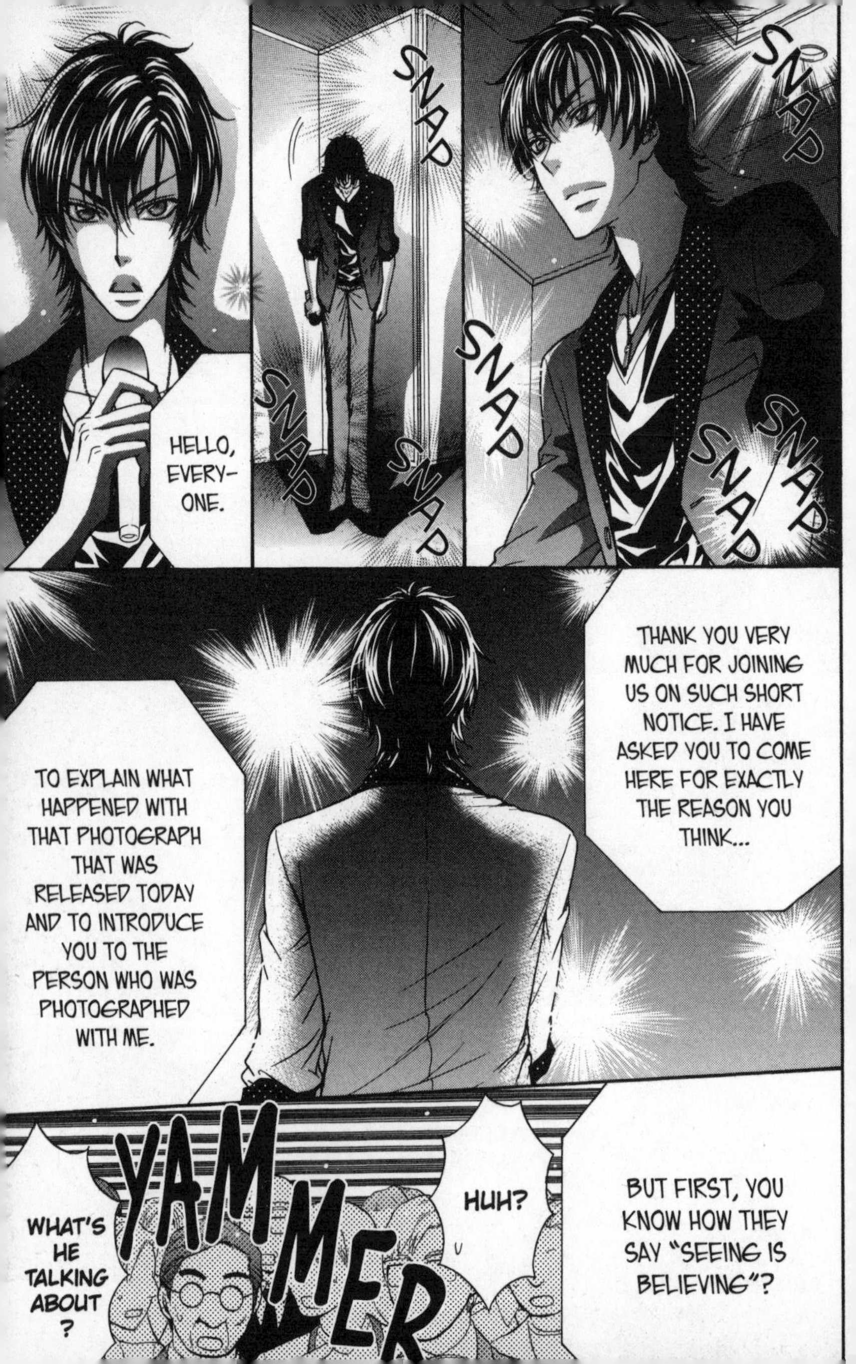
SNAP
SNAP
SNAP
SNAP
SNAP
SNAP
SNAP
HELLO, EVERY-ONE.
THANK YOU VERY MUCH FOR JOINING US ON SUCH SHORT NOTICE. I HAVE ASKED YOU TO COME HERE FOR EXACTLY THE REASON YOU THINK...
TO EXPLAIN WHAT HAPPENED WITH THAT PHOTOGRAPH THAT WAS RELEASED TODAY AND TO INTRODUCE YOU TO THE PERSON WHO WAS PHOTOGRAPHED WITH ME.
BUT FIRST, YOU KNOW HOW THEY SAY "SEEING IS BELIEVING"?
HUH?
YAMMER
WHAT'S HE TALKING ABOUT?

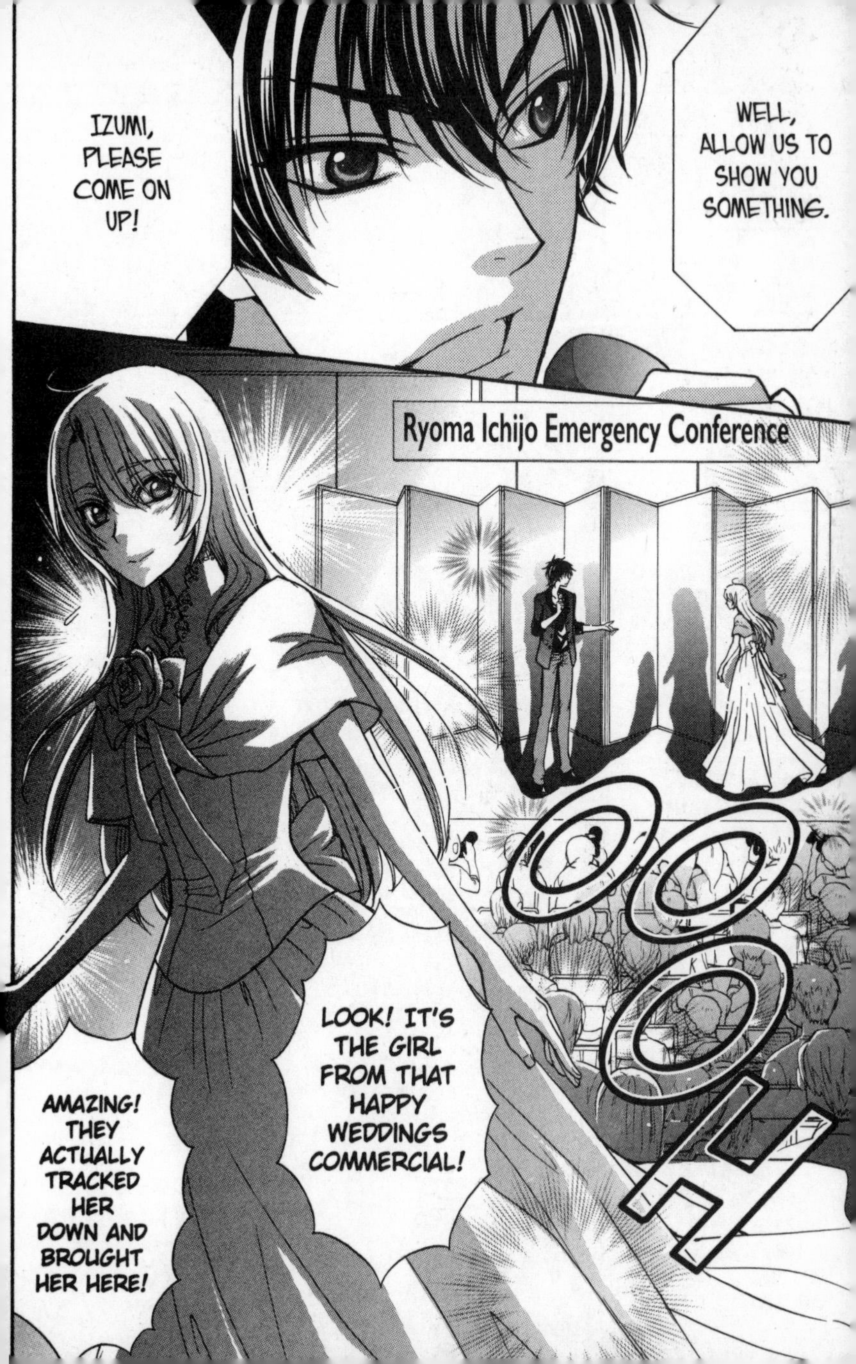
WELL, ALLOW US TO SHOW YOU SOMETHING.
IZUMI, PLEASE COME ON UP!
Ryoma Ichijo Emergency Conference
OOOH
LOOK! IT'S THE GIRL FROM THAT HAPPY WEDDINGS COMMERCIAL!
AMAZING! THEY ACTUALLY TRACKED HER DOWN AND BROUGHT HER HERE!

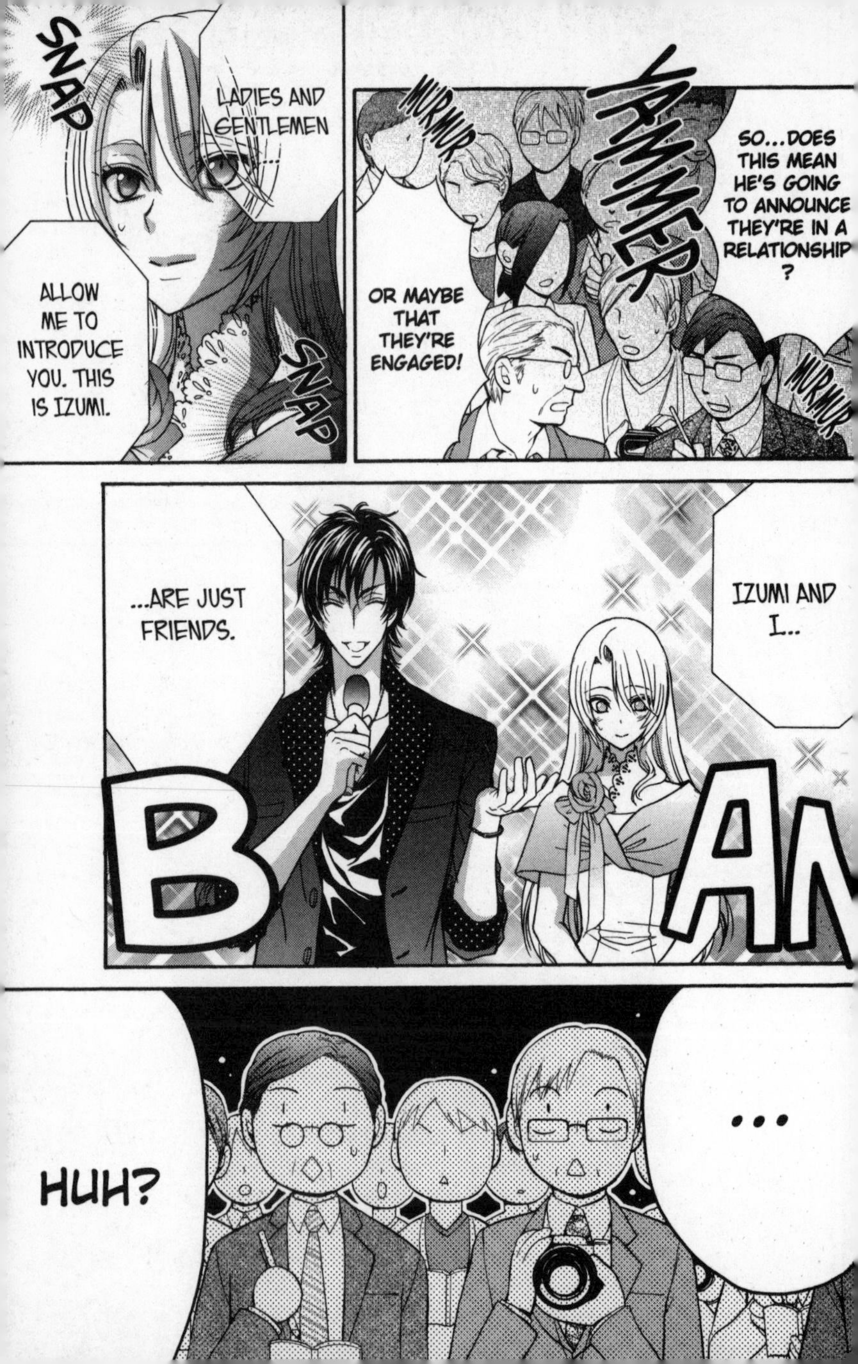

YAMMER
MURMUR
SO...DOES THIS MEAN HE'S GOING TO ANNOUNCE THEY'RE IN A RELATIONSHIP?
OR MAYBE THAT THEY'RE ENGAGED!
MURMUR
SNAP
LADIES AND GENTLEMEN
ALLOW ME TO INTRODUCE YOU. THIS IS IZUMI.
SNAP
IZUMI AND I...
...ARE JUST FRIENDS.
B
A
...
HUH?

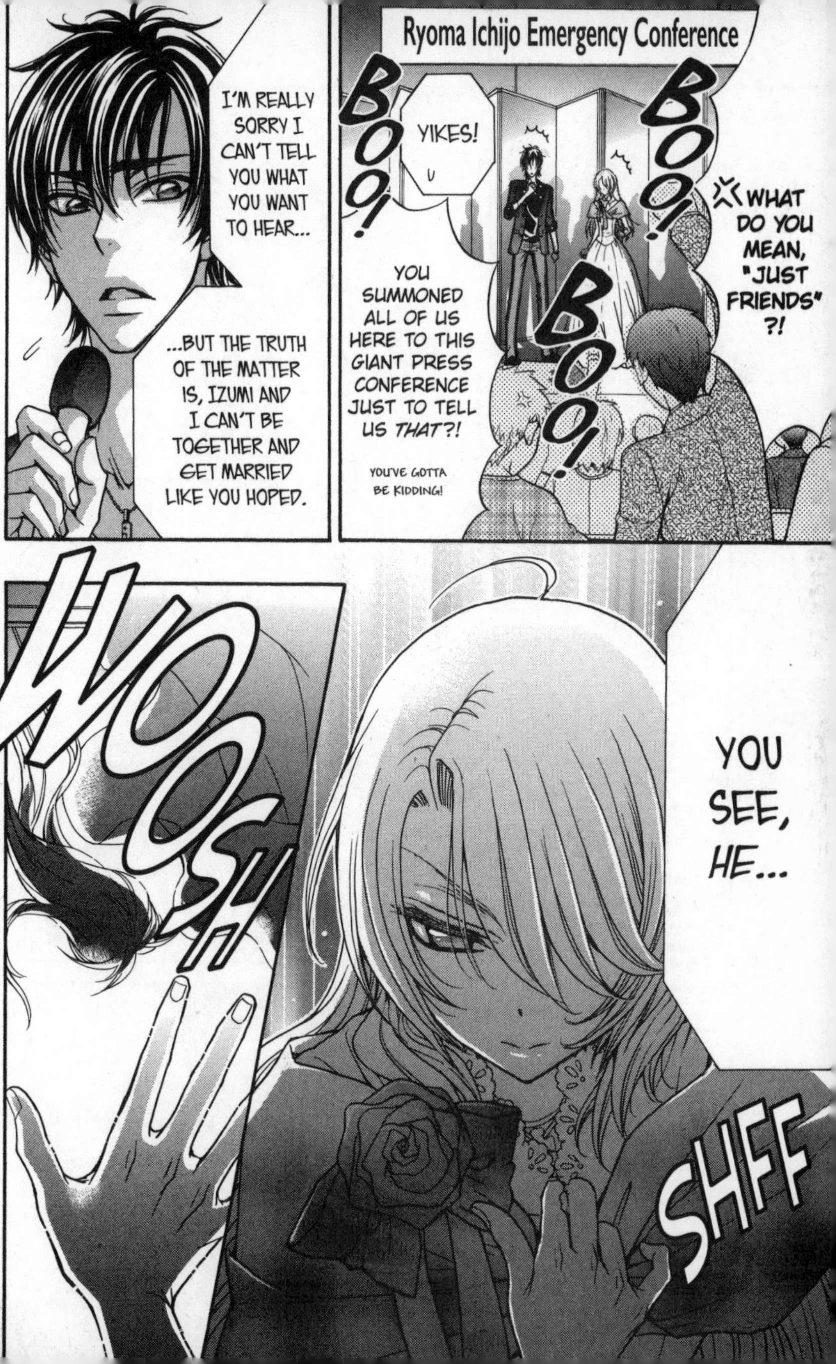
Ryoma Ichijo Emergency Conference
BOO!
BOO!
BOO!
BOO!
WHAT DO YOU MEAN, "JUST FRIENDS"?!
YIKES!
YOU SUMMONED ALL OF US HERE TO THIS GIANT PRESS CONFERENCE JUST TO TELL US *THAT*?!
YOU'VE GOTTA BE KIDDING!
I'M REALLY SORRY I CAN'T TELL YOU WHAT YOU WANT TO HEAR...
...BUT THE TRUTH OF THE MATTER IS, IZUMI AND I CAN'T BE TOGETHER AND GET MARRIED LIKE YOU HOPED.
YOU SEE, HE...
SHFF
WOOSH

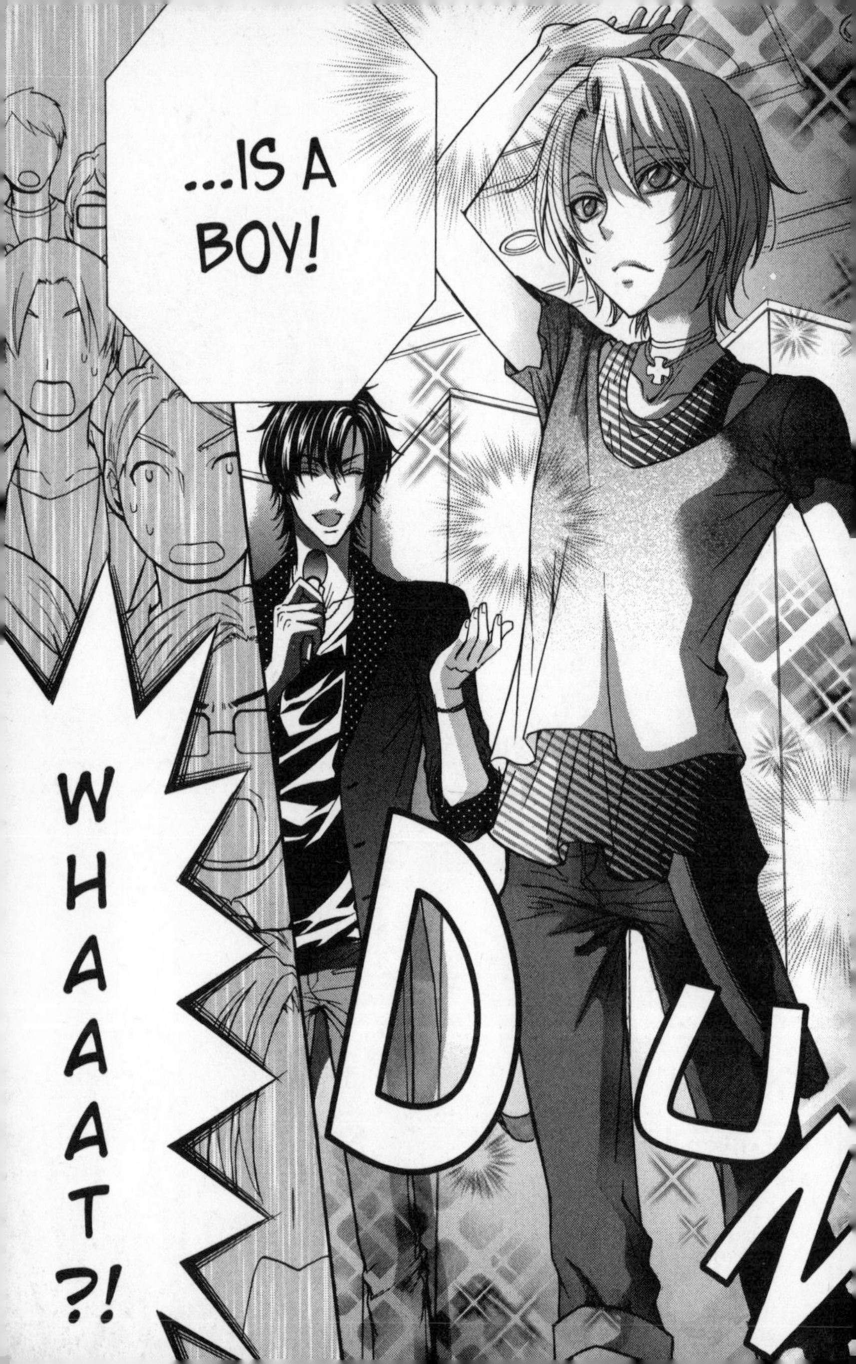
...IS A BOY!
WHAAAT?!
DUN

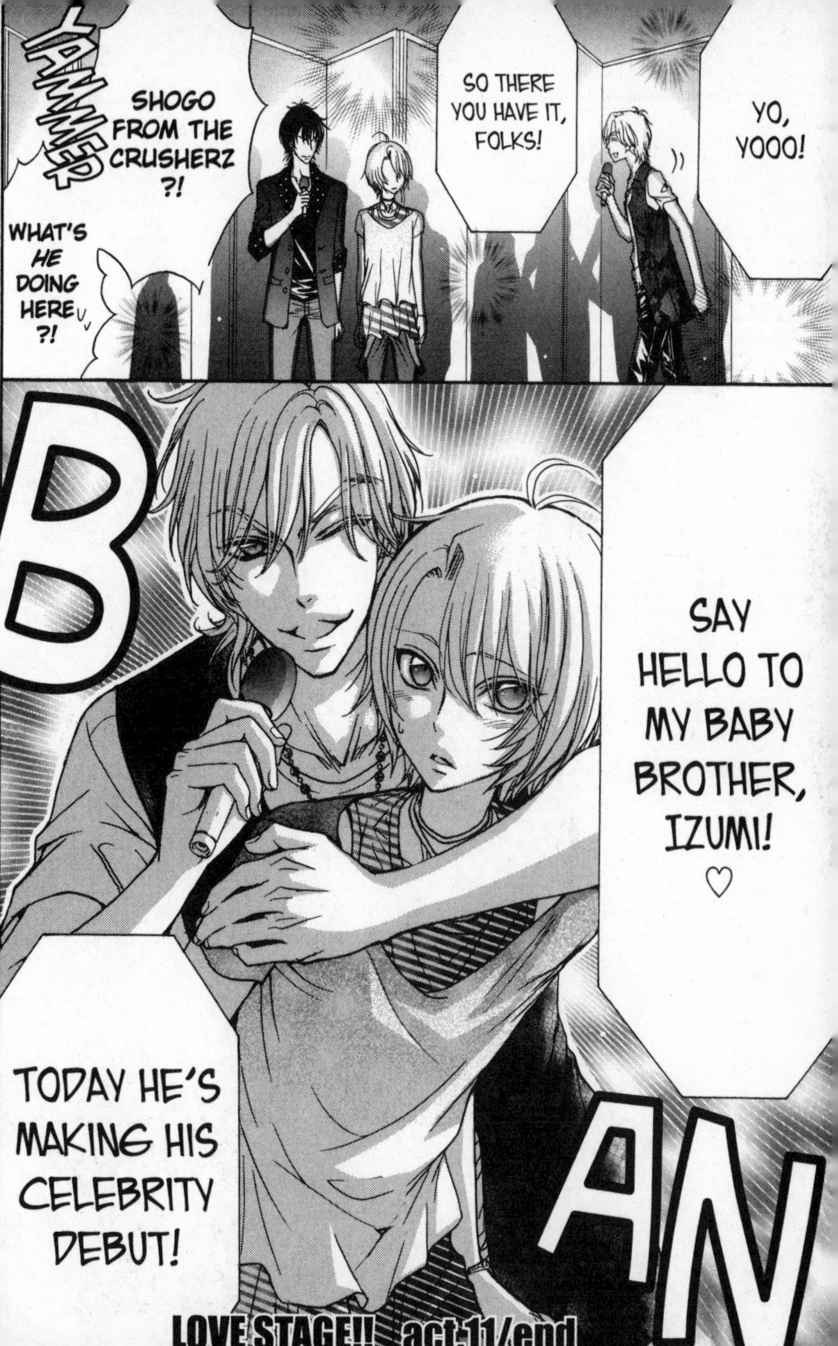
YO, YOOO!
SO THERE YOU HAVE IT, FOLKS!
YAMMER
SHOGO FROM THE CRUSHERZ ?!
WHAT'S HE DOING HERE ?!
SAY HELLO TO MY BABY BROTHER, IZUMI! ♡
TODAY HE'S MAKING HIS CELEBRITY DEBUT!
B
AN

LOVE STAGE!! act.11/end

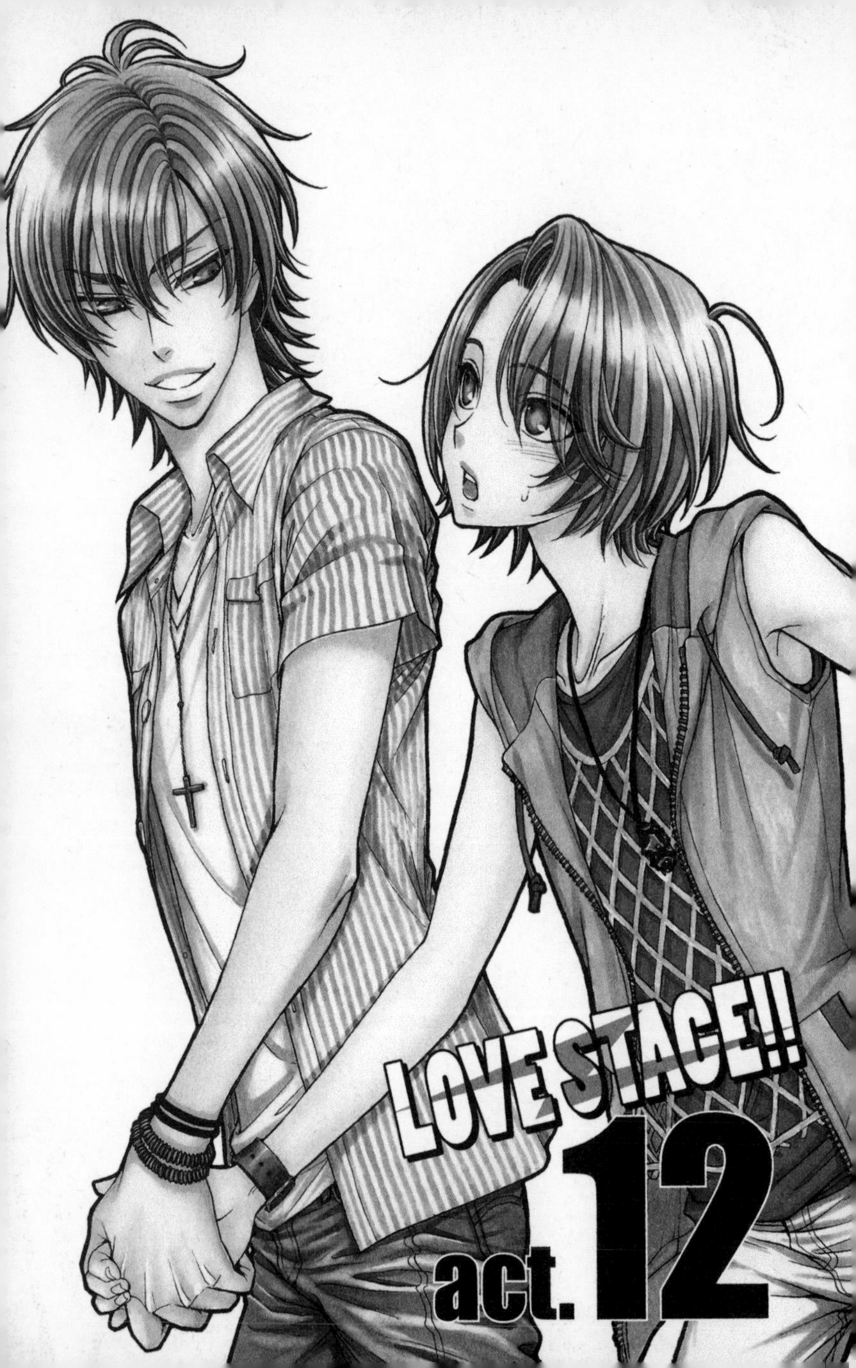
LOVE STAGE!!
act. 12

LOVE STAGE!!

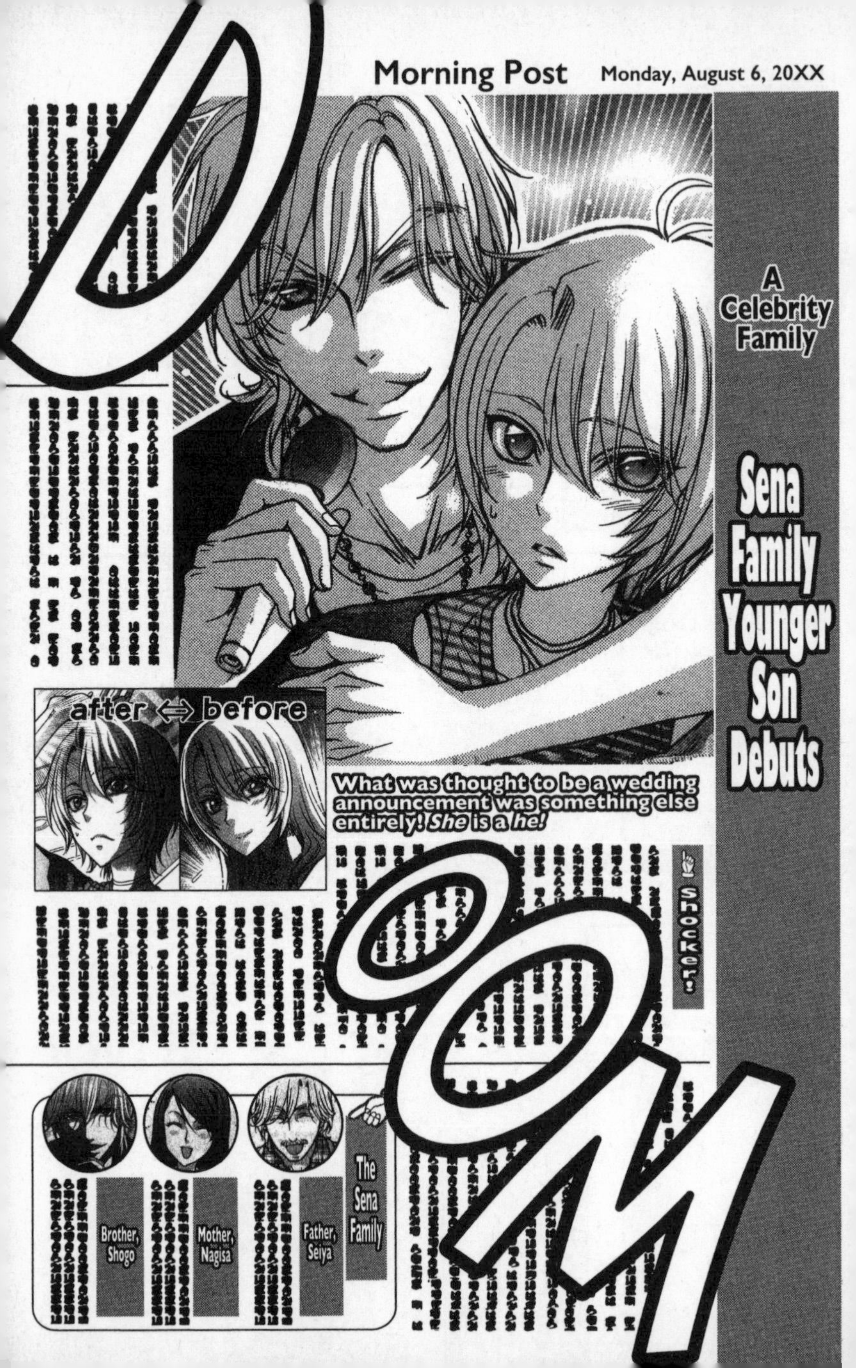
Morning Post
Monday, August 6, 20XX
A Celebrity Family
Sena Family Younger Son Debuts
What was thought to be a wedding announcement was something else entirely! She is a he!
after ⇔ before
Shocker!
DOOM
The Sena Family
Father, Seiya
Mother, Nagisa
Brother, Shogo

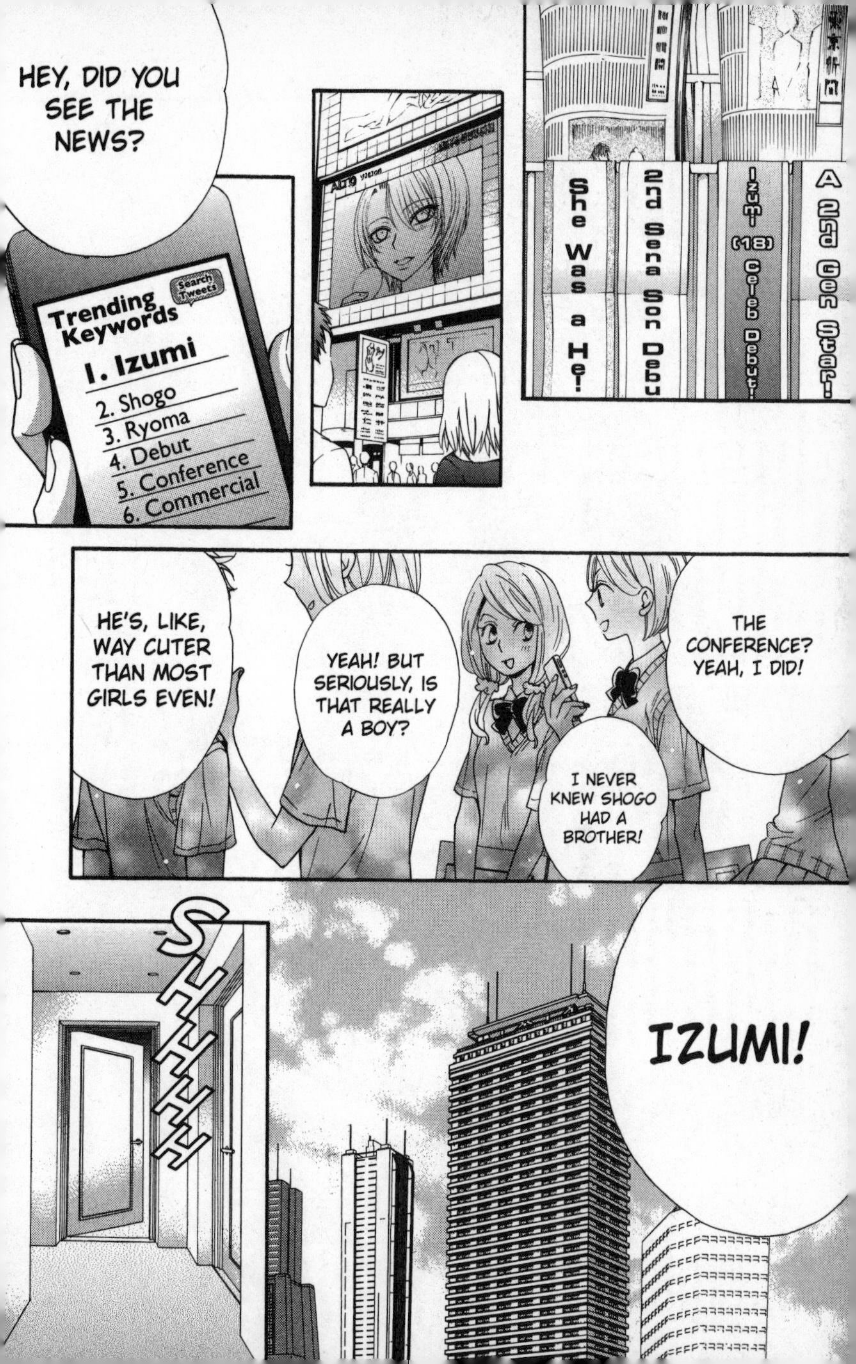
A 2nd Gen Star!
Izumi (18) Celeb Debut!
2nd Sena Son Debu
She Was a He!
HEY, DID YOU SEE THE NEWS?
Search Tweets
Trending Keywords
1. Izumi
2. Shogo
3. Ryoma
4. Debut
5. Conference
6. Commercial
THE CONFERENCE? YEAH, I DID!
I NEVER KNEW SHOGO HAD A BROTHER!
YEAH! BUT SERIOUSLY, IS THAT REALLY A BOY?
HE'S, LIKE, WAY CUTER THAN MOST GIRLS EVEN!
IZUMI!
SHHHHH

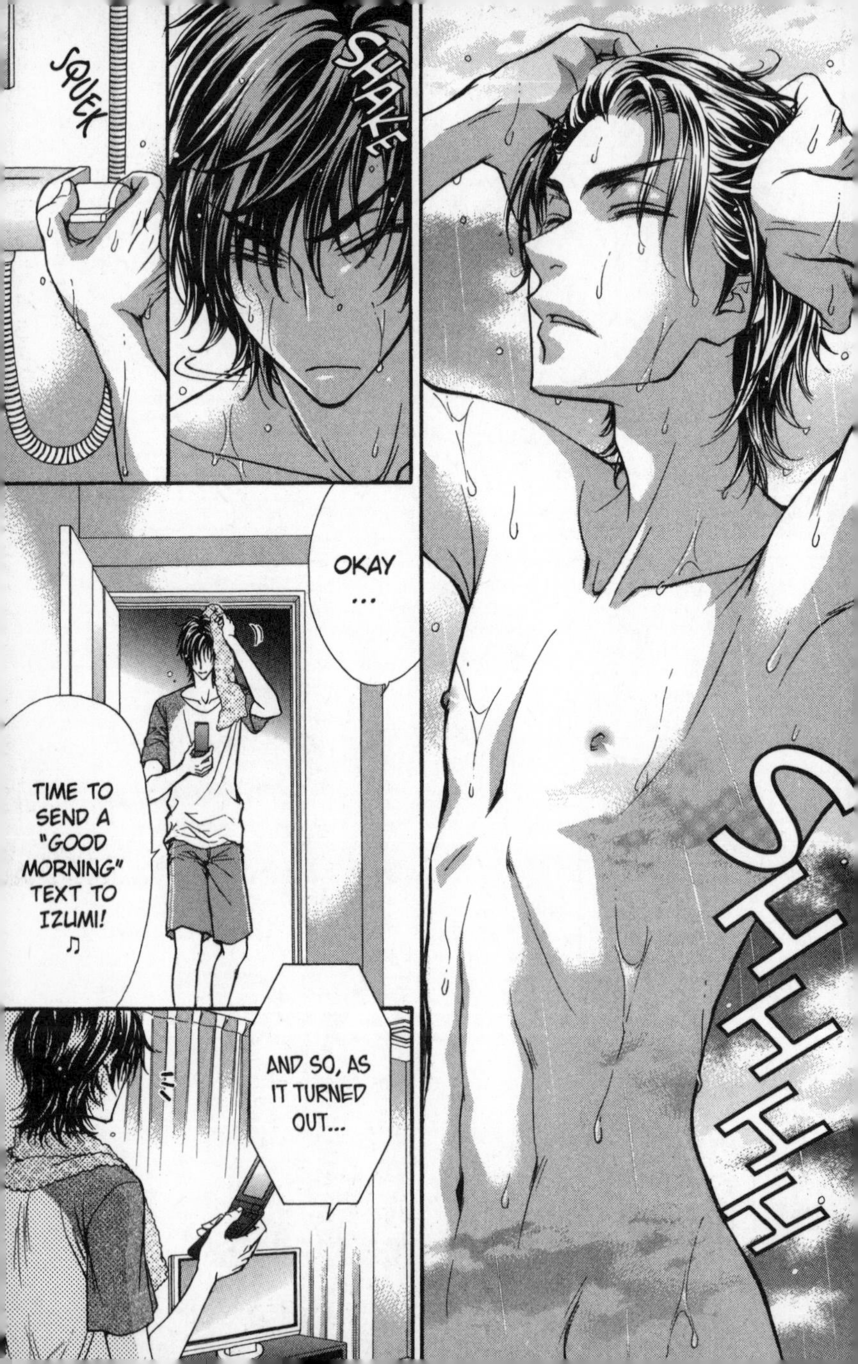
SHHHH
SHAKE
SQUECK
OKAY ...
TIME TO SEND A "GOOD MORNING" TEXT TO IZUMI! ♫
!!
AND SO, AS IT TURNED OUT...

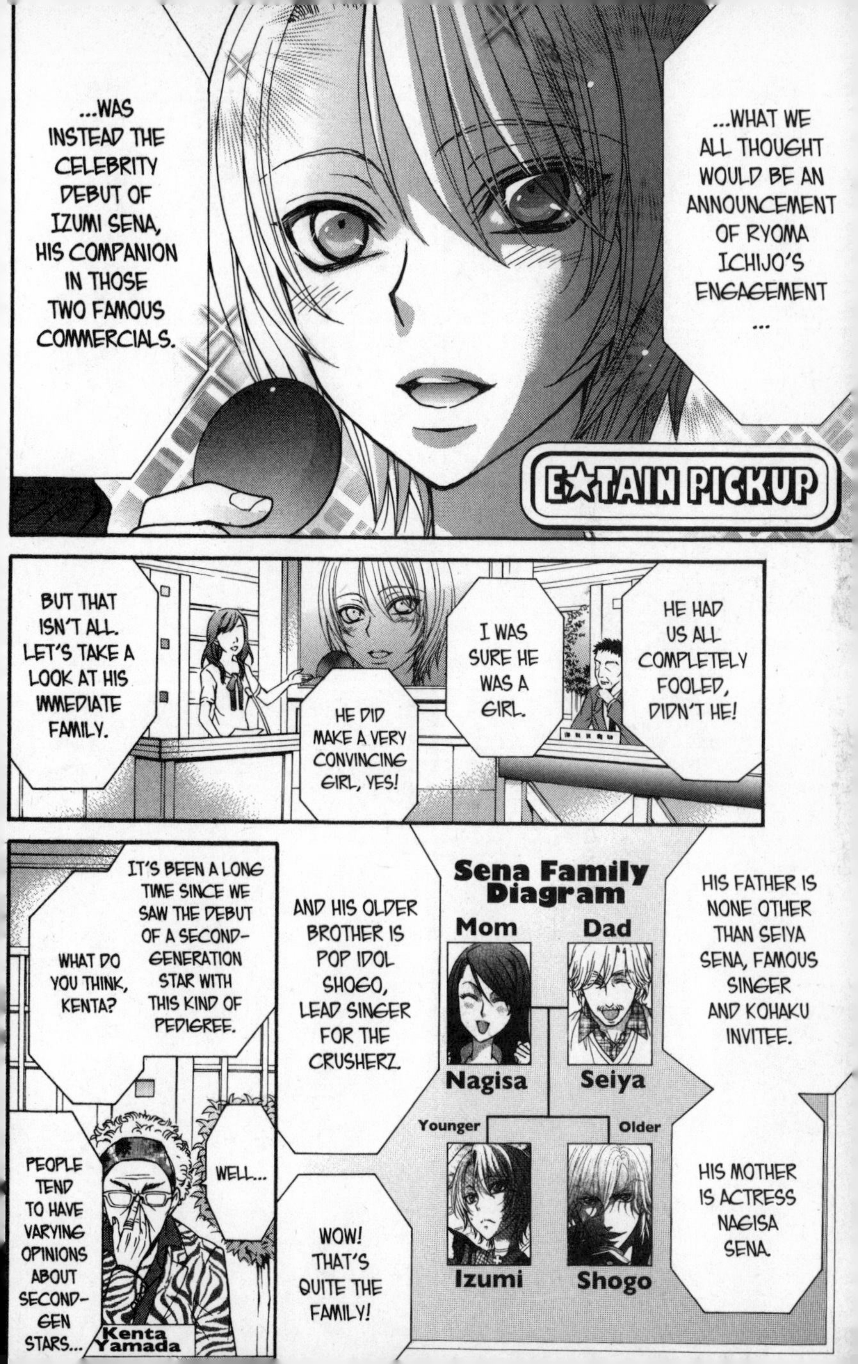
...WHAT WE ALL THOUGHT WOULD BE AN ANNOUNCEMENT OF RYOMA ICHIJO'S ENGAGEMENT ...
...WAS INSTEAD THE CELEBRITY DEBUT OF IZUMI SENA, HIS COMPANION IN THOSE TWO FAMOUS COMMERCIALS.
E★TAIN PICKUP
HE HAD US ALL COMPLETELY FOOLED, DIDN'T HE!
I WAS SURE HE WAS A GIRL.
HE DID MAKE A VERY CONVINCING GIRL, YES!
BUT THAT ISN'T ALL. LET'S TAKE A LOOK AT HIS IMMEDIATE FAMILY.
HIS FATHER IS NONE OTHER THAN SEIYA SENA, FAMOUS SINGER AND KOHAKU INVITEE.
Sena Family Diagram
Mom
Dad
Nagisa
Seiya
Younger
Older
Izumi
Shogo
HIS MOTHER IS ACTRESS NAGISA SENA.
AND HIS OLDER BROTHER IS POP IDOL SHOGO, LEAD SINGER FOR THE CRUSHERZ.
WOW! THAT'S QUITE THE FAMILY!
IT'S BEEN A LONG TIME SINCE WE SAW THE DEBUT OF A SECOND-GENERATION STAR WITH THIS KIND OF PEDIGREE.
WHAT DO YOU THINK, KENTA?
WELL...
PEOPLE TEND TO HAVE VARYING OPINIONS ABOUT SECOND-GEN STARS...
Kenta Yamada

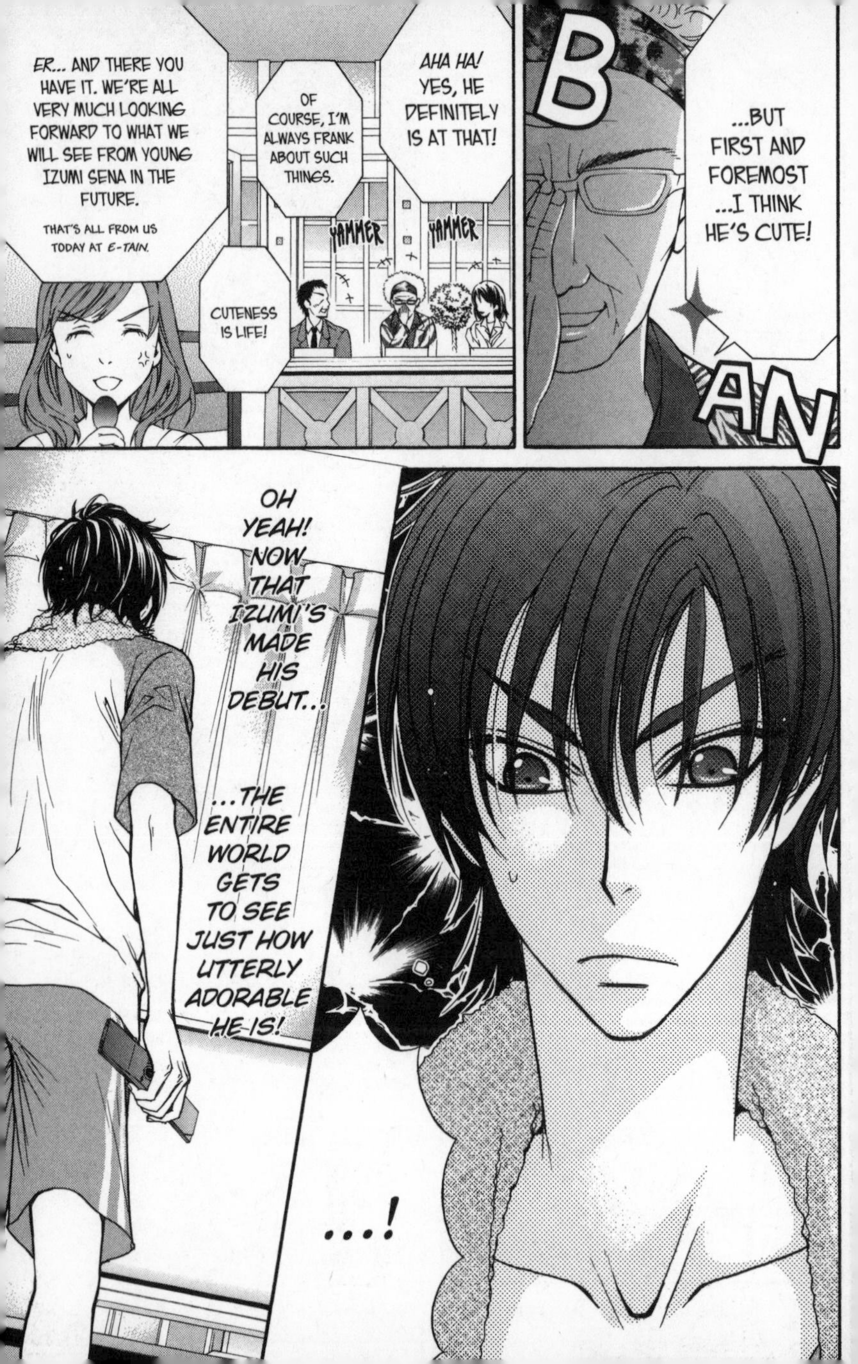
B
...BUT FIRST AND FOREMOST ...I THINK HE'S CUTE!
AN
CUTENESS IS LIFE!
OF COURSE, I'M ALWAYS FRANK ABOUT SUCH THINGS.
AHA HA! YES, HE DEFINITELY IS AT THAT!
YAMMER
YAMMER
ER... AND THERE YOU HAVE IT. WE'RE ALL VERY MUCH LOOKING FORWARD TO WHAT WE WILL SEE FROM YOUNG IZUMI SENA IN THE FUTURE.
THAT'S ALL FROM US TODAY AT E-TAIN.
OH YEAH! NOW THAT IZUMI'S MADE HIS DEBUT...
...THE ENTIRE WORLD GETS TO SEE JUST HOW UTTERLY ADORABLE HE IS!
...!

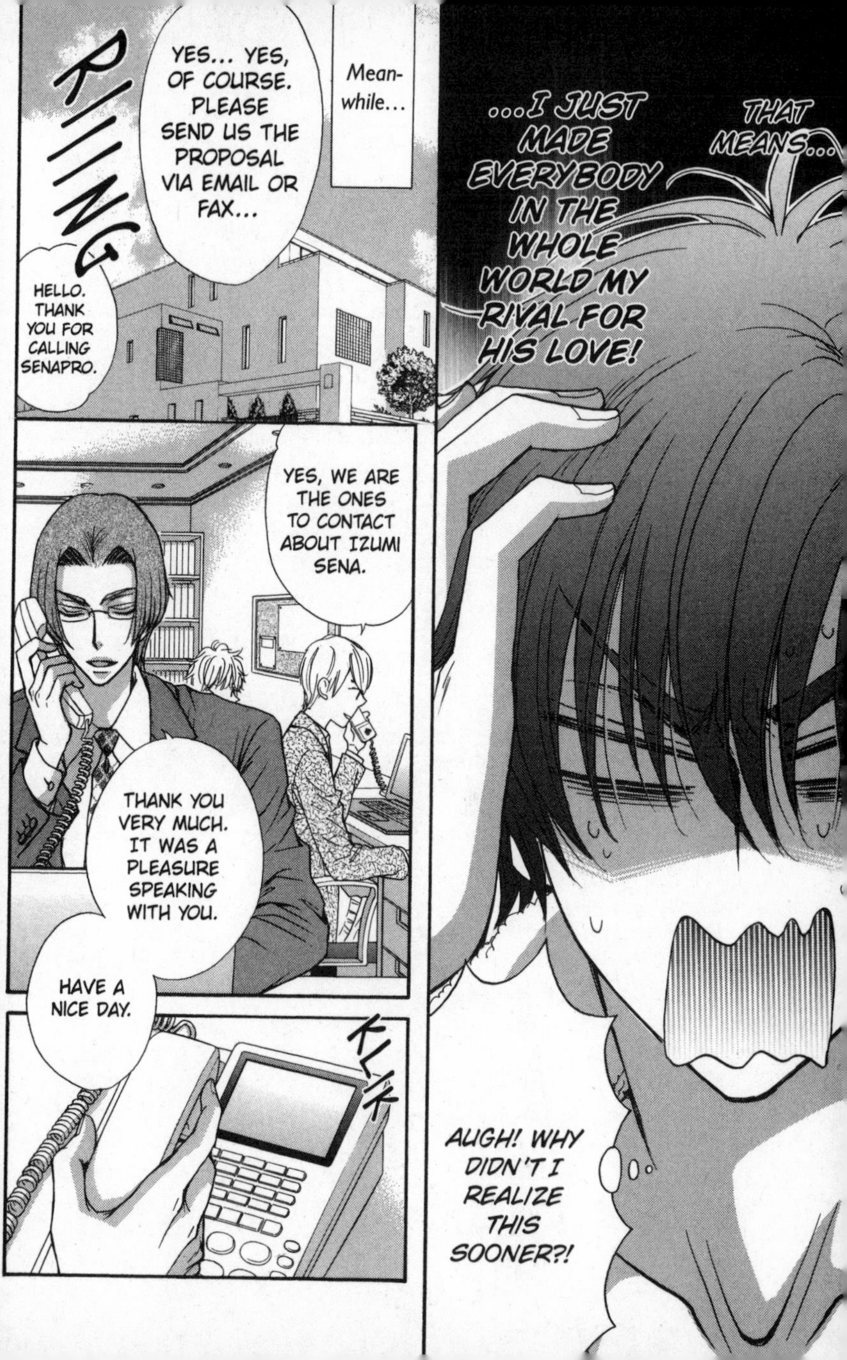
THAT MEANS...
...I JUST MADE EVERYBODY IN THE WHOLE WORLD MY RIVAL FOR HIS LOVE!
AUGH! WHY DIDN'T I REALIZE THIS SOONER?!
Mean-while...
YES... YES, OF COURSE. PLEASE SEND US THE PROPOSAL VIA EMAIL OR FAX...
RIIING
HELLO. THANK YOU FOR CALLING SENAPRO.
YES, WE ARE THE ONES TO CONTACT ABOUT IZUMI SENA.
THANK YOU VERY MUCH. IT WAS A PLEASURE SPEAKING WITH YOU.
HAVE A NICE DAY.
KLIK

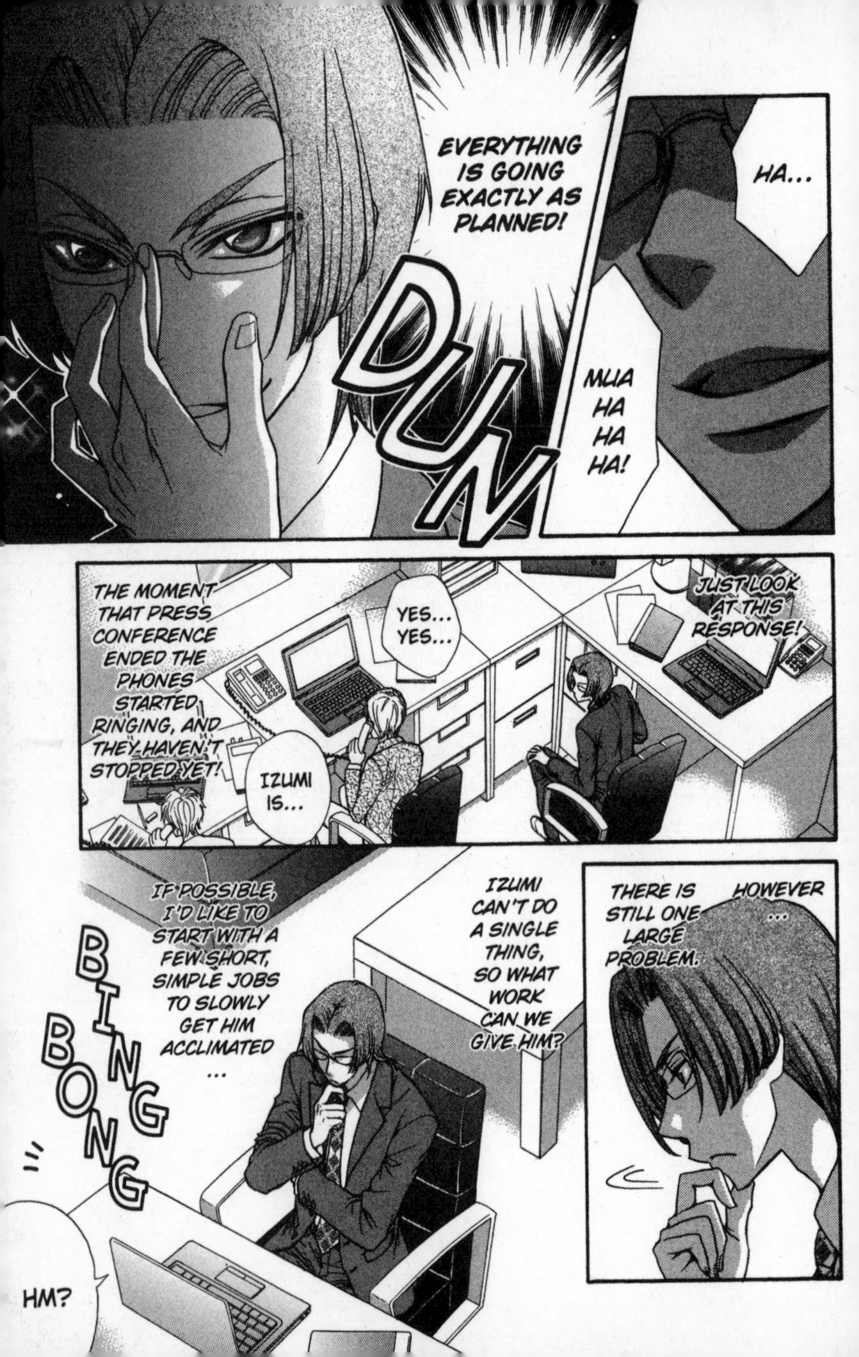
HA...
MUA HA HA HA!
EVERYTHING IS GOING EXACTLY AS PLANNED!
DUN
JUST LOOK AT THIS RESPONSE!
YES... YES...
THE MOMENT THAT PRESS CONFERENCE ENDED THE PHONES STARTED RINGING, AND THEY HAVEN'T STOPPED YET!
IZUMI IS...
HOWEVER...
THERE IS STILL ONE LARGE PROBLEM.
IZUMI CAN'T DO A SINGLE THING, SO WHAT WORK CAN WE GIVE HIM?
IF POSSIBLE, I'D LIKE TO START WITH A FEW SHORT, SIMPLE JOBS TO SLOWLY GET HIM ACCLIMATED...
BING BONG
HM?

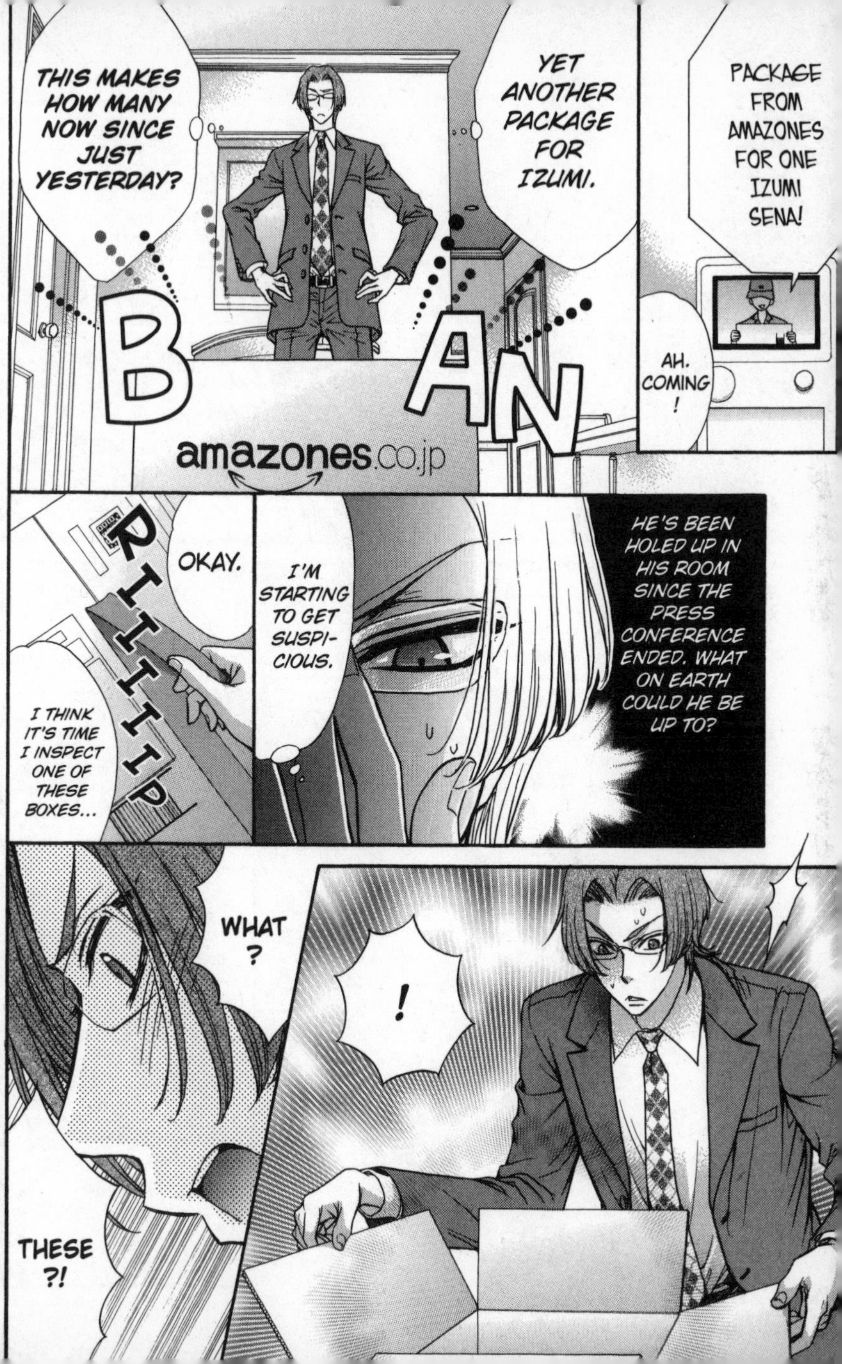
PACKAGE FROM AMAZONES FOR ONE IZUMI SENA!
AH. COMING!
YET ANOTHER PACKAGE FOR IZUMI.
THIS MAKES HOW MANY NOW SINCE JUST YESTERDAY?
BAN
amazones.co.jp
HE'S BEEN HOLED UP IN HIS ROOM SINCE THE PRESS CONFERENCE ENDED. WHAT ON EARTH COULD HE BE UP TO?
I'M STARTING TO GET SUSPICIOUS.
OKAY.
RIIIIP
I THINK IT'S TIME I INSPECT ONE OF THESE BOXES...
!
WHAT?
THESE?!

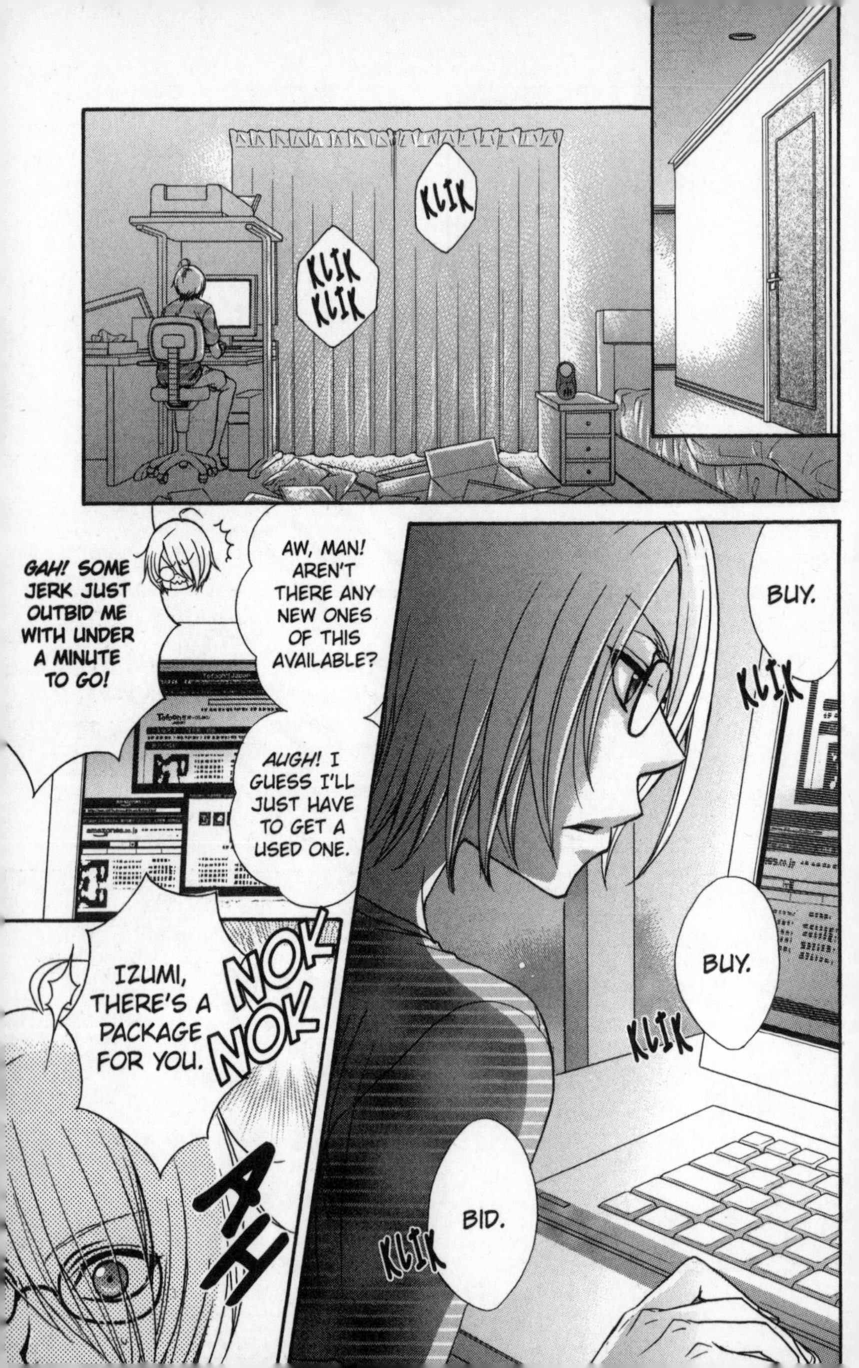
KLIK
KLIK KLIK
BUY.
KLIK
BUY.
KLIK
BID.
KLIK
AW, MAN! AREN'T THERE ANY NEW ONES OF THIS AVAILABLE?
GAH! SOME JERK JUST OUTBID ME WITH UNDER A MINUTE TO GO!
AUGH! I GUESS I'LL JUST HAVE TO GET A USED ONE.
NOK NOK
IZUMI, THERE'S A PACKAGE FOR YOU.
AH

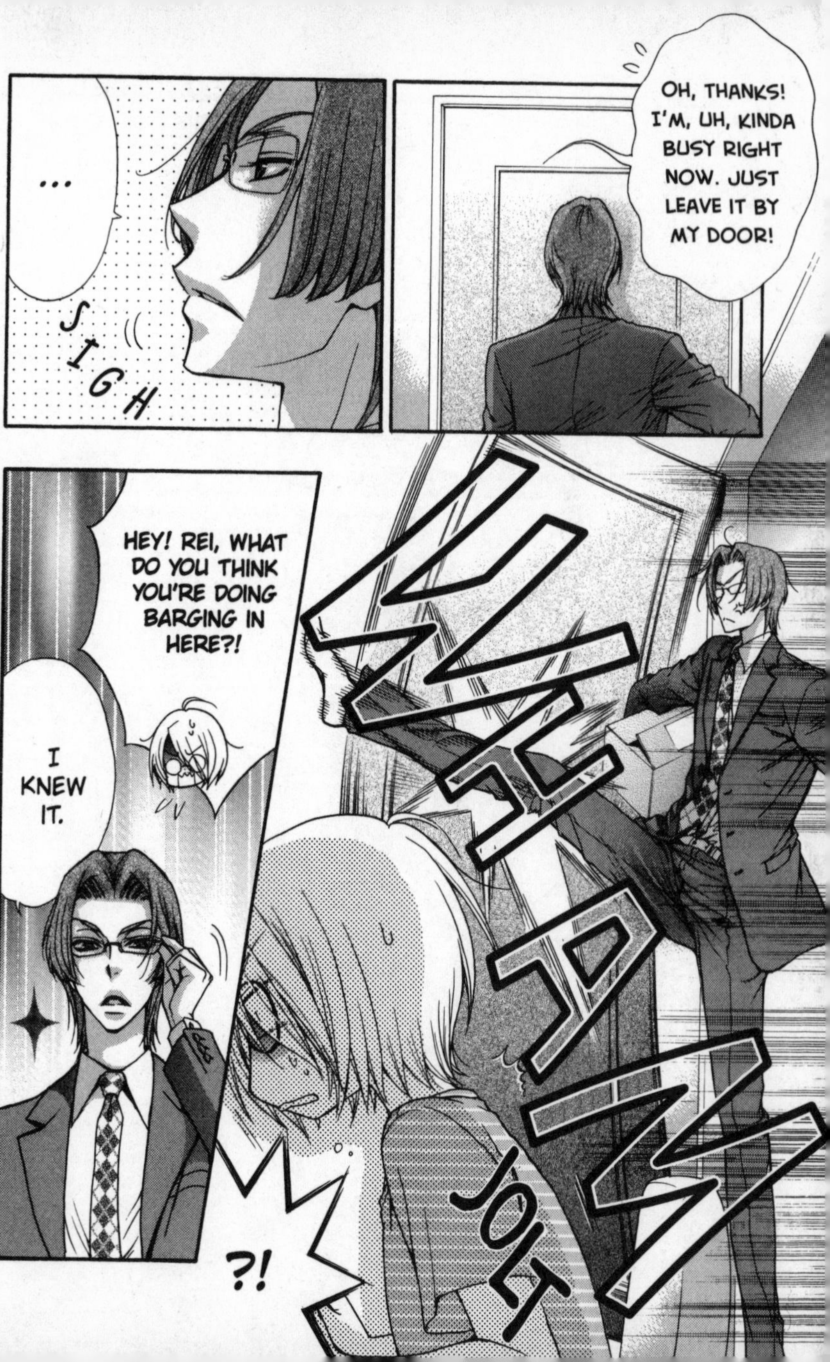
OH, THANKS! I'M, UH, KINDA BUSY RIGHT NOW. JUST LEAVE IT BY MY DOOR!
...
SIGH
WHAM
JOLT
?!
HEY! REI, WHAT DO YOU THINK YOU'RE DOING BARGING IN HERE?!
I KNEW IT.

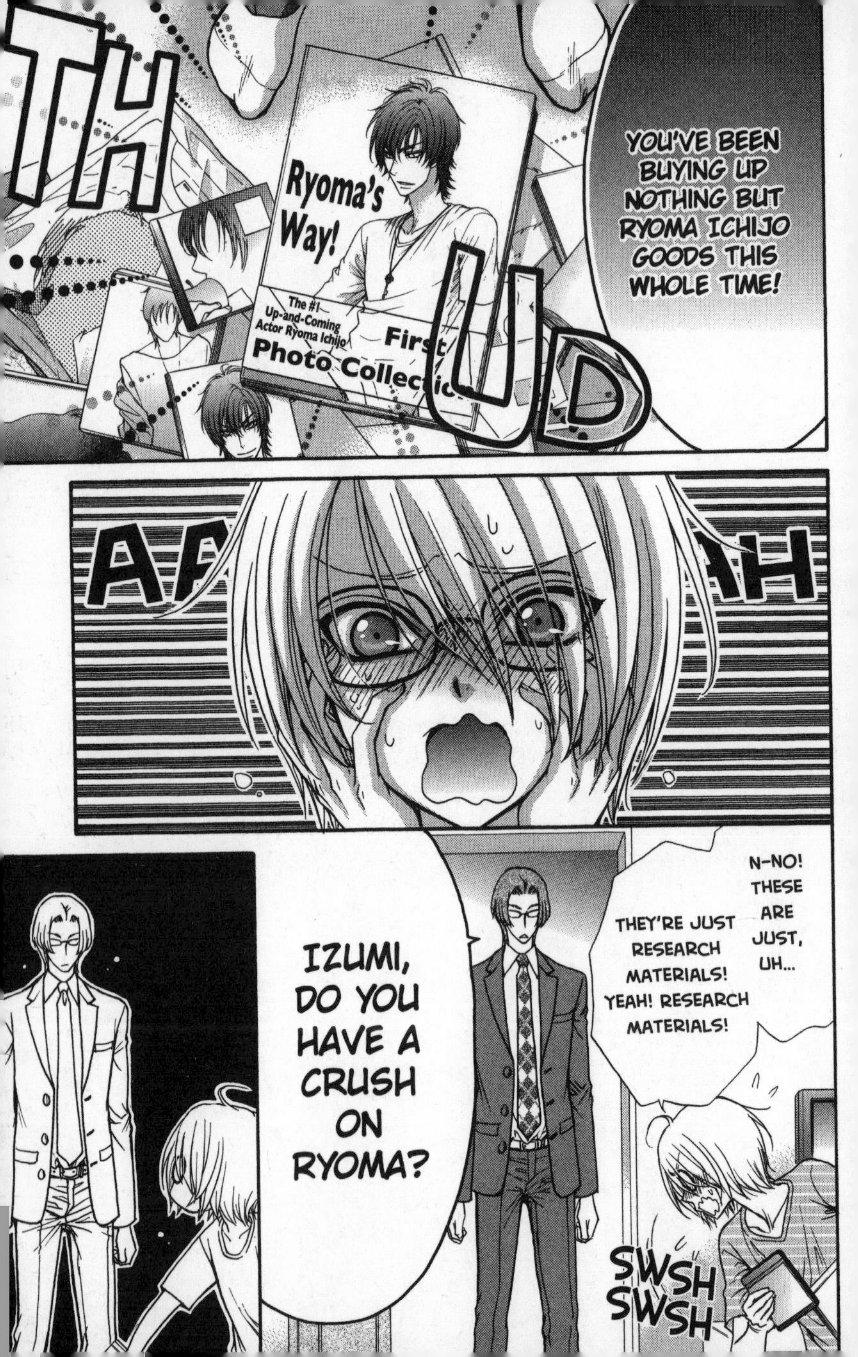
YOU'VE BEEN BUYING UP NOTHING BUT RYOMA ICHIJO GOODS THIS WHOLE TIME!
Ryoma's Way!
The #1 Up-and-Coming Actor Ryoma Ichijo
First Photo Collectio
TH
UD
AA
AH
N-NO! THESE ARE JUST, UH...
THEY'RE JUST RESEARCH MATERIALS! YEAH! RESEARCH MATERIALS!
SWSH SWSH
IZUMI, DO YOU HAVE A CRUSH ON RYOMA?

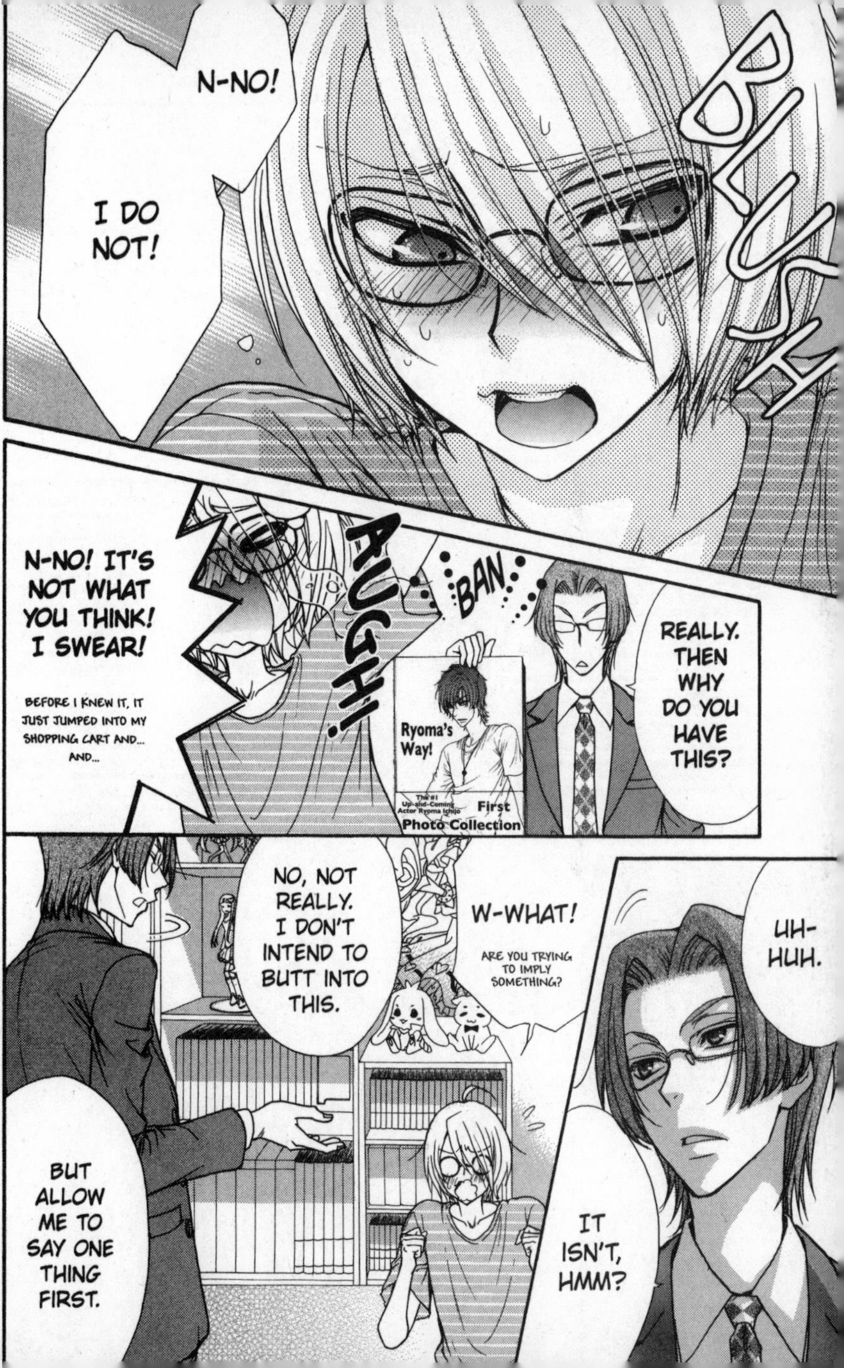
BLUSH
N-NO!
I DO NOT!
REALLY. THEN WHY DO YOU HAVE THIS?
BAN
Ryoma's Way!
The #1 Up-and-Coming Actor Ryoma Ichijo
First Photo Collection
AUGH!
N-NO! IT'S NOT WHAT YOU THINK! I SWEAR!
BEFORE I KNEW IT, IT JUST JUMPED INTO MY SHOPPING CART AND... AND...
UH-HUH.
IT ISN'T, HMM?
W-WHAT!
ARE YOU TRYING TO IMPLY SOMETHING?
NO, NOT REALLY. I DON'T INTEND TO BUTT INTO THIS.
BUT ALLOW ME TO SAY ONE THING FIRST.

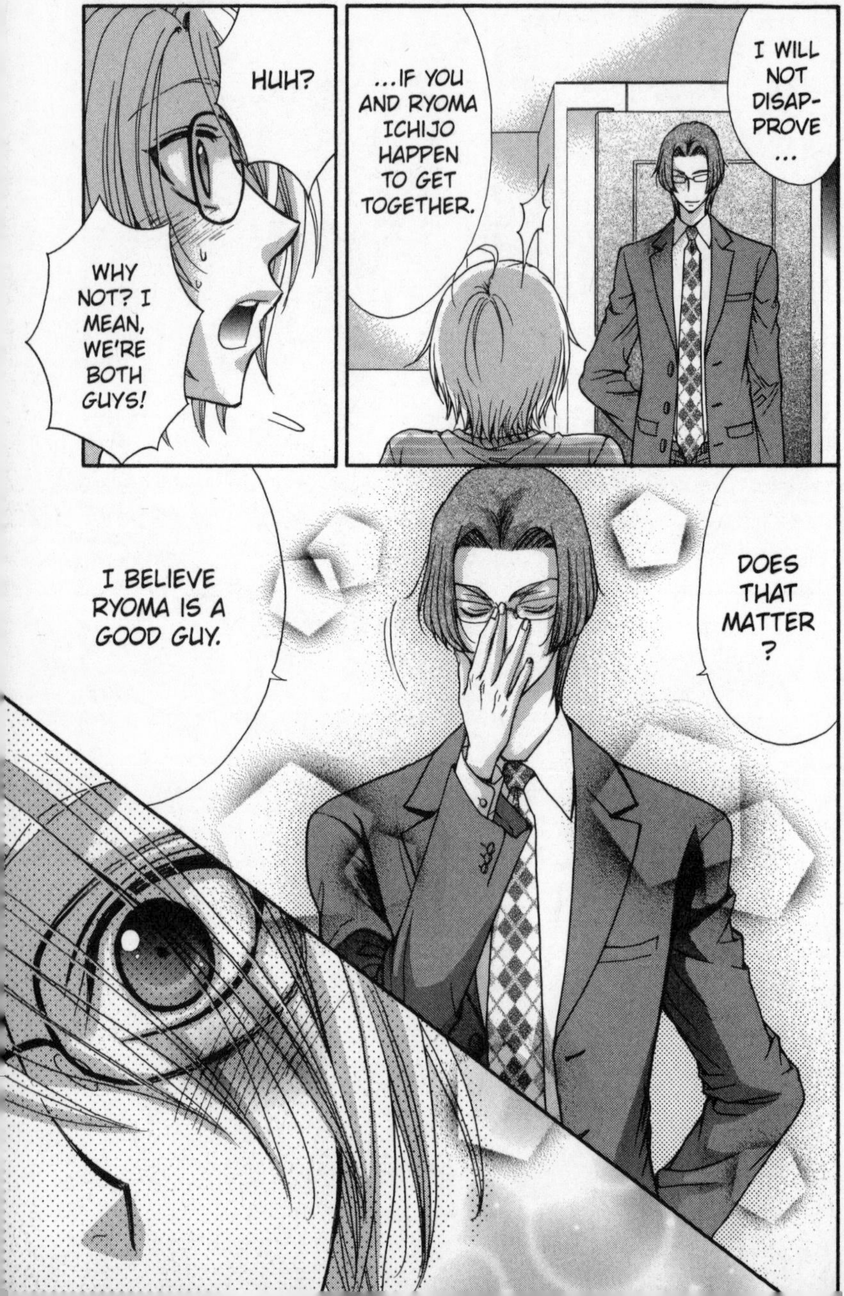
I WILL NOT DISAPPROVE...
...IF YOU AND RYOMA ICHIJO HAPPEN TO GET TOGETHER.
HUH?
WHY NOT? I MEAN, WE'RE BOTH GUYS!
DOES THAT MATTER?
I BELIEVE RYOMA IS A GOOD GUY.

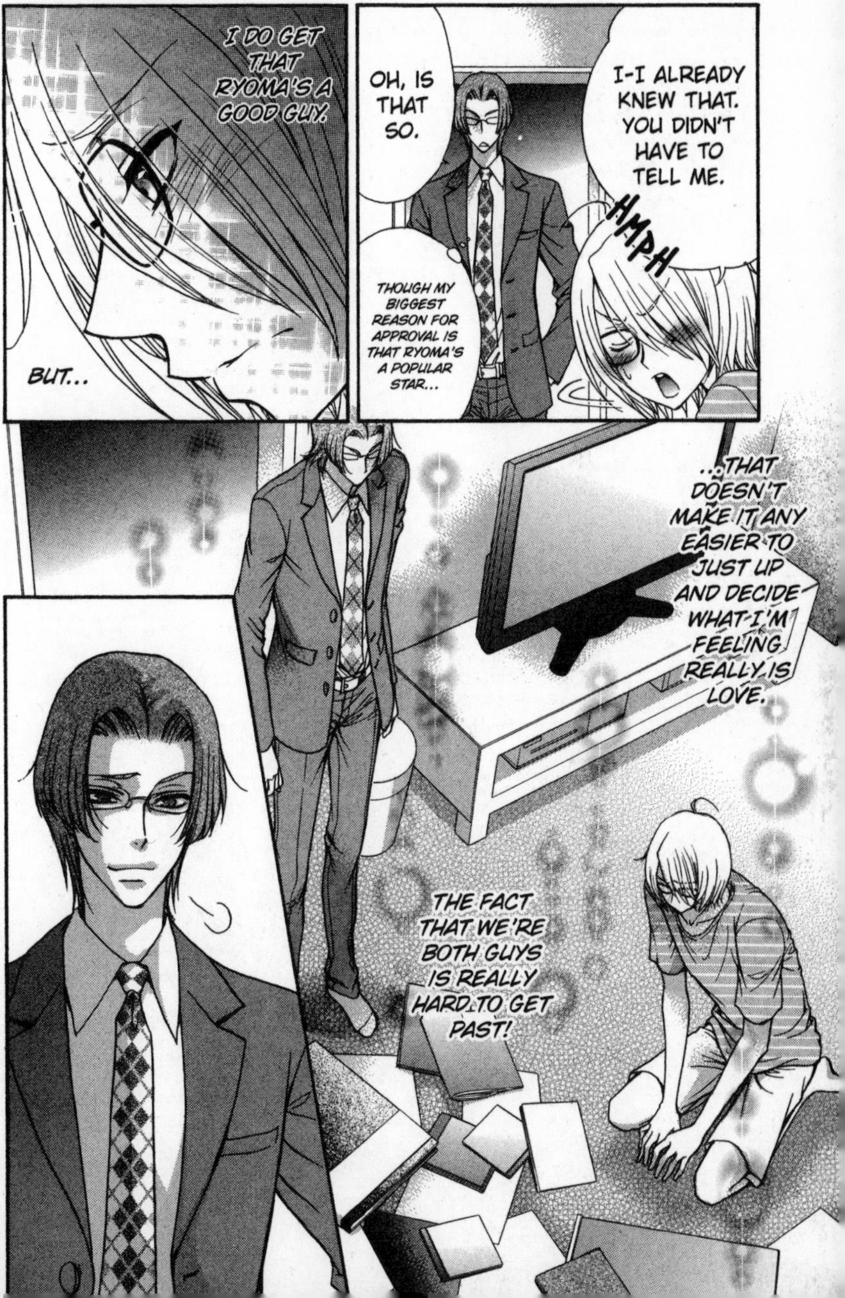
I-I ALREADY KNEW THAT. YOU DIDN'T HAVE TO TELL ME.
HMPH
OH, IS THAT SO.
THOUGH MY BIGGEST REASON FOR APPROVAL IS THAT RYOMA'S A POPULAR STAR...
I DO GET THAT RYOMA'S A GOOD GUY.
BUT...
...THAT DOESN'T MAKE IT ANY EASIER TO JUST UP AND DECIDE WHAT I'M FEELING REALLY IS LOVE.
THE FACT THAT WE'RE BOTH GUYS IS REALLY HARD TO GET PAST!

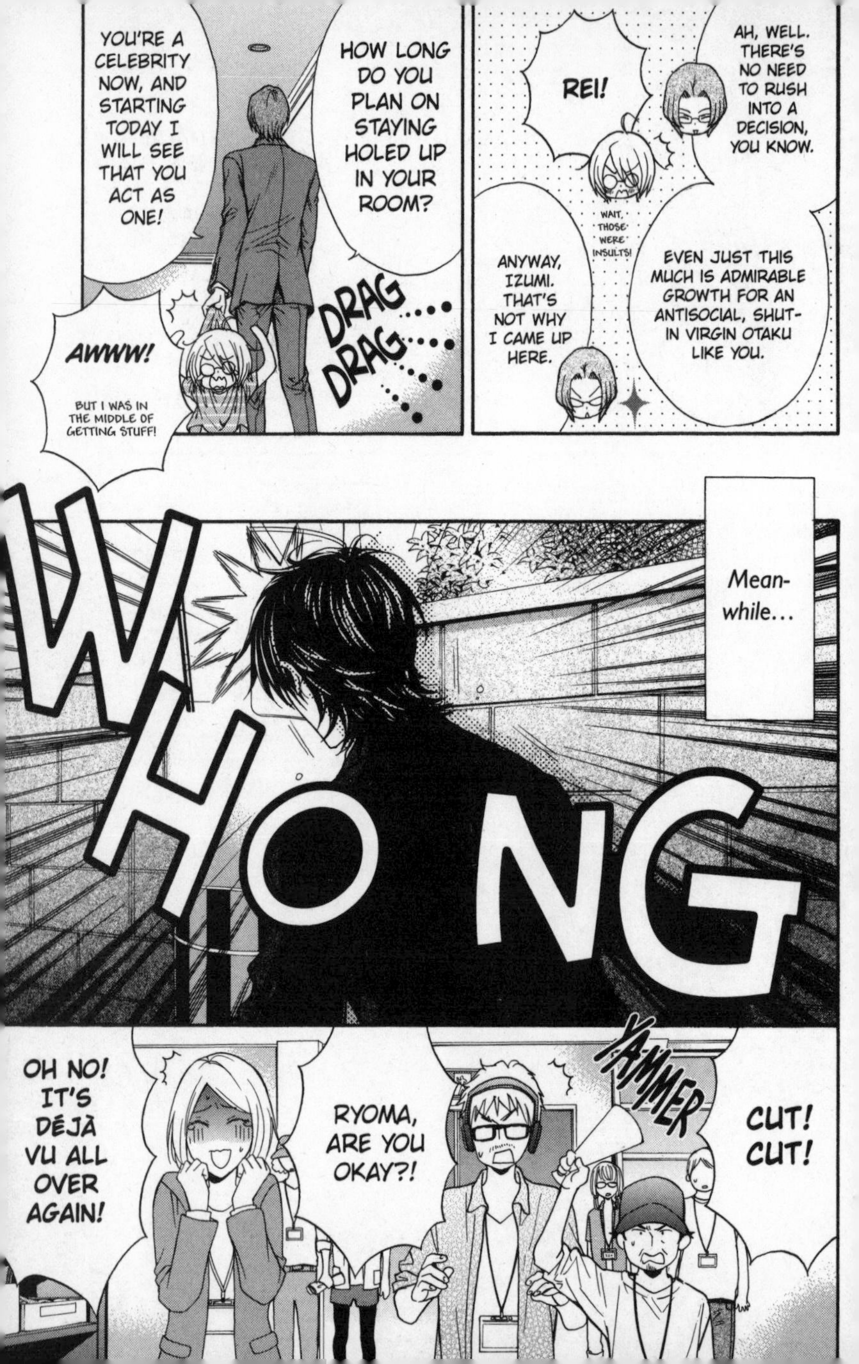
REI!
AH, WELL. THERE'S NO NEED TO RUSH INTO A DECISION, YOU KNOW.
EVEN JUST THIS MUCH IS ADMIRABLE GROWTH FOR AN ANTISOCIAL, SHUT-IN VIRGIN OTAKU LIKE YOU.
WAIT, THOSE WERE INSULTS!
ANYWAY, IZUMI. THAT'S NOT WHY I CAME UP HERE.
HOW LONG DO YOU PLAN ON STAYING HOLED UP IN YOUR ROOM?
YOU'RE A CELEBRITY NOW, AND STARTING TODAY I WILL SEE THAT YOU ACT AS ONE!
DRAG DRAG
AWWW!
BUT I WAS IN THE MIDDLE OF GETTING STUFF!
Mean-while...
WHONG
CUT! CUT!
YAMMER
RYOMA, ARE YOU OKAY?!
OH NO! IT'S DÉJÀ VU ALL OVER AGAIN!

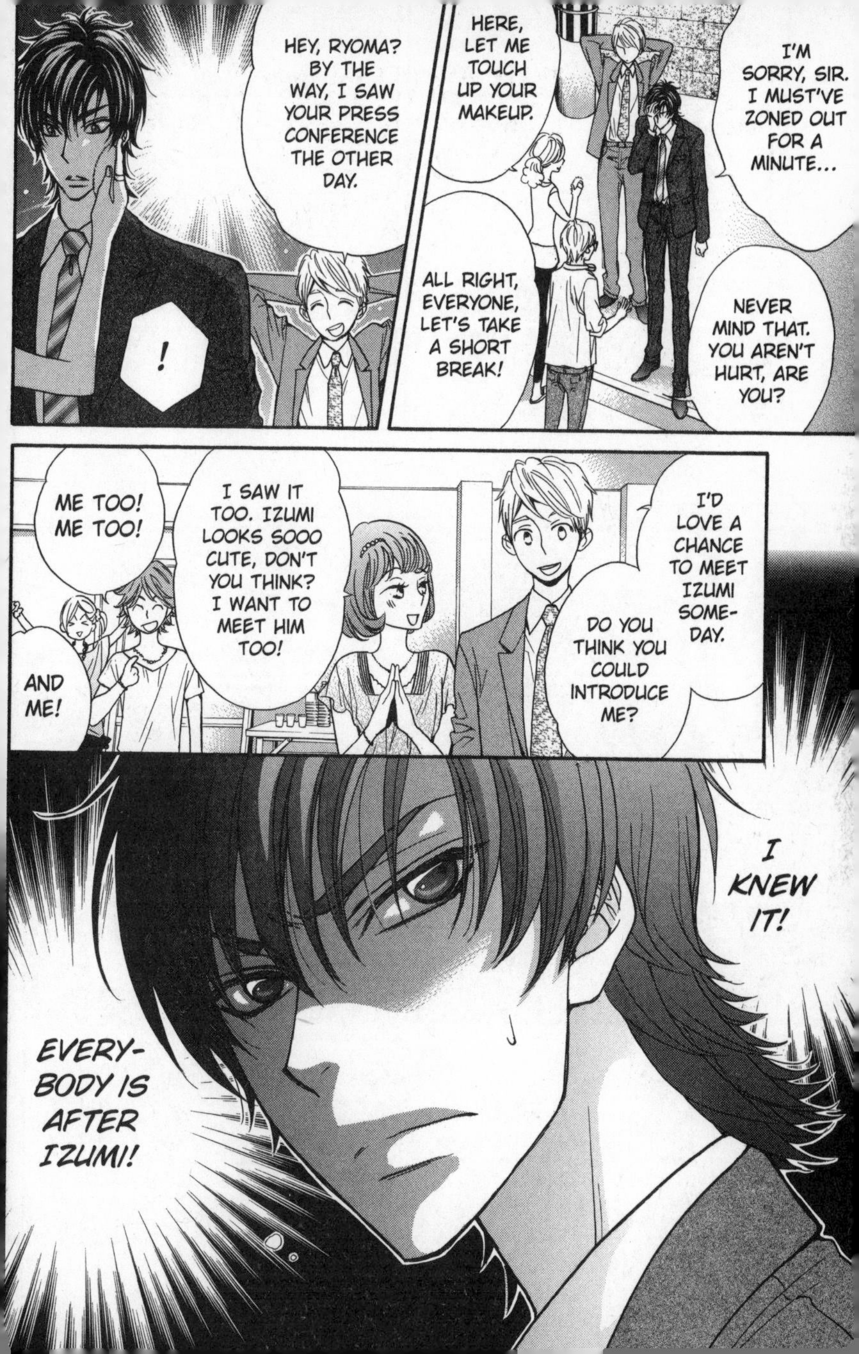
I'M SORRY, SIR. I MUST'VE ZONED OUT FOR A MINUTE...
NEVER MIND THAT. YOU AREN'T HURT, ARE YOU?
HERE, LET ME TOUCH UP YOUR MAKEUP.
ALL RIGHT, EVERYONE, LET'S TAKE A SHORT BREAK!
HEY, RYOMA? BY THE WAY, I SAW YOUR PRESS CONFERENCE THE OTHER DAY.
!
I'D LOVE A CHANCE TO MEET IZUMI SOME-DAY.
DO YOU THINK YOU COULD INTRODUCE ME?
I SAW IT TOO. IZUMI LOOKS SOOO CUTE, DON'T YOU THINK? I WANT TO MEET HIM TOO!
ME TOO! ME TOO!
AND ME!
I KNEW IT!
EVERY-BODY IS AFTER IZUMI!

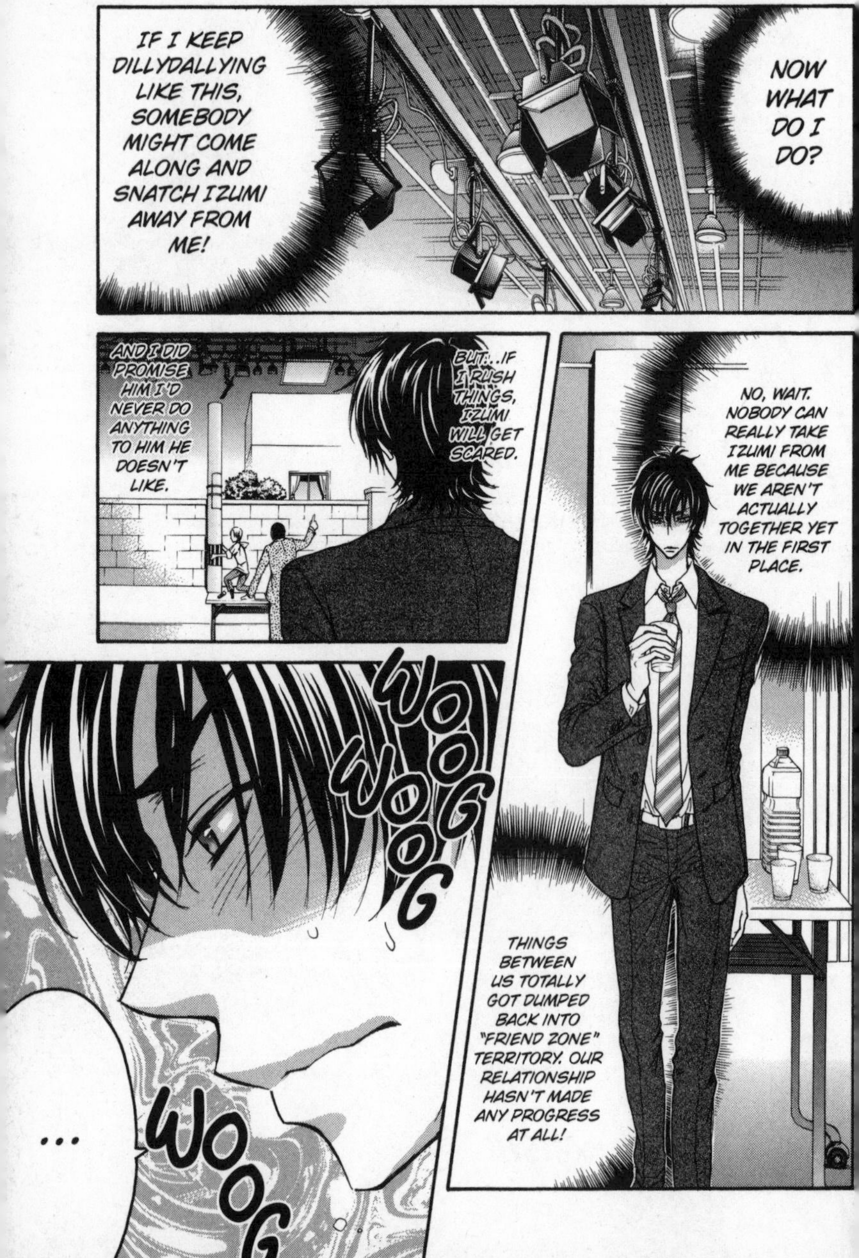
NOW WHAT DO I DO?
IF I KEEP DILLYDALLYING LIKE THIS, SOMEBODY MIGHT COME ALONG AND SNATCH IZUMI AWAY FROM ME!
NO, WAIT. NOBODY CAN REALLY TAKE IZUMI FROM ME BECAUSE WE AREN'T ACTUALLY TOGETHER YET IN THE FIRST PLACE.
THINGS BETWEEN US TOTALLY GOT DUMPED BACK INTO "FRIEND ZONE" TERRITORY. OUR RELATIONSHIP HASN'T MADE ANY PROGRESS AT ALL!
BUT...IF I RUSH THINGS, IZUMI WILL GET SCARED.
AND I DID PROMISE HIM I'D NEVER DO ANYTHING TO HIM HE DOESN'T LIKE.
WOOG WOOG WOOG
...
WOOG

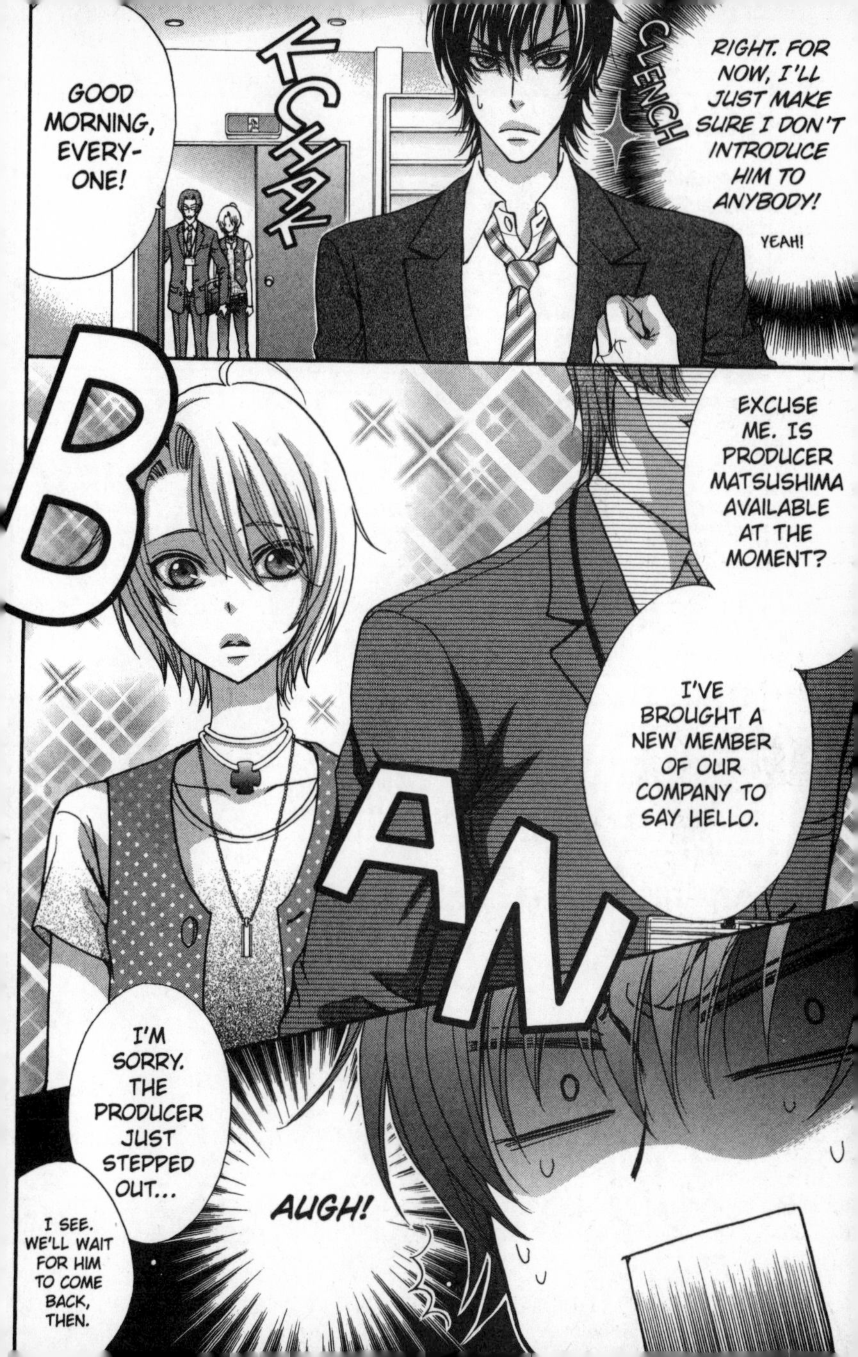
RIGHT. FOR NOW, I'LL JUST MAKE SURE I DON'T INTRODUCE HIM TO ANYBODY!
YEAH!
CLENCH
KCHAK
GOOD MORNING, EVERY-ONE!
EXCUSE ME. IS PRODUCER MATSUSHIMA AVAILABLE AT THE MOMENT?
I'VE BROUGHT A NEW MEMBER OF OUR COMPANY TO SAY HELLO.
BAN
I'M SORRY. THE PRODUCER JUST STEPPED OUT...
AUGH!
I SEE. WE'LL WAIT FOR HIM TO COME BACK, THEN.

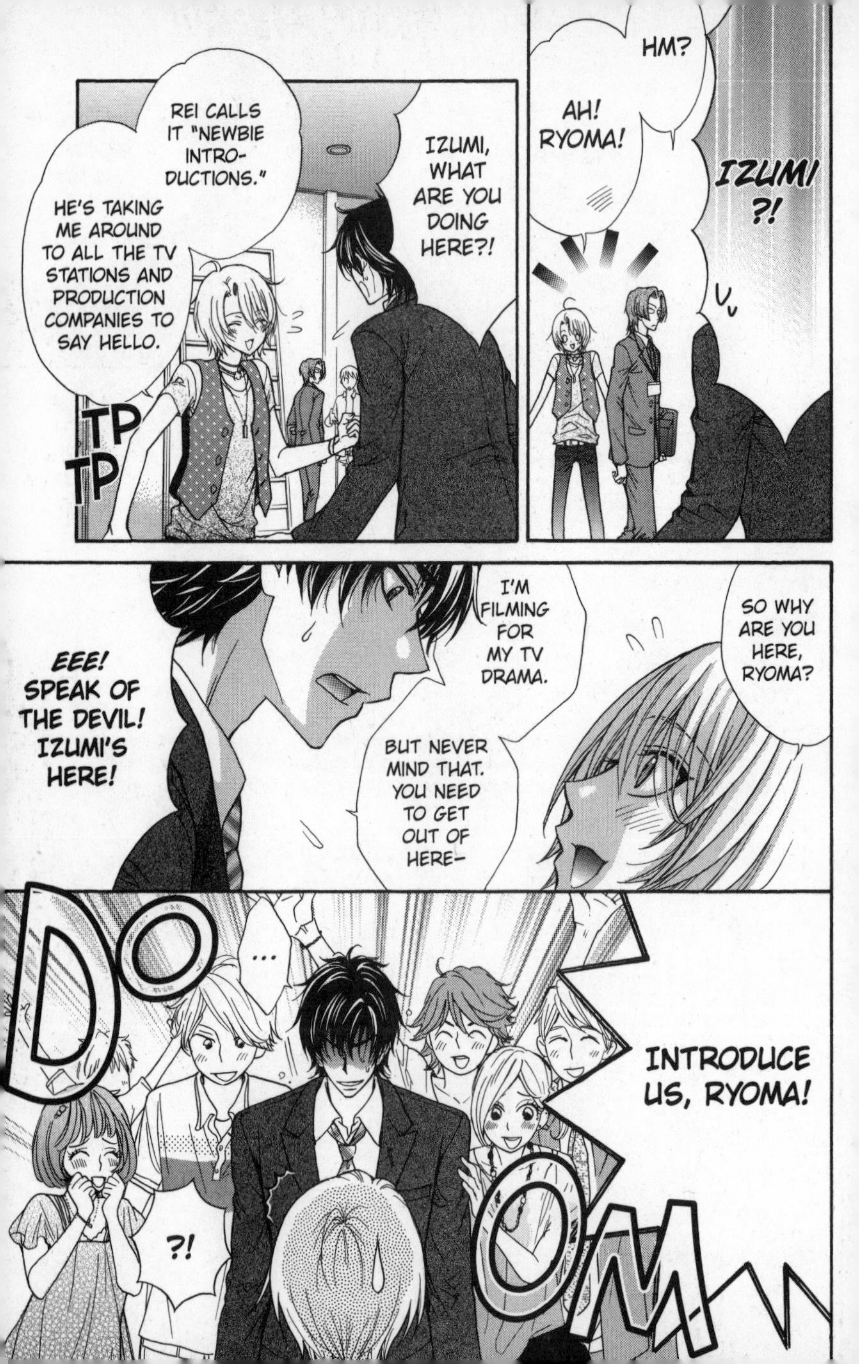
HM?
AH! RYOMA!
IZUMI ?!
IZUMI, WHAT ARE YOU DOING HERE?!
REI CALLS IT "NEWBIE INTRO-DUCTIONS."
HE'S TAKING ME AROUND TO ALL THE TV STATIONS AND PRODUCTION COMPANIES TO SAY HELLO.
TP TP
SO WHY ARE YOU HERE, RYOMA?
I'M FILMING FOR MY TV DRAMA.
BUT NEVER MIND THAT. YOU NEED TO GET OUT OF HERE–
EEE! SPEAK OF THE DEVIL! IZUMI'S HERE!
INTRODUCE US, RYOMA!
DOOOM
...
?!

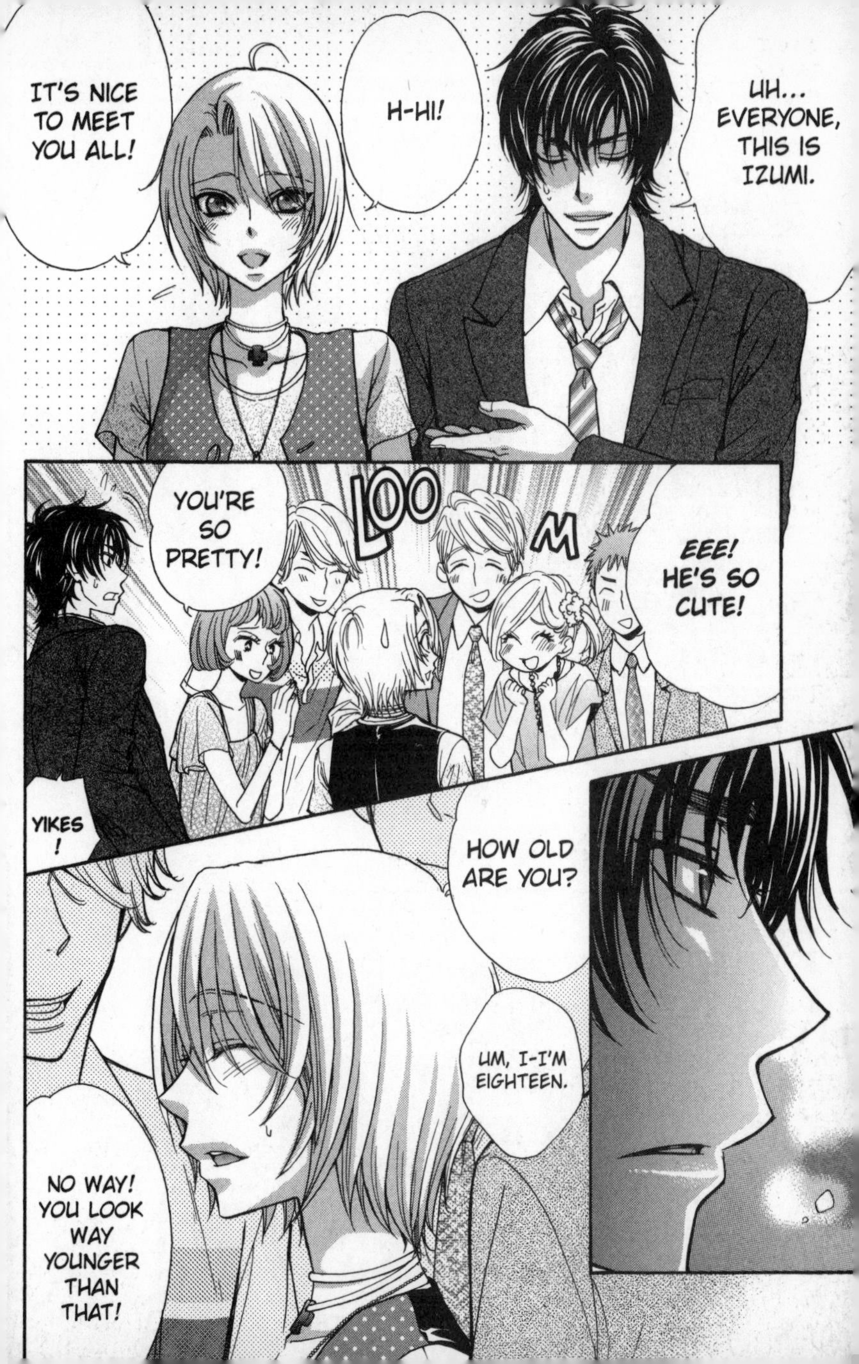
UH... EVERYONE, THIS IS IZUMI.
H-HI!
IT'S NICE TO MEET YOU ALL!
EEE! HE'S SO CUTE!
LOOM
YOU'RE SO PRETTY!
YIKES!
HOW OLD ARE YOU?
UM, I-I'M EIGHTEEN.
NO WAY! YOU LOOK WAY YOUNGER THAN THAT!

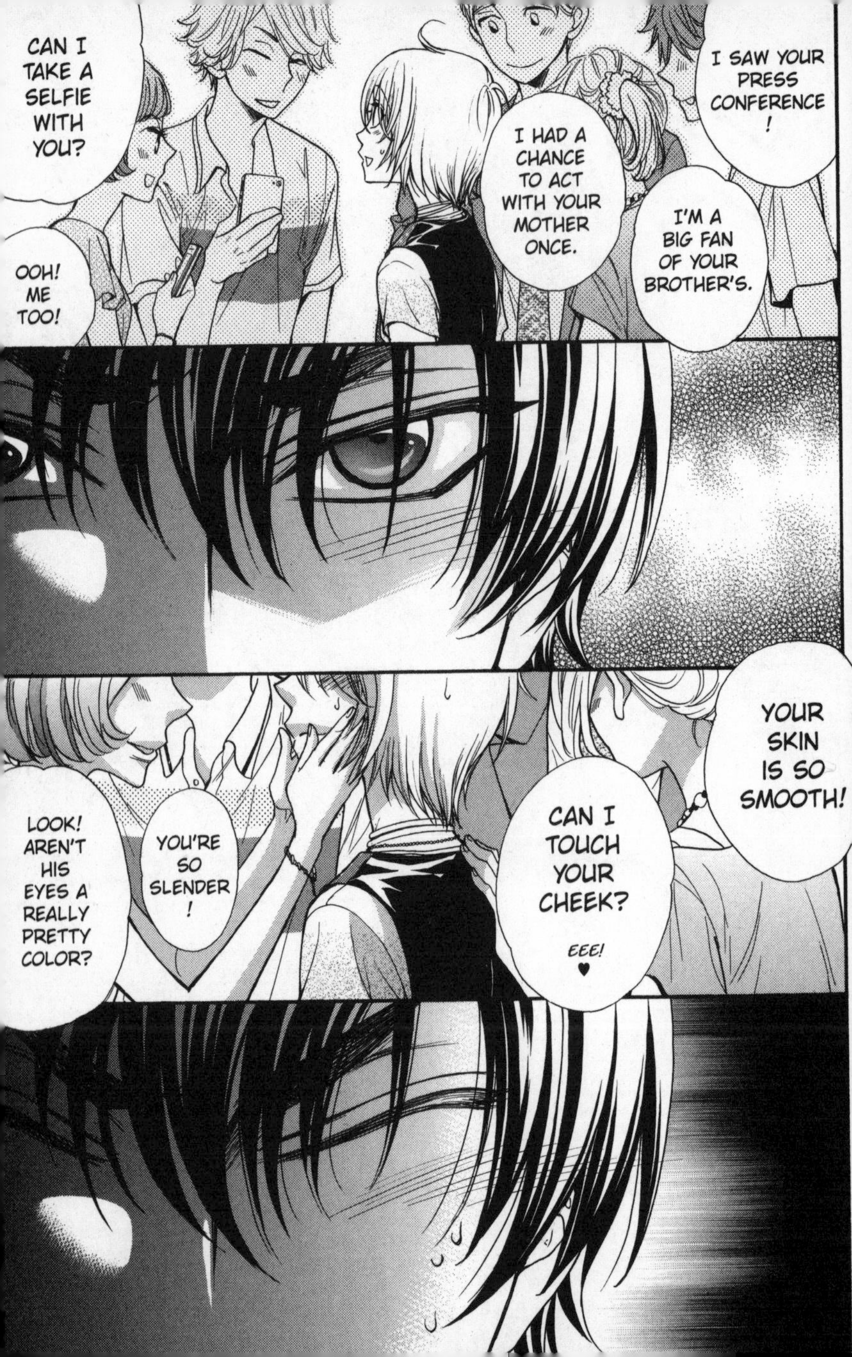
I SAW YOUR PRESS CONFERENCE!
I'M A BIG FAN OF YOUR BROTHER'S.
I HAD A CHANCE TO ACT WITH YOUR MOTHER ONCE.
CAN I TAKE A SELFIE WITH YOU?
OOH! ME TOO!
YOUR SKIN IS SO SMOOTH!
CAN I TOUCH YOUR CHEEK?
EEE! ♥
YOU'RE SO SLENDER!
LOOK! AREN'T HIS EYES A REALLY PRETTY COLOR?

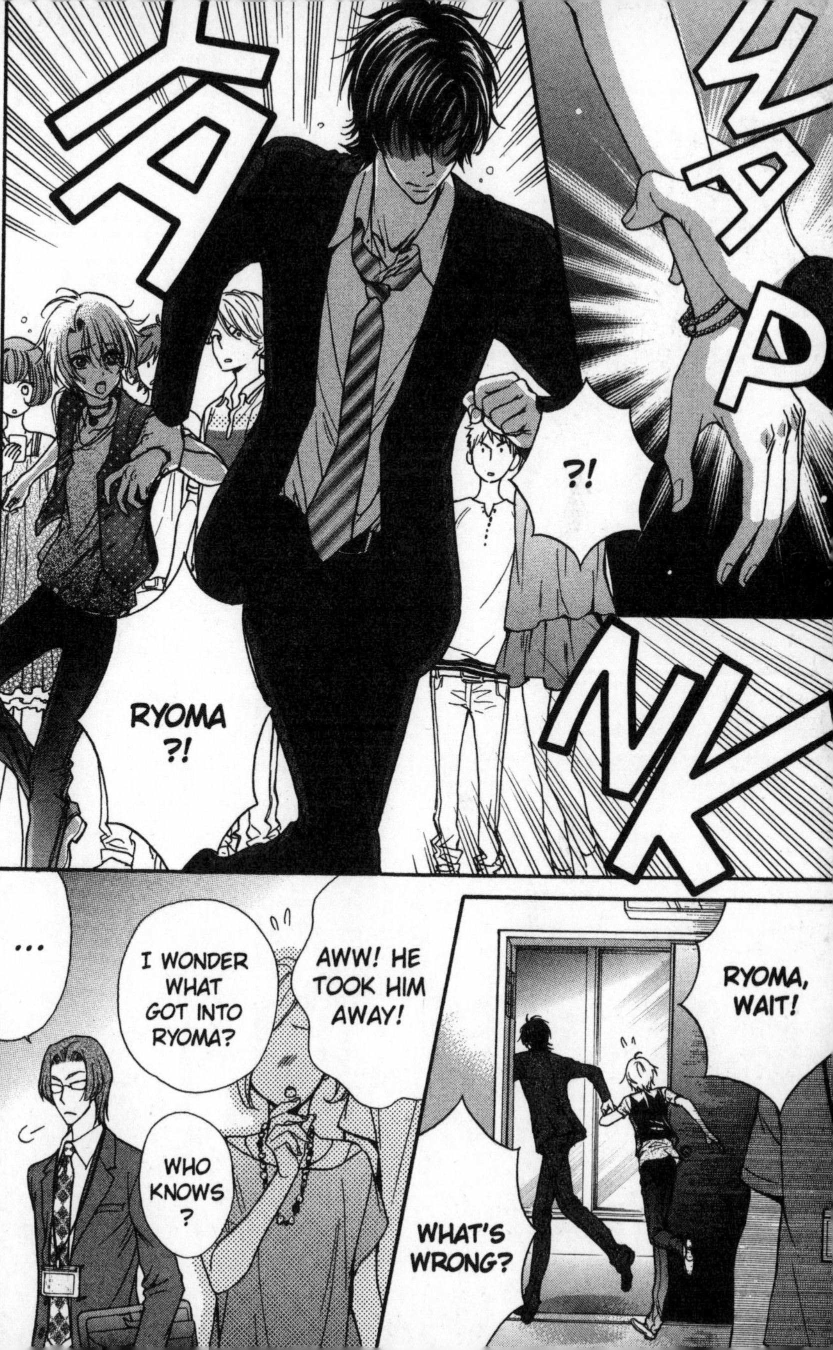
WAP
?!
YA
NK
RYOMA ?!
RYOMA, WAIT!
WHAT'S WRONG?
AWW! HE TOOK HIM AWAY!
I WONDER WHAT GOT INTO RYOMA?
...
WHO KNOWS ?

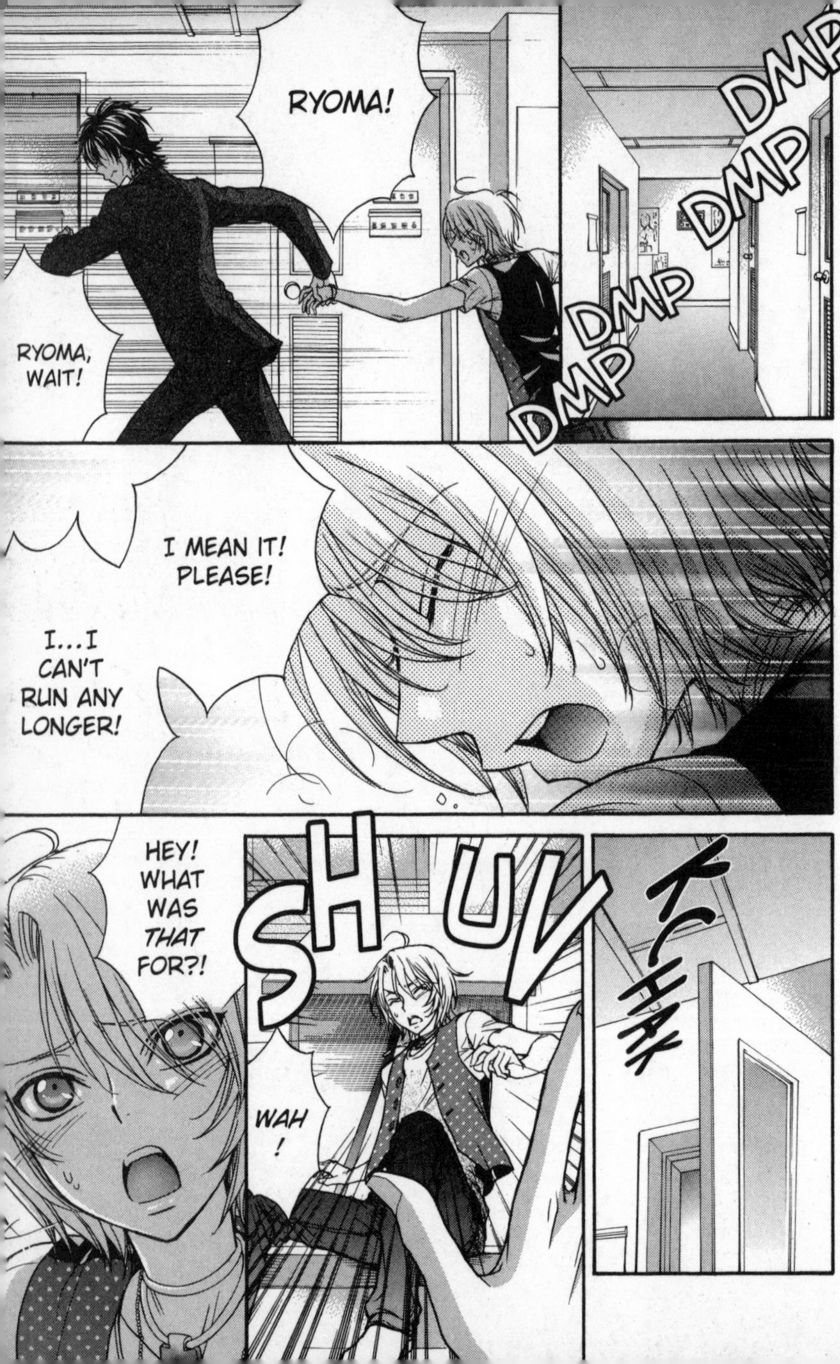
DMP
DMP
DMP
DMP
DMP
DMP
RYOMA!
RYOMA, WAIT!
I MEAN IT! PLEASE!
I...I CAN'T RUN ANY LONGER!
K-CHAK
SHUV
WAH!
HEY! WHAT WAS *THAT* FOR?!

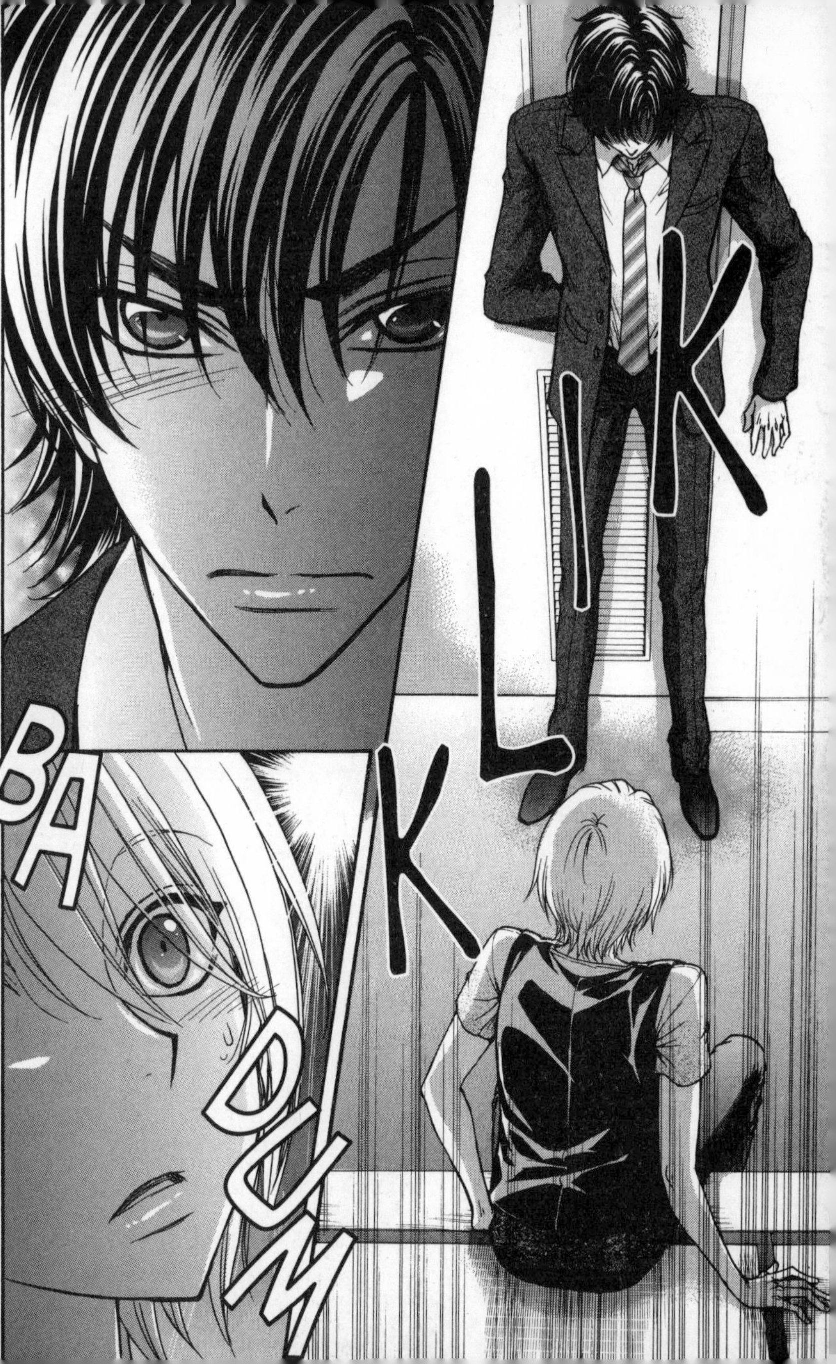
KLIK
BA DUM

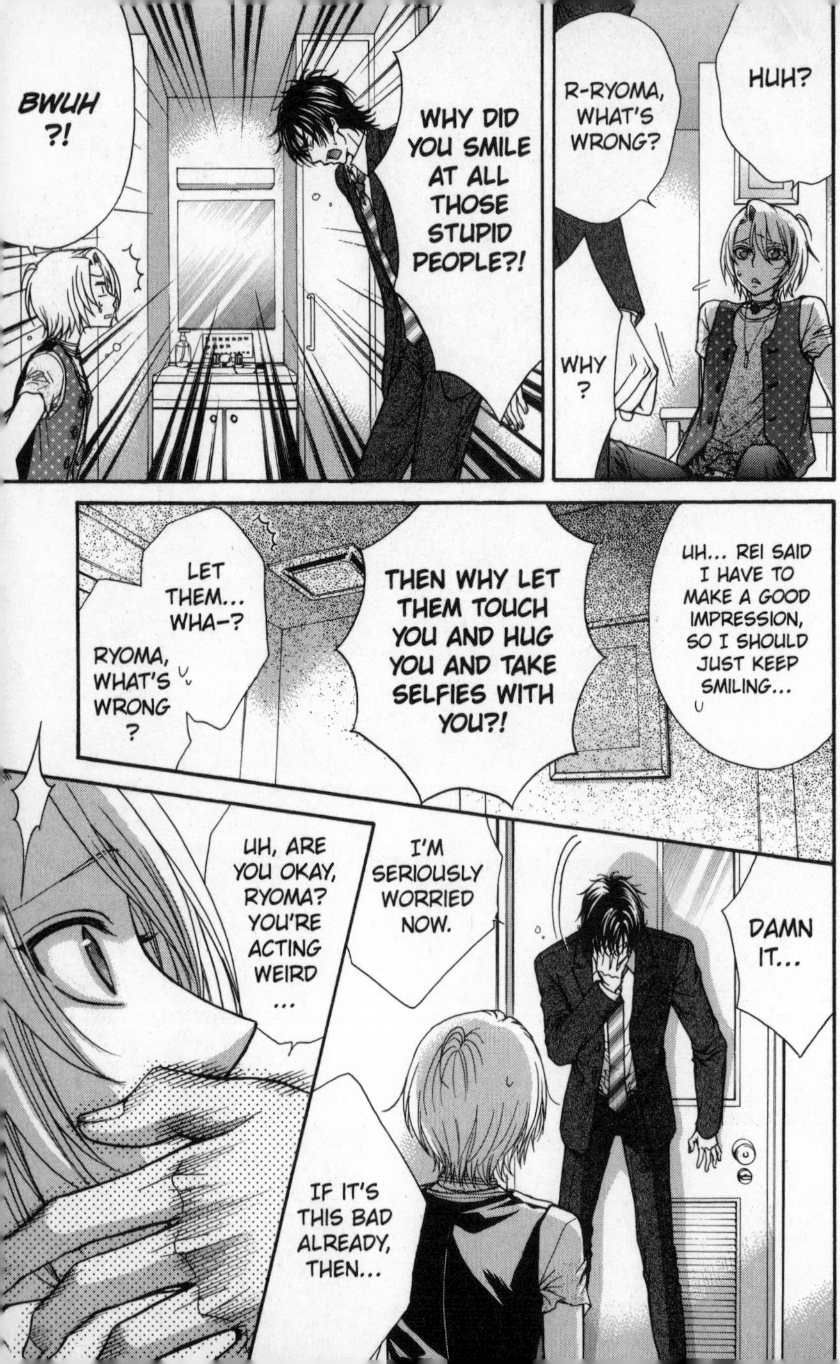
HUH?
R-RYOMA, WHAT'S WRONG?
WHY?
WHY DID YOU SMILE AT ALL THOSE STUPID PEOPLE?!
BWUH ?!
UH... REI SAID I HAVE TO MAKE A GOOD IMPRESSION, SO I SHOULD JUST KEEP SMILING...
THEN WHY LET THEM TOUCH YOU AND HUG YOU AND TAKE SELFIES WITH YOU?!
LET THEM... WHA-?
RYOMA, WHAT'S WRONG?
DAMN IT...
I'M SERIOUSLY WORRIED NOW.
UH, ARE YOU OKAY, RYOMA? YOU'RE ACTING WEIRD...
IF IT'S THIS BAD ALREADY, THEN...

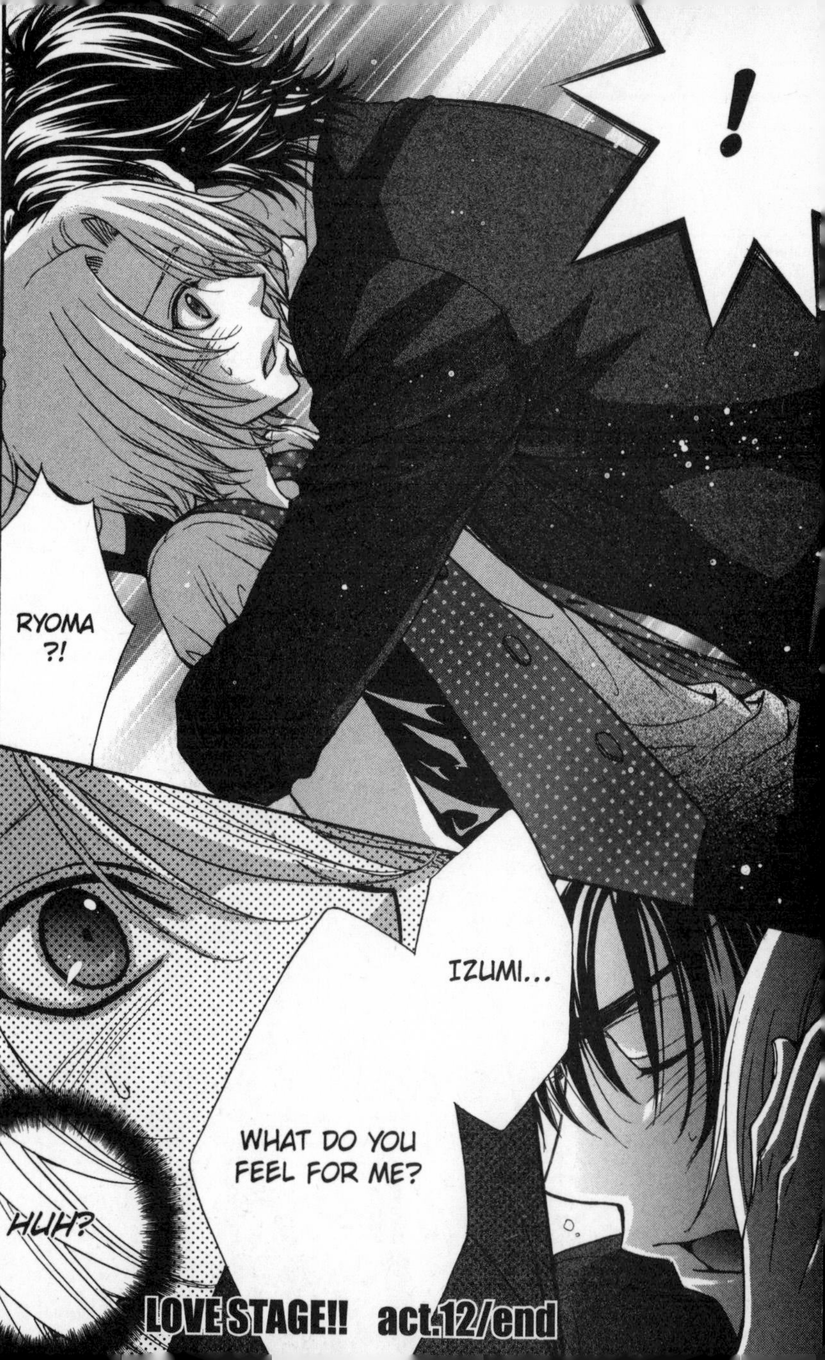
!
RYOMA ?!
IZUMI...
WHAT DO YOU FEEL FOR ME?
HUH?
LOVE STAGE!! act.12/end

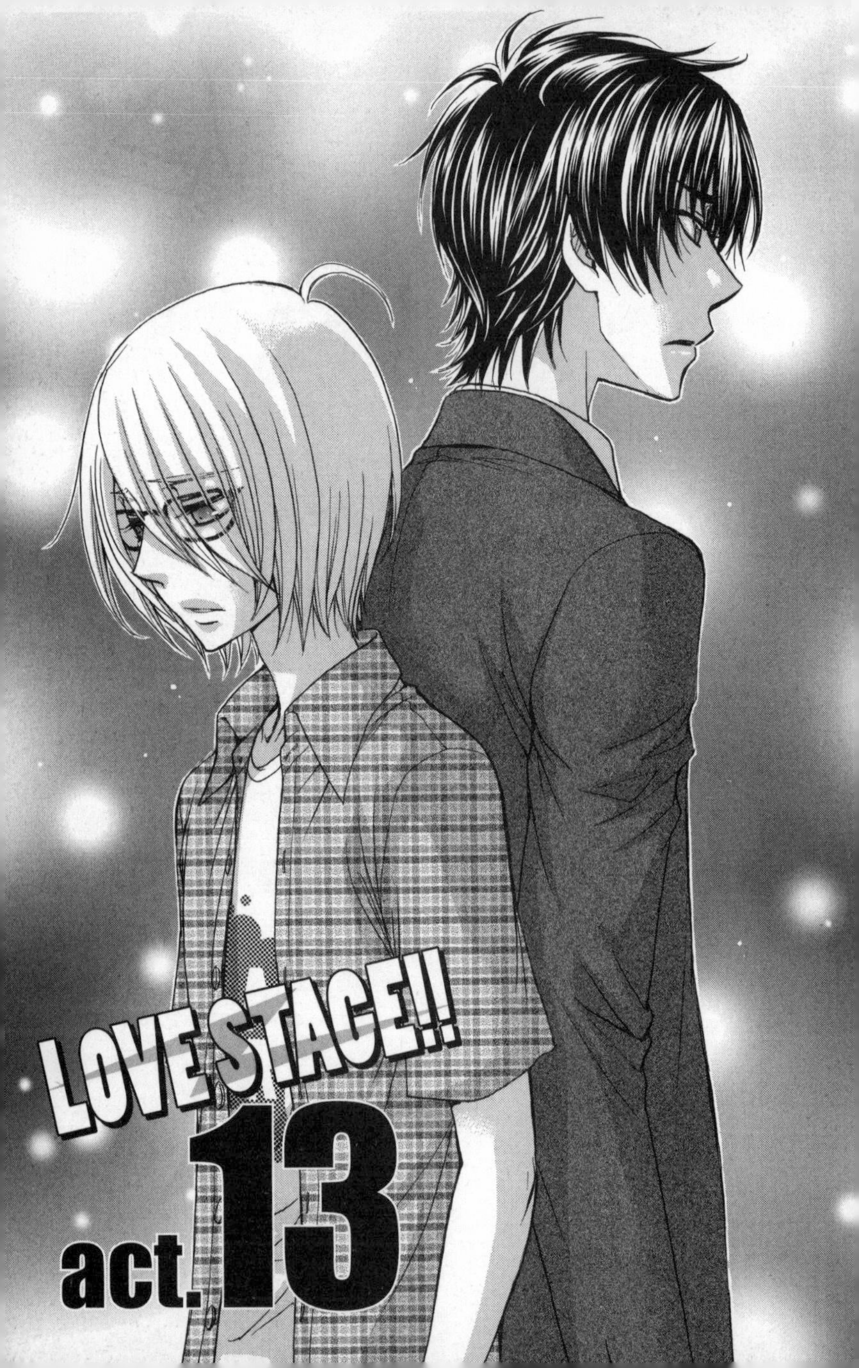
LOVE STAGE!!
act.13

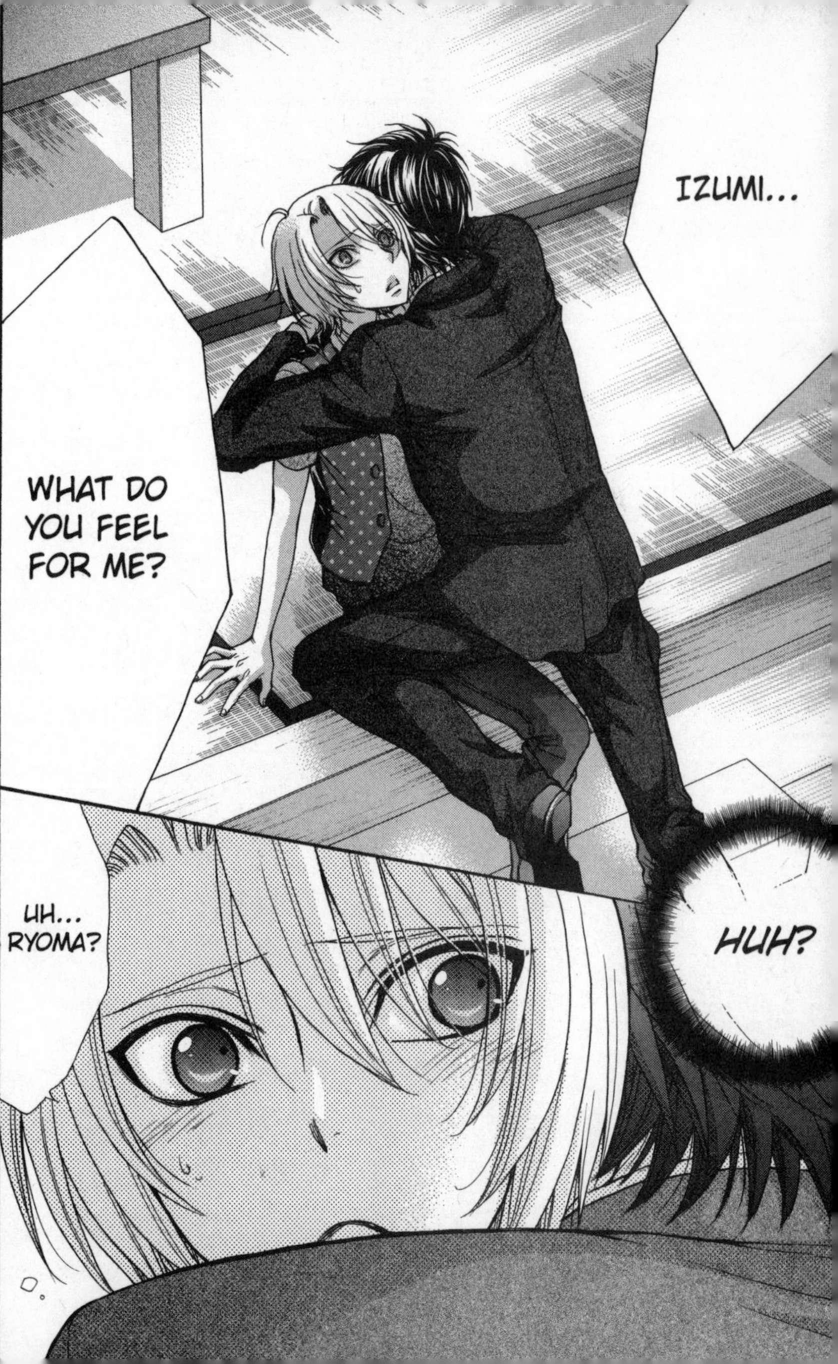
IZUMI...
WHAT DO YOU FEEL FOR ME?
HUH?
UH... RYOMA?

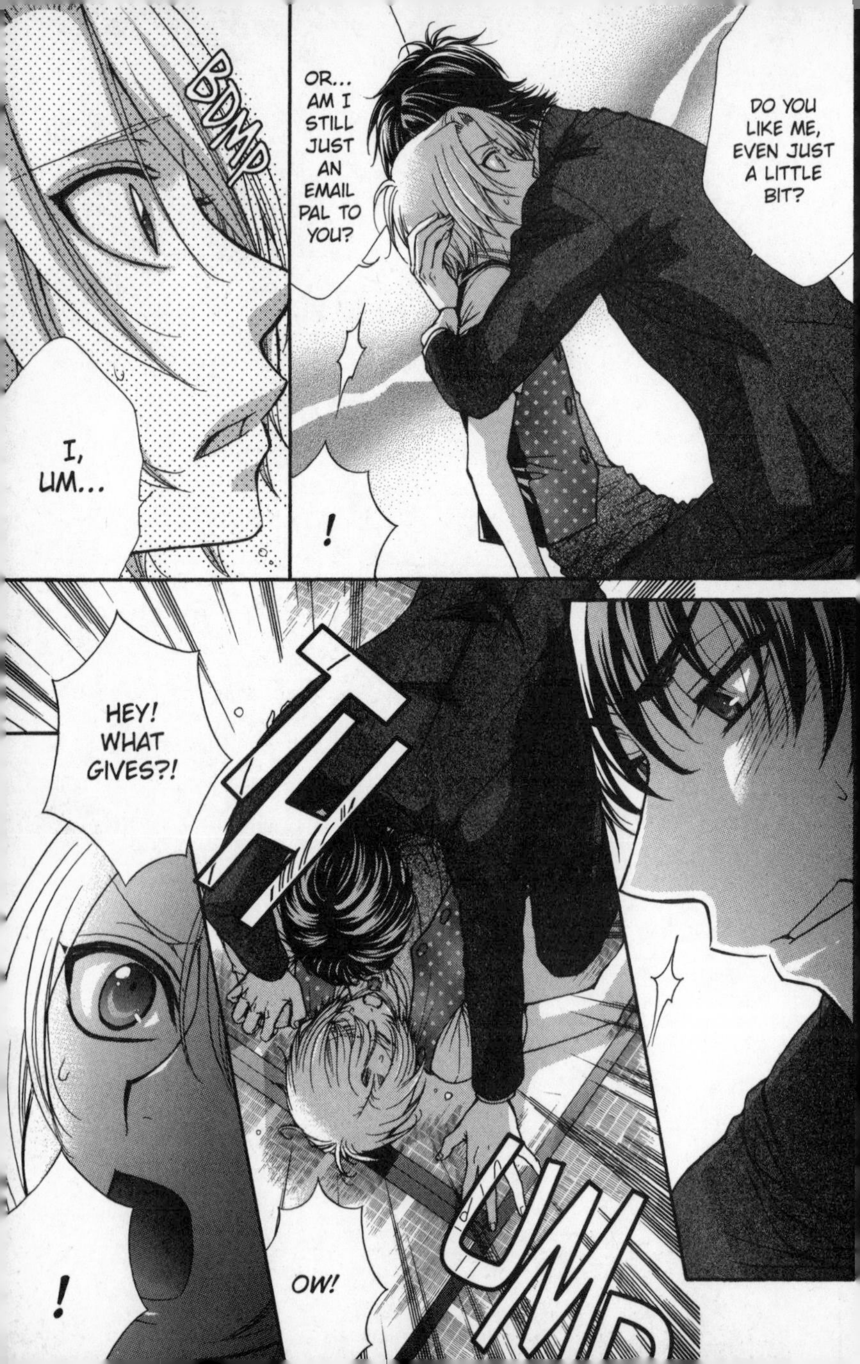
DO YOU LIKE ME, EVEN JUST A LITTLE BIT?
OR... AM I STILL JUST AN EMAIL PAL TO YOU?
!
BDMP
I, UM...
HEY! WHAT GIVES?!
OW!
!

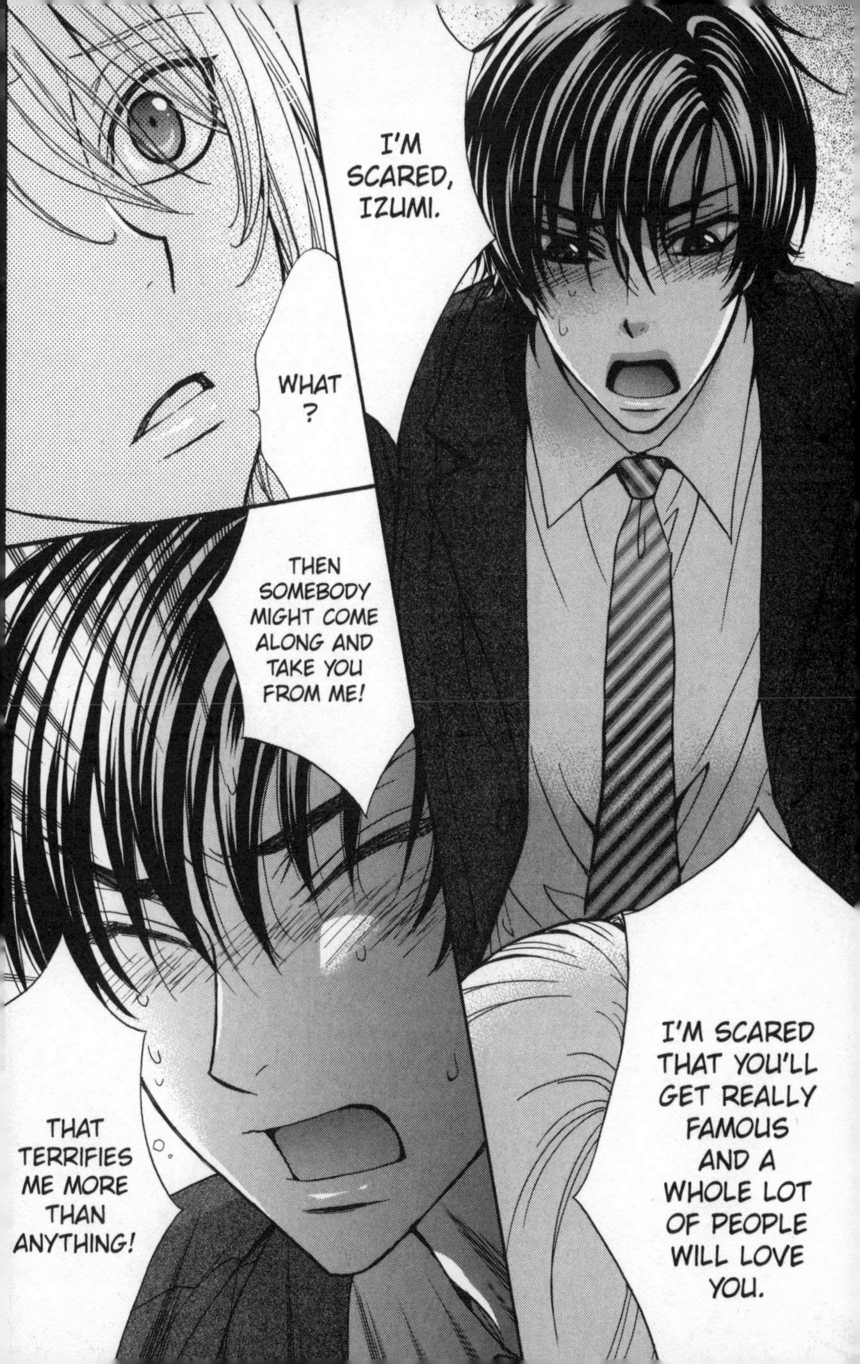
I'M SCARED, IZUMI.
WHAT?
I'M SCARED THAT YOU'LL GET REALLY FAMOUS AND A WHOLE LOT OF PEOPLE WILL LOVE YOU.
THEN SOMEBODY MIGHT COME ALONG AND TAKE YOU FROM ME!
THAT TERRIFIES ME MORE THAN ANYTHING!

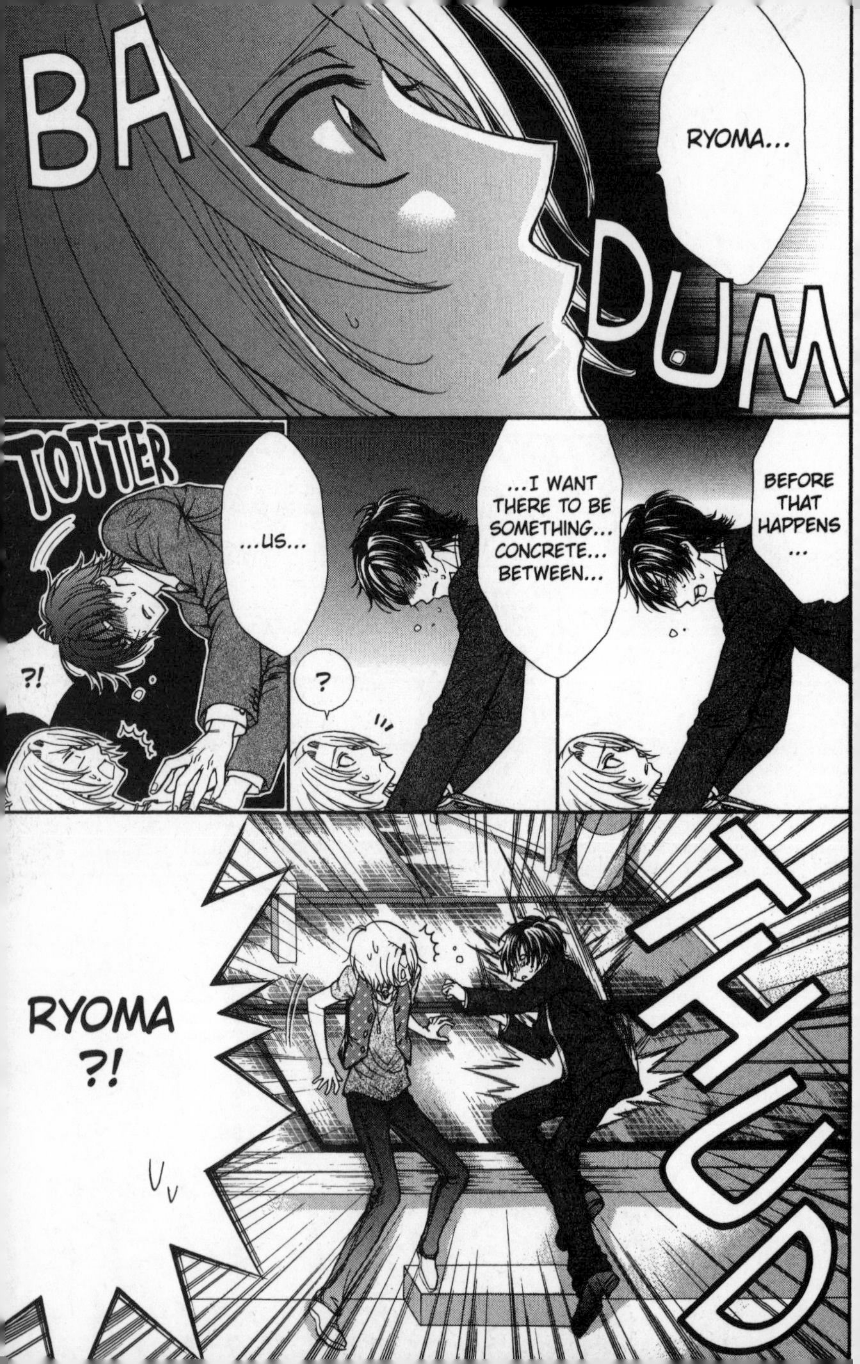
RYOMA...
BA DUM
BEFORE THAT HAPPENS ...
...I WANT THERE TO BE SOMETHING... CONCRETE... BETWEEN...
?
...US...
TOTTER
?!
THUD
RYOMA ?!

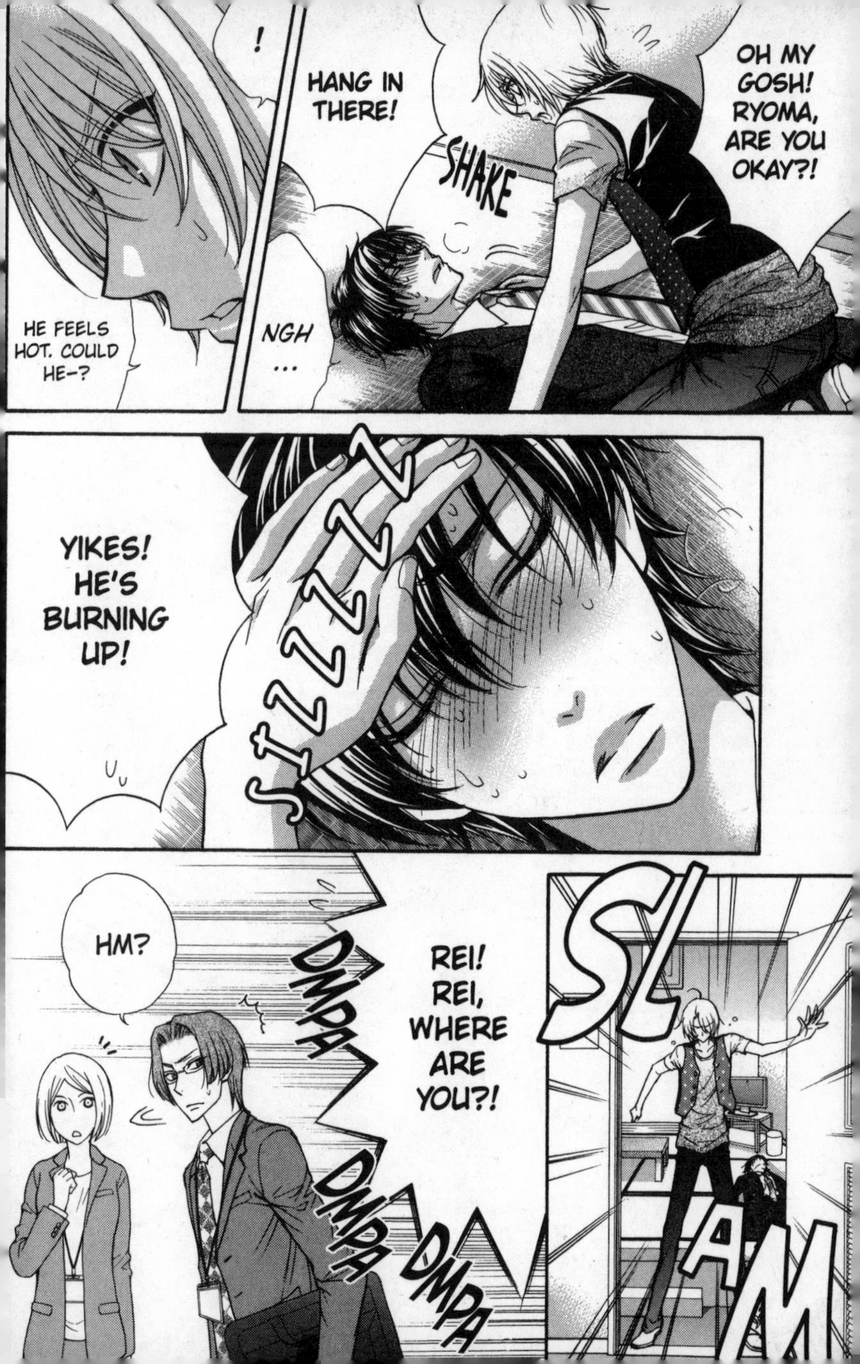
OH MY GOSH! RYOMA, ARE YOU OKAY?!
SHAKE
HANG IN THERE!
NGH ...
!
HE FEELS HOT. COULD HE-?
SIZZZZZ
YIKES! HE'S BURNING UP!
SLAM
REI! REI, WHERE ARE YOU?!
DMPA DMPA DMPA DMPA
HM?

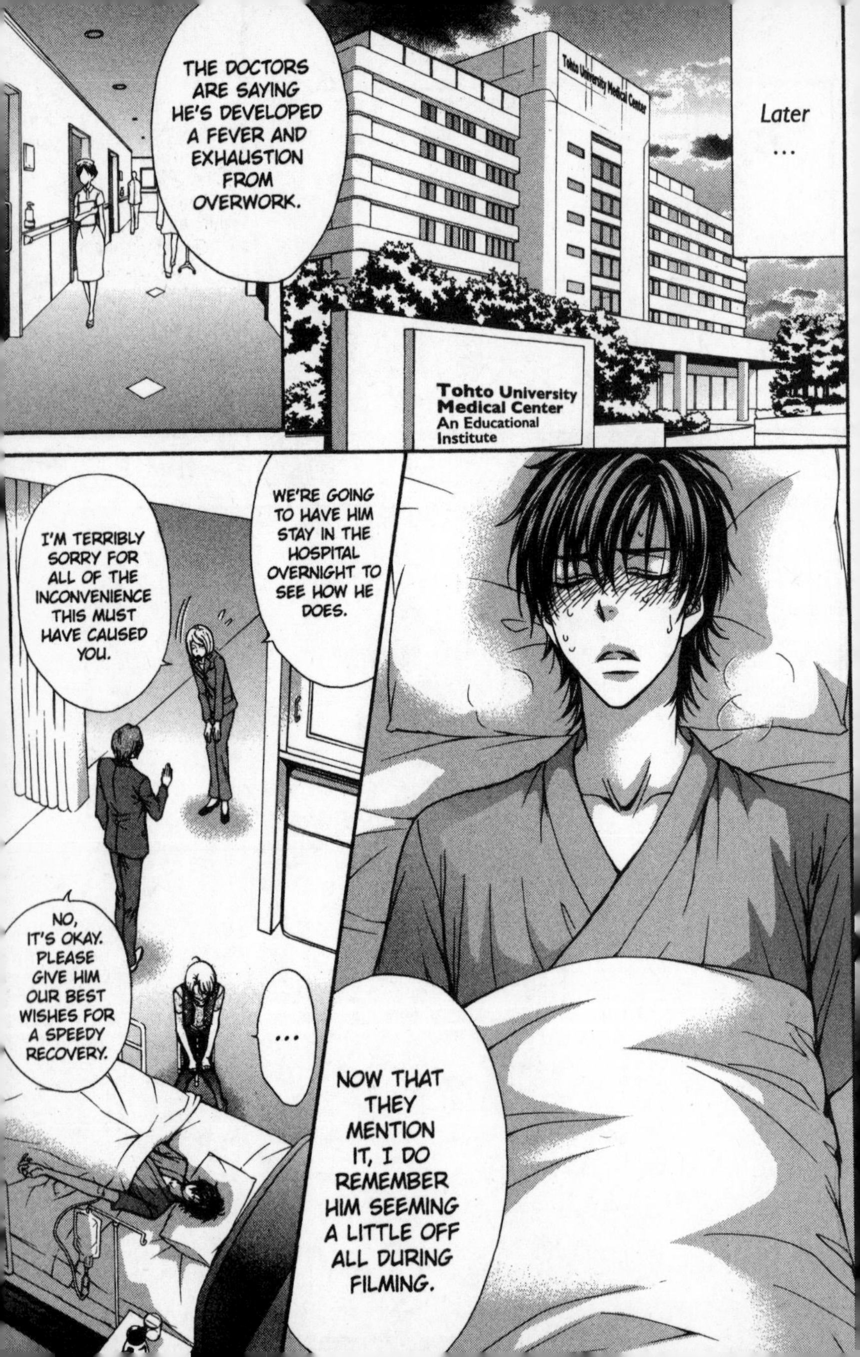
Later ...
Tohto University Medical Center
Tohto University Medical Center An Educational Institute
THE DOCTORS ARE SAYING HE'S DEVELOPED A FEVER AND EXHAUSTION FROM OVERWORK.
WE'RE GOING TO HAVE HIM STAY IN THE HOSPITAL OVERNIGHT TO SEE HOW HE DOES.
I'M TERRIBLY SORRY FOR ALL OF THE INCONVENIENCE THIS MUST HAVE CAUSED YOU.
NO, IT'S OKAY. PLEASE GIVE HIM OUR BEST WISHES FOR A SPEEDY RECOVERY.
...
NOW THAT THEY MENTION IT, I DO REMEMBER HIM SEEMING A LITTLE OFF ALL DURING FILMING.

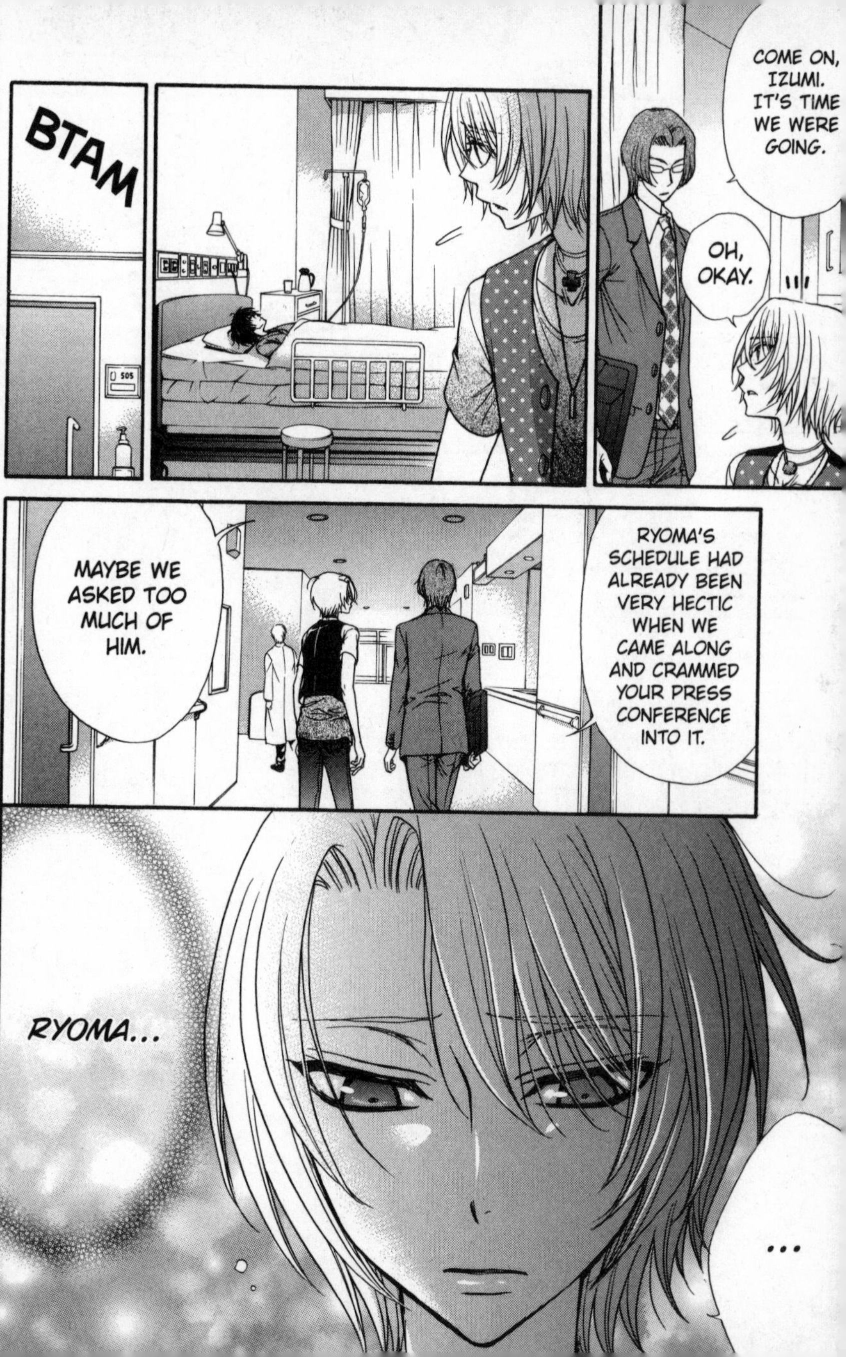
COME ON, IZUMI. IT'S TIME WE WERE GOING.
OH, OKAY.
BTAM
RYOMA'S SCHEDULE HAD ALREADY BEEN VERY HECTIC WHEN WE CAME ALONG AND CRAMMED YOUR PRESS CONFERENCE INTO IT.
MAYBE WE ASKED TOO MUCH OF HIM.
RYOMA...
...

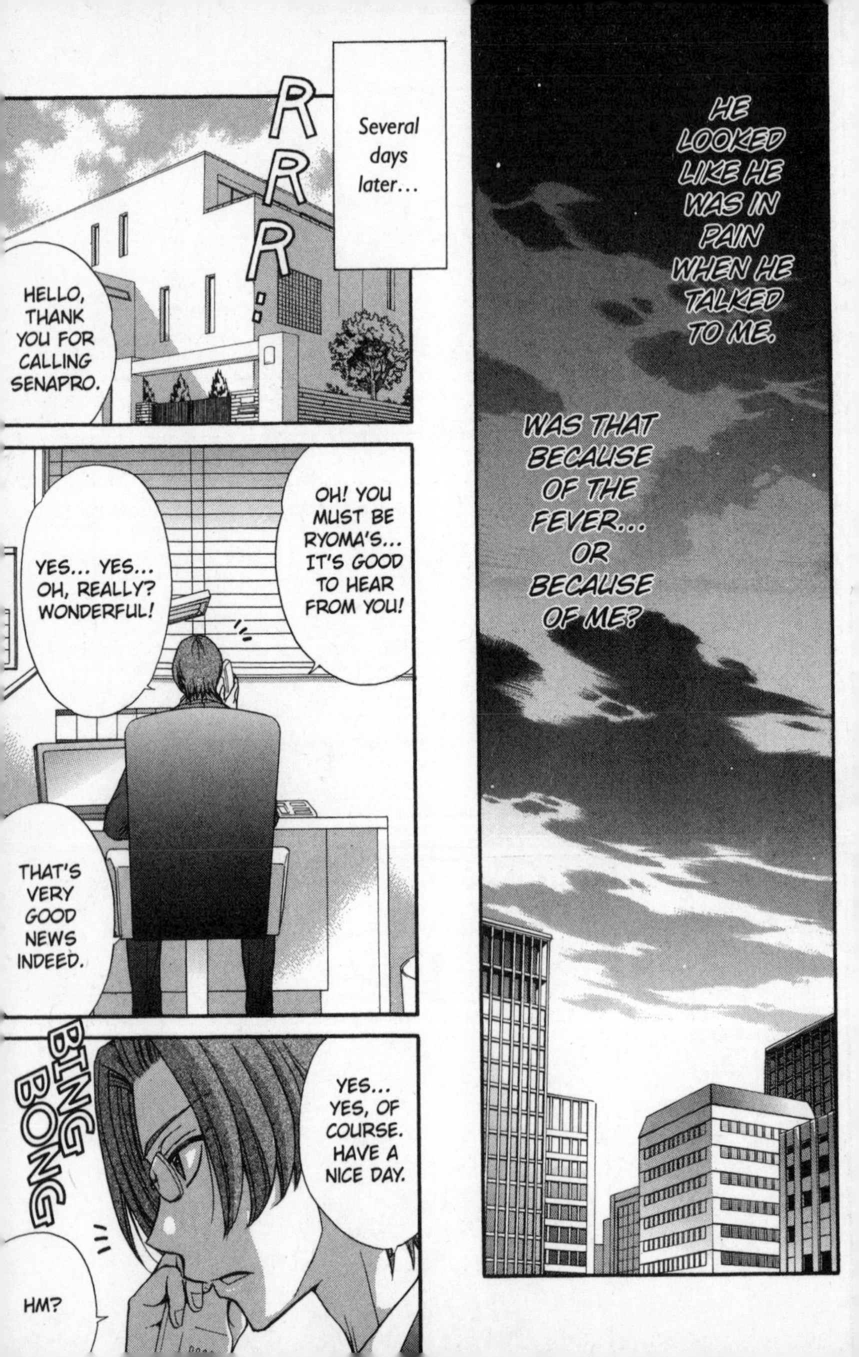
HE LOOKED LIKE HE WAS IN PAIN WHEN HE TALKED TO ME.
WAS THAT BECAUSE OF THE FEVER... OR BECAUSE OF ME?
Several days later…
RRR
HELLO, THANK YOU FOR CALLING SENAPRO.
OH! YOU MUST BE RYOMA'S... IT'S GOOD TO HEAR FROM YOU!
YES... YES... OH, REALLY? WONDERFUL!
THAT'S VERY GOOD NEWS INDEED.
YES... YES, OF COURSE. HAVE A NICE DAY.
BING BONG
HM?

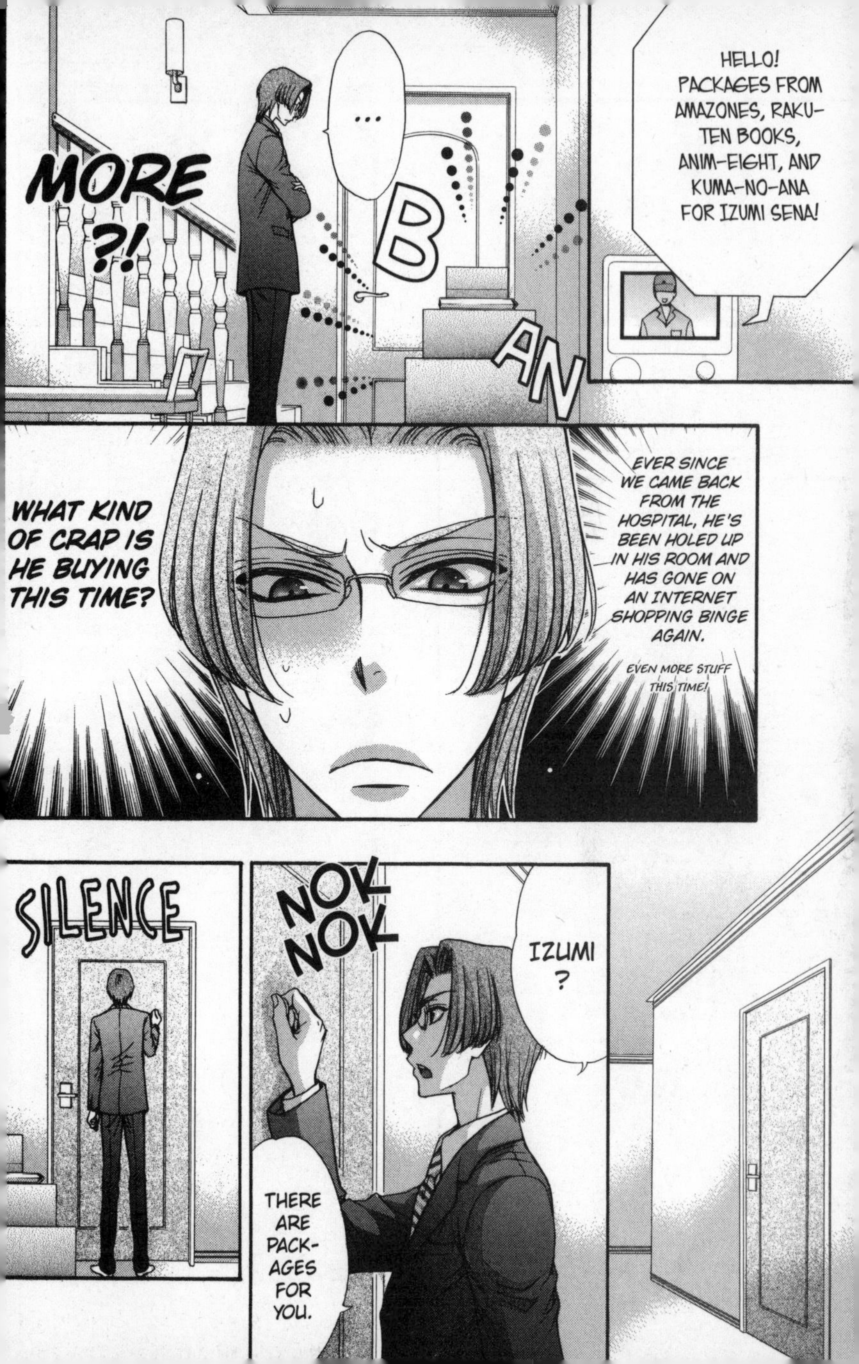
HELLO! PACKAGES FROM AMAZONES, RAKU-TEN BOOKS, ANIM-EIGHT, AND KUMA-NO-ANA FOR IZUMI SENA!
BAN
...
MORE ?!
EVER SINCE WE CAME BACK FROM THE HOSPITAL, HE'S BEEN HOLED UP IN HIS ROOM AND HAS GONE ON AN INTERNET SHOPPING BINGE AGAIN.
EVEN MORE STUFF THIS TIME!
WHAT KIND OF CRAP IS HE BUYING THIS TIME?
NOK NOK
IZUMI ?
THERE ARE PACK-AGES FOR YOU.
SILENCE

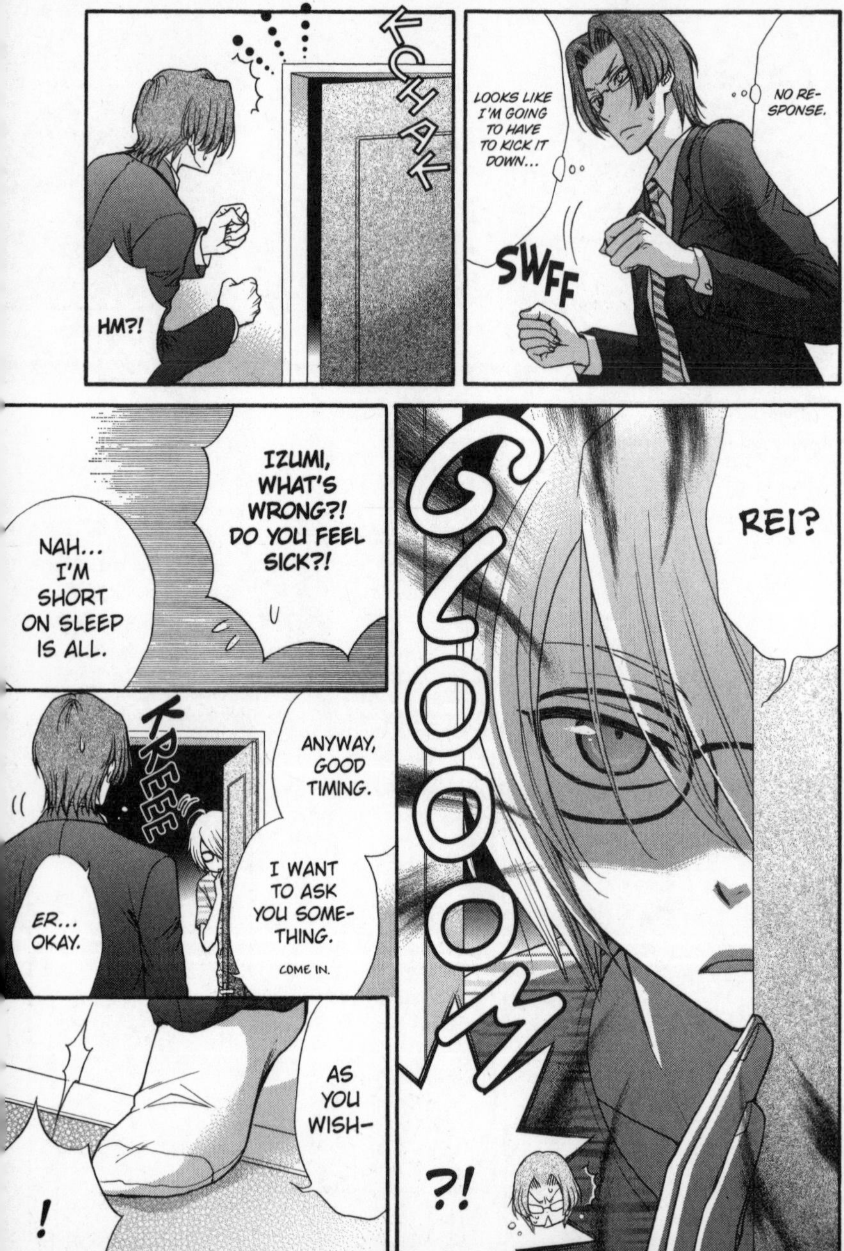
NO RE-SPONSE.
LOOKS LIKE I'M GOING TO HAVE TO KICK IT DOWN...
SWFF
KCHAK
HM?!
GLOOOM
REI?
?!
IZUMI, WHAT'S WRONG?! DO YOU FEEL SICK?!
NAH... I'M SHORT ON SLEEP IS ALL.
KREEE
ANYWAY, GOOD TIMING.
I WANT TO ASK YOU SOMETHING.
COME IN.
ER... OKAY.
AS YOU WISH-
!

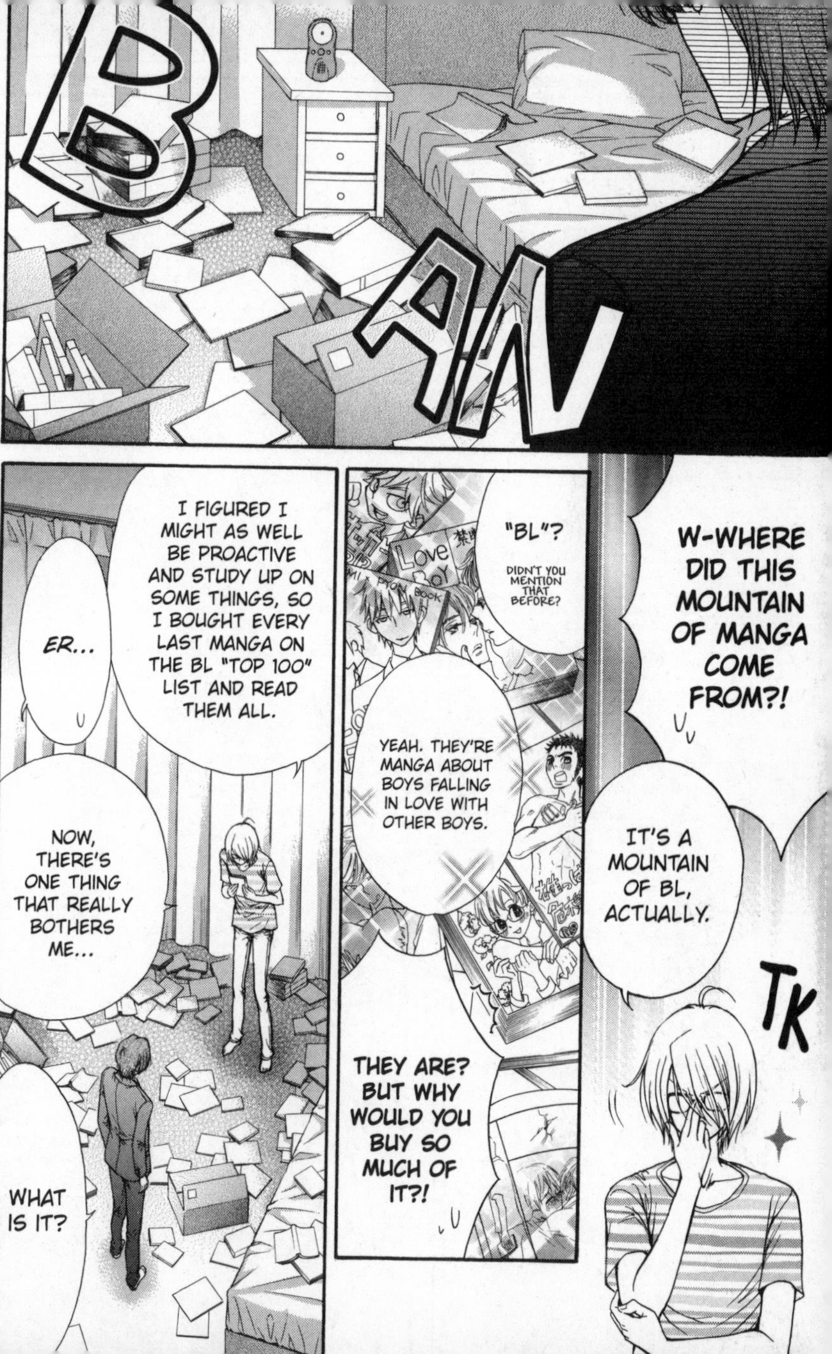
BAN
W-WHERE DID THIS MOUNTAIN OF MANGA COME FROM?!
IT'S A MOUNTAIN OF BL, ACTUALLY.
TK
"BL"? DIDN'T YOU MENTION THAT BEFORE?
YEAH. THEY'RE MANGA ABOUT BOYS FALLING IN LOVE WITH OTHER BOYS.
THEY ARE? BUT WHY WOULD YOU BUY SO MUCH OF IT?!
I FIGURED I MIGHT AS WELL BE PROACTIVE AND STUDY UP ON SOME THINGS, SO I BOUGHT EVERY LAST MANGA ON THE BL "TOP 100" LIST AND READ THEM ALL.
ER...
NOW, THERE'S ONE THING THAT REALLY BOTHERS ME...
WHAT IS IT?

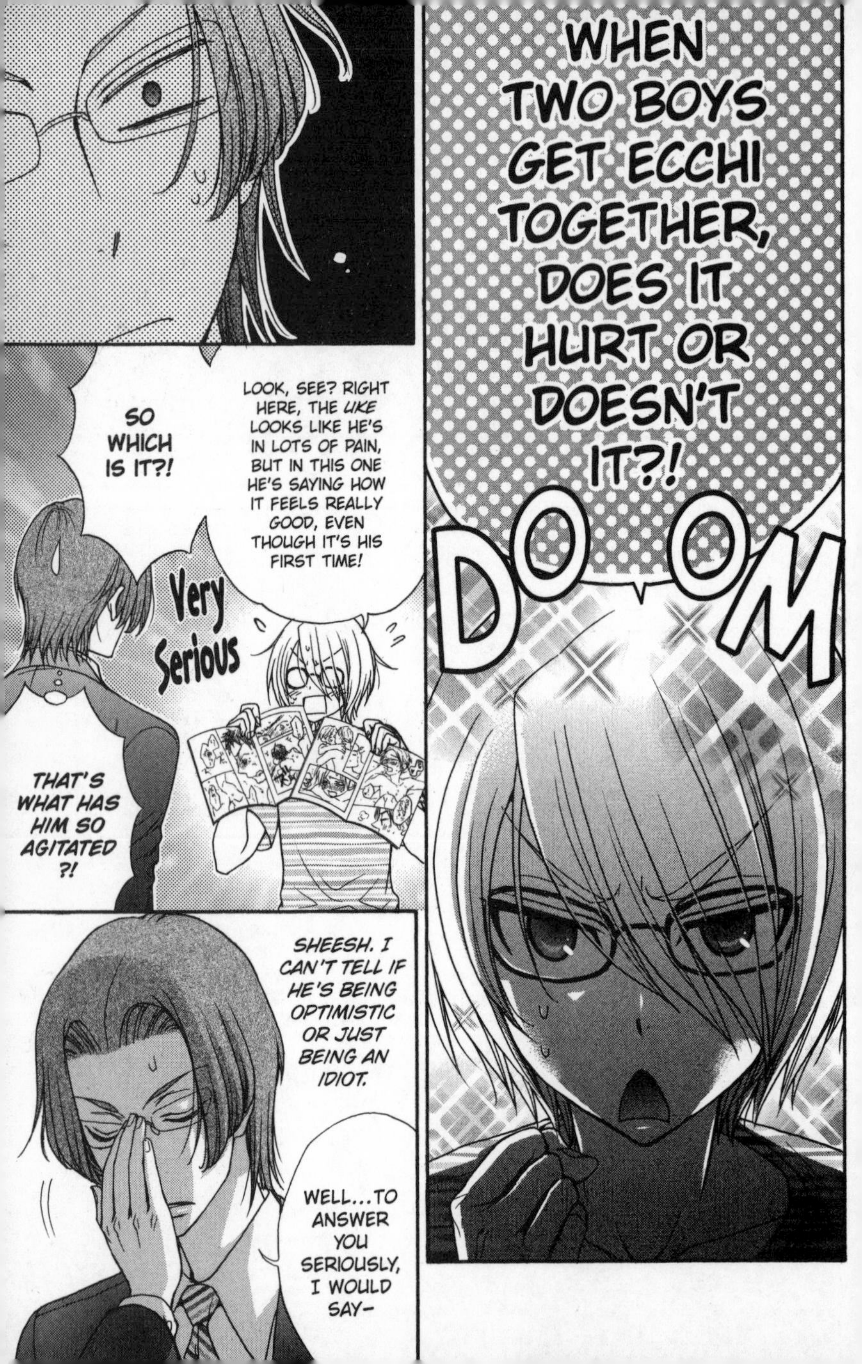
WHEN TWO BOYS GET ECCHI TOGETHER, DOES IT HURT OR DOESN'T IT?!
DOOM
SO WHICH IS IT?!
LOOK, SEE? RIGHT HERE, THE *UKE* LOOKS LIKE HE'S IN LOTS OF PAIN, BUT IN THIS ONE HE'S SAYING HOW IT FEELS REALLY GOOD, EVEN THOUGH IT'S HIS FIRST TIME!
Very Serious
THAT'S WHAT HAS HIM SO AGITATED ?!
SHEESH. I CAN'T TELL IF HE'S BEING OPTIMISTIC OR JUST BEING AN IDIOT.
WELL...TO ANSWER YOU SERIOUSLY, I WOULD SAY-

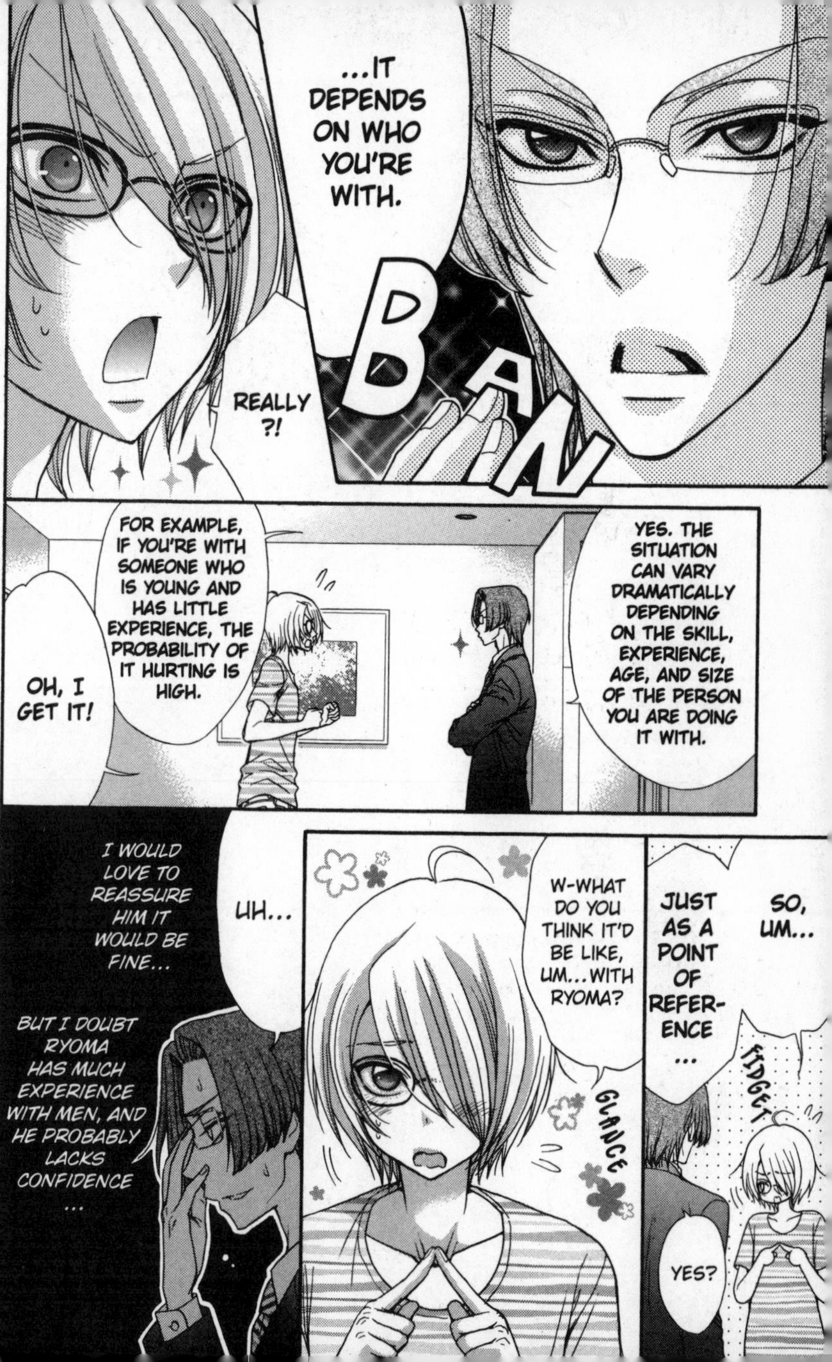
...IT DEPENDS ON WHO YOU'RE WITH.
BAN
REALLY ?!
YES. THE SITUATION CAN VARY DRAMATICALLY DEPENDING ON THE SKILL, EXPERIENCE, AGE, AND SIZE OF THE PERSON YOU ARE DOING IT WITH.
FOR EXAMPLE, IF YOU'RE WITH SOMEONE WHO IS YOUNG AND HAS LITTLE EXPERIENCE, THE PROBABILITY OF IT HURTING IS HIGH.
OH, I GET IT!
SO, UM...
JUST AS A POINT OF REFER-ENCE ...
FIDGET
YES?
W-WHAT DO YOU THINK IT'D BE LIKE, UM...WITH RYOMA?
GLANCE
UH...
I WOULD LOVE TO REASSURE HIM IT WOULD BE FINE...
BUT I DOUBT RYOMA HAS MUCH EXPERIENCE WITH MEN, AND HE PROBABLY LACKS CONFIDENCE ...

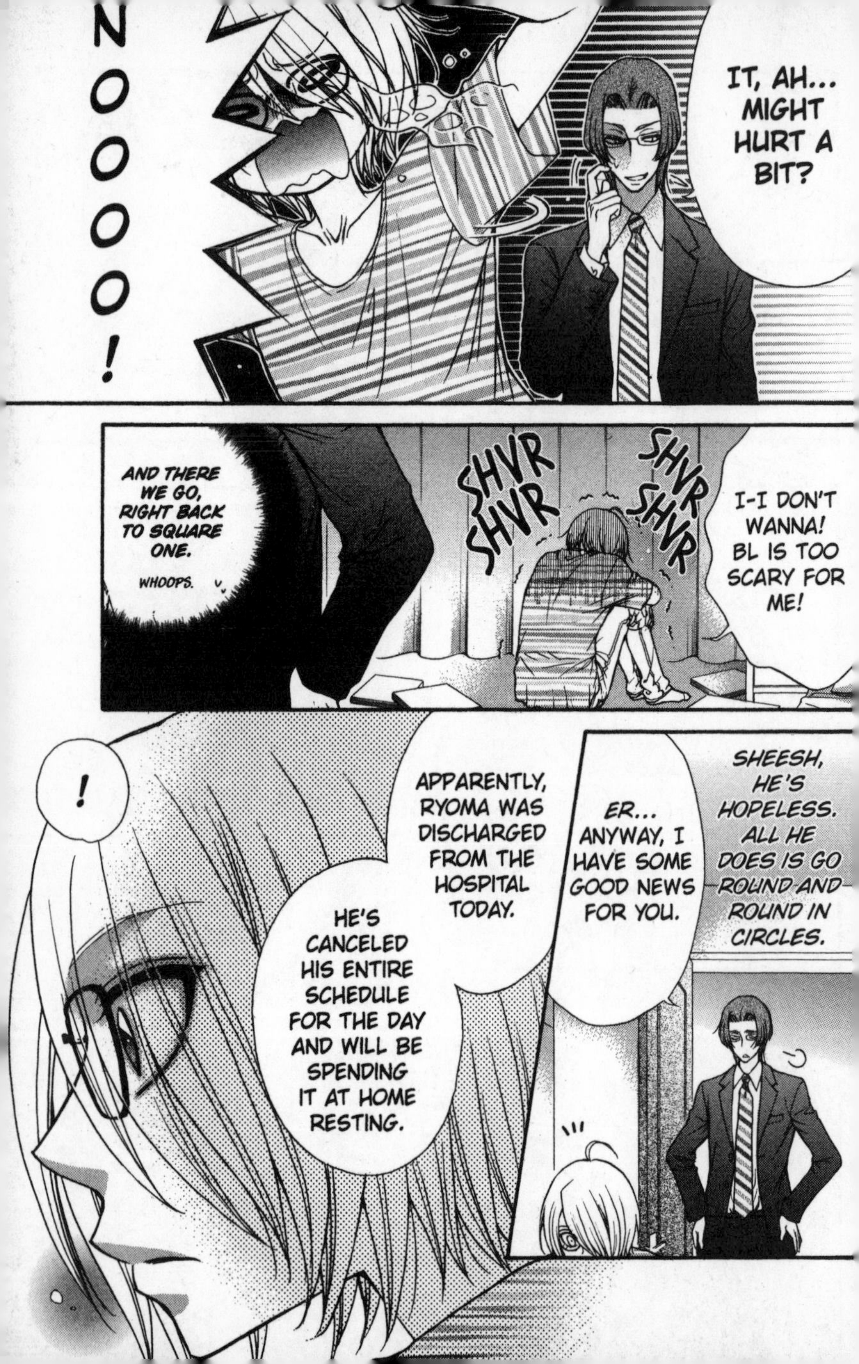
IT, AH... MIGHT HURT A BIT?
NOOOOO!
I-I DON'T WANNA! BL IS TOO SCARY FOR ME!
SHVR SHVR
SHVR SHVR
AND THERE WE GO, RIGHT BACK TO SQUARE ONE.
WHOOPS.
SHEESH, HE'S HOPELESS. ALL HE DOES IS GO ROUND AND ROUND IN CIRCLES.
ER... ANYWAY, I HAVE SOME GOOD NEWS FOR YOU.
APPARENTLY, RYOMA WAS DISCHARGED FROM THE HOSPITAL TODAY.
HE'S CANCELED HIS ENTIRE SCHEDULE FOR THE DAY AND WILL BE SPENDING IT AT HOME RESTING.
!

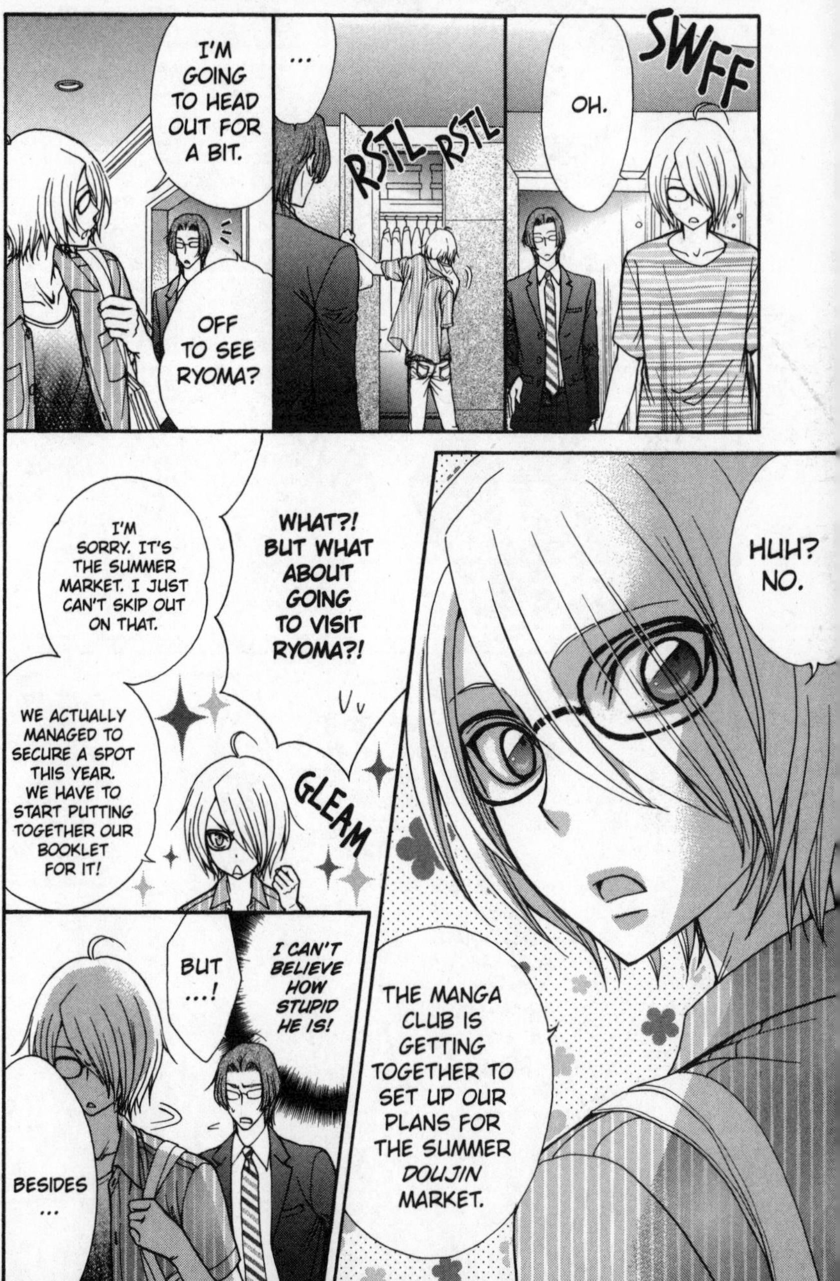
SWFF
OH.
...
RSTL RSTL
I'M GOING TO HEAD OUT FOR A BIT.
OFF TO SEE RYOMA?
HUH? NO.
THE MANGA CLUB IS GETTING TOGETHER TO SET UP OUR PLANS FOR THE SUMMER *DOUJIN* MARKET.
WHAT?! BUT WHAT ABOUT GOING TO VISIT RYOMA?!
I'M SORRY. IT'S THE SUMMER MARKET. I JUST CAN'T SKIP OUT ON THAT.
GLEAM
WE ACTUALLY MANAGED TO SECURE A SPOT THIS YEAR. WE HAVE TO START PUTTING TOGETHER OUR BOOKLET FOR IT!
I CAN'T BELIEVE HOW STUPID HE IS!
BUT ...!
BESIDES ...

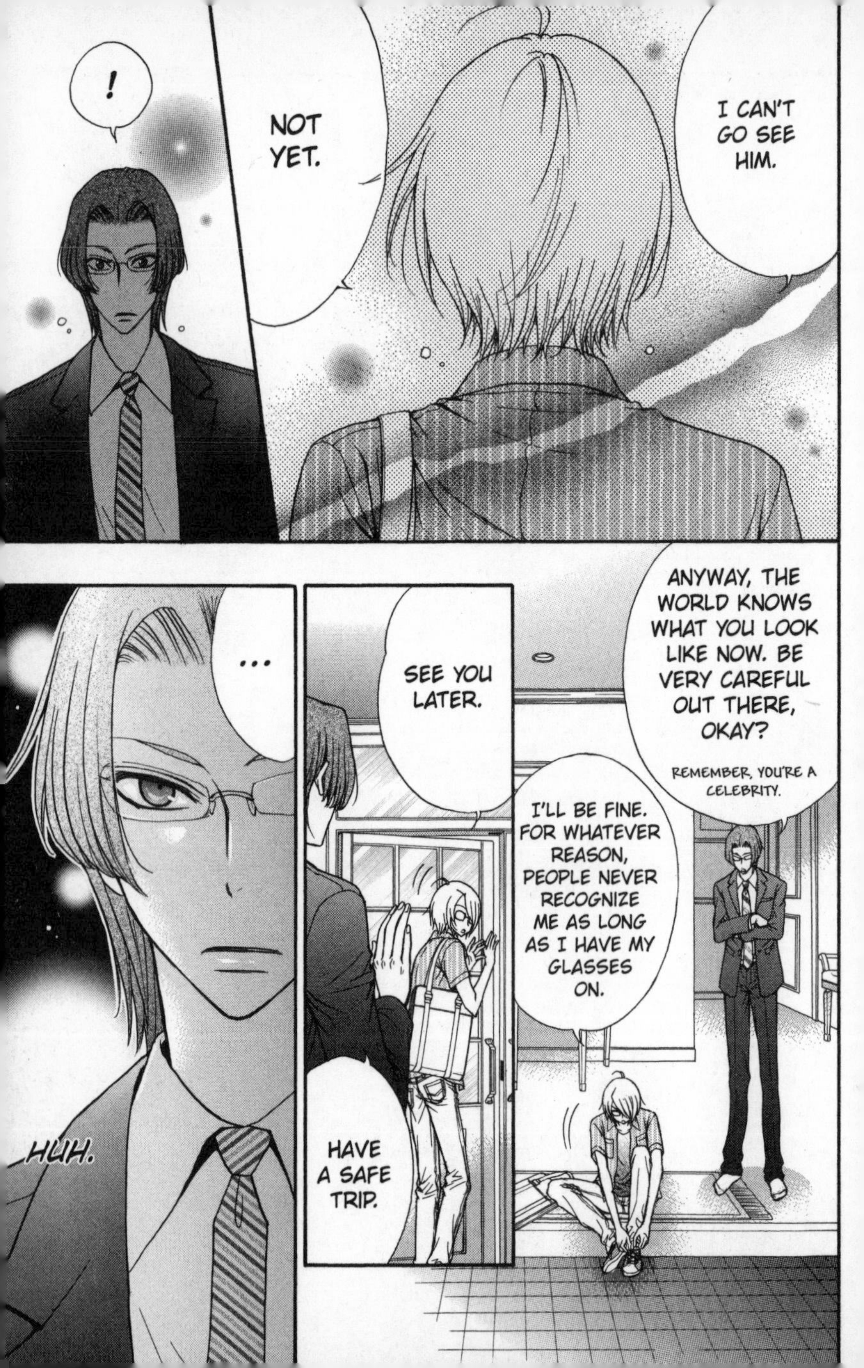
I CAN'T GO SEE HIM.
NOT YET.
!
ANYWAY, THE WORLD KNOWS WHAT YOU LOOK LIKE NOW. BE VERY CAREFUL OUT THERE, OKAY?
REMEMBER, YOU'RE A CELEBRITY.
I'LL BE FINE. FOR WHATEVER REASON, PEOPLE NEVER RECOGNIZE ME AS LONG AS I HAVE MY GLASSES ON.
SEE YOU LATER.
HAVE A SAFE TRIP.
...
HUH.

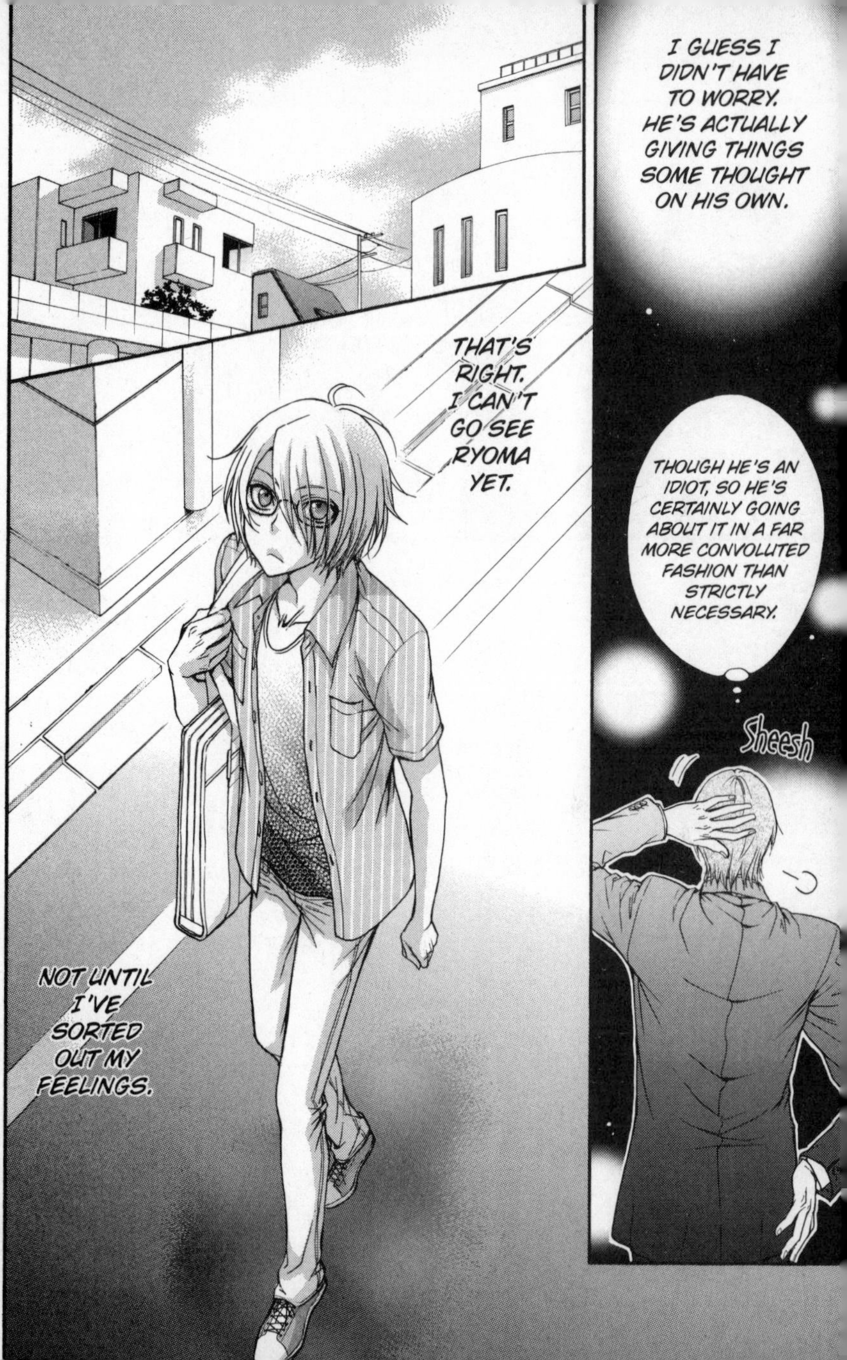
I GUESS I DIDN'T HAVE TO WORRY. HE'S ACTUALLY GIVING THINGS SOME THOUGHT ON HIS OWN.
THOUGH HE'S AN IDIOT, SO HE'S CERTAINLY GOING ABOUT IT IN A FAR MORE CONVOLUTED FASHION THAN STRICTLY NECESSARY.
Sheesh
THAT'S RIGHT. I CAN'T GO SEE RYOMA YET.
NOT UNTIL I'VE SORTED OUT MY FEELINGS.

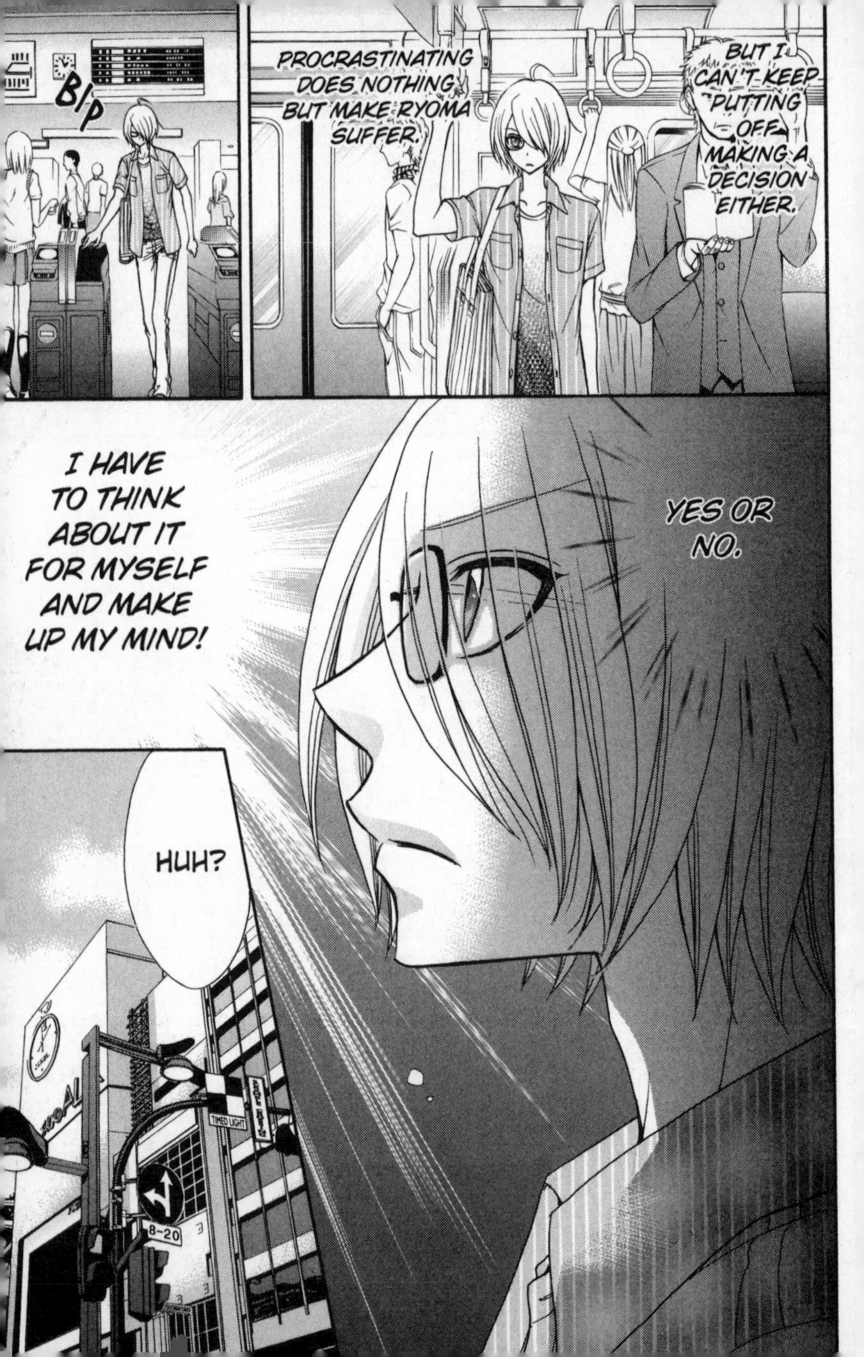
PROCRASTINATING DOES NOTHING BUT MAKE RYOMA SUFFER.
BUT I CAN'T KEEP PUTTING OFF MAKING A DECISION EITHER.
BIP
YES OR NO.
I HAVE TO THINK ABOUT IT FOR MYSELF AND MAKE UP MY MIND!
HUH?
TIMED LIGHT
8-20

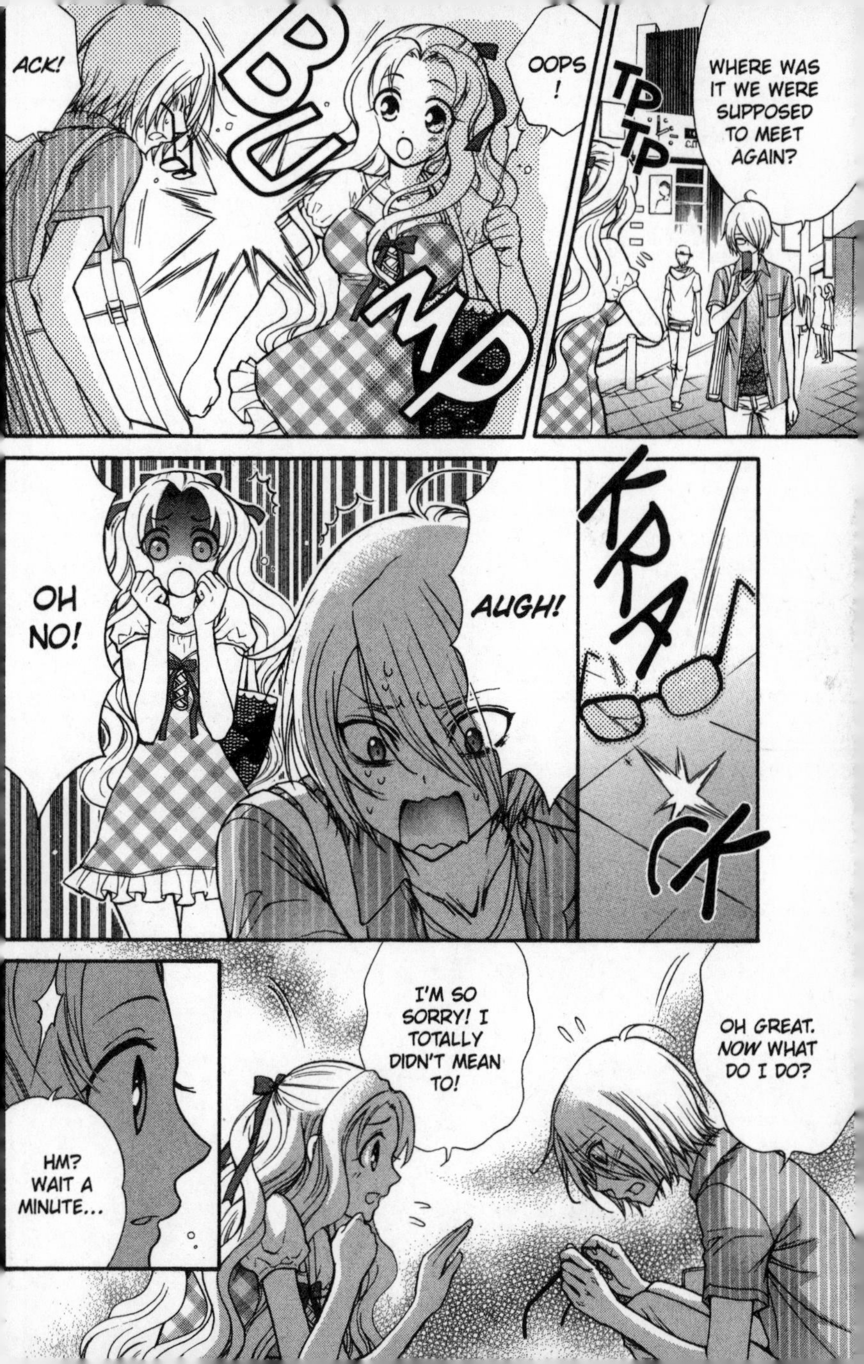
WHERE WAS IT WE WERE SUPPOSED TO MEET AGAIN?
TP TP
OOPS!
BUMP
ACK!
KRACK
AUGH!
OH NO!
OH GREAT. NOW WHAT DO I DO?
I'M SO SORRY! I TOTALLY DIDN'T MEAN TO!
HM? WAIT A MINUTE...

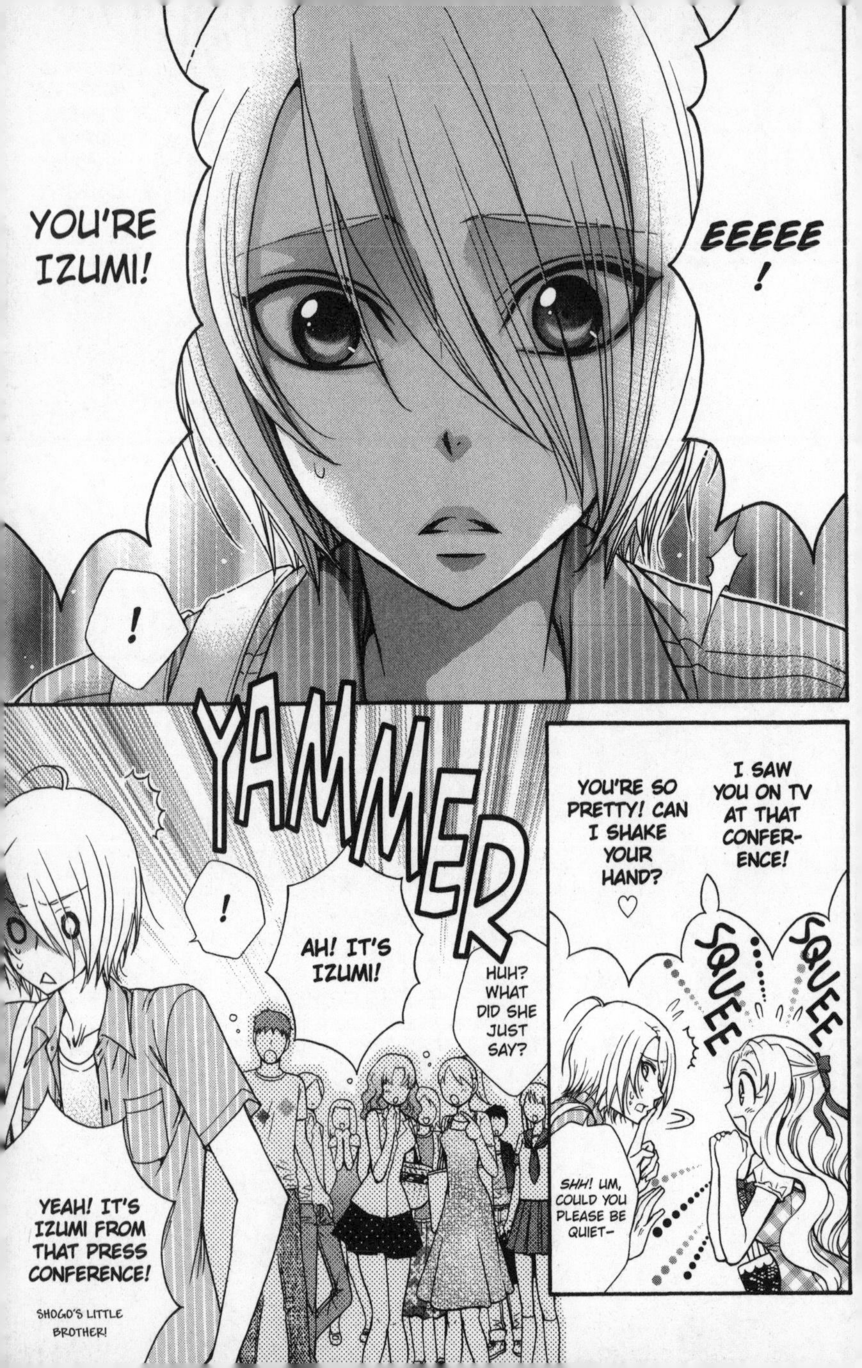
EEEEE!
YOU'RE IZUMI!
!
I SAW YOU ON TV AT THAT CONFERENCE!
YOU'RE SO PRETTY! CAN I SHAKE YOUR HAND? ♡
SQUEE
SQUEE
SHH! UM, COULD YOU PLEASE BE QUIET-
YAMMER
HUH? WHAT DID SHE JUST SAY?
AH! IT'S IZUMI!
!
YEAH! IT'S IZUMI FROM THAT PRESS CONFERENCE!
SHOGO'S LITTLE BROTHER!

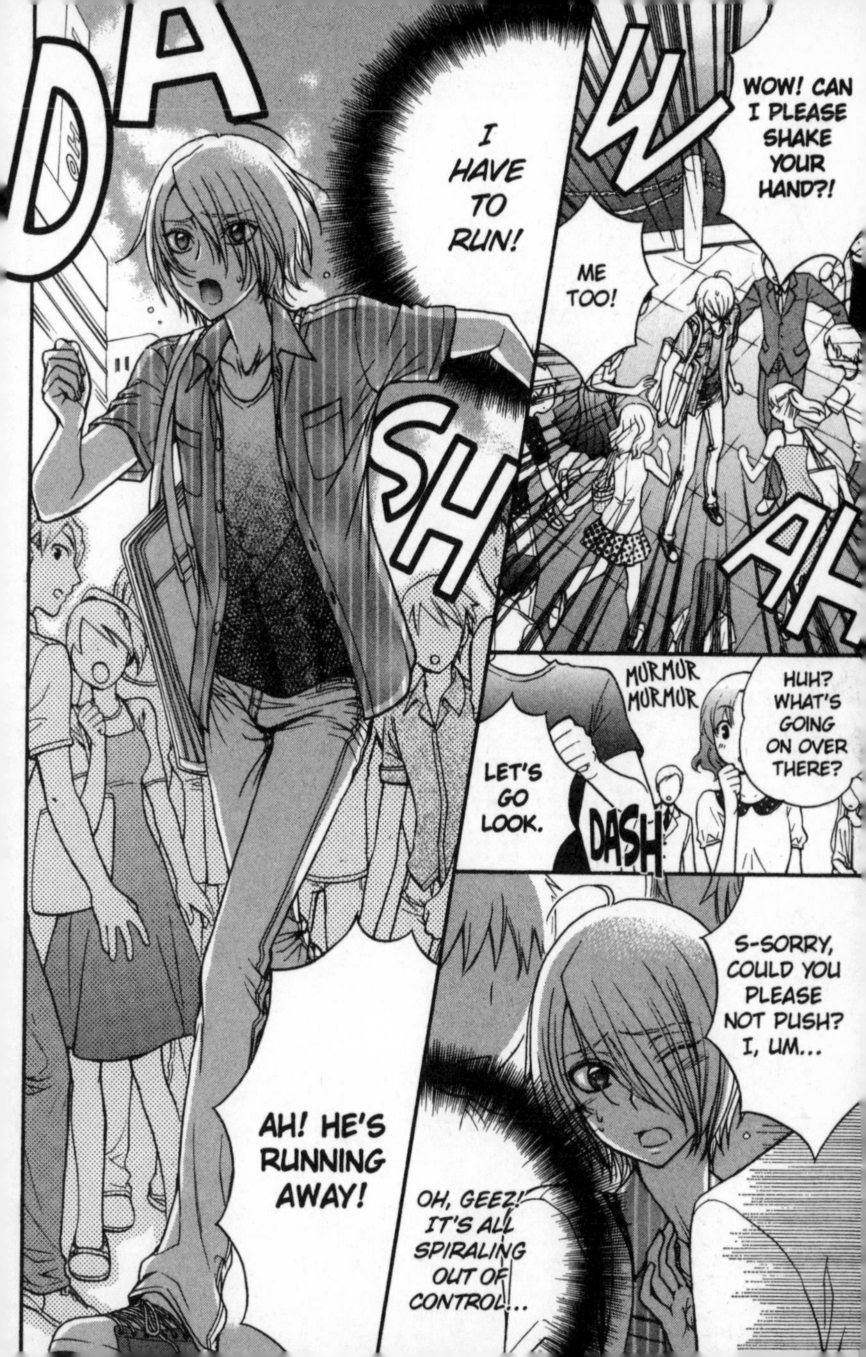
WOW! CAN I PLEASE SHAKE YOUR HAND?!
ME TOO!
W
AH
HUH? WHAT'S GOING ON OVER THERE?
MURMUR MURMUR
LET'S GO LOOK.
DASH
S-SORRY, COULD YOU PLEASE NOT PUSH? I, UM...
OH, GEEZ! IT'S ALL SPIRALING OUT OF CONTROL...
DA
I HAVE TO RUN!
SH
AH! HE'S RUNNING AWAY!

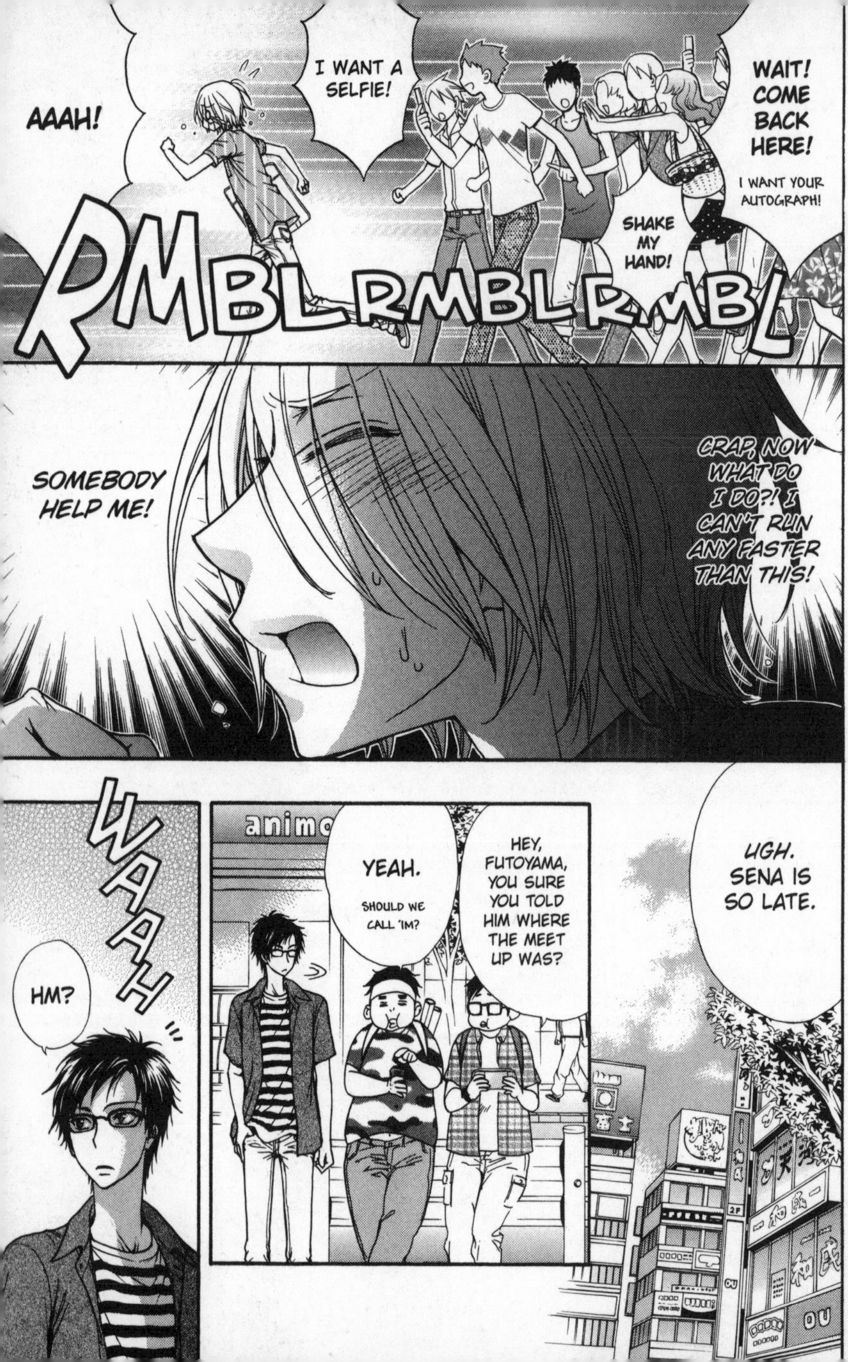
WAIT! COME BACK HERE!
I WANT YOUR AUTOGRAPH!
SHAKE MY HAND!
I WANT A SELFIE!
AAAH!
RMBLRMBLRMBL
CRAP, NOW WHAT DO I DO?! I CAN'T RUN ANY FASTER THAN THIS!
SOMEBODY HELP ME!
UGH. SENA IS SO LATE.
HEY, FUTOYAMA, YOU SURE YOU TOLD HIM WHERE THE MEET UP WAS?
YEAH.
SHOULD WE CALL 'IM?
animo
WAAAH
HM?

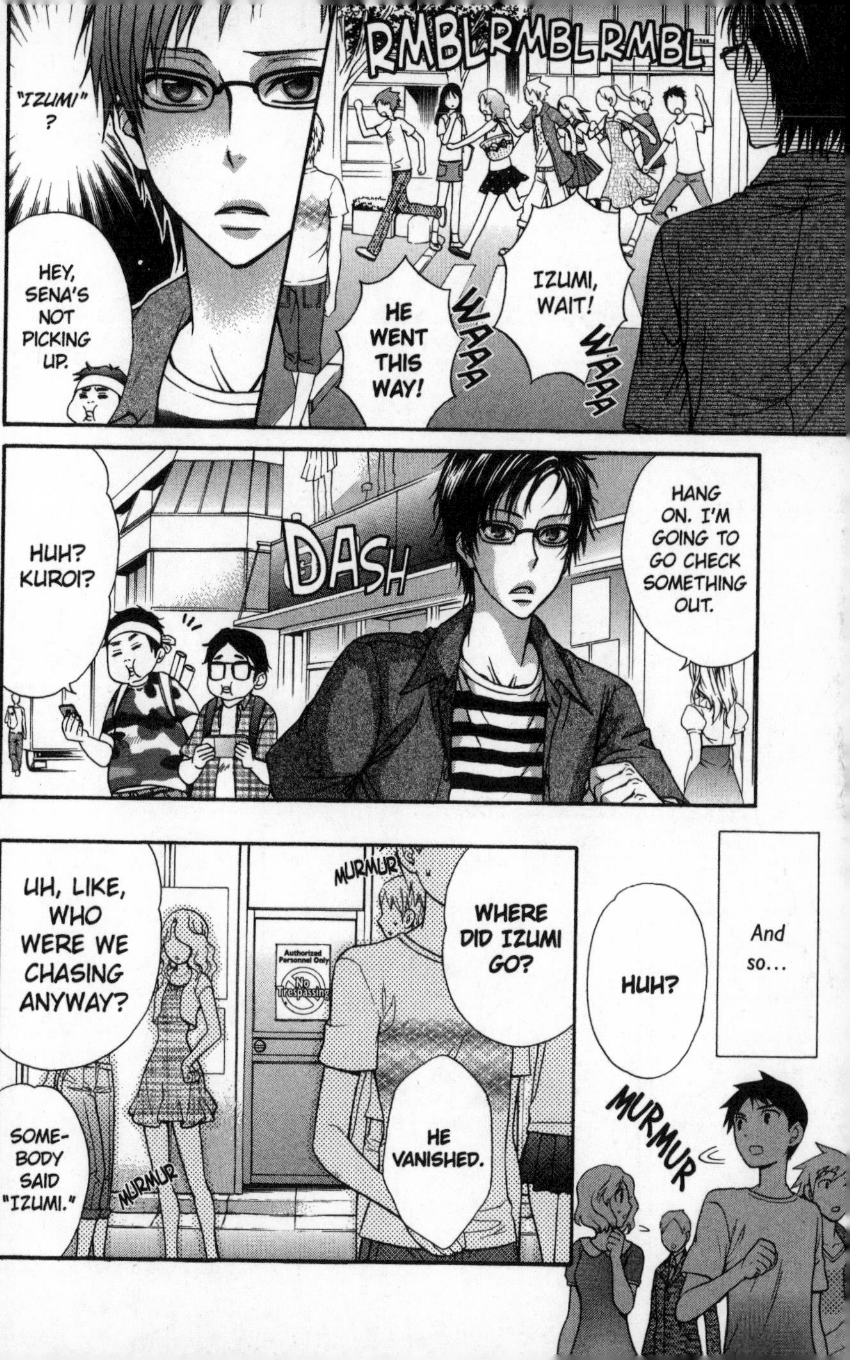
RMBLRMBLRMBL
IZUMI, WAIT!
WAAA
HE WENT THIS WAY!
WAAA
"IZUMI"?
HEY, SENA'S NOT PICKING UP.
HANG ON. I'M GOING TO GO CHECK SOMETHING OUT.
DASH
HUH? KUROI?
And so…
HUH?
MURMUR
WHERE DID IZUMI GO?
MURMUR
Authorized Personnel Only
No Trespassing
HE VANISHED.
UH, LIKE, WHO WERE WE CHASING ANYWAY?
SOME-BODY SAID "IZUMI."
MURMUR

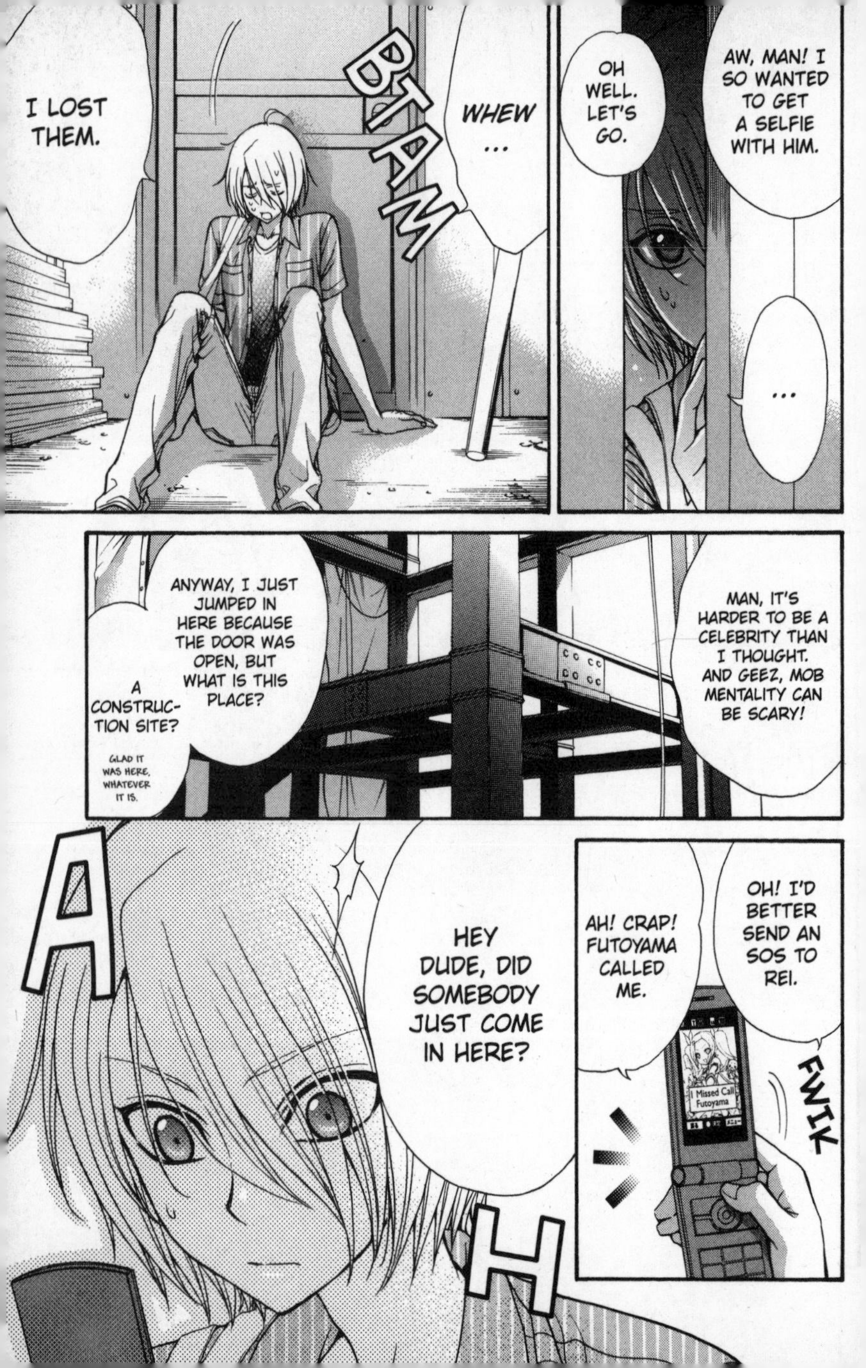
AW, MAN! I SO WANTED TO GET A SELFIE WITH HIM.
OH WELL. LET'S GO.
...
BTAM
WHEW ...
I LOST THEM.
MAN, IT'S HARDER TO BE A CELEBRITY THAN I THOUGHT. AND GEEZ, MOB MENTALITY CAN BE SCARY!
ANYWAY, I JUST JUMPED IN HERE BECAUSE THE DOOR WAS OPEN, BUT WHAT IS THIS PLACE?
A CONSTRUCTION SITE?
GLAD IT WAS HERE, WHATEVER IT IS.
OH! I'D BETTER SEND AN SOS TO REI.
FWIK
Missed Call
Futoyama
AH! CRAP! FUTOYAMA CALLED ME.
AH
HEY DUDE, DID SOMEBODY JUST COME IN HERE?

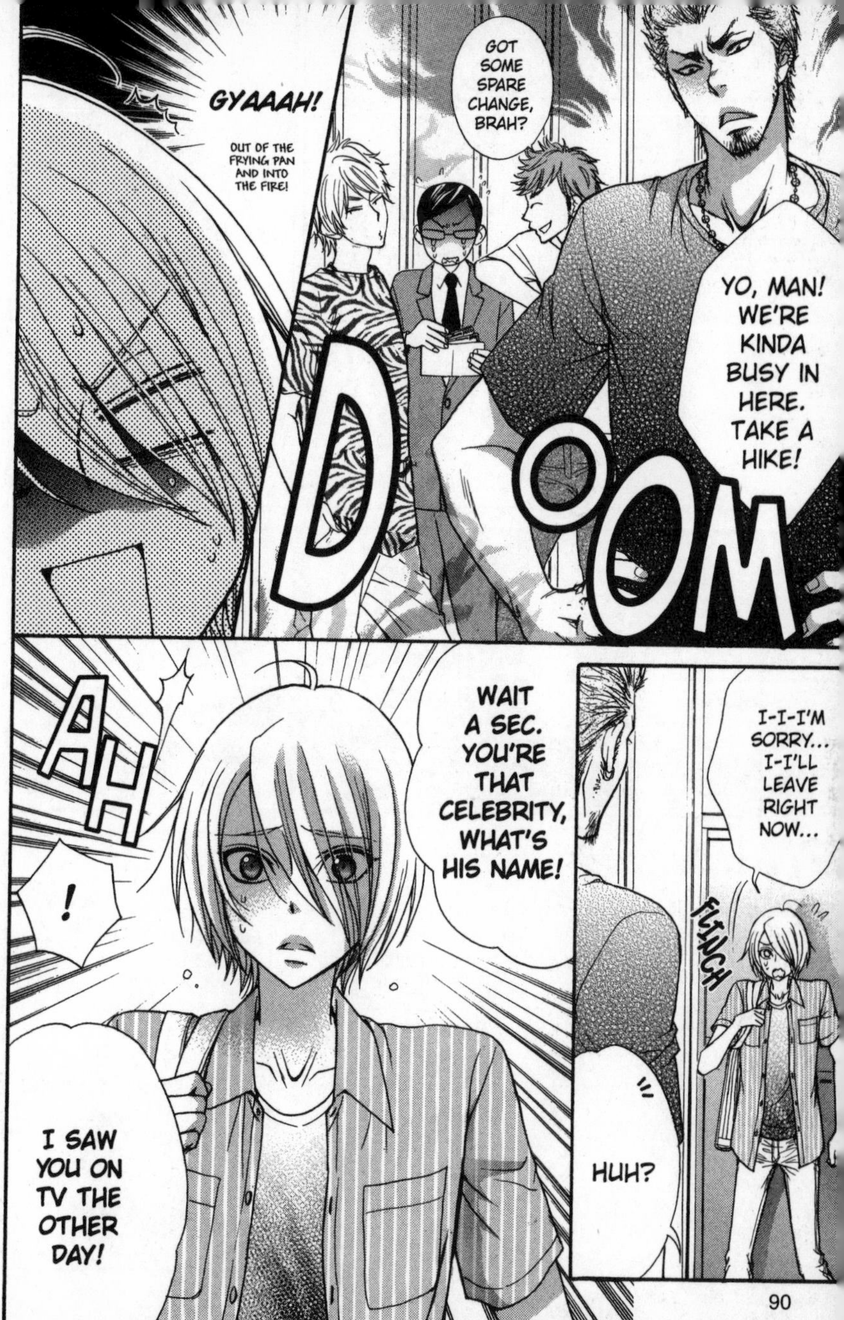
GOT SOME SPARE CHANGE, BRAH?
DOOM
YO, MAN! WE'RE KINDA BUSY IN HERE. TAKE A HIKE!
GYAAAH!
OUT OF THE FRYING PAN AND INTO THE FIRE!
I-I-I'M SORRY... I-I'LL LEAVE RIGHT NOW...
FLINCH
HUH?
AH
!
WAIT A SEC. YOU'RE THAT CELEBRITY, WHAT'S HIS NAME!
I SAW YOU ON TV THE OTHER DAY!

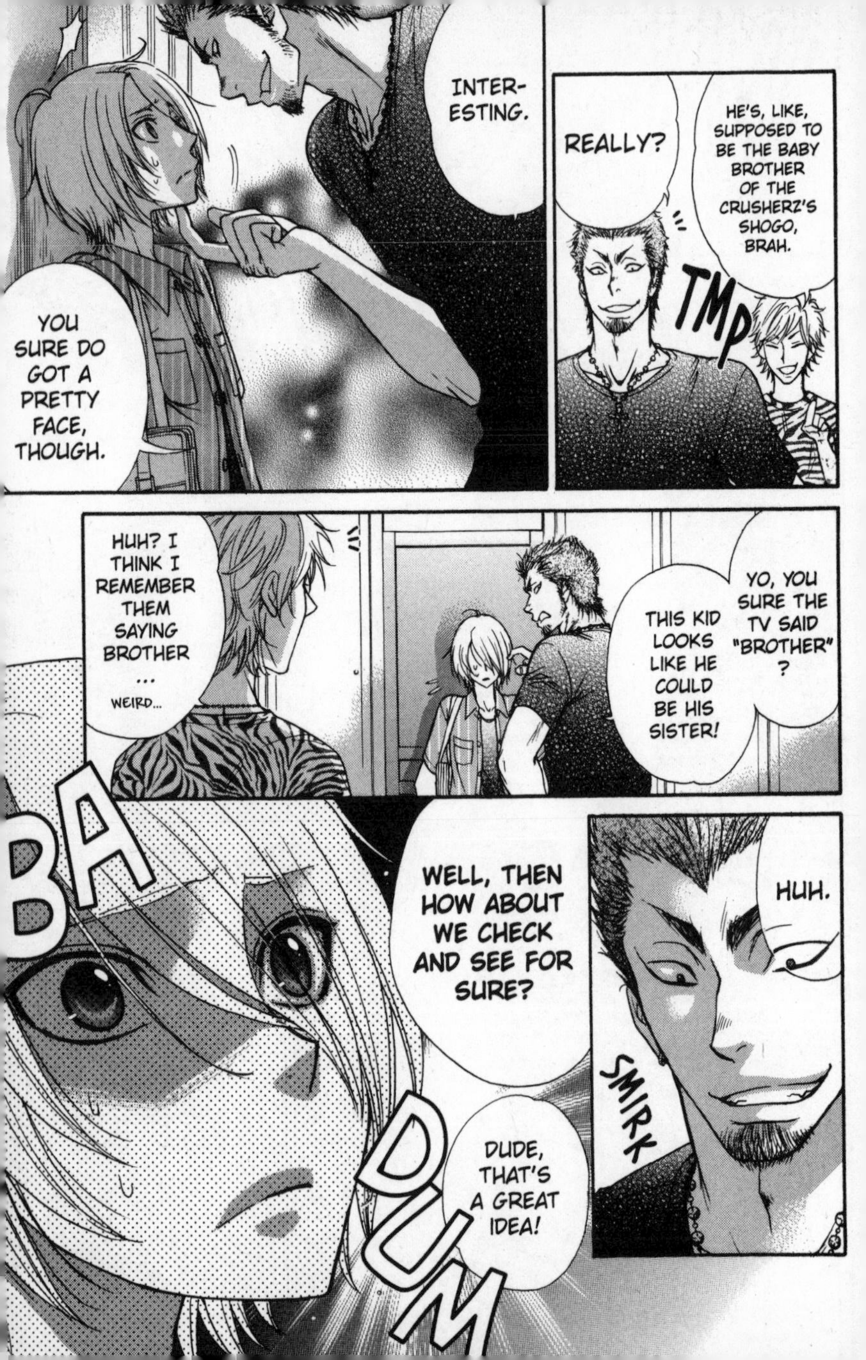
HE'S, LIKE, SUPPOSED TO BE THE BABY BROTHER OF THE CRUSHERZ'S SHOGO, BRAH.
REALLY?
TMP
INTER-ESTING.
YOU SURE DO GOT A PRETTY FACE, THOUGH.
YO, YOU SURE THE TV SAID "BROTHER"?
THIS KID LOOKS LIKE HE COULD BE HIS SISTER!
HUH? I THINK I REMEMBER THEM SAYING BROTHER ... WEIRD...
HUH.
SMIRK
WELL, THEN HOW ABOUT WE CHECK AND SEE FOR SURE?
DUDE, THAT'S A GREAT IDEA!
BA
DUM

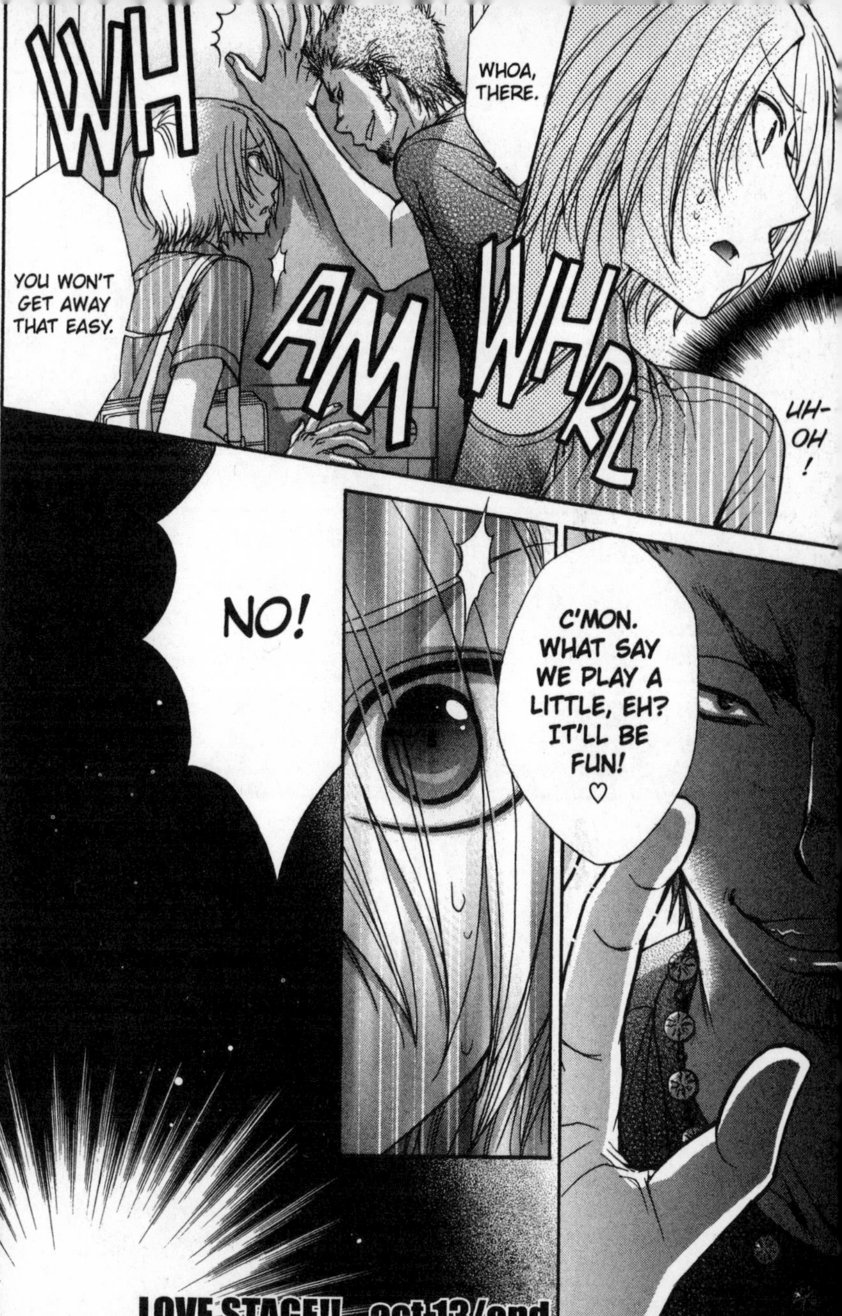
WH
AM
WHOA, THERE.
WHRL
UH-OH!
YOU WON'T GET AWAY THAT EASY.
C'MON. WHAT SAY WE PLAY A LITTLE, EH? IT'LL BE FUN! ♡
NO!

LOVE STAGE!! act.13/end

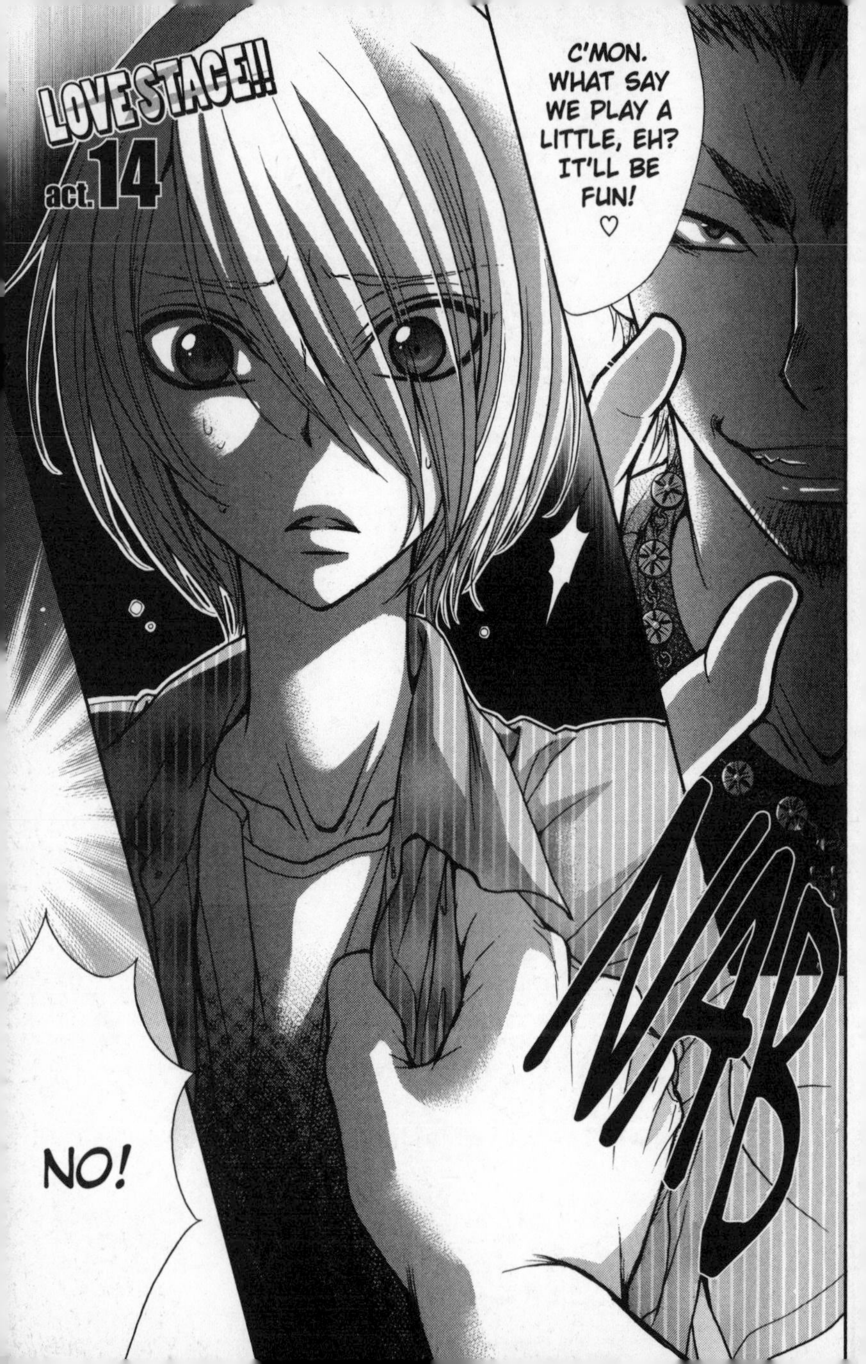
C'MON. WHAT SAY WE PLAY A LITTLE, EH? IT'LL BE FUN! ♡
LOVE STAGE!!
act.14
NO!

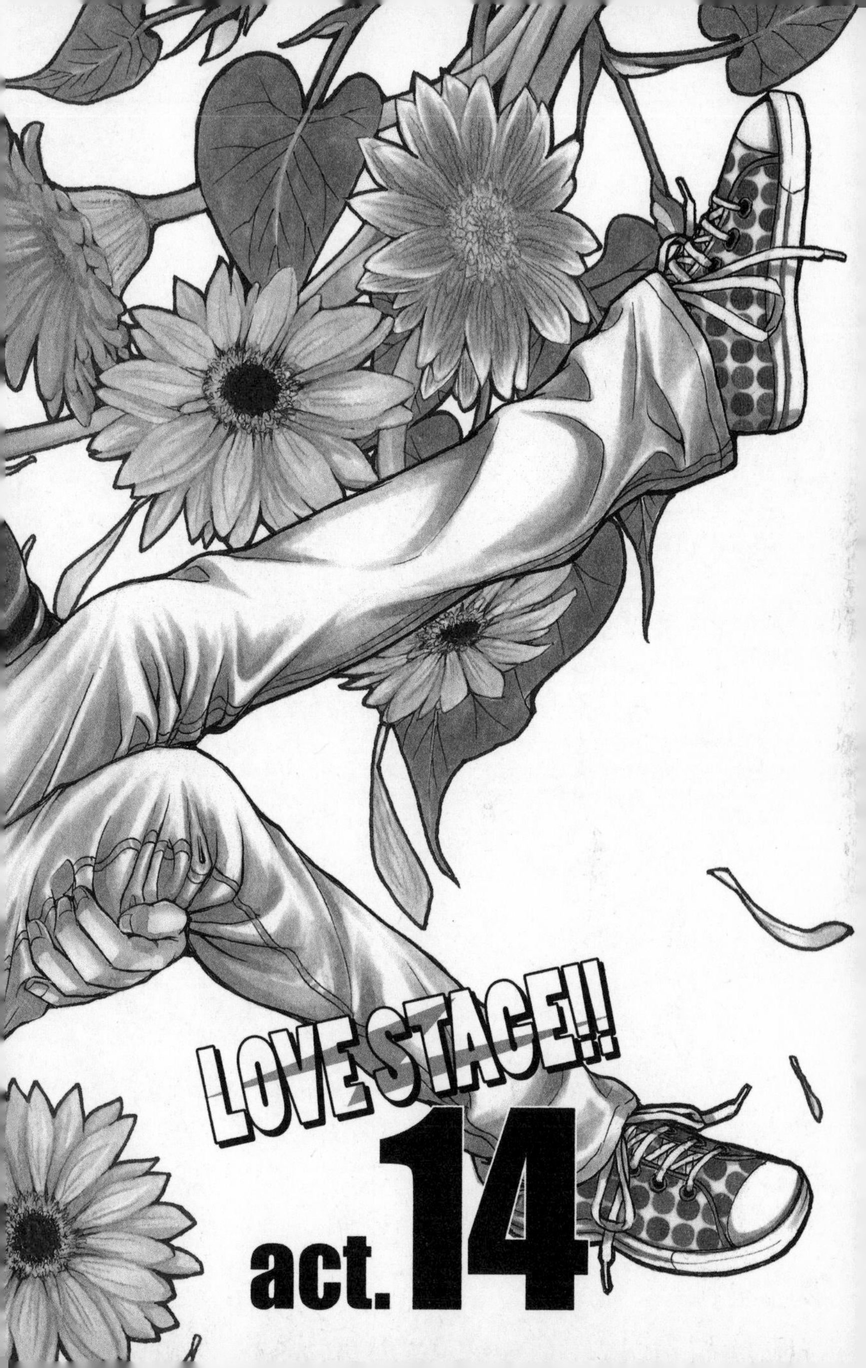
LOVE STAGE!!
act. 14

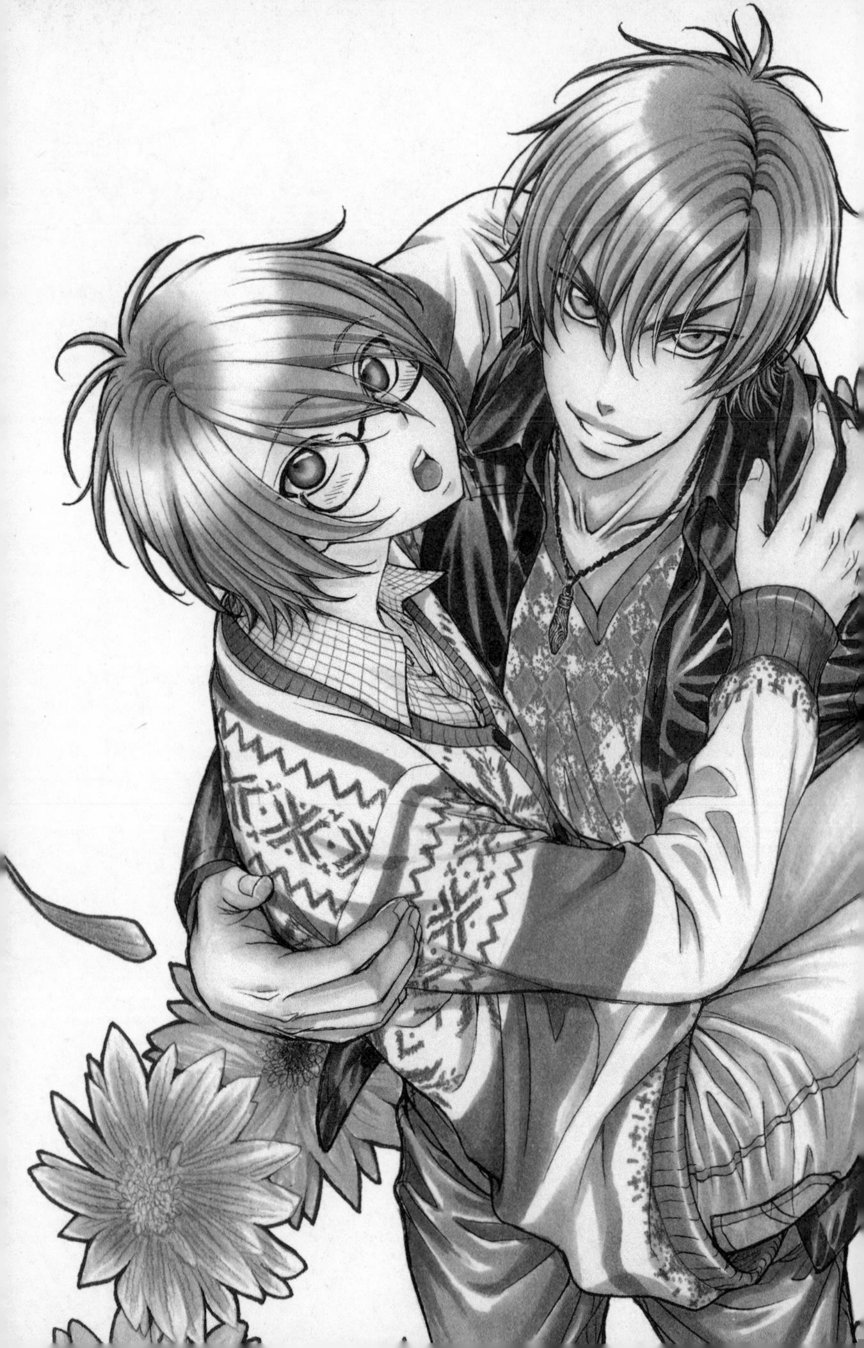

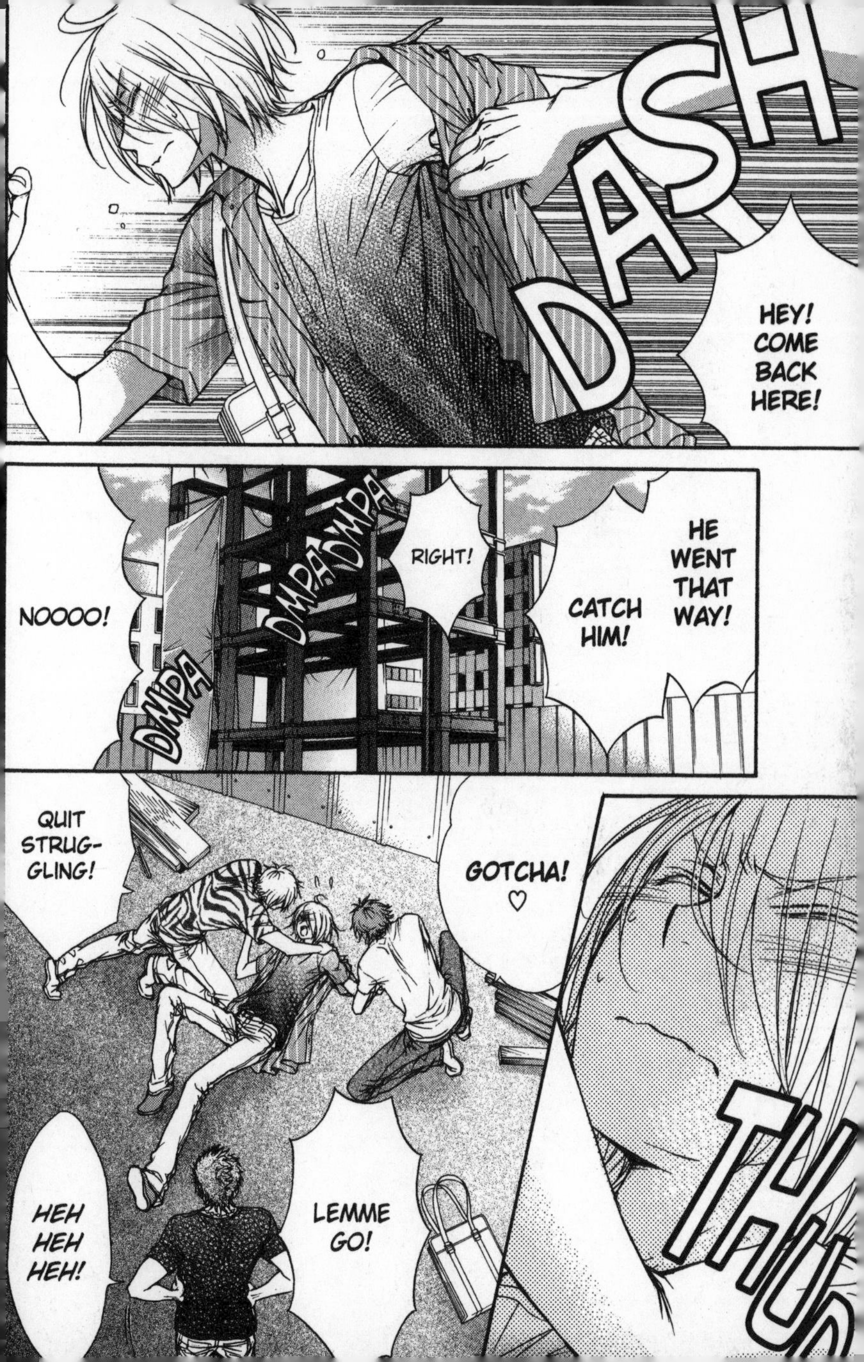

DASH
HEY! COME BACK HERE!
HE WENT THAT WAY!
CATCH HIM!
RIGHT!
DMPADMPA
DMPA
DMPA
NOOOO!
THUS
GOTCHA! ♡
QUIT STRUG-GLING!
LEMME GO!
HEH HEH HEH!

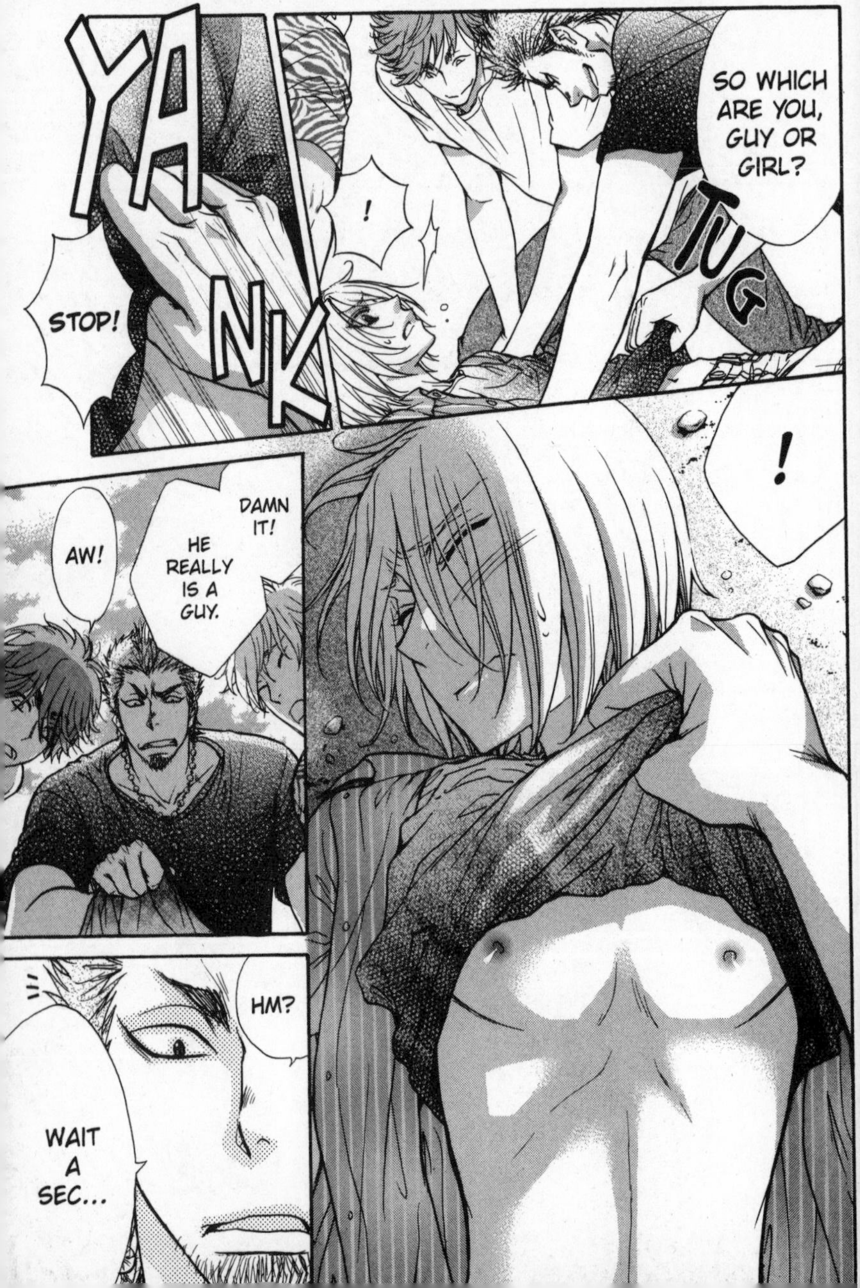
SO WHICH ARE YOU, GUY OR GIRL?
!
TUG
YANK
STOP!
!
DAMN IT! HE REALLY IS A GUY.
AW!
HM?
WAIT A SEC...

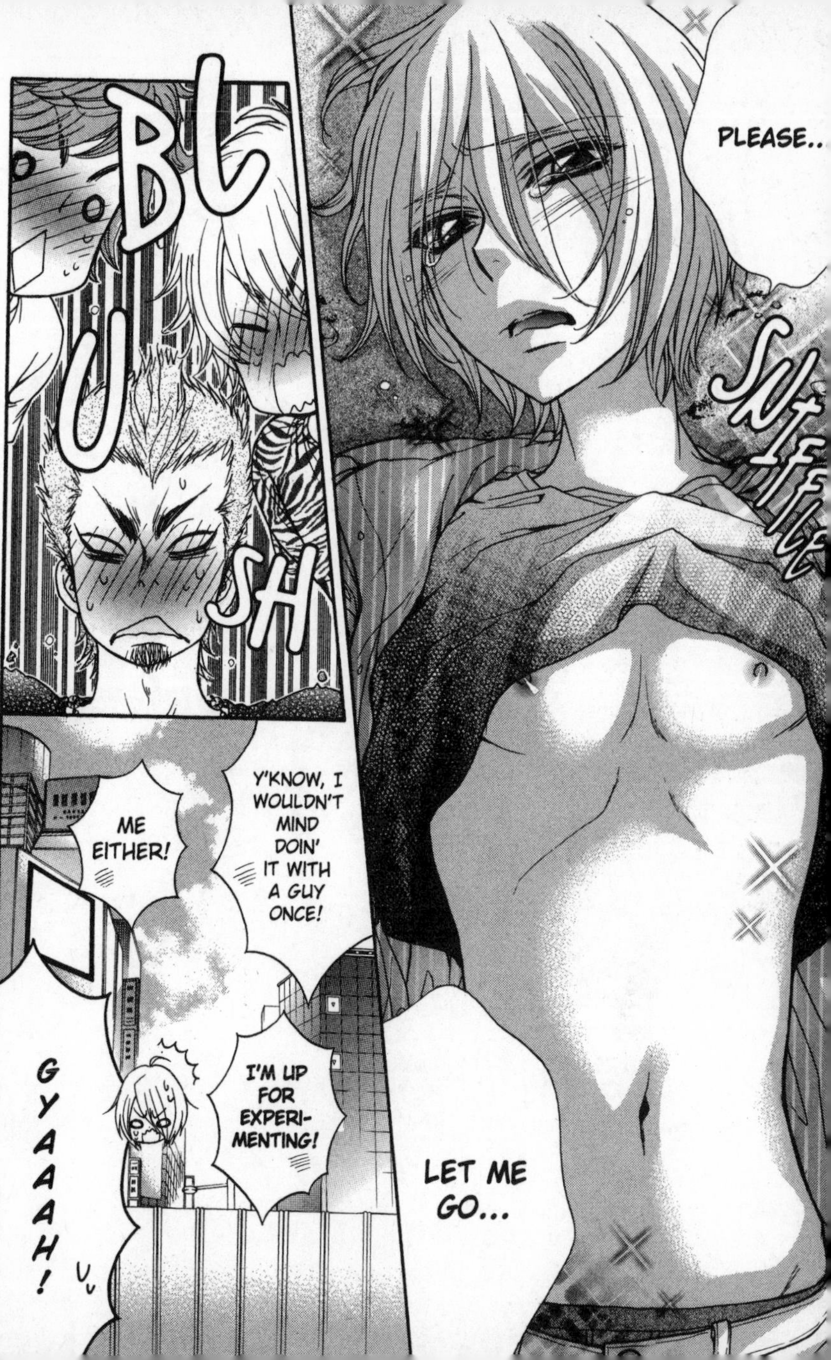
PLEASE...
SNIFFLE
LET ME GO...
BLUSH
Y'KNOW, I WOULDN'T MIND DOIN' IT WITH A GUY ONCE!
ME EITHER!
I'M UP FOR EXPERI-MENTING!
GYAAAAH!

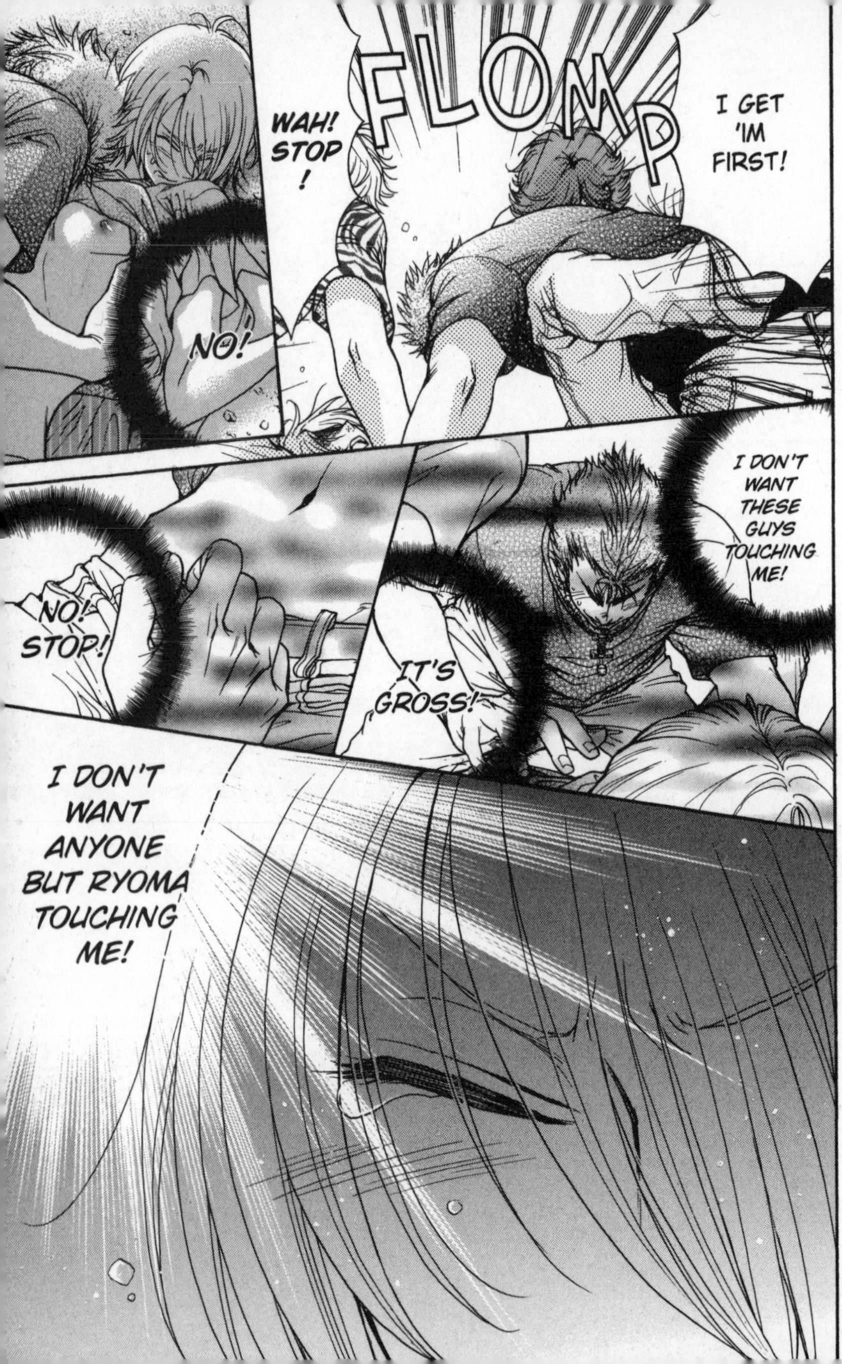
I GET 'IM FIRST!
FLOMP
WAH! STOP!
NO!
I DON'T WANT THESE GUYS TOUCHING ME!
IT'S GROSS!
NO! STOP!
I DON'T WANT ANYONE BUT RYOMA TOUCHING ME!

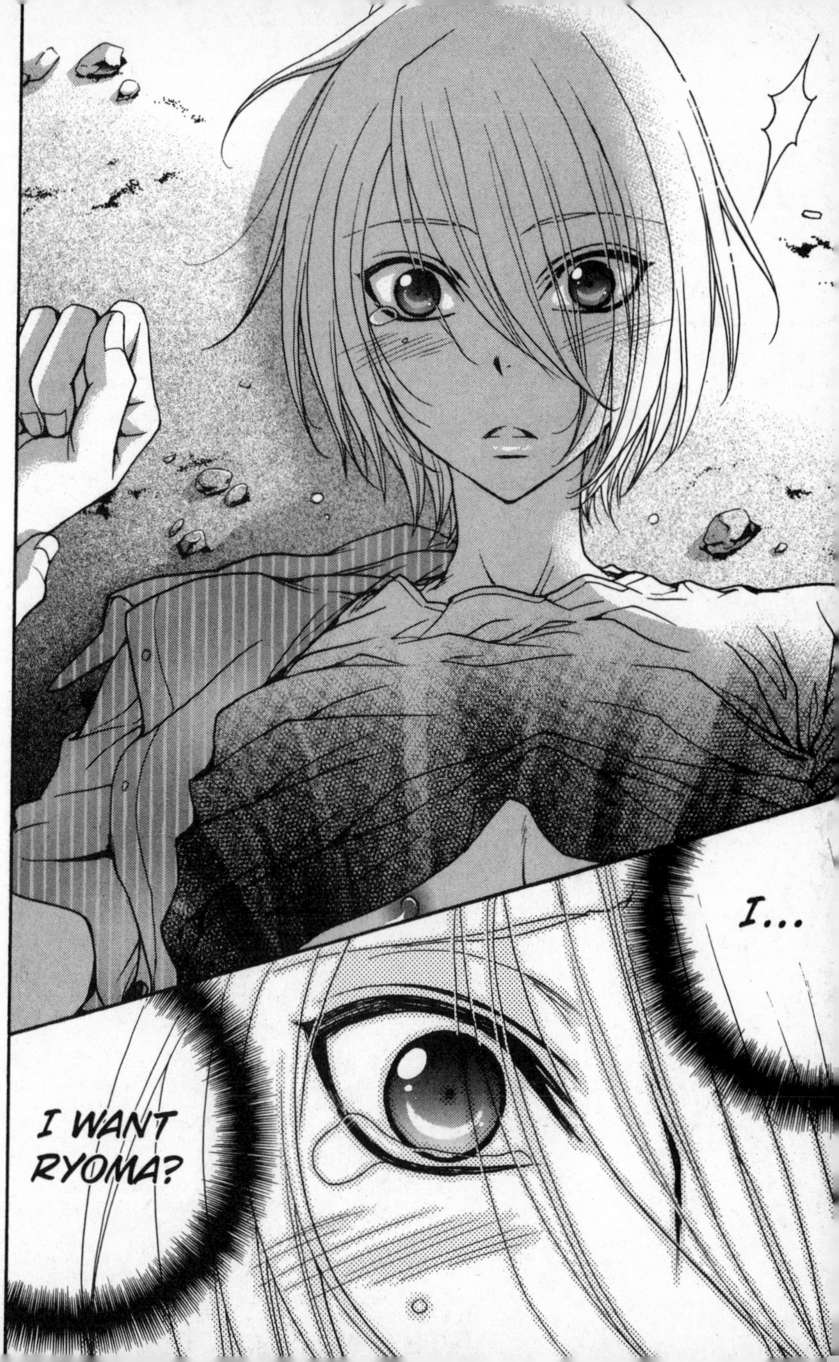
I...
I WANT RYOMA?

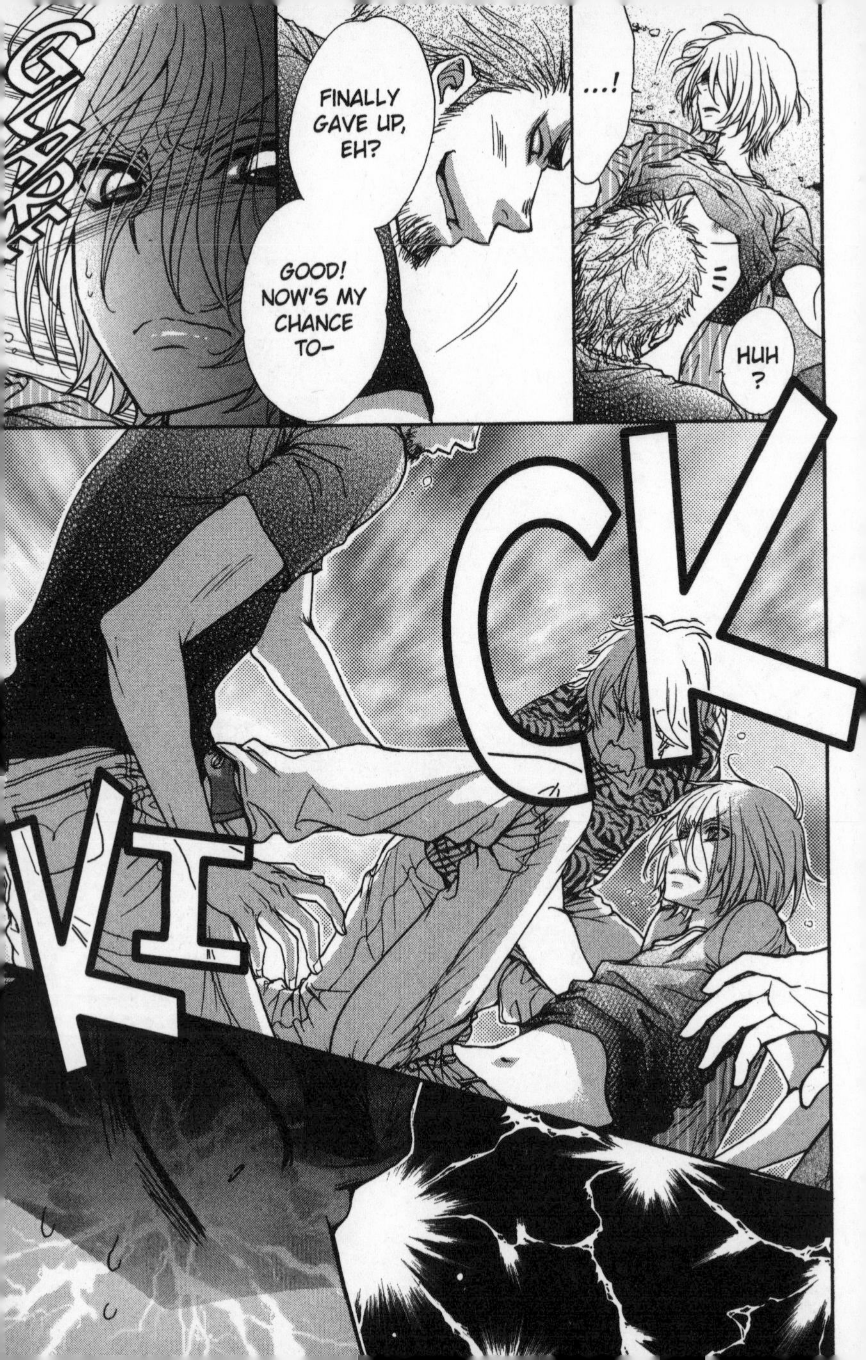
...!
HUH ?
FINALLY GAVE UP, EH?
GOOD! NOW'S MY CHANCE TO-
GLARE
VICK

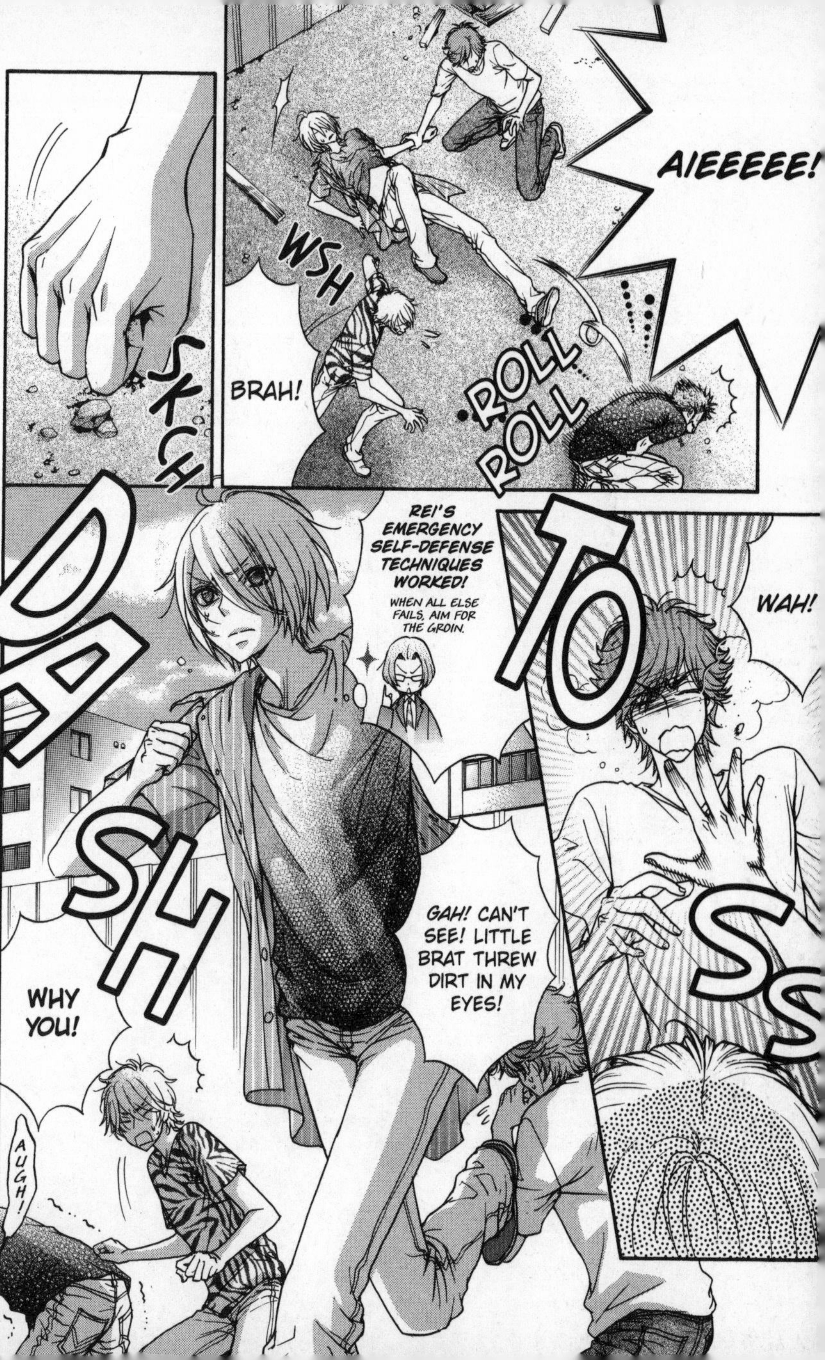
AIEEEEE!
WSH
BRAH!
ROLL ROLL
SKCH
TOSS
WAH!
DASH
REI'S EMERGENCY SELF-DEFENSE TECHNIQUES WORKED!
WHEN ALL ELSE FAILS, AIM FOR THE GROIN.
GAH! CAN'T SEE! LITTLE BRAT THREW DIRT IN MY EYES!
WHY YOU!
AUGH!

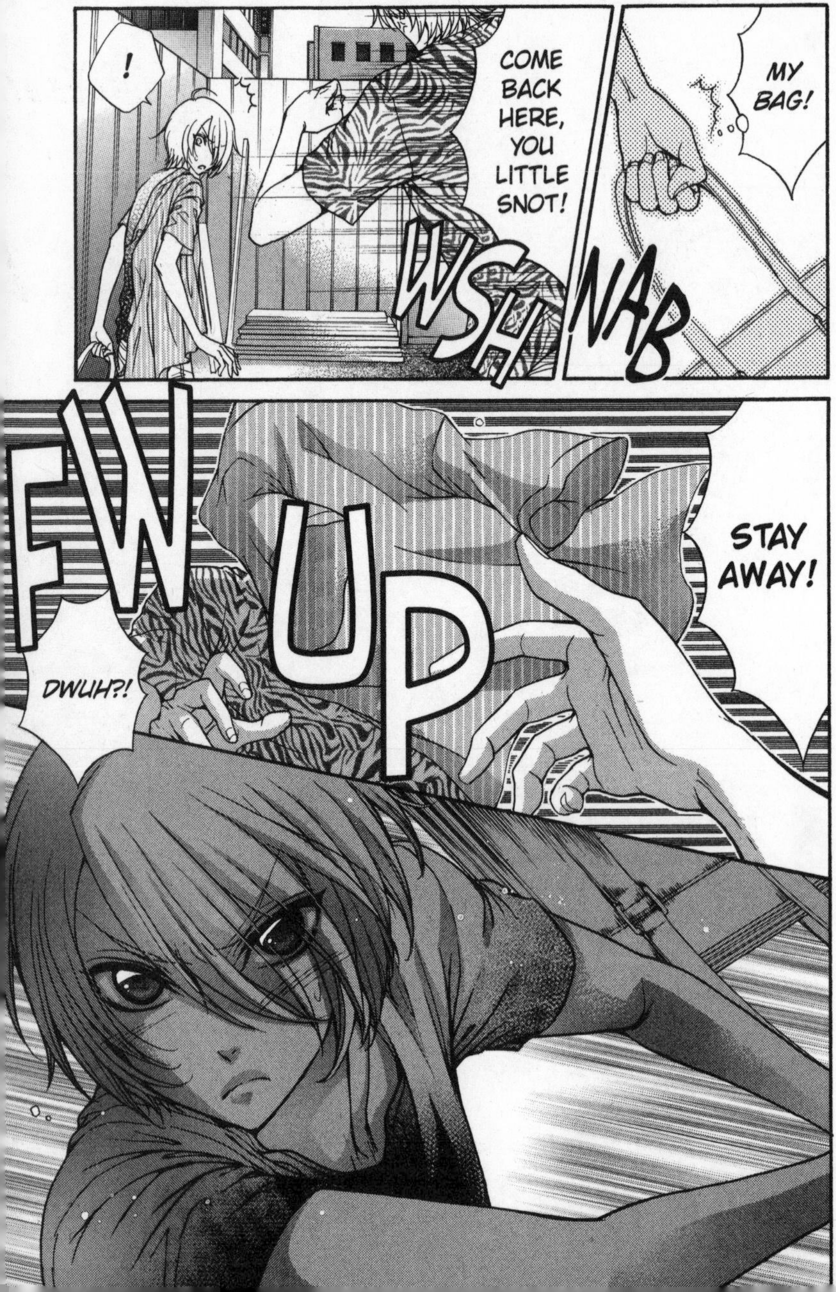
MY BAG!
NAB
!
COME BACK HERE, YOU LITTLE SNOT!
WSH
STAY AWAY!
FWUP
DWUH?!

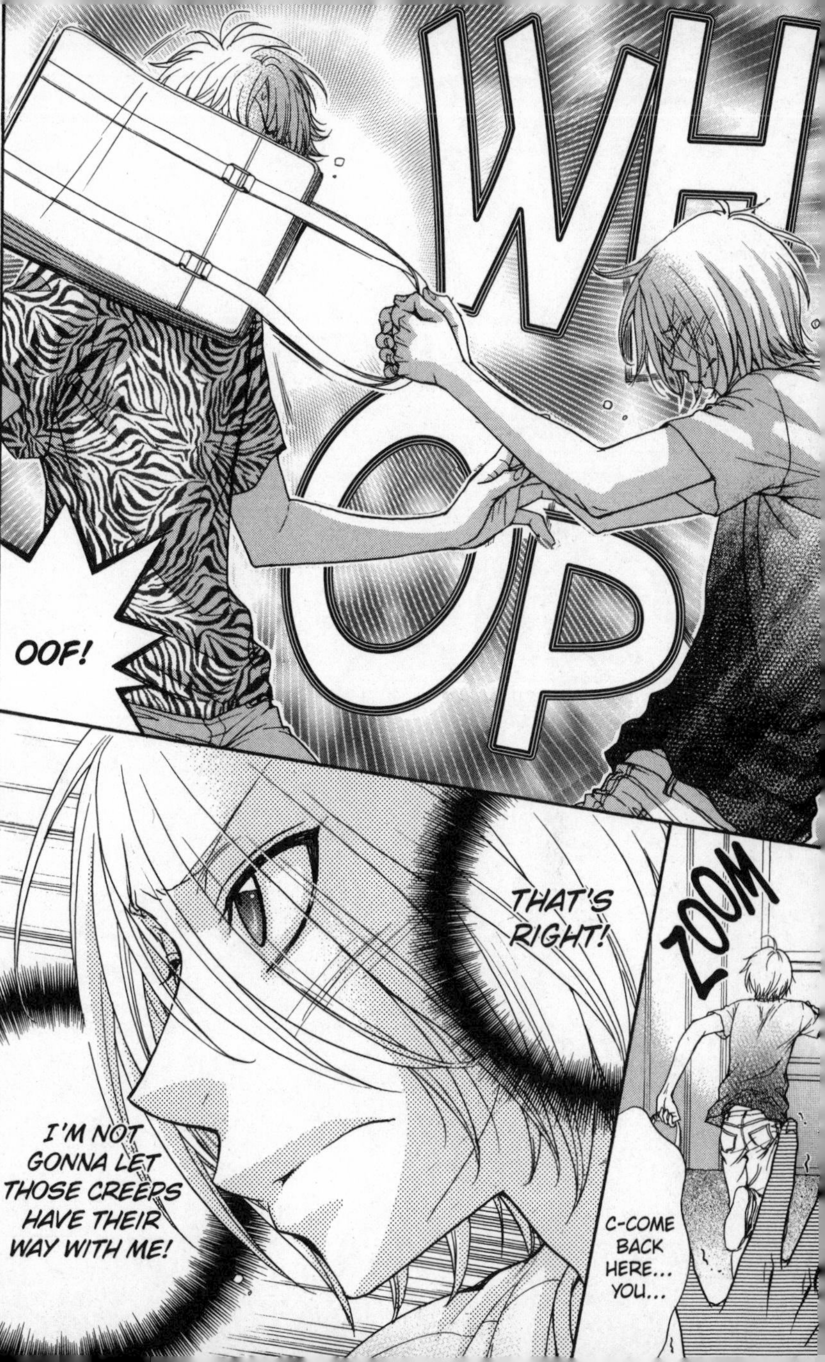
WHOOP
OOF!
ZOOM
C-COME BACK HERE... YOU...
THAT'S RIGHT!
I'M NOT GONNA LET THOSE CREEPS HAVE THEIR WAY WITH ME!

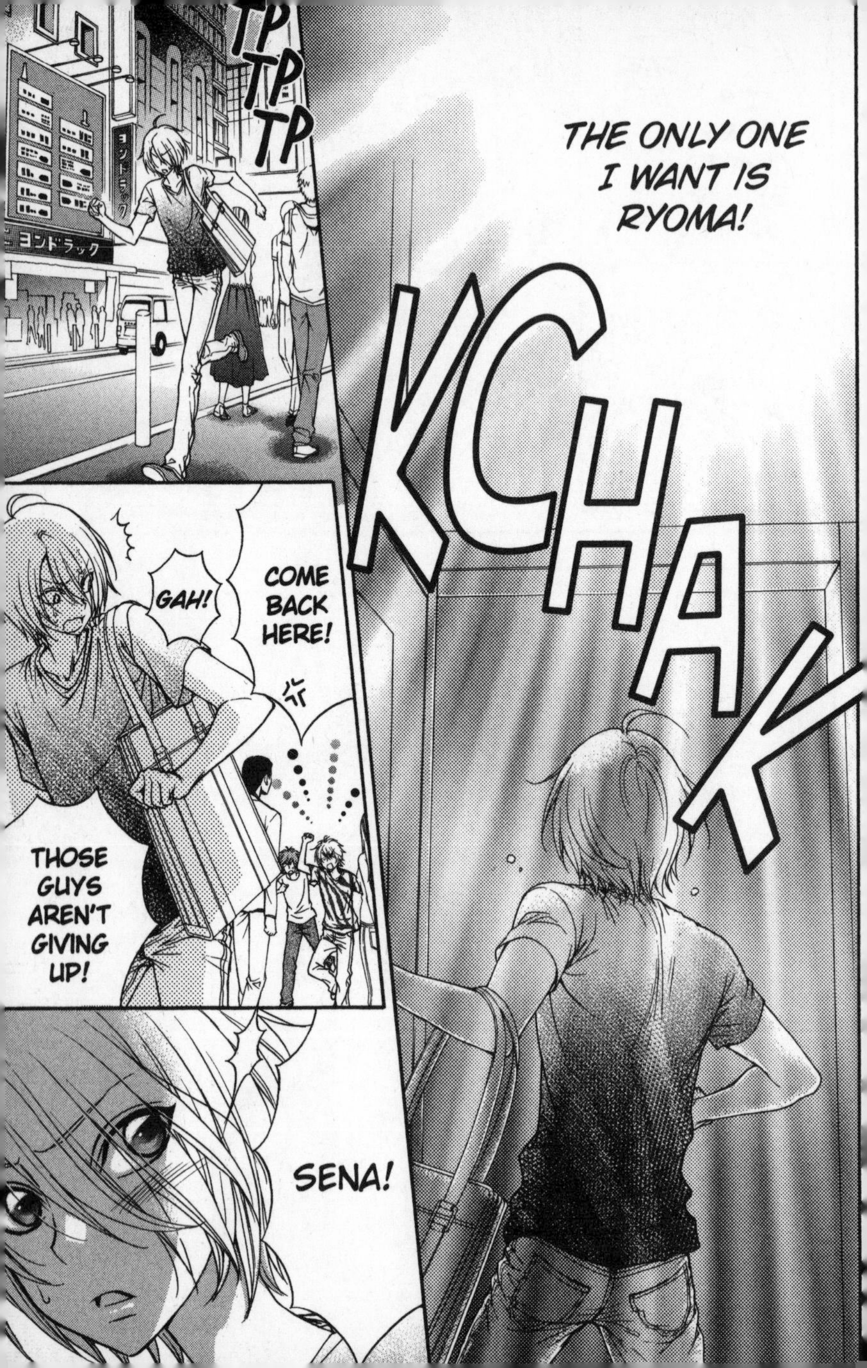
THE ONLY ONE I WANT IS RYOMA!
KCHAK
TP TP TP
ヨントラック
ヨンドラック
GAH!
COME BACK HERE!
THOSE GUYS AREN'T GIVING UP!
SENA!

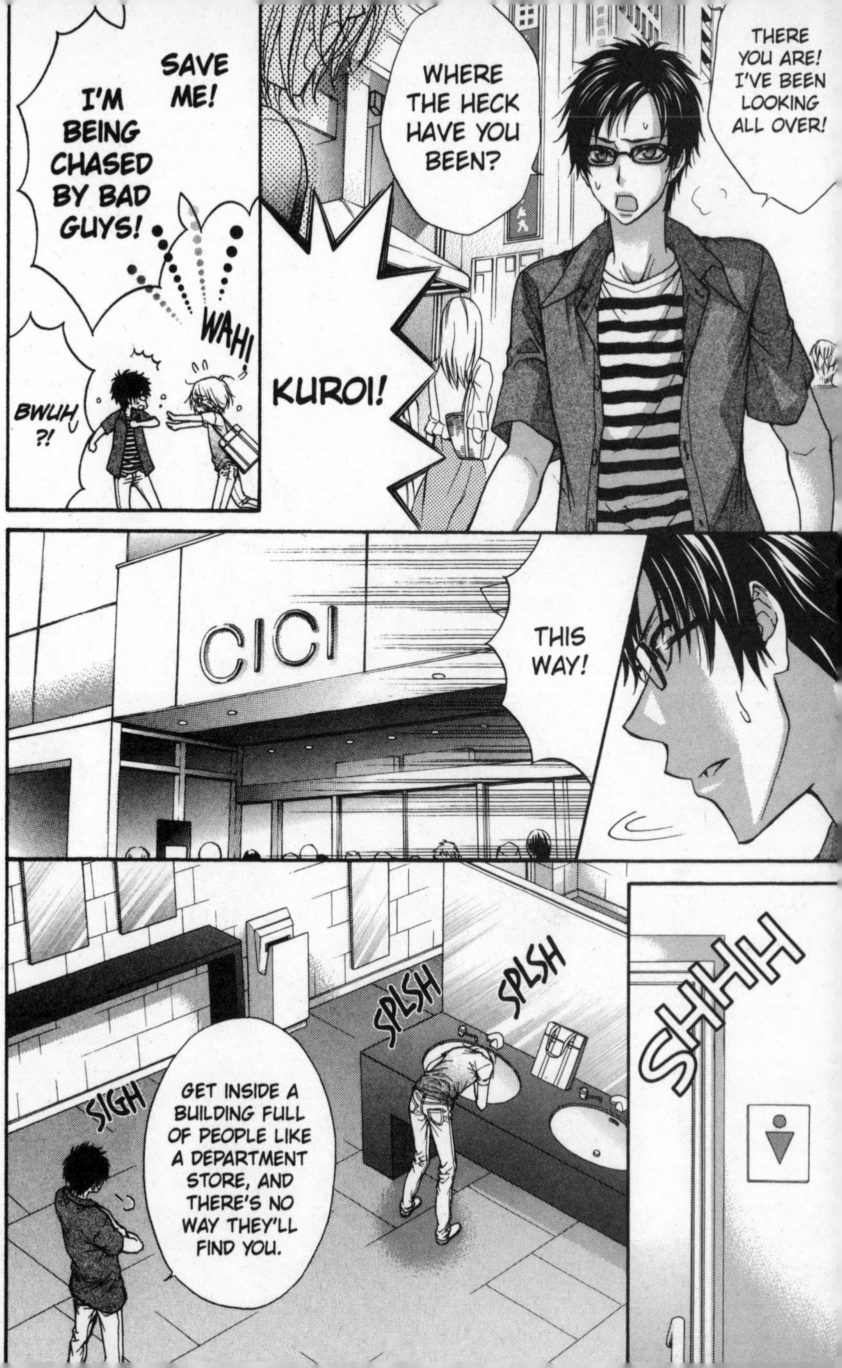
THERE YOU ARE! I'VE BEEN LOOKING ALL OVER!
WHERE THE HECK HAVE YOU BEEN?
KUROI!
SAVE ME! I'M BEING CHASED BY BAD GUYS!
WAH!
BWUH ?!
THIS WAY!
SHHH
SPLSH
SPLSH
GET INSIDE A BUILDING FULL OF PEOPLE LIKE A DEPARTMENT STORE, AND THERE'S NO WAY THEY'LL FIND YOU.
SIGH
CICI

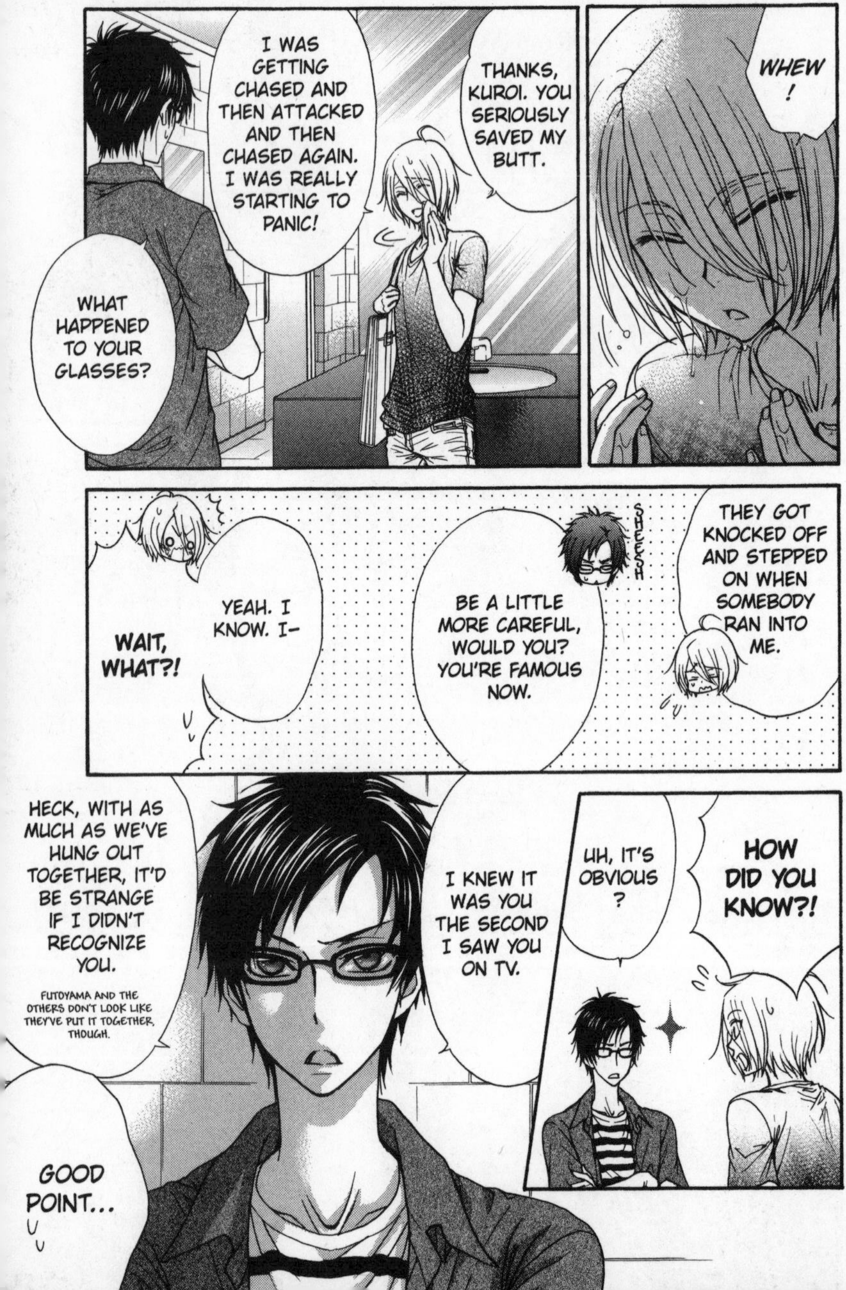
WHEW!
THANKS, KUROI. YOU SERIOUSLY SAVED MY BUTT.
I WAS GETTING CHASED AND THEN ATTACKED AND THEN CHASED AGAIN. I WAS REALLY STARTING TO PANIC!
WHAT HAPPENED TO YOUR GLASSES?
THEY GOT KNOCKED OFF AND STEPPED ON WHEN SOMEBODY RAN INTO ME.
SHEESH
BE A LITTLE MORE CAREFUL, WOULD YOU? YOU'RE FAMOUS NOW.
YEAH. I KNOW. I—
WAIT, WHAT?!
HOW DID YOU KNOW?!
UH, IT'S OBVIOUS?
I KNEW IT WAS YOU THE SECOND I SAW YOU ON TV.
HECK, WITH AS MUCH AS WE'VE HUNG OUT TOGETHER, IT'D BE STRANGE IF I DIDN'T RECOGNIZE YOU.
FUTOYAMA AND THE OTHERS DON'T LOOK LIKE THEY'VE PUT IT TOGETHER, THOUGH.
GOOD POINT...

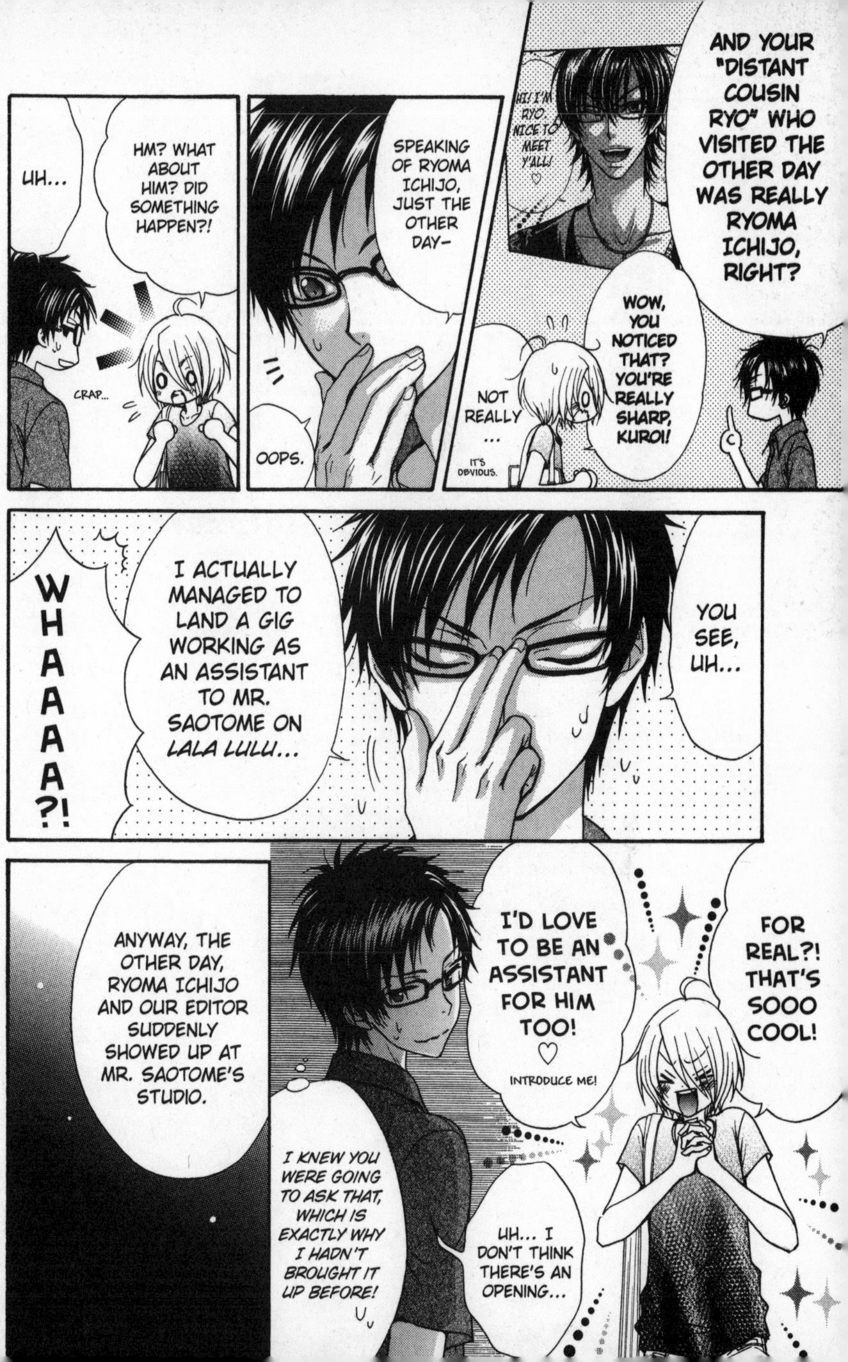
AND YOUR "DISTANT COUSIN RYO" WHO VISITED THE OTHER DAY WAS REALLY RYOMA ICHIJO, RIGHT?
HI! I'M RYO. NICE TO MEET Y'ALL! ♡
WOW, YOU NOTICED THAT? YOU'RE REALLY SHARP, KUROI!
NOT REALLY...
IT'S OBVIOUS.
SPEAKING OF RYOMA ICHIJO, JUST THE OTHER DAY—
OOPS.
HM? WHAT ABOUT HIM? DID SOMETHING HAPPEN?!
UH...
CRAP...
YOU SEE, UH...
I ACTUALLY MANAGED TO LAND A GIG WORKING AS AN ASSISTANT TO MR. SAOTOME ON *LALA LULU*...
WHAAAAA?!
FOR REAL?! THAT'S SOOO COOL!
I'D LOVE TO BE AN ASSISTANT FOR HIM TOO! ♡
INTRODUCE ME!
UH... I DON'T THINK THERE'S AN OPENING...
I KNEW YOU WERE GOING TO ASK THAT, WHICH IS EXACTLY WHY I HADN'T BROUGHT IT UP BEFORE!
ANYWAY, THE OTHER DAY, RYOMA ICHIJO AND OUR EDITOR SUDDENLY SHOWED UP AT MR. SAOTOME'S STUDIO.

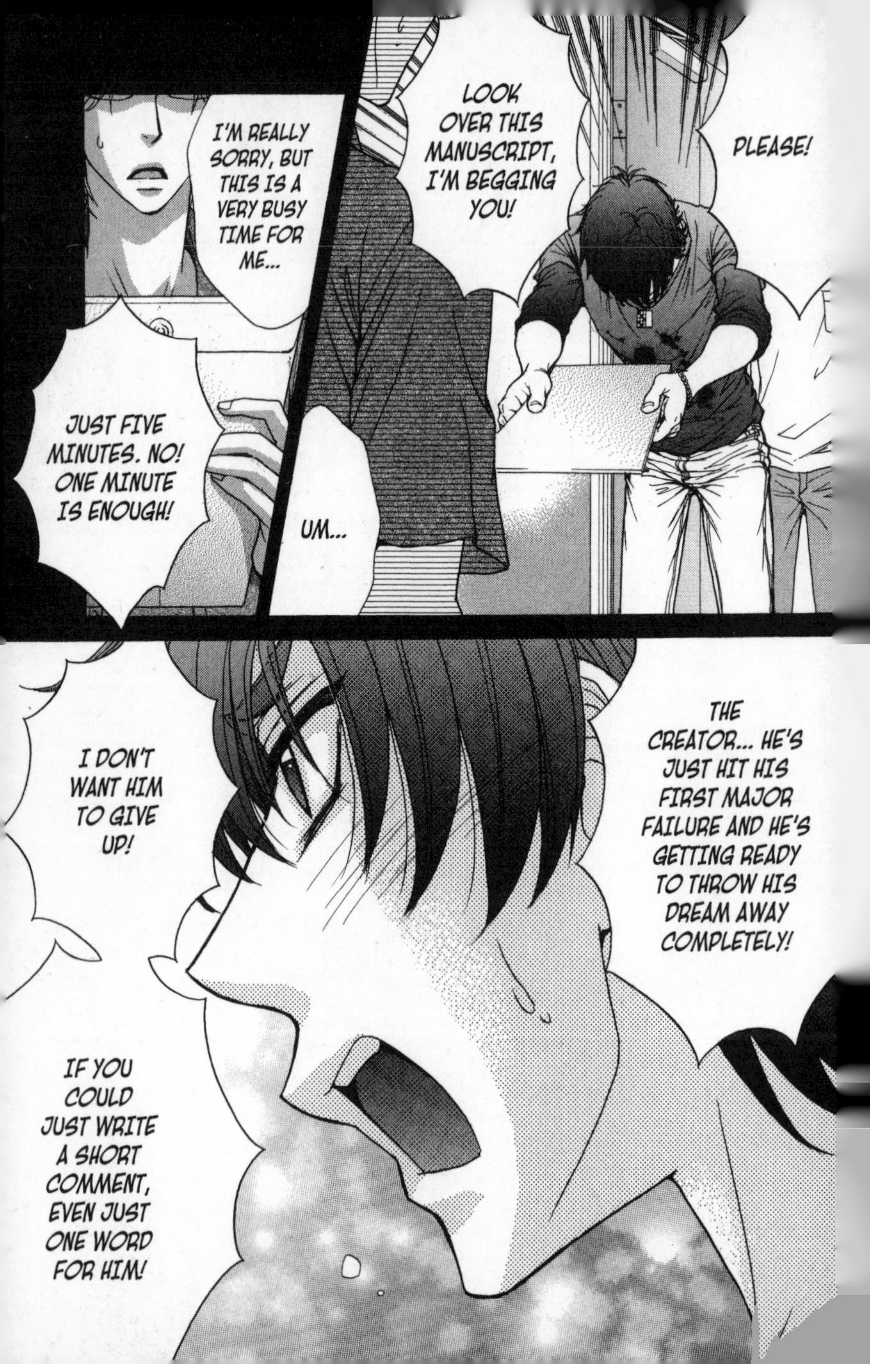
LOOK OVER THIS MANUSCRIPT, I'M BEGGING YOU!
PLEASE!
UM...
I'M REALLY SORRY, BUT THIS IS A VERY BUSY TIME FOR ME...
JUST FIVE MINUTES. NO! ONE MINUTE IS ENOUGH!
THE CREATOR... HE'S JUST HIT HIS FIRST MAJOR FAILURE AND HE'S GETTING READY TO THROW HIS DREAM AWAY COMPLETELY!
I DON'T WANT HIM TO GIVE UP!
IF YOU COULD JUST WRITE A SHORT COMMENT, EVEN JUST ONE WORD FOR HIM!

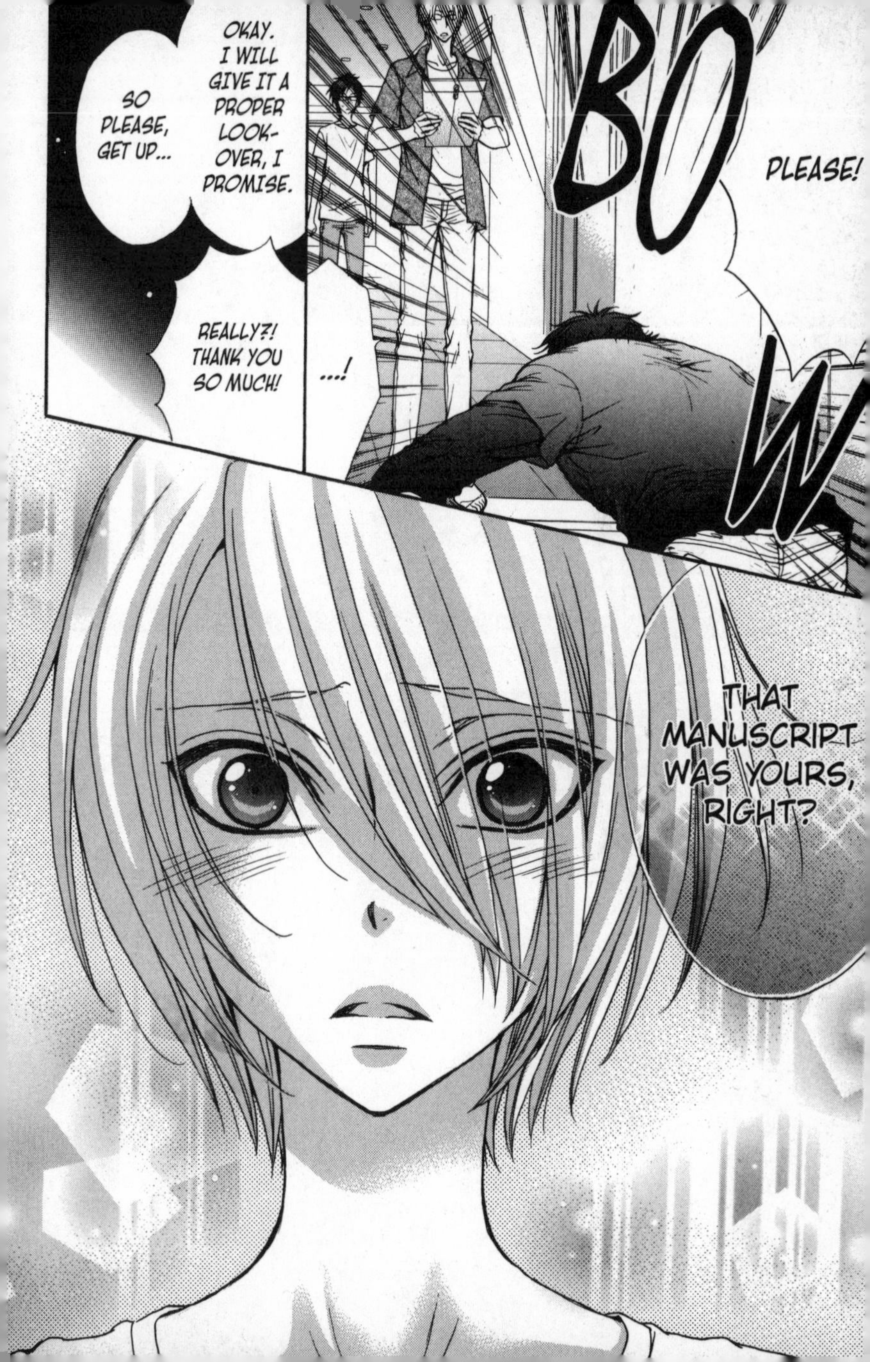
BOW
PLEASE!
...!
OKAY. I WILL GIVE IT A PROPER LOOK-OVER, I PROMISE.
SO PLEASE, GET UP...
REALLY?! THANK YOU SO MUCH!
THAT MANUSCRIPT WAS YOURS, RIGHT?

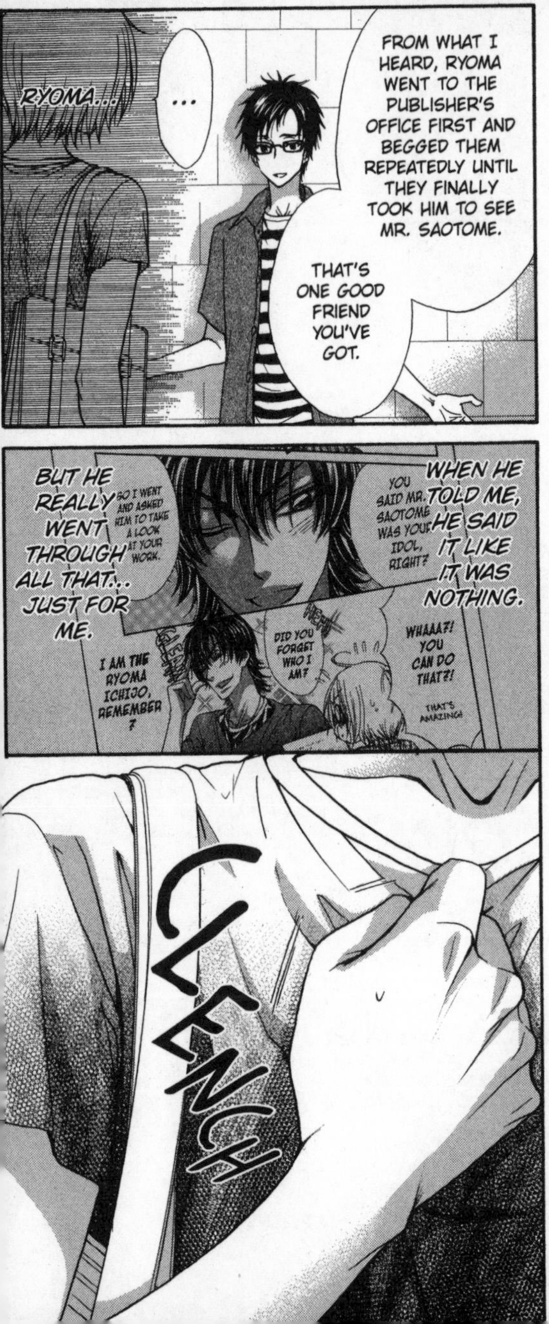
FROM WHAT I HEARD, RYOMA WENT TO THE PUBLISHER'S OFFICE FIRST AND BEGGED THEM REPEATEDLY UNTIL THEY FINALLY TOOK HIM TO SEE MR. SAOTOME.
THAT'S ONE GOOD FRIEND YOU'VE GOT.
...
RYOMA...
WHEN HE TOLD ME, HE SAID IT LIKE IT WAS NOTHING.
YOU SAID MR. SAOTOME WAS YOUR IDOL, RIGHT?
SO I WENT AND ASKED HIM TO TAKE A LOOK AT YOUR WORK.
WHAAA?! YOU CAN DO THAT?!
THAT'S AMAZING!
HEH
DID YOU FORGET WHO I AM?
I AM THE RYOMA ICHIJO, REMEMBER?
BUT HE REALLY WENT THROUGH ALL THAT... JUST FOR ME.
CLENCH

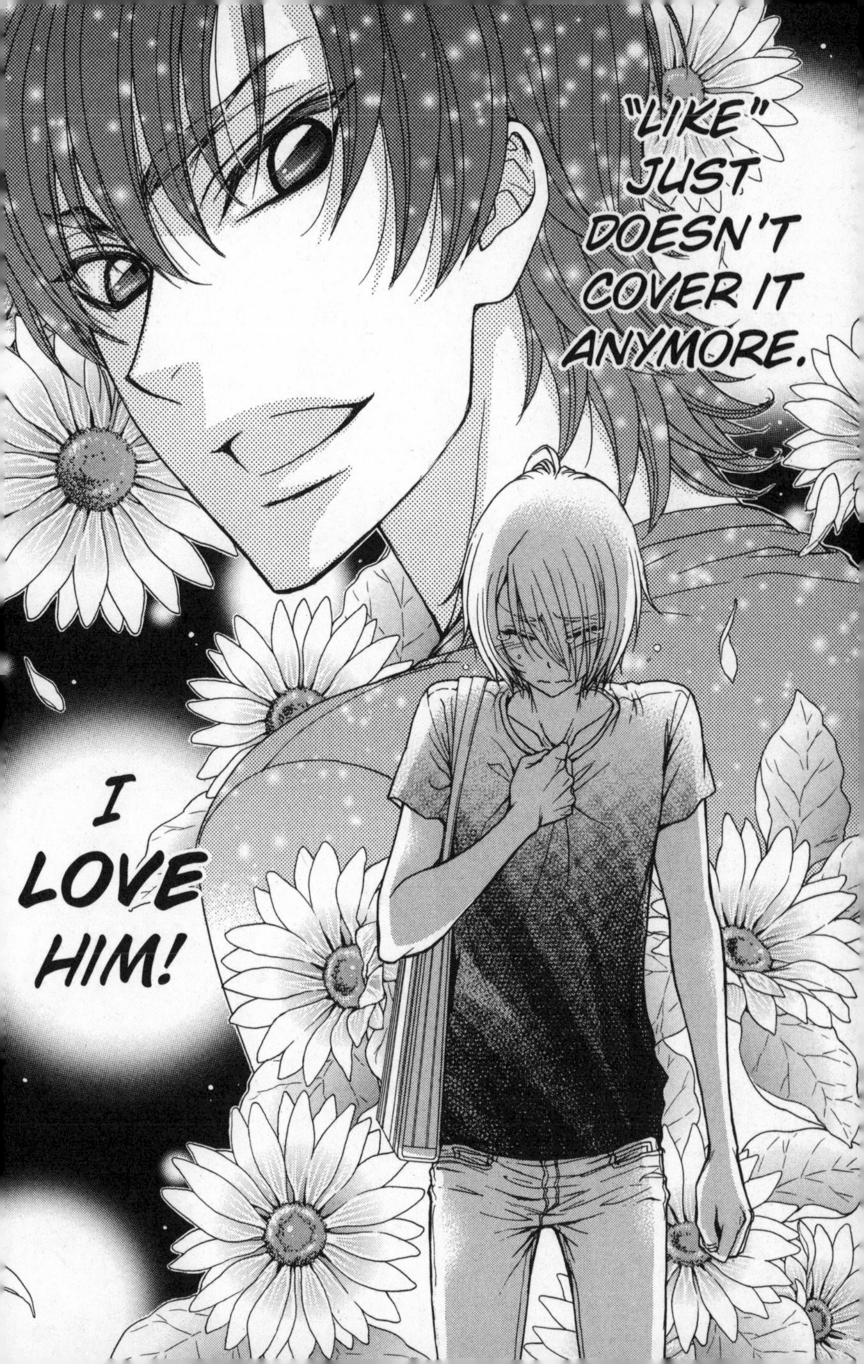
"LIKE" JUST DOESN'T COVER IT ANYMORE.
I LOVE HIM!

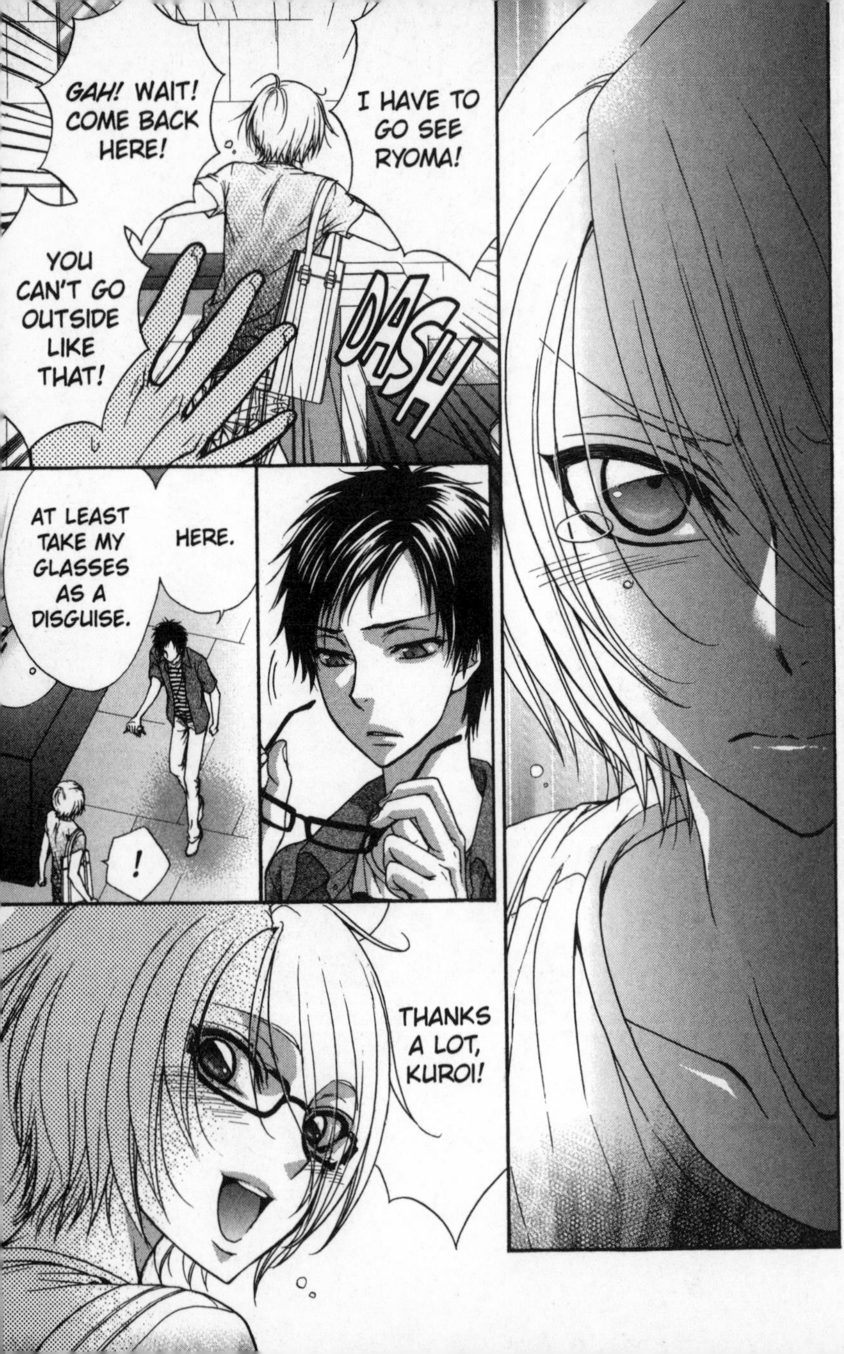
I HAVE TO GO SEE RYOMA!
GAH! WAIT! COME BACK HERE!
YOU CAN'T GO OUTSIDE LIKE THAT!
DASH
AT LEAST TAKE MY GLASSES AS A DISGUISE.
HERE.
!
THANKS A LOT, KUROI!

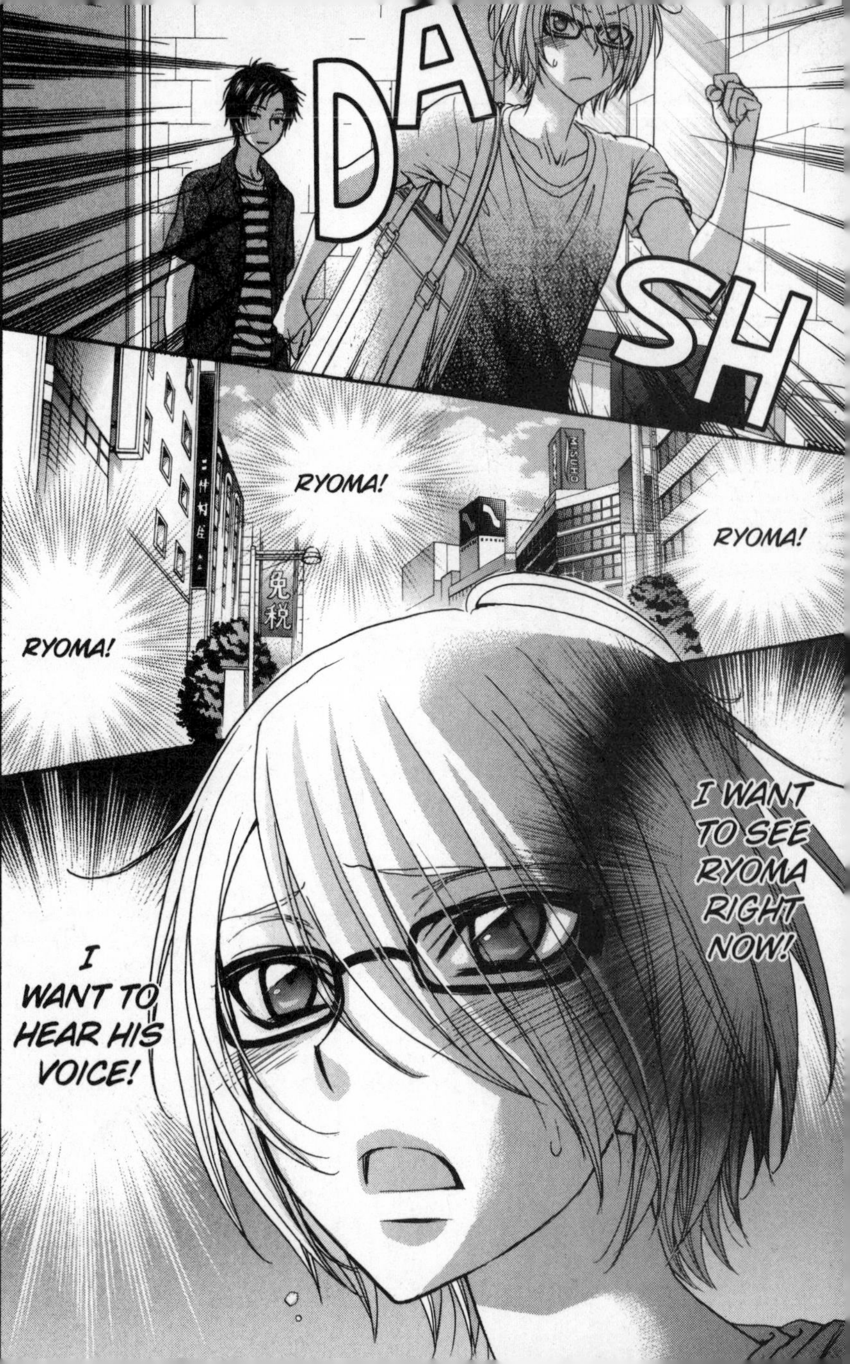
DASH
RYOMA!
RYOMA!
MISUHO
免税
RYOMA!
I WANT TO SEE RYOMA RIGHT NOW!
I WANT TO HEAR HIS VOICE!

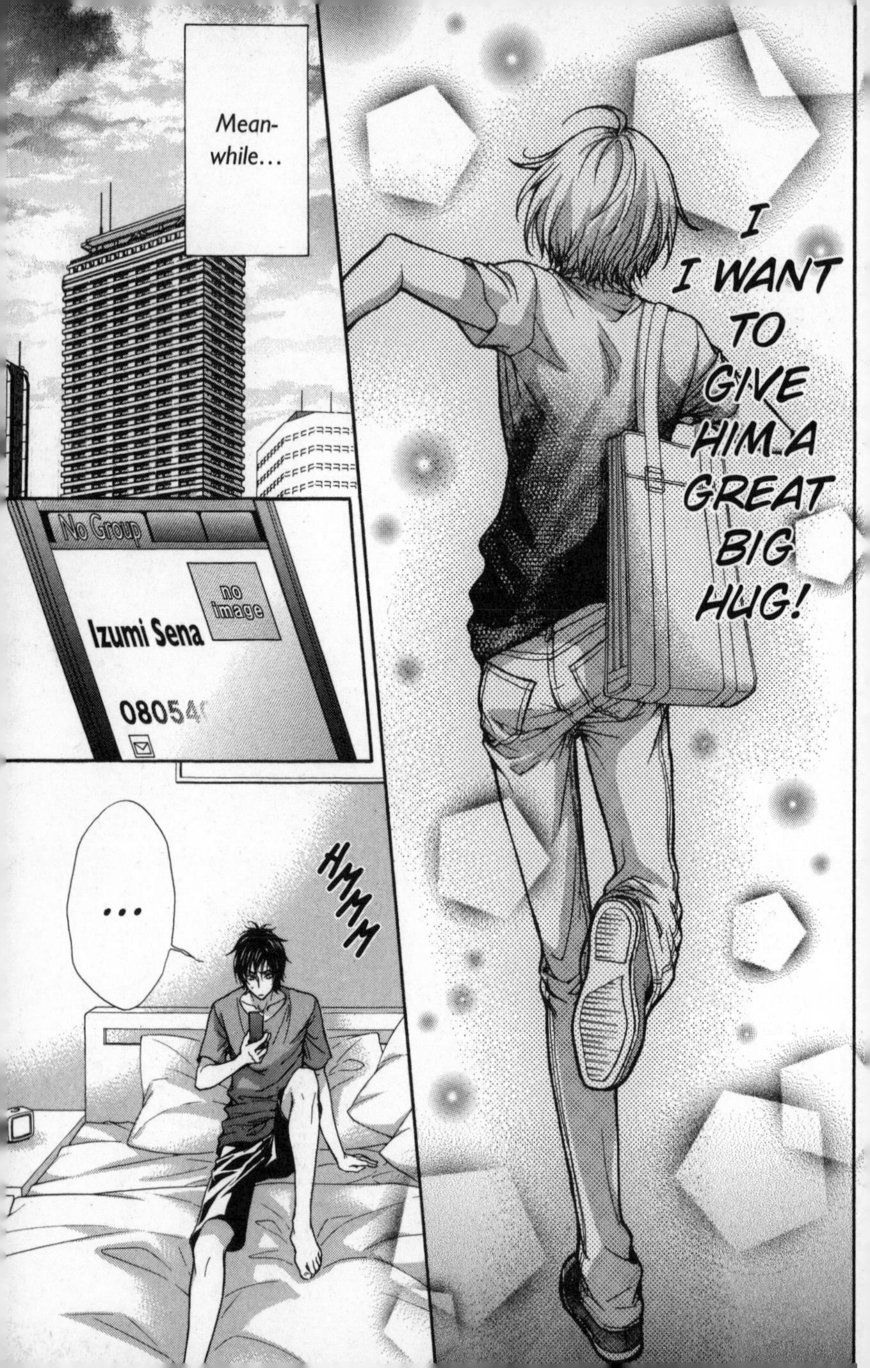
I
I WANT TO GIVE HIM A GREAT BIG HUG!
Mean-while...
No Group
no image
Izumi Sena
08054
...
HMMM

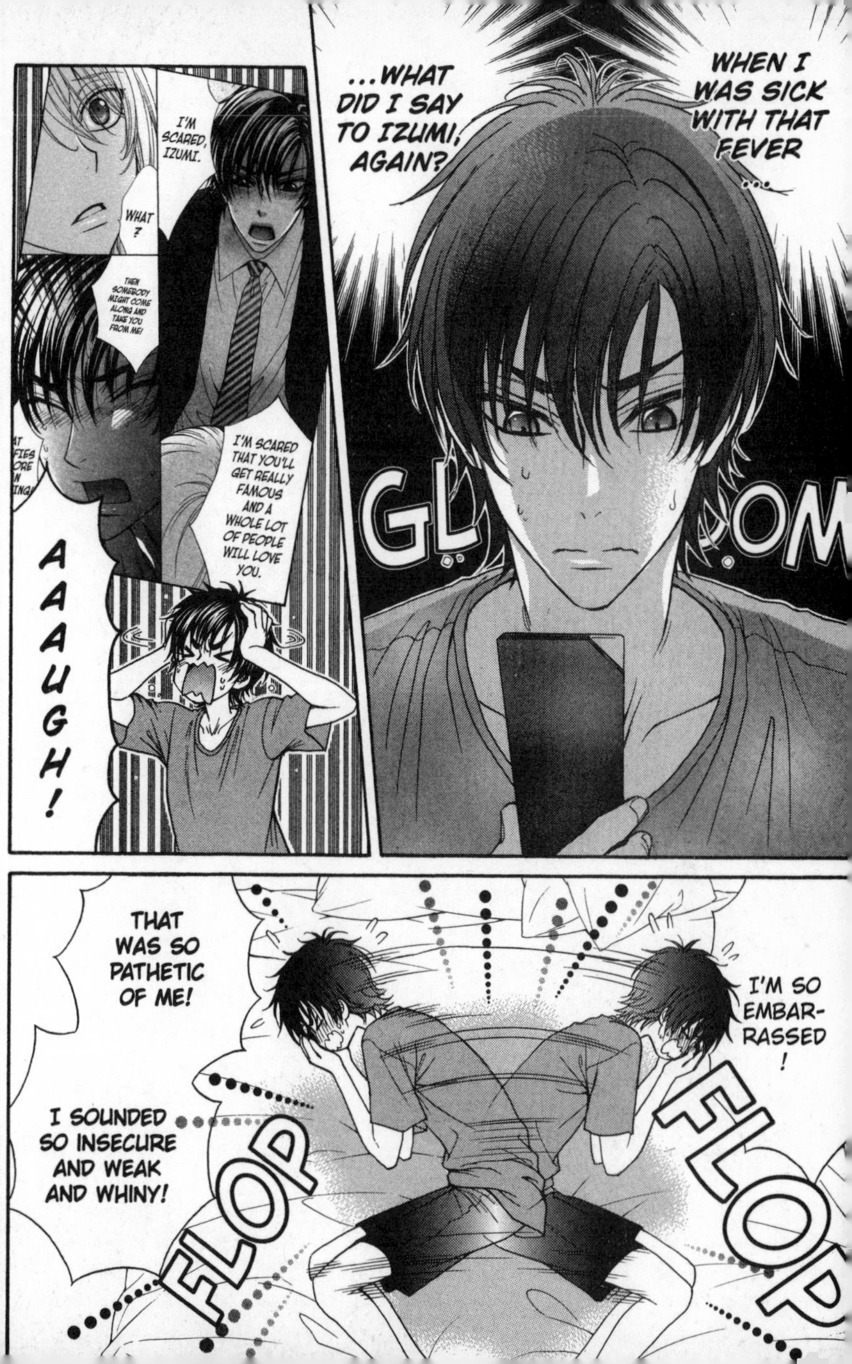
WHEN I WAS SICK WITH THAT FEVER...
...WHAT DID I SAY TO IZUMI, AGAIN?
I'M SCARED, IZUMI.
WHAT?
THEN SOMEBODY MIGHT COME ALONG AND TAKE YOU FROM ME!
I'M SCARED THAT YOU'LL GET REALLY FAMOUS AND A WHOLE LOT OF PEOPLE WILL LOVE YOU.
AAAAUGH!
I'M SO EMBARRASSED!
THAT WAS SO PATHETIC OF ME!
I SOUNDED SO INSECURE AND WEAK AND WHINY!
FLOP
FLOP

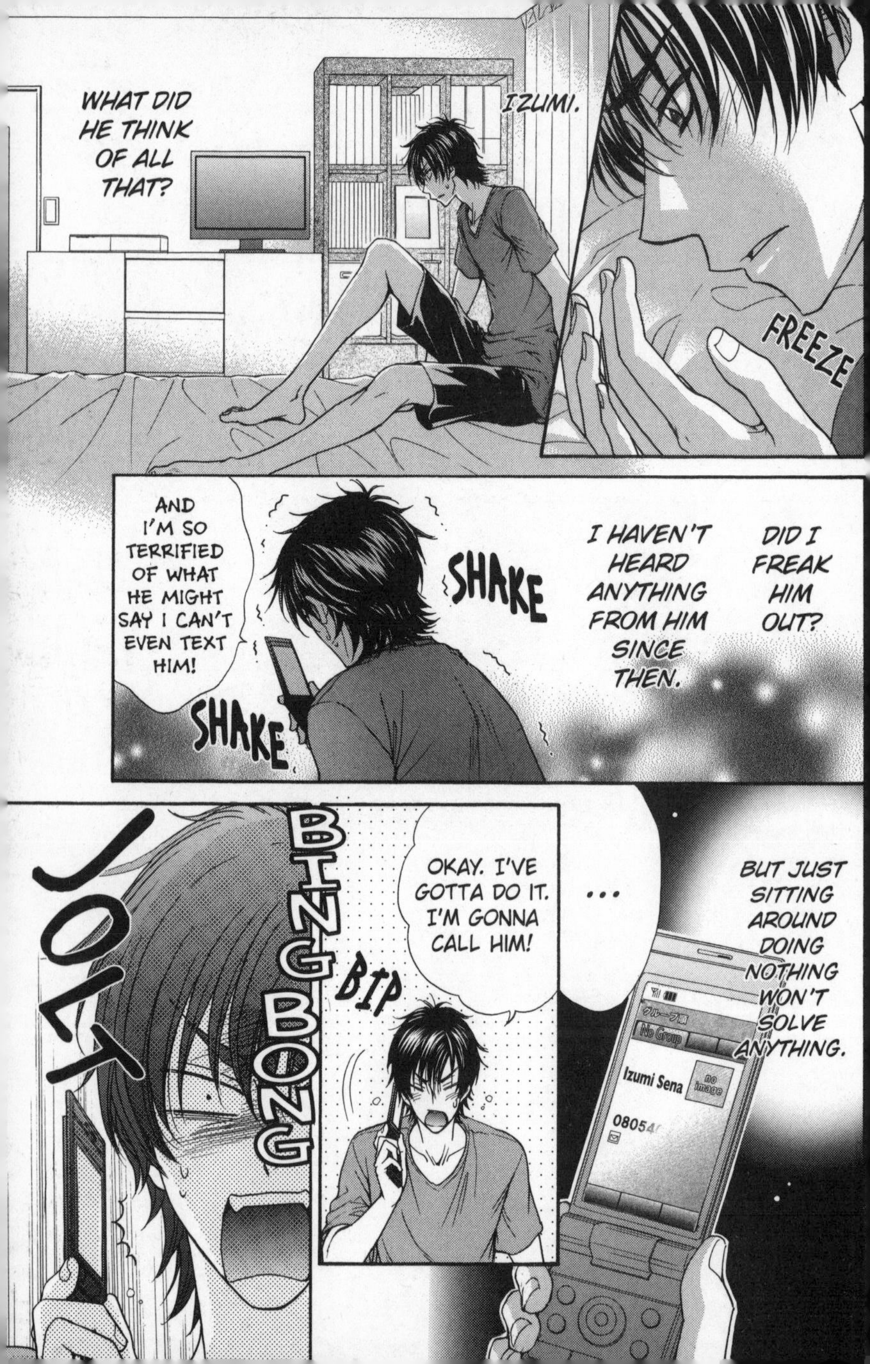
IZUMI.
FREEZE
WHAT DID HE THINK OF ALL THAT?
DID I FREAK HIM OUT?
I HAVEN'T HEARD ANYTHING FROM HIM SINCE THEN.
SHAKE
SHAKE
AND I'M SO TERRIFIED OF WHAT HE MIGHT SAY I CAN'T EVEN TEXT HIM!
BUT JUST SITTING AROUND DOING NOTHING WON'T SOLVE ANYTHING.
...
No Group
Izumi Sena
no image
OKAY. I'VE GOTTA DO IT. I'M GONNA CALL HIM!
BIP
BING BONG
JOLT

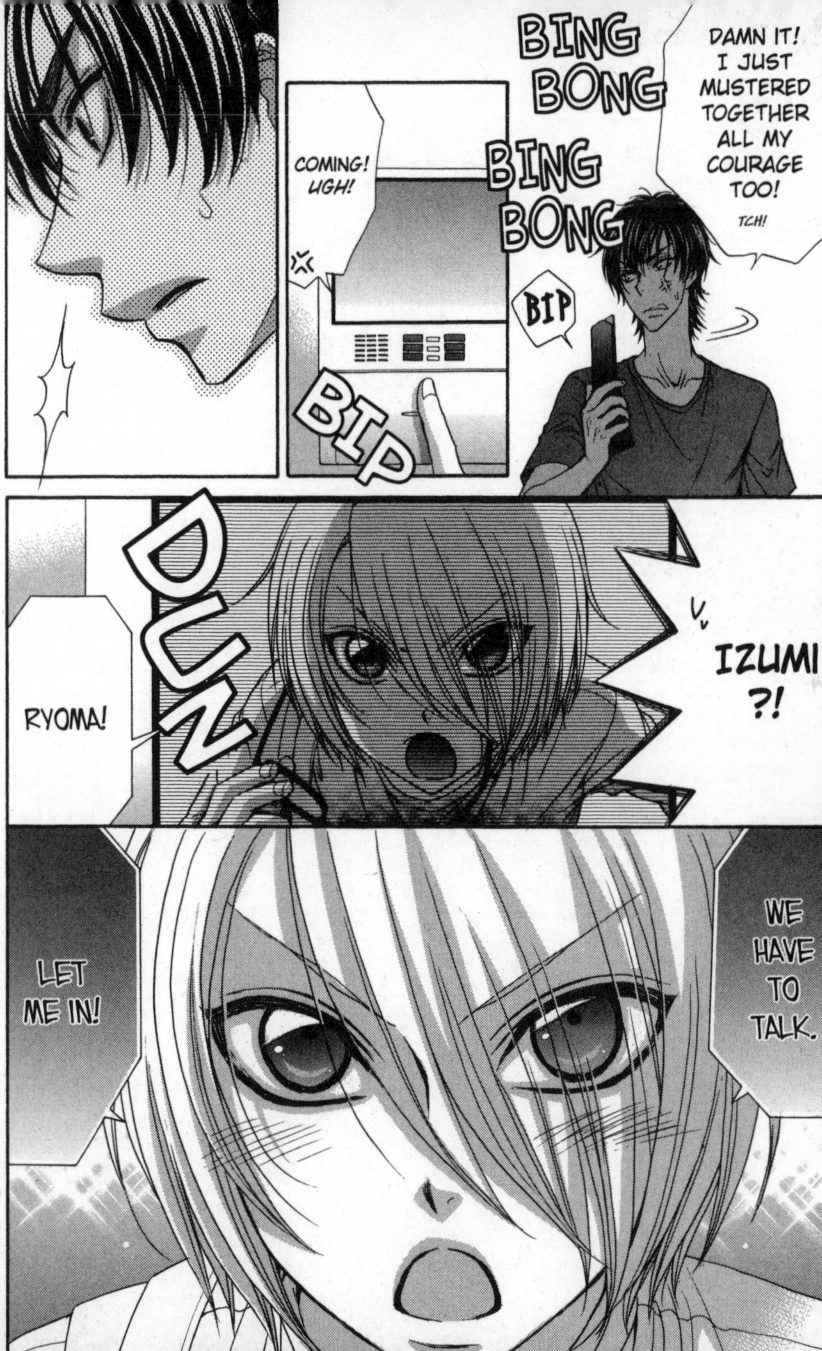
DAMN IT! I JUST MUSTERED TOGETHER ALL MY COURAGE TOO!
TCH!
BING BONG
BING BONG
BIP
COMING! UGH!
BIP
IZUMI ?!
DUN
RYOMA!
WE HAVE TO TALK.
LET ME IN!

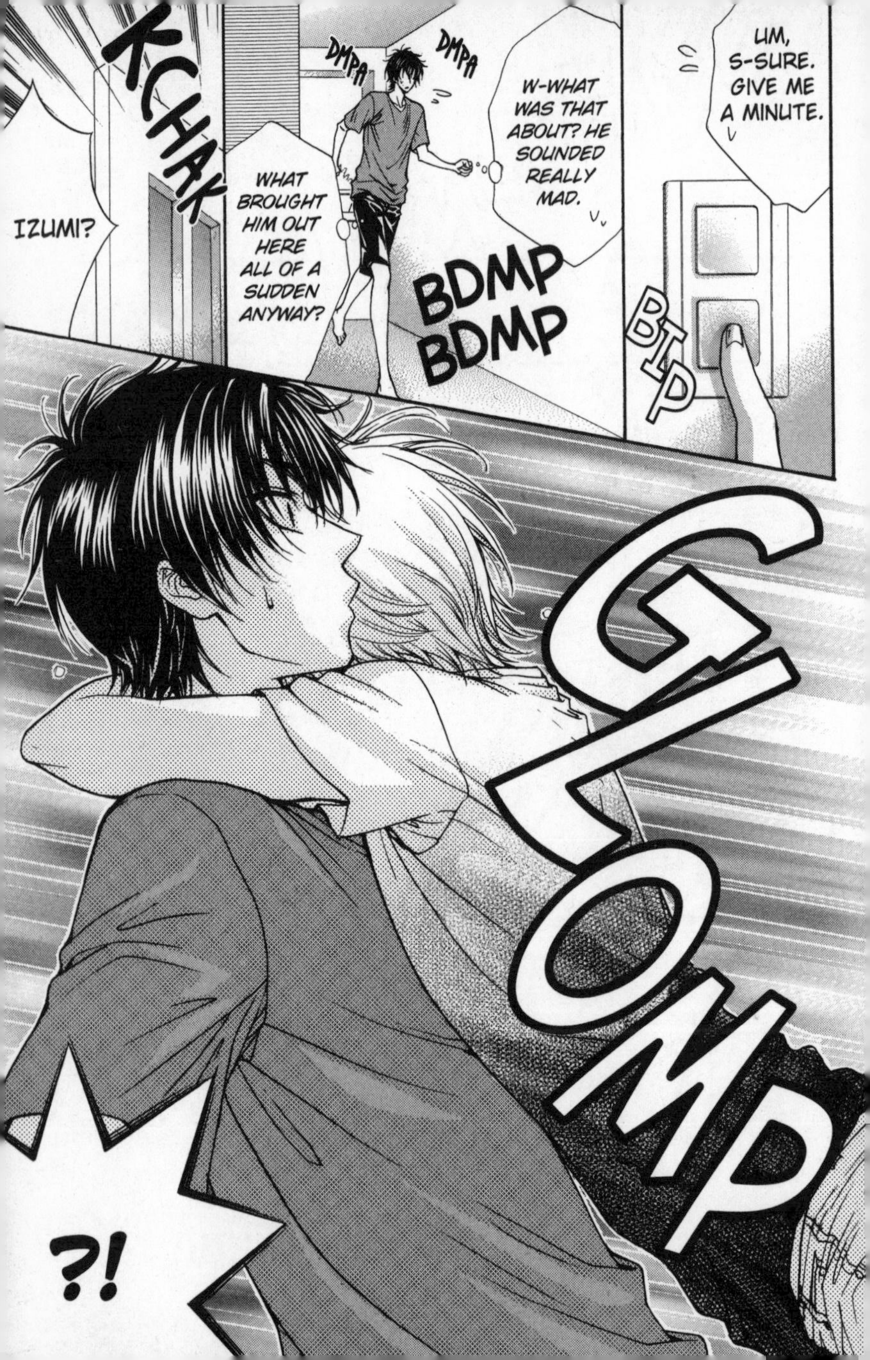
UM, S-SURE. GIVE ME A MINUTE.
BIP
W-WHAT WAS THAT ABOUT? HE SOUNDED REALLY MAD.
DMPA
DMPA
BDMP BDMP
WHAT BROUGHT HIM OUT HERE ALL OF A SUDDEN ANYWAY?
KCHAK
IZUMI?
GLOMP
?!

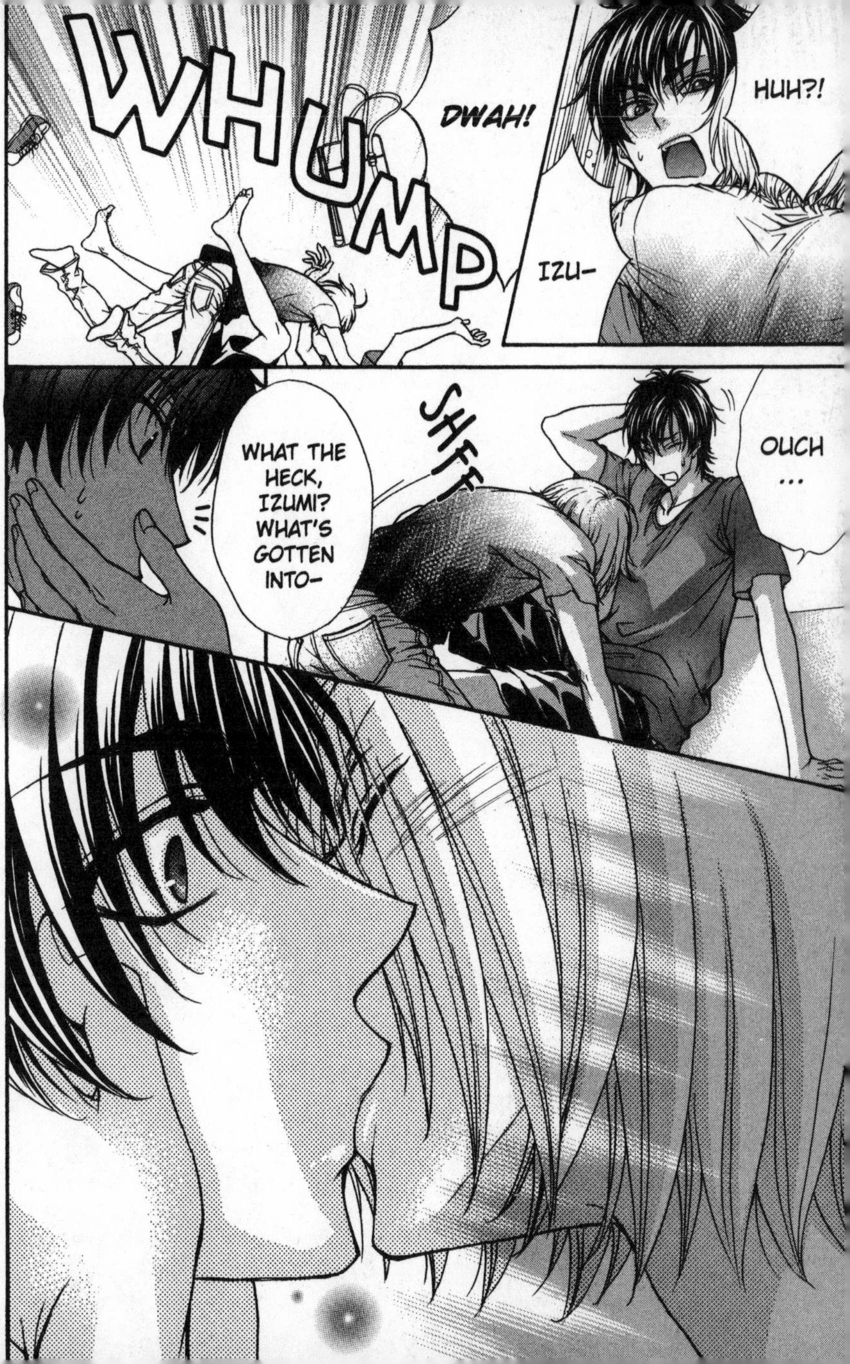
HUH?!
IZU-
WHUMP
DWAH!
OUCH ...
SHFF
WHAT THE HECK, IZUMI? WHAT'S GOTTEN INTO-

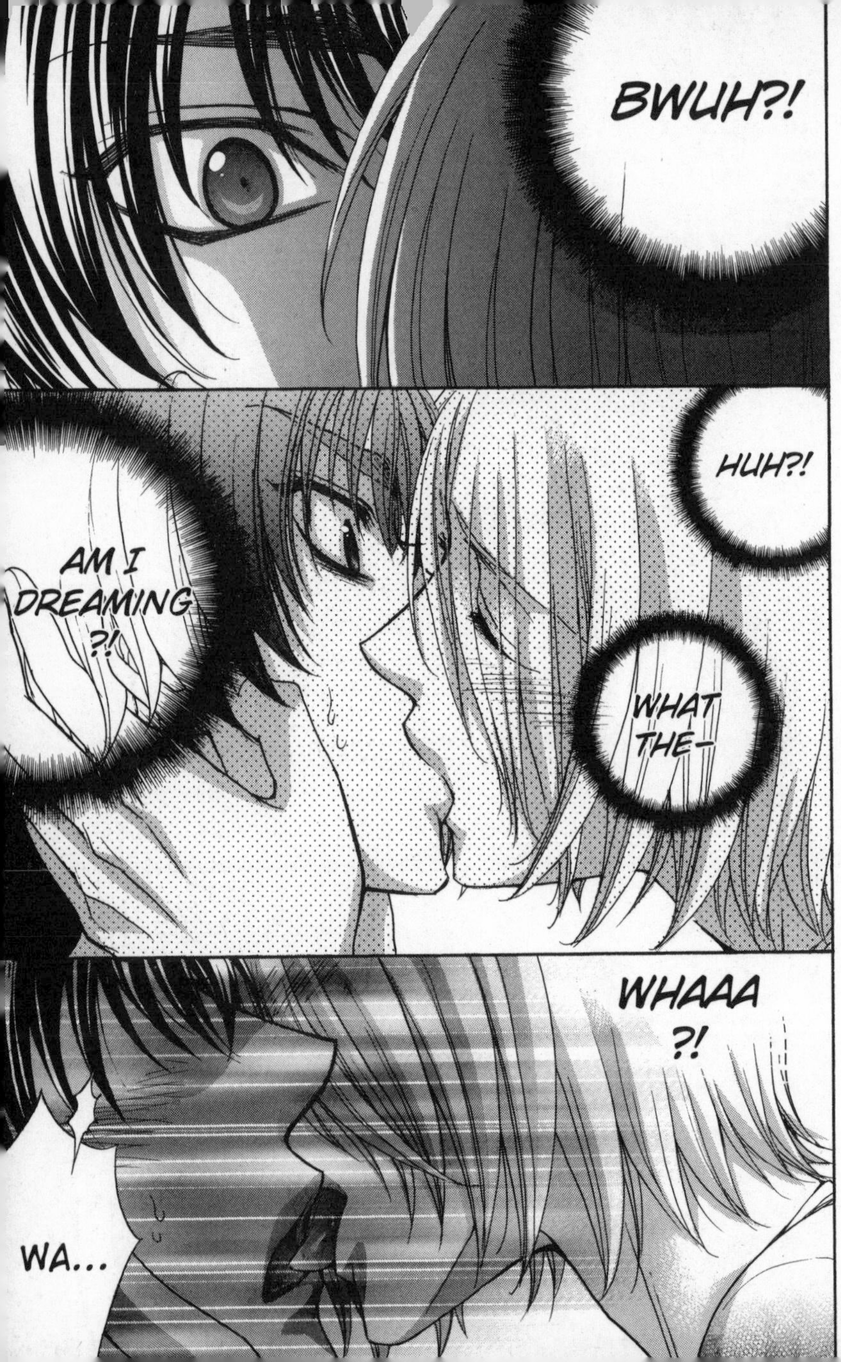
BWUH?!
HUH?!
WHAT THE-
AM I DREAMING ?!
WHAAA ?!
WA...

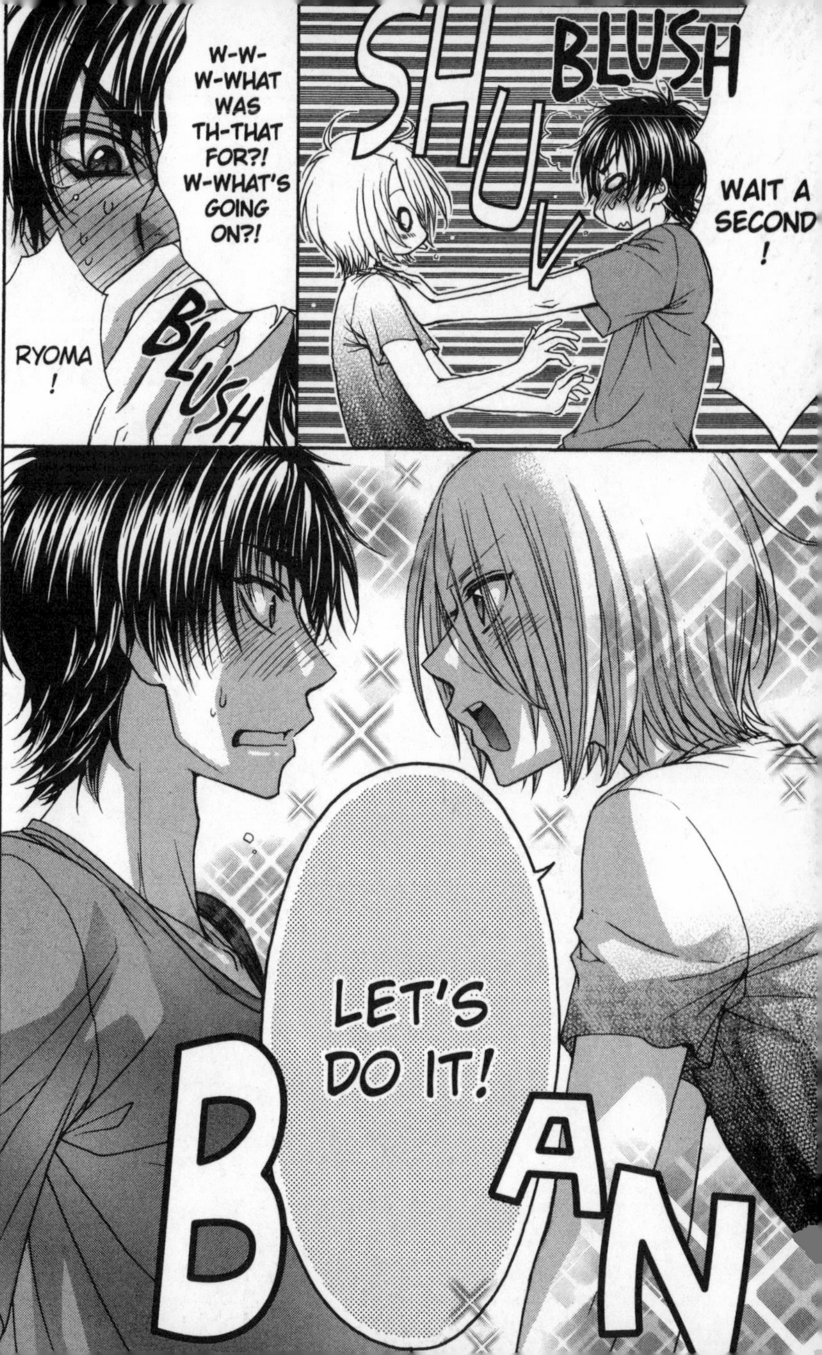
BLUSH
WAIT A SECOND!
SHUV
W-W-W-WHAT WAS TH-THAT FOR?! W-WHAT'S GOING ON?!
BLUSH
RYOMA!
LET'S DO IT!
BAN

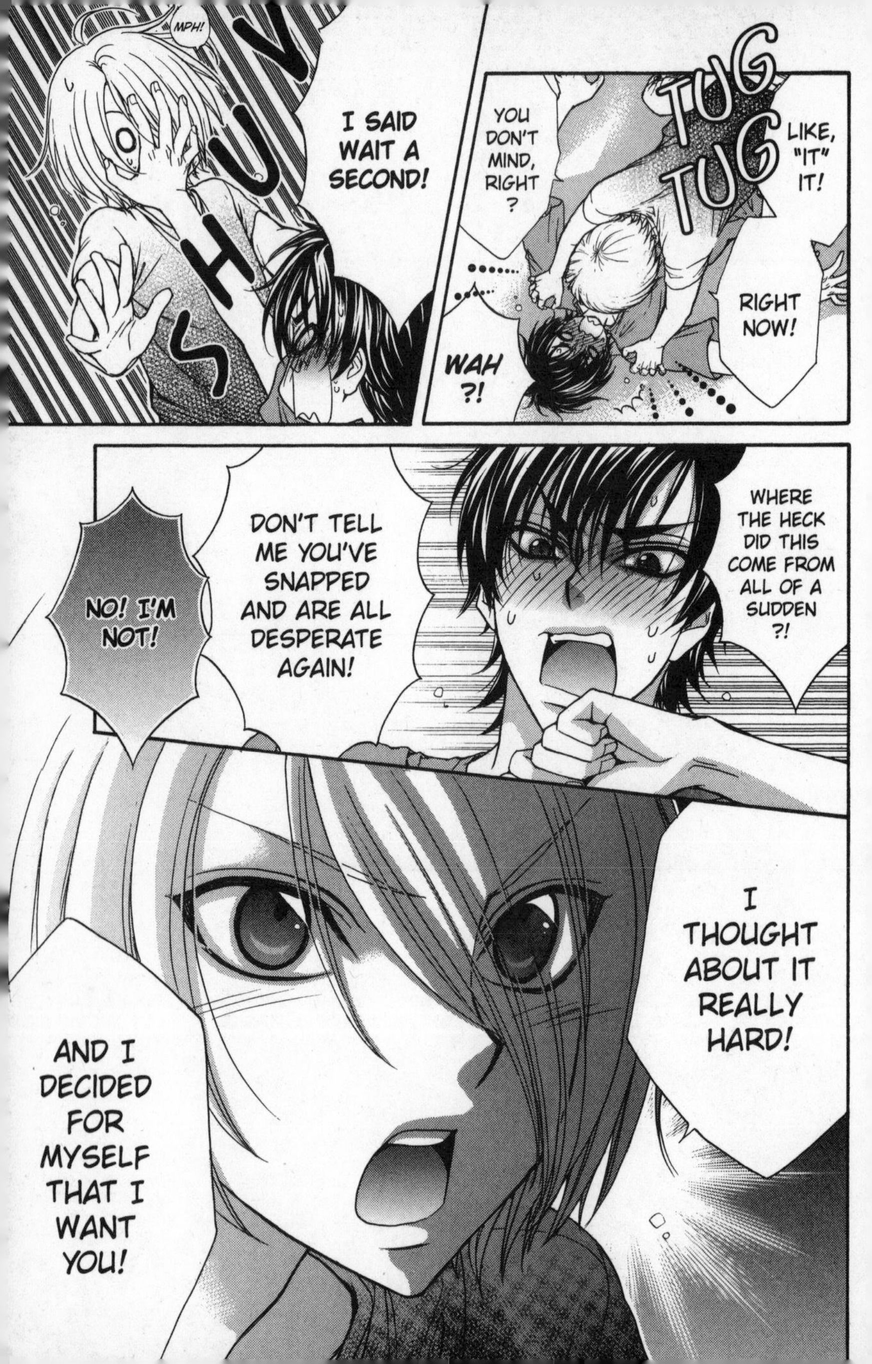
TUG TUG
LIKE, "IT" IT!
RIGHT NOW!
YOU DON'T MIND, RIGHT?
......
......
WAH?!
I SAID WAIT A SECOND!
SHUV
MPH!
WHERE THE HECK DID THIS COME FROM ALL OF A SUDDEN?!
DON'T TELL ME YOU'VE SNAPPED AND ARE ALL DESPERATE AGAIN!
NO! I'M NOT!
I THOUGHT ABOUT IT REALLY HARD!
AND I DECIDED FOR MYSELF THAT I WANT YOU!

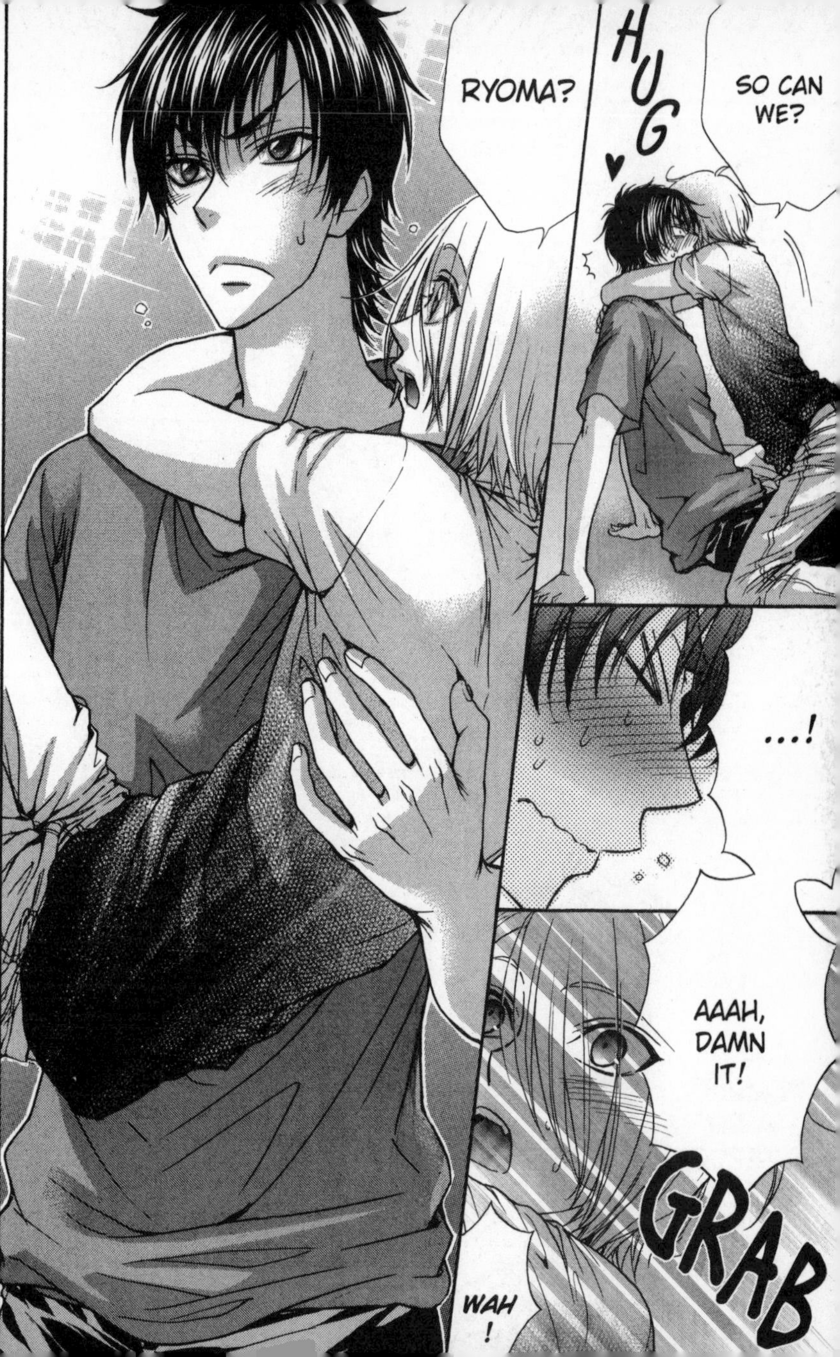
SO CAN WE?
HUG ♥
...!
AAAH, DAMN IT!
GRAB
WAH!
RYOMA?

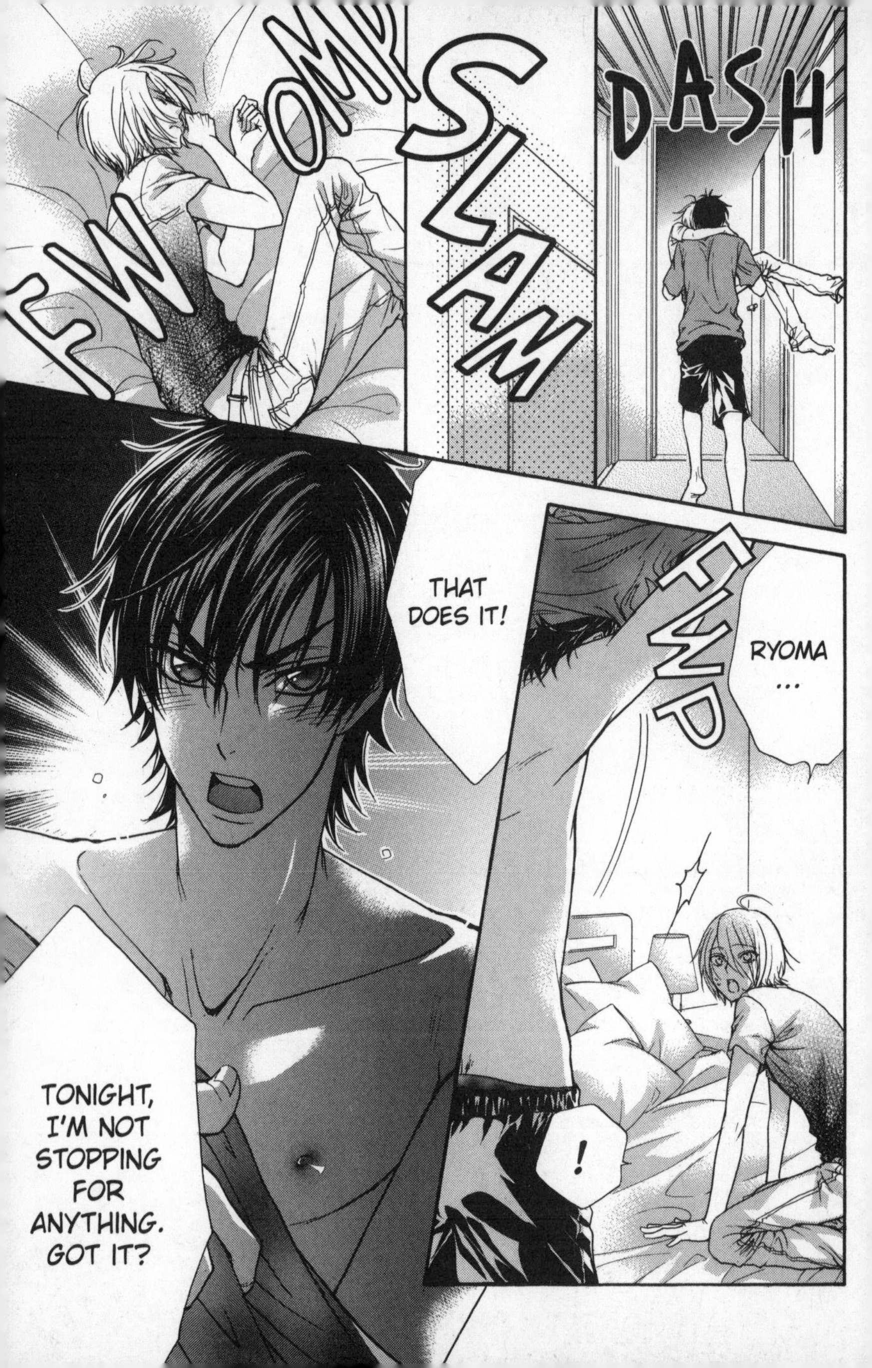
DASH
SLAM
WOMP
FWP
RYOMA ...
!
THAT DOES IT!
TONIGHT, I'M NOT STOPPING FOR ANYTHING. GOT IT?

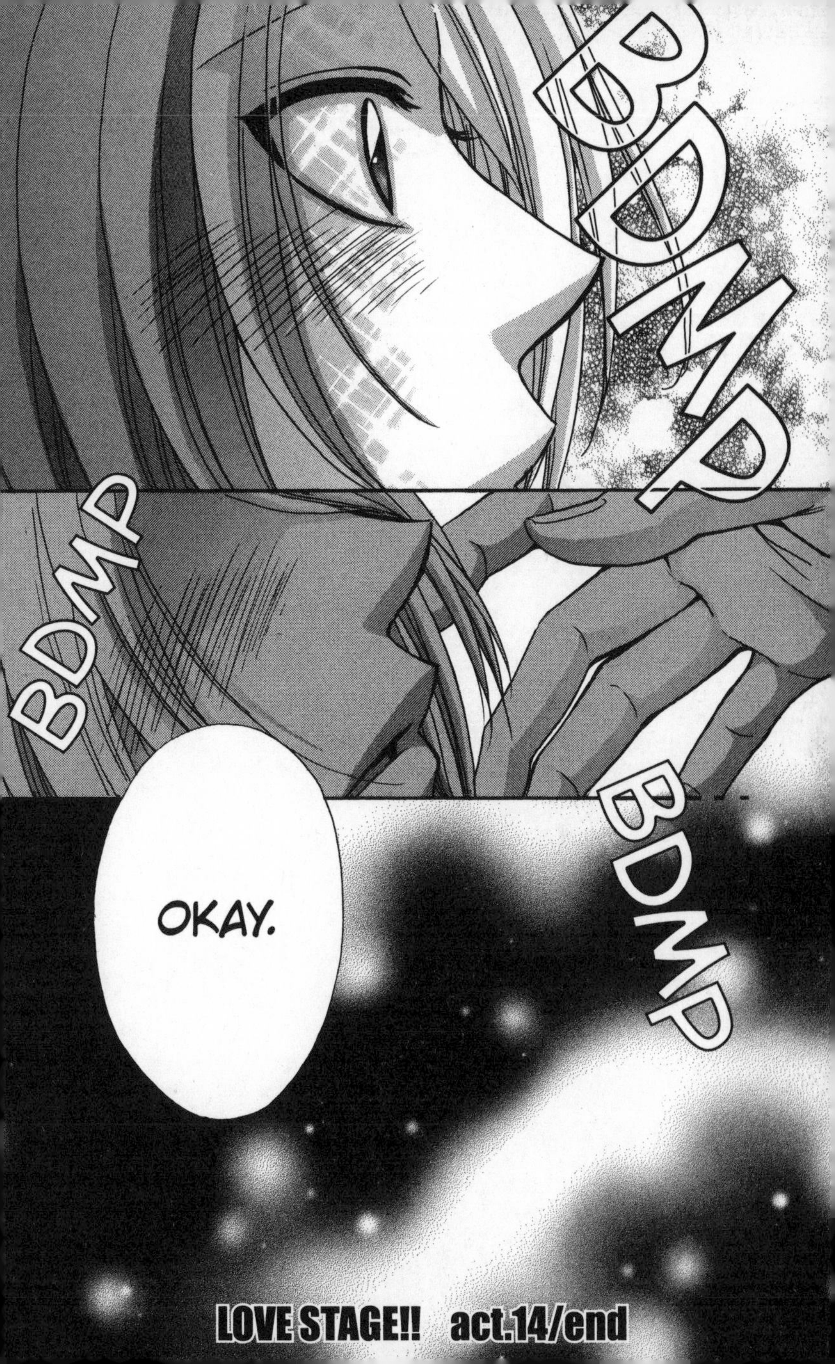
BDMP
BDMP
BDMP
OKAY.
LOVE STAGE!! act.14/end

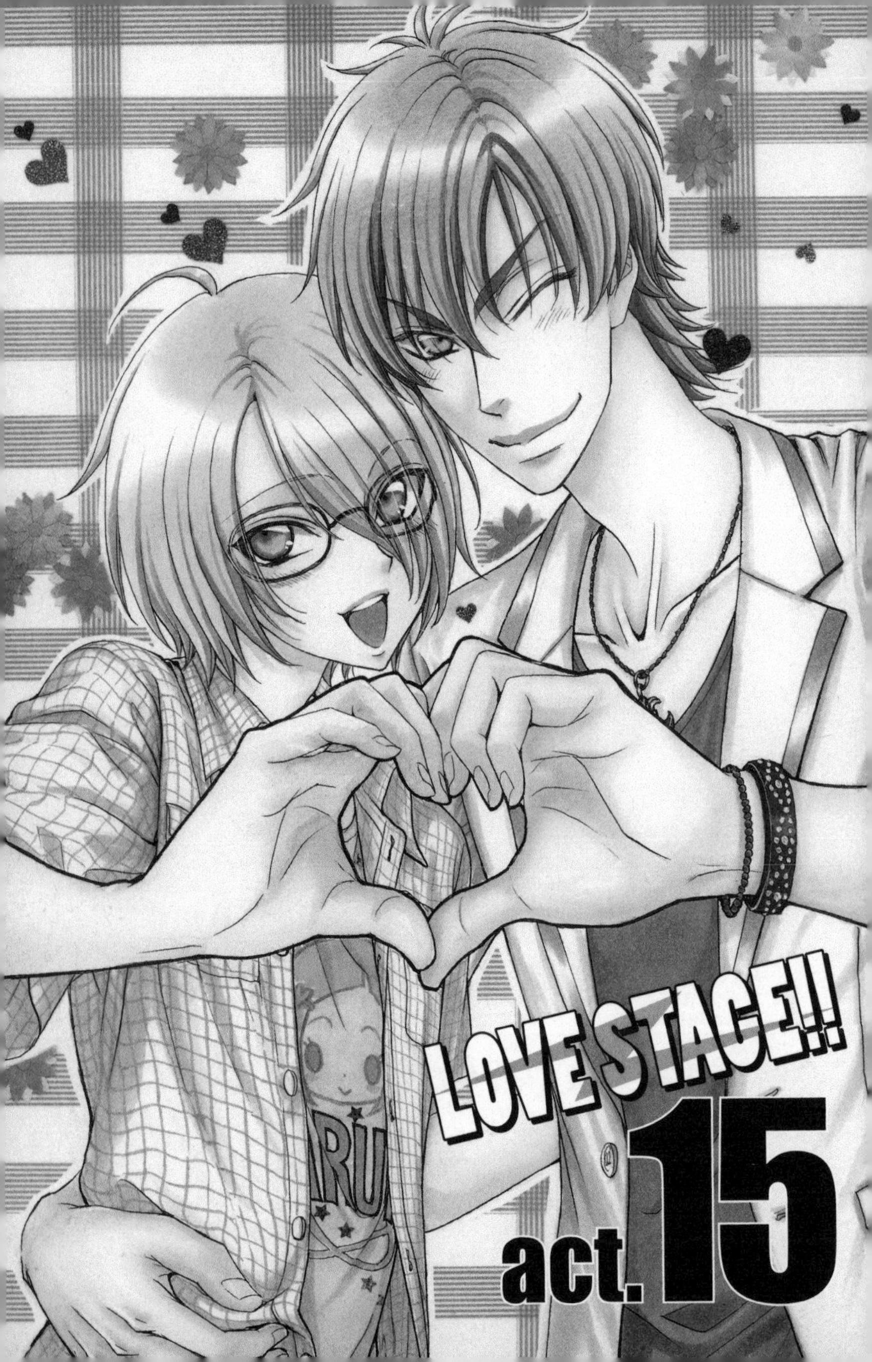
LOVE STAGE!!
act.15

LOVE STAGE!!

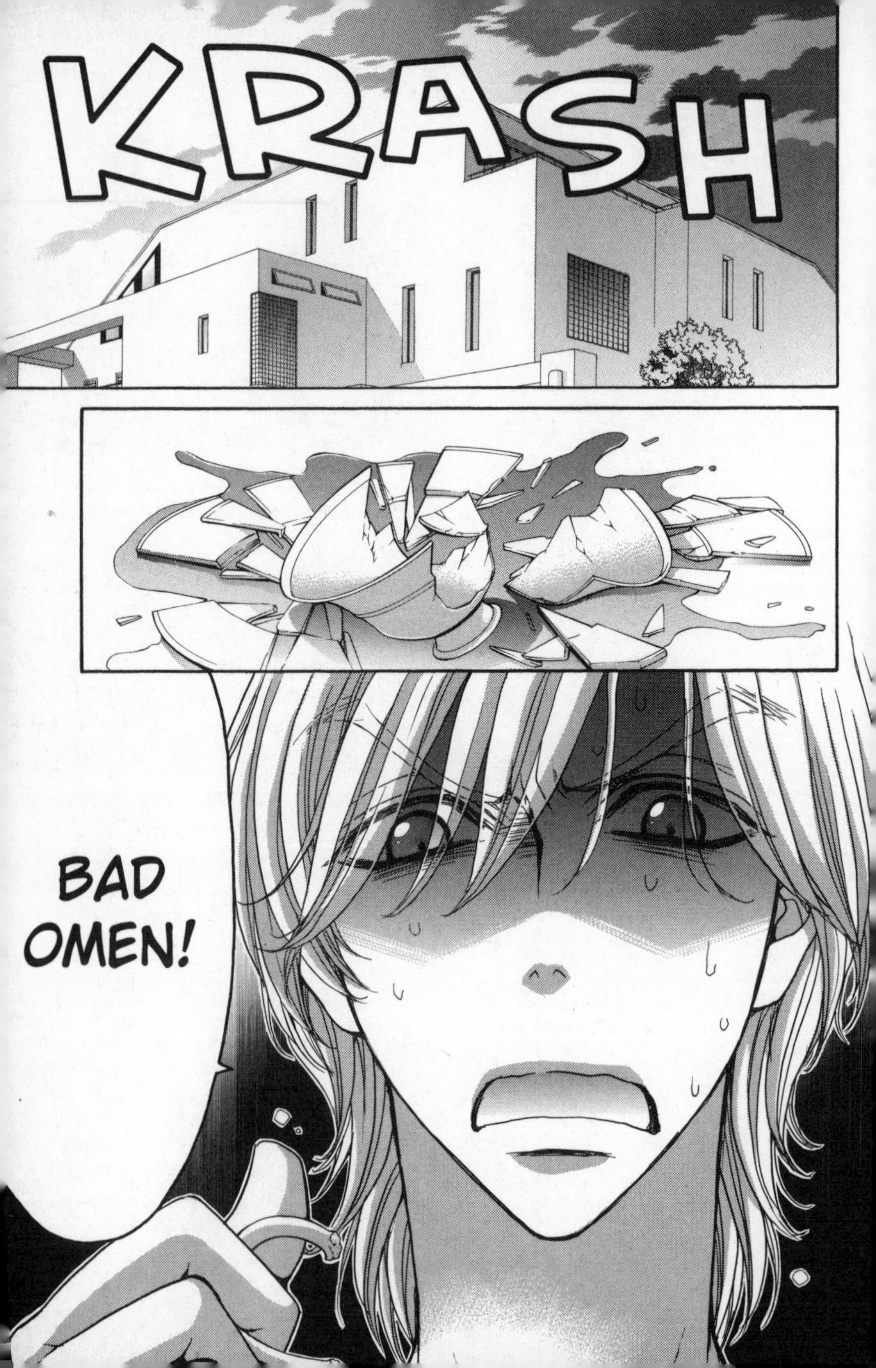
KRASH
BAD OMEN!

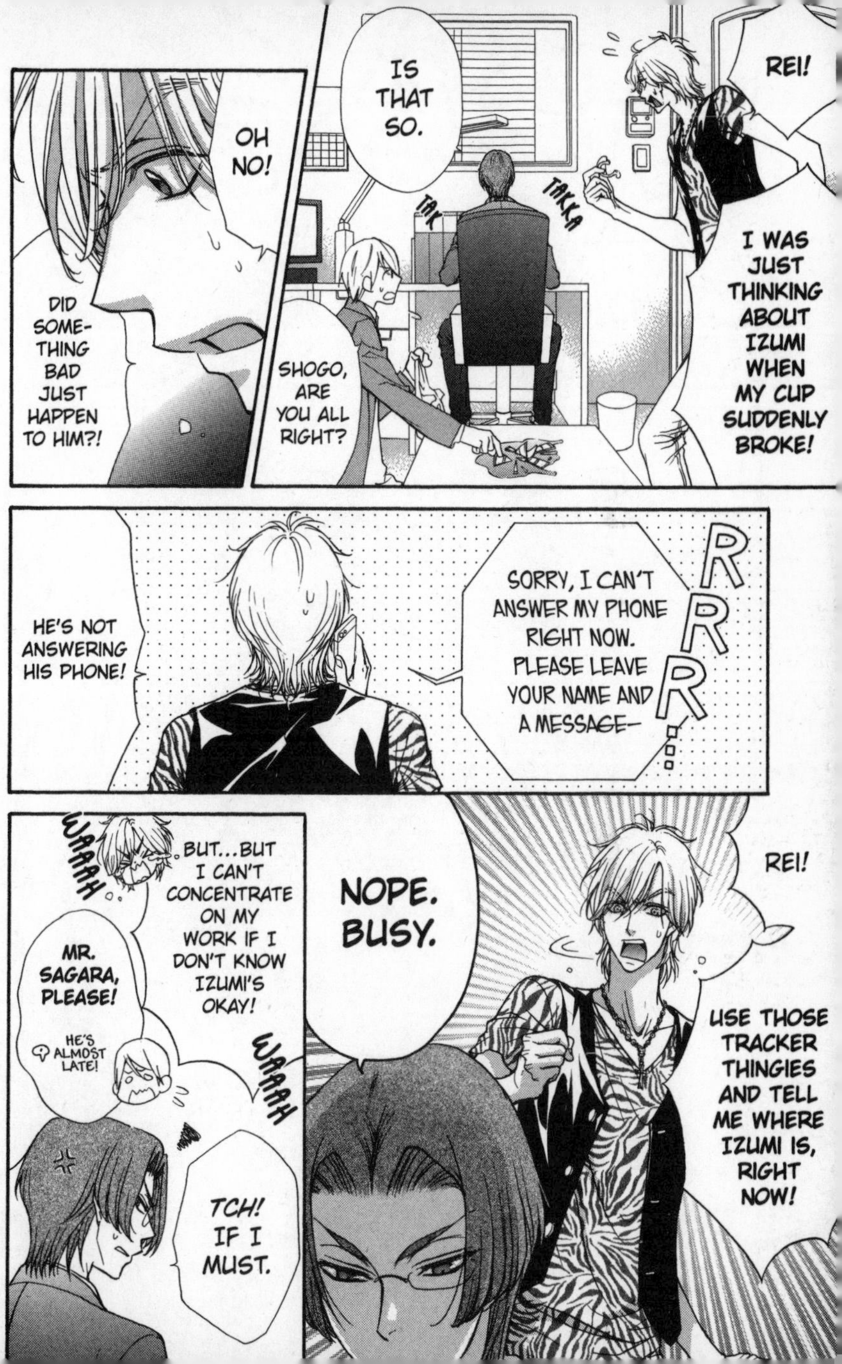
REI!
I WAS JUST THINKING ABOUT IZUMI WHEN MY CUP SUDDENLY BROKE!
IS THAT SO.
TAKKA
TAK
SHOGO, ARE YOU ALL RIGHT?
OH NO!
DID SOME-THING BAD JUST HAPPEN TO HIM?!
RRR
SORRY, I CAN'T ANSWER MY PHONE RIGHT NOW. PLEASE LEAVE YOUR NAME AND A MESSAGE—
HE'S NOT ANSWERING HIS PHONE!
REI!
USE THOSE TRACKER THINGIES AND TELL ME WHERE IZUMI IS, RIGHT NOW!
NOPE. BUSY.
WAAAAH
BUT...BUT I CAN'T CONCENTRATE ON MY WORK IF I DON'T KNOW IZUMI'S OKAY!
WAAAAH
MR. SAGARA, PLEASE!
HE'S ALMOST LATE!
TCH! IF I MUST.

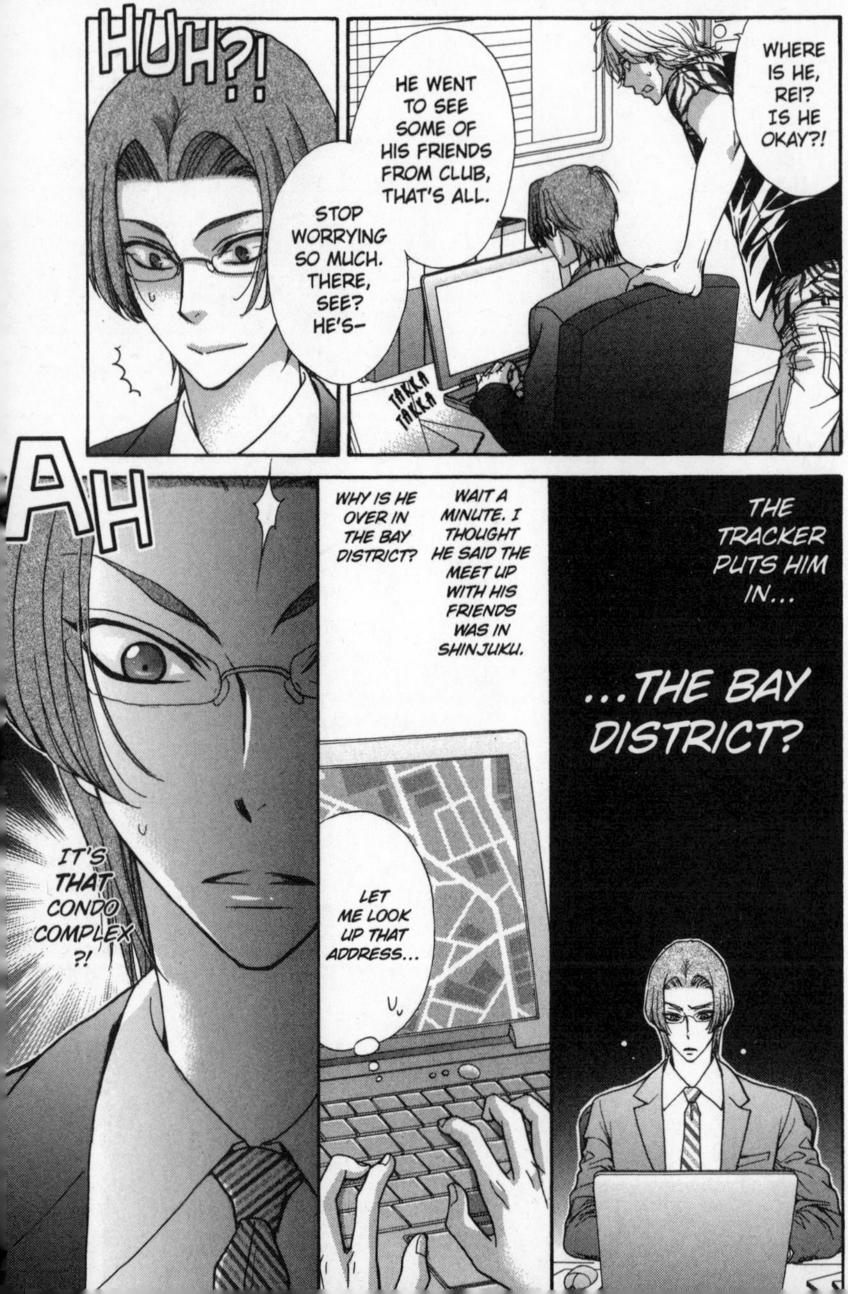
WHERE IS HE, REI? IS HE OKAY?!
HE WENT TO SEE SOME OF HIS FRIENDS FROM CLUB, THAT'S ALL.
STOP WORRYING SO MUCH. THERE, SEE? HE'S-
TAKKA TAKKA
HUH?!
THE TRACKER PUTS HIM IN...
...THE BAY DISTRICT?
WAIT A MINUTE. I THOUGHT HE SAID THE MEET UP WITH HIS FRIENDS WAS IN SHINJUKU.
WHY IS HE OVER IN THE BAY DISTRICT?
LET ME LOOK UP THAT ADDRESS...
AH
IT'S THAT CONDO COMPLEX ?!

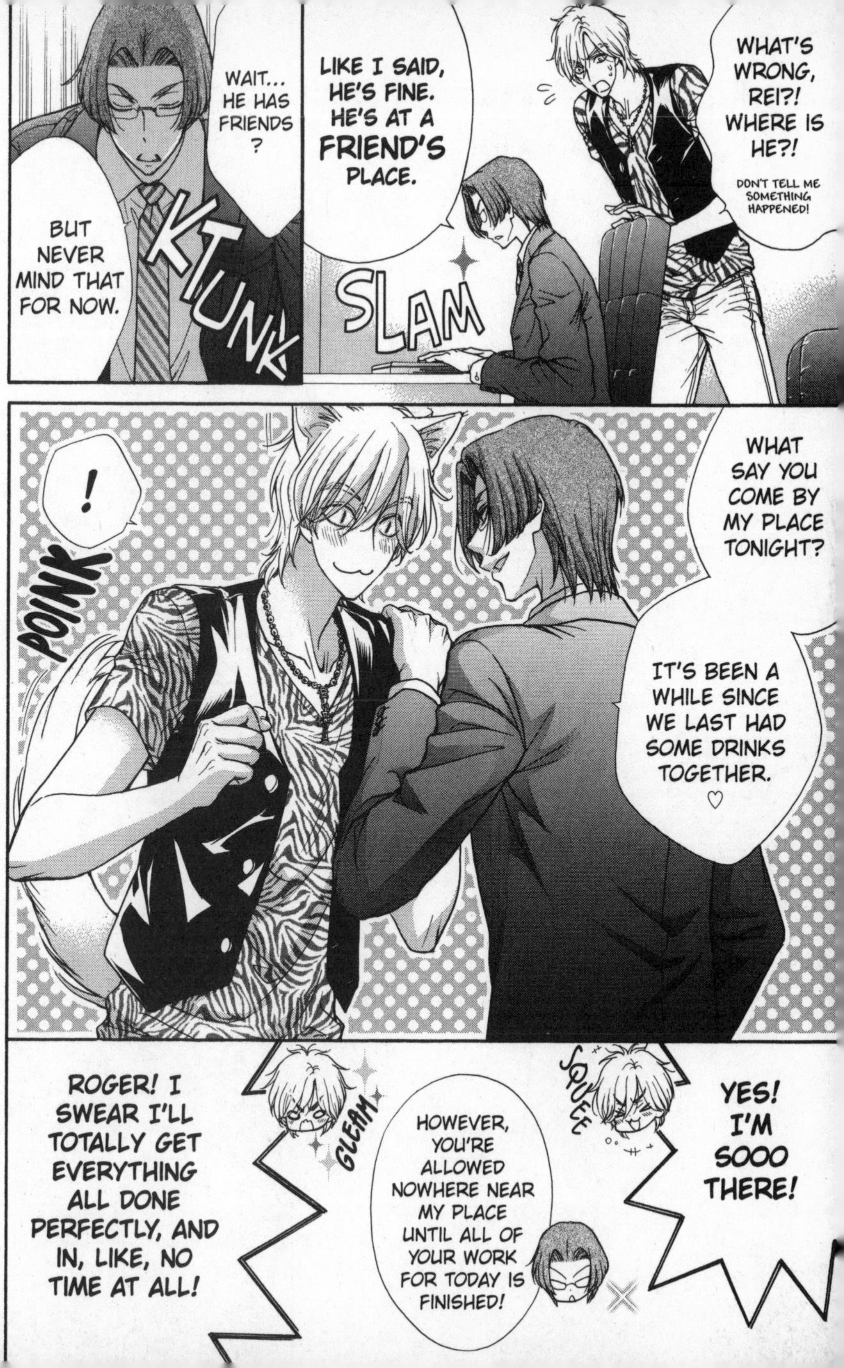
WHAT'S WRONG, REI?! WHERE IS HE?!
DON'T TELL ME SOMETHING HAPPENED!
LIKE I SAID, HE'S FINE. HE'S AT A FRIEND'S PLACE.
SLAM
WAIT... HE HAS FRIENDS ?
BUT NEVER MIND THAT FOR NOW.
KTUNK
WHAT SAY YOU COME BY MY PLACE TONIGHT?
IT'S BEEN A WHILE SINCE WE LAST HAD SOME DRINKS TOGETHER. ♡
!
POINK
YES! I'M SOOO THERE!
SQUEE
HOWEVER, YOU'RE ALLOWED NOWHERE NEAR MY PLACE UNTIL ALL OF YOUR WORK FOR TODAY IS FINISHED!
GLEAM
ROGER! I SWEAR I'LL TOTALLY GET EVERYTHING ALL DONE PERFECTLY, AND IN, LIKE, NO TIME AT ALL!

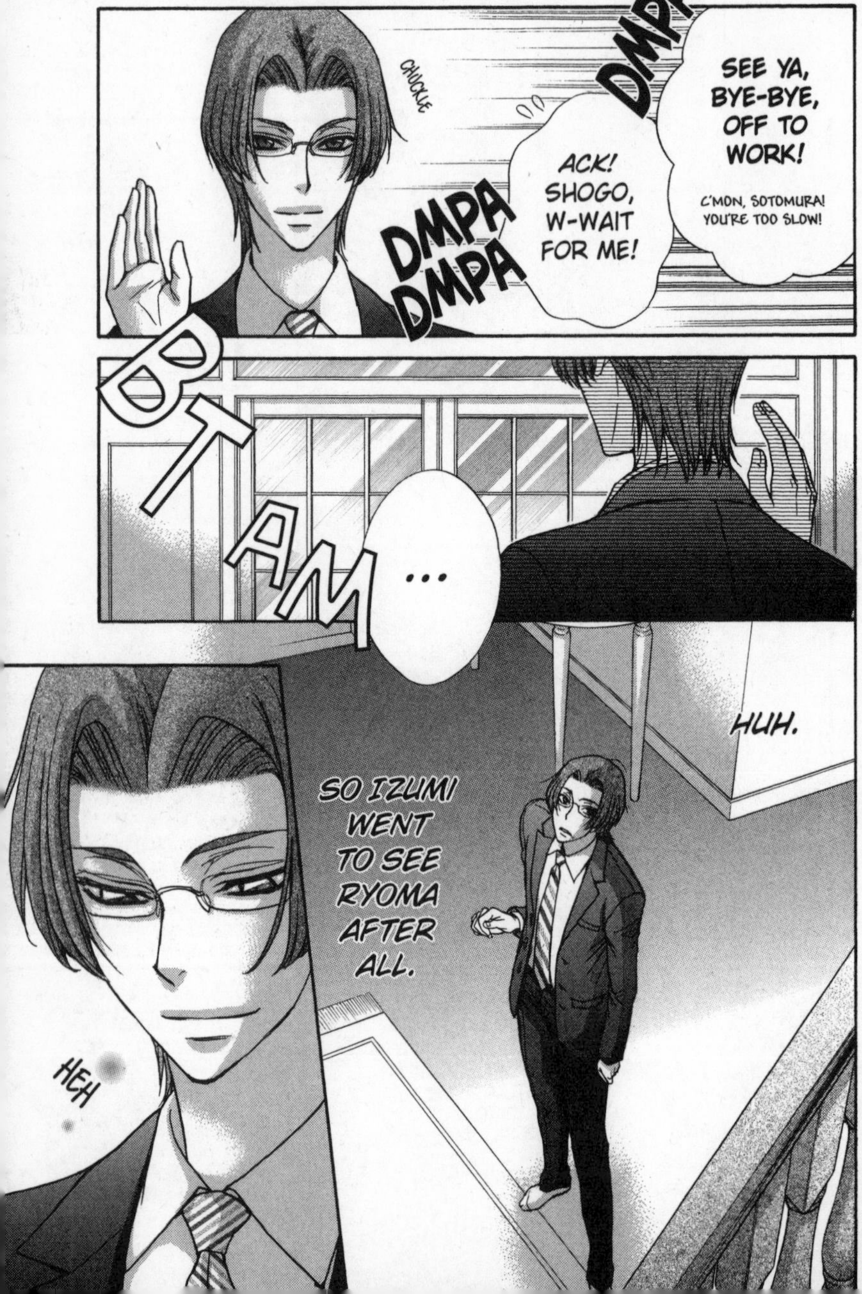
SEE YA, BYE-BYE, OFF TO WORK!
C'MON, SOTOMURA! YOU'RE TOO SLOW!
DMPA
ACK! SHOGO, W-WAIT FOR ME!
DMPA DMPA DMPA
CHUCKLE
BTAM
...
HUH.
SO IZUMI WENT TO SEE RYOMA AFTER ALL.
HEH

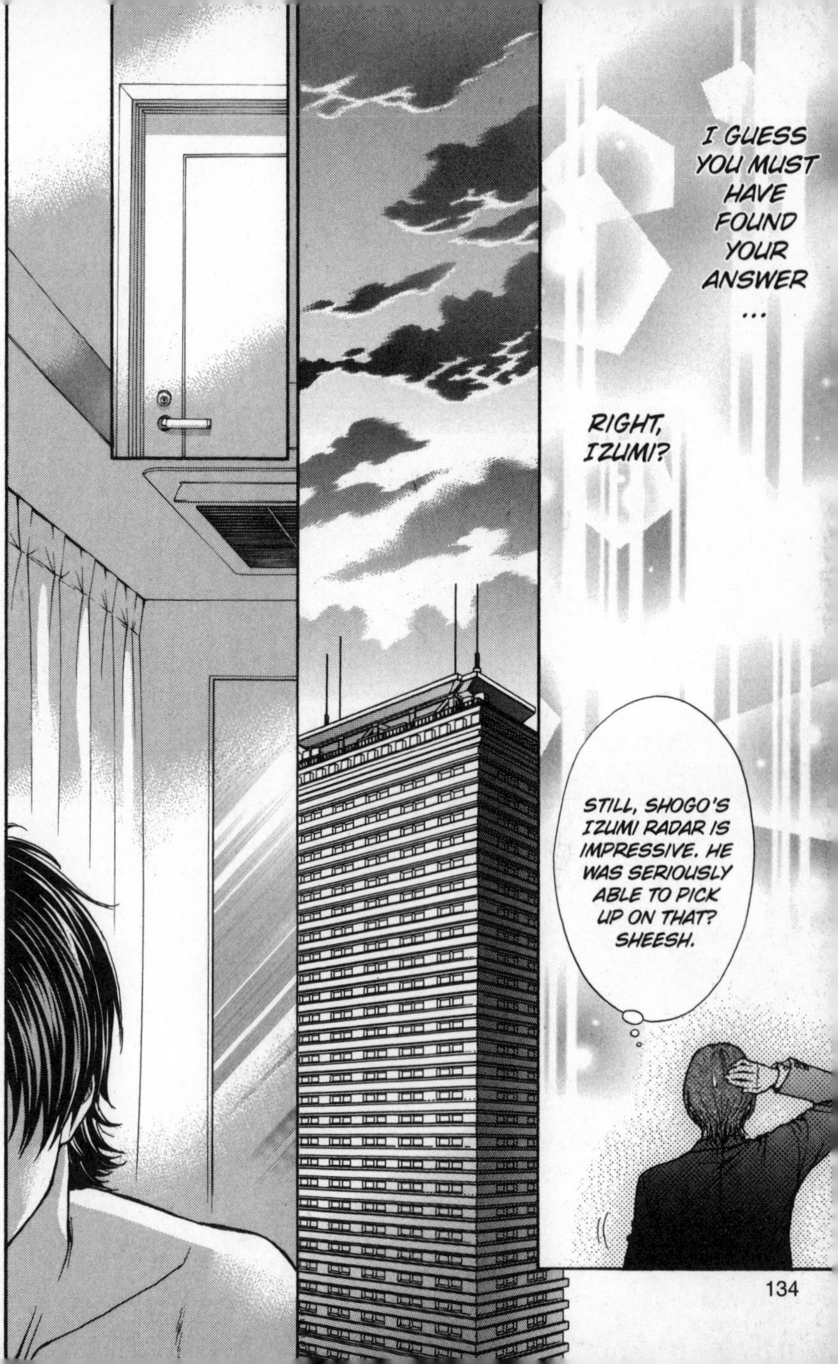
I GUESS YOU MUST HAVE FOUND YOUR ANSWER ...
RIGHT, IZUMI?
STILL, SHOGO'S IZUMI RADAR IS IMPRESSIVE. HE WAS SERIOUSLY ABLE TO PICK UP ON THAT? SHEESH.

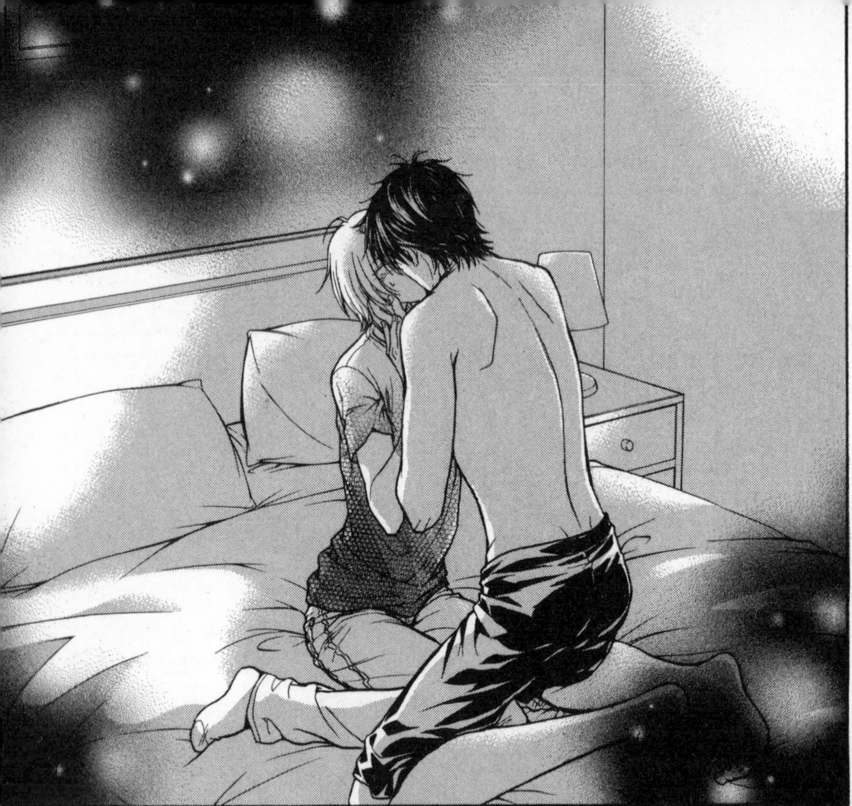
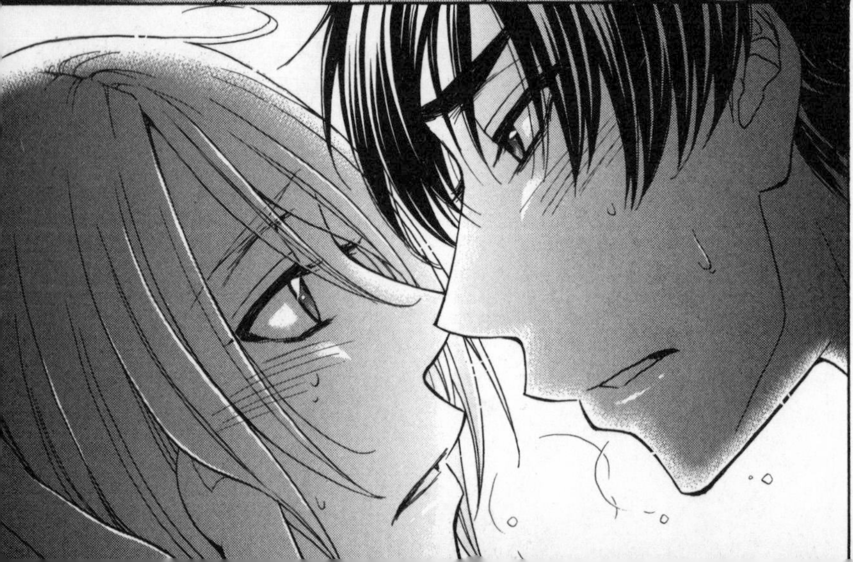

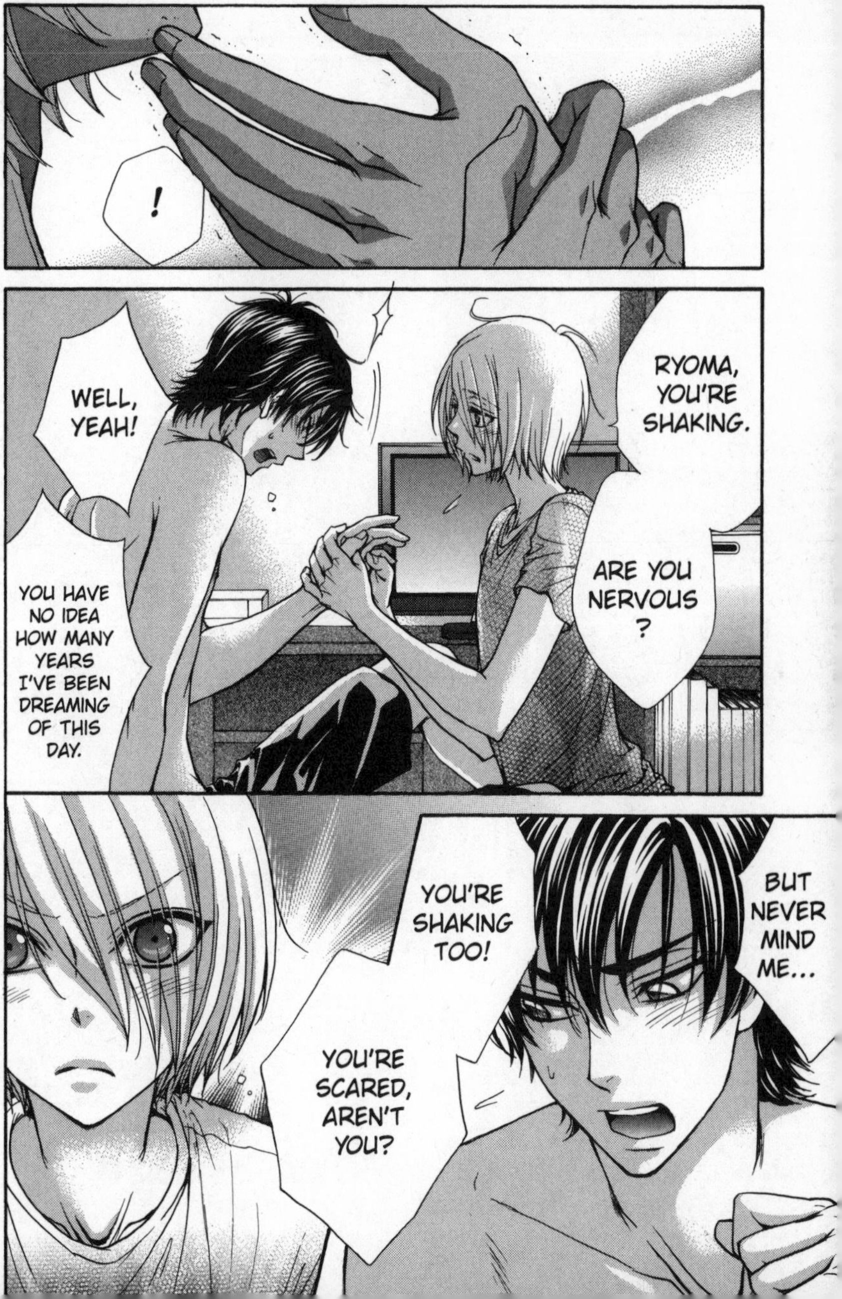
!
RYOMA, YOU'RE SHAKING.
ARE YOU NERVOUS?
WELL, YEAH!
YOU HAVE NO IDEA HOW MANY YEARS I'VE BEEN DREAMING OF THIS DAY.
BUT NEVER MIND ME...
YOU'RE SHAKING TOO!
YOU'RE SCARED, AREN'T YOU?

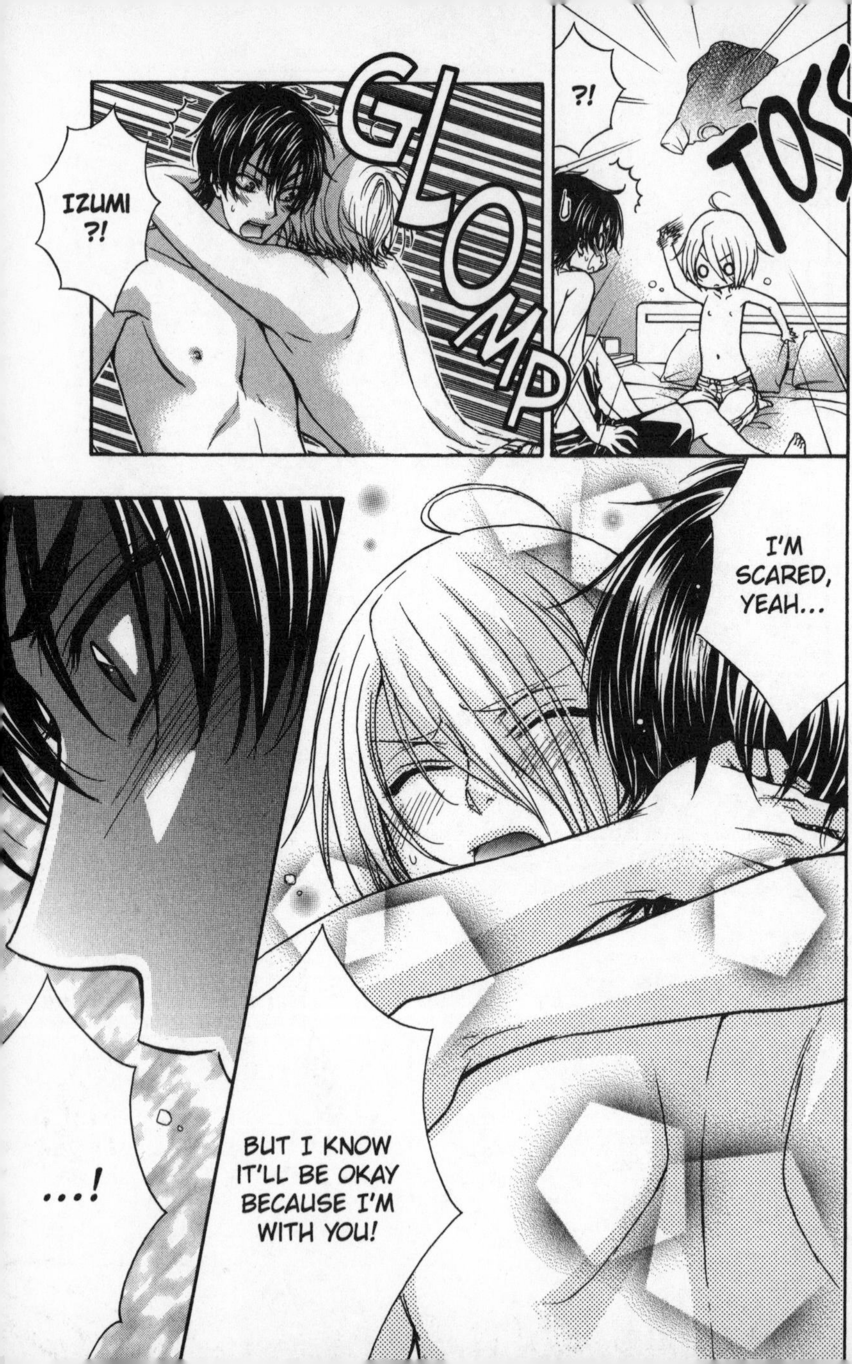
?!
TOSS
GLOMP
IZUMI ?!
I'M SCARED, YEAH...
BUT I KNOW IT'LL BE OKAY BECAUSE I'M WITH YOU!
...!

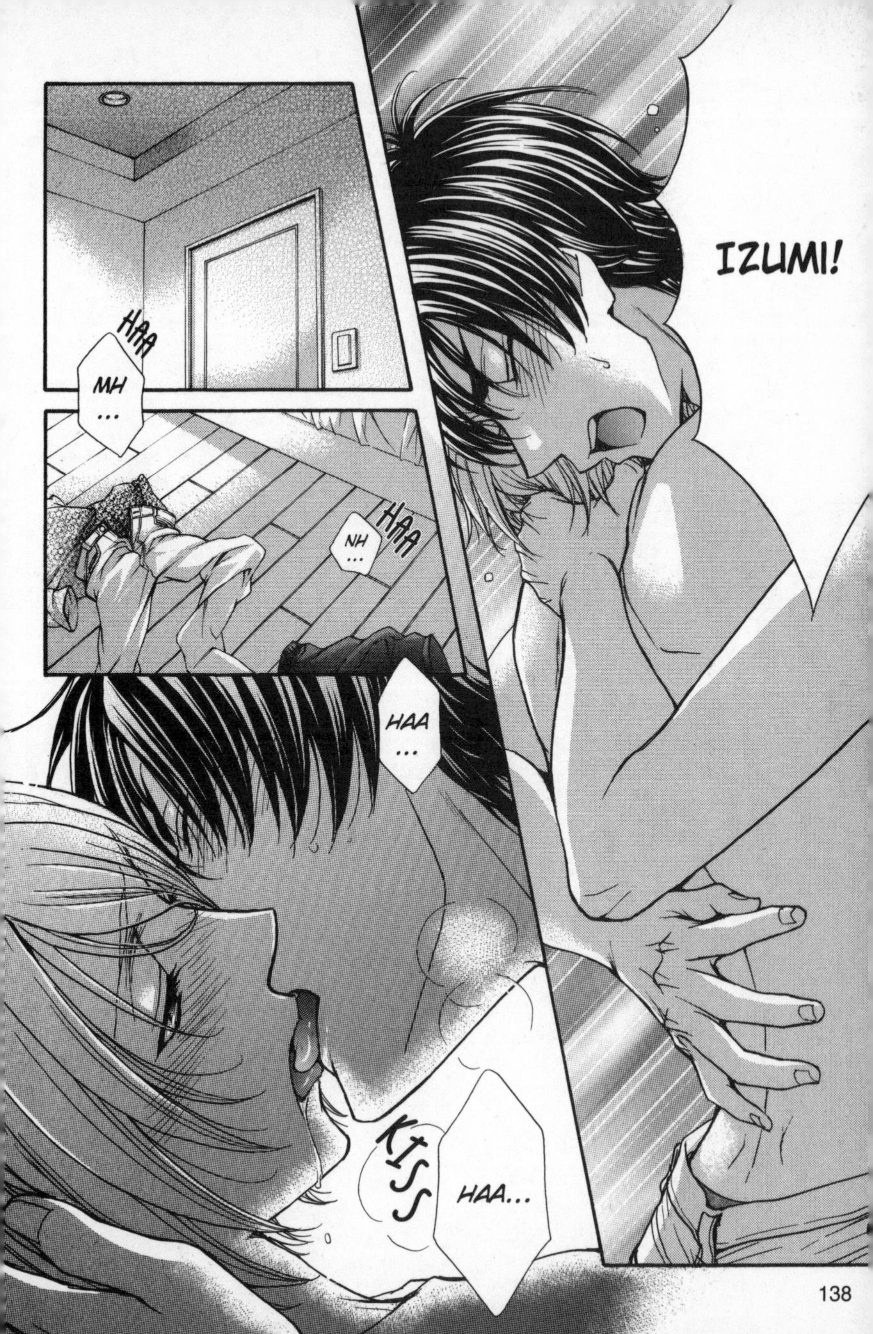
IZUMI!
HAA
MH ...
HAA
NH ...
HAA ...
KISS
HAA...

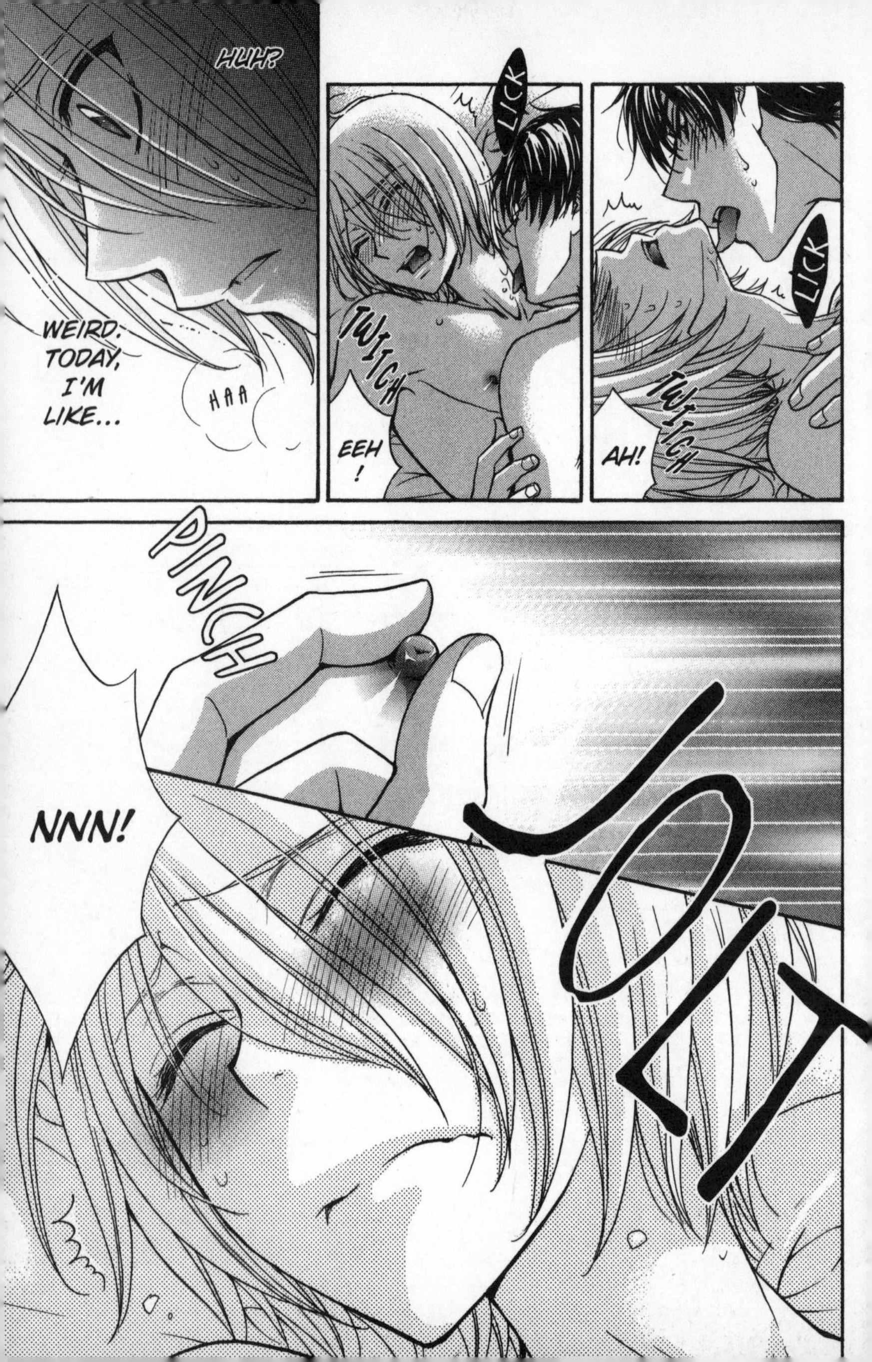
LICK
MU
TWITCH
AH!
LICK
MU
TWITCH
EEH!
HUH?
WEIRD. TODAY, I'M LIKE...
HAA
PINCH
JOLT
NNN!

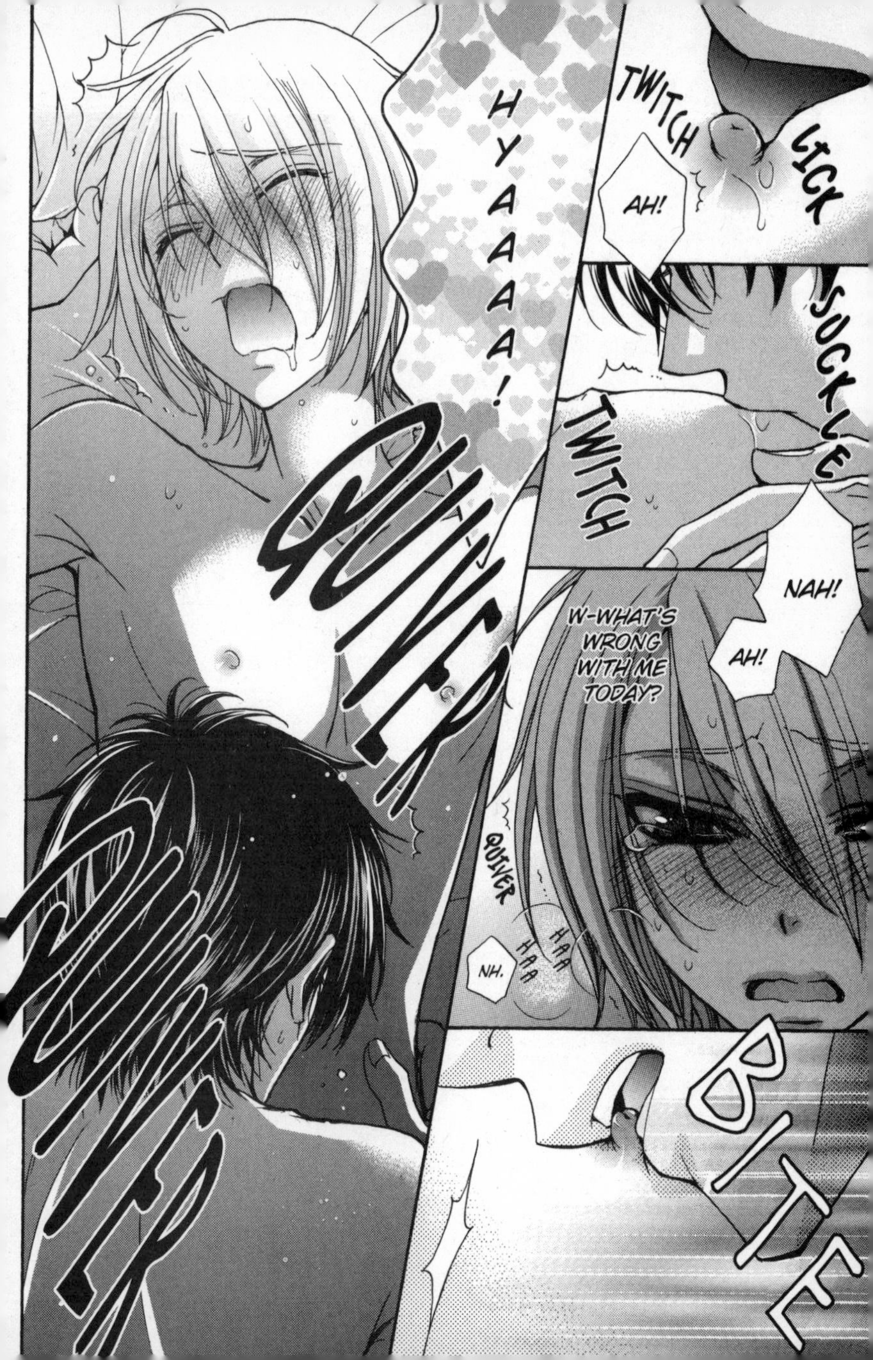
LICK
TWITCH
AH!
SUCKLE
TWITCH
NAH!
AH!
W-WHAT'S WRONG WITH ME TODAY?
QUIVER
HAA HAA HAA
NH.
BITE
HYAAAAAA!
QUIVER
QUIVER

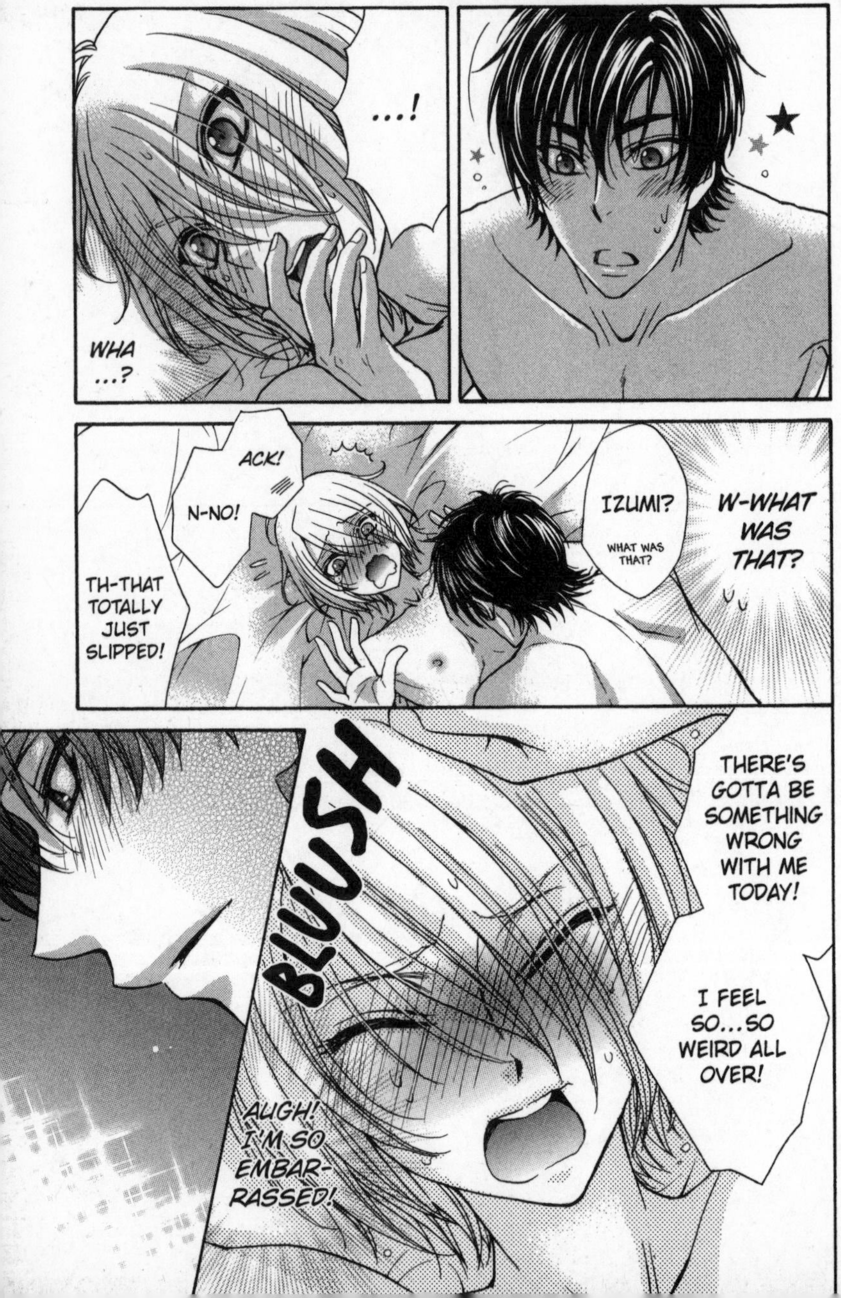
...!
WHA ...?
W-WHAT WAS THAT?
IZUMI?
WHAT WAS THAT?
ACK!
N-NO!
TH-THAT TOTALLY JUST SLIPPED!
THERE'S GOTTA BE SOMETHING WRONG WITH ME TODAY!
BLUUSH
I FEEL SO...SO WEIRD ALL OVER!
AUGH! I'M SO EMBAR-RASSED!

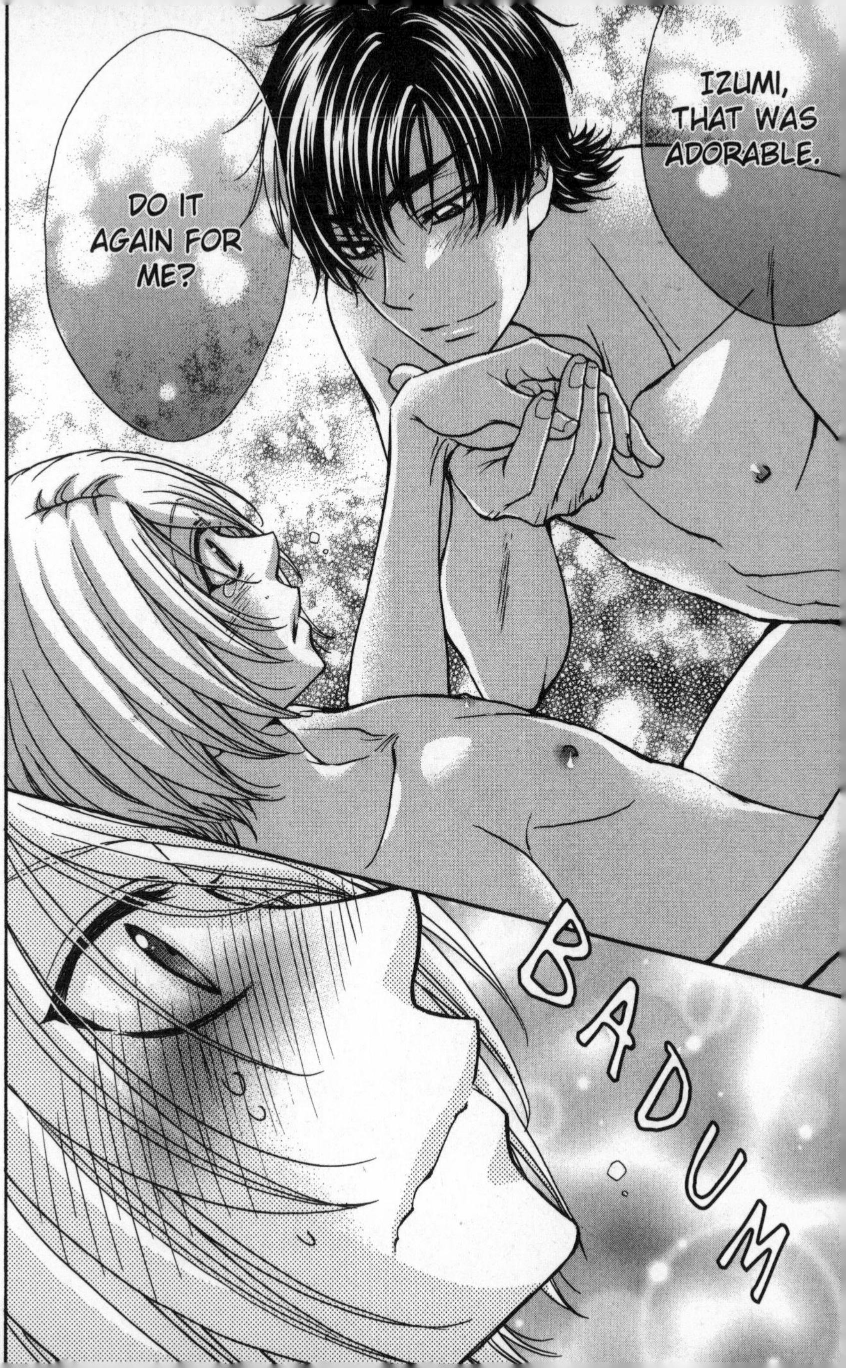
IZUMI, THAT WAS ADORABLE.
DO IT AGAIN FOR ME?
BADUM

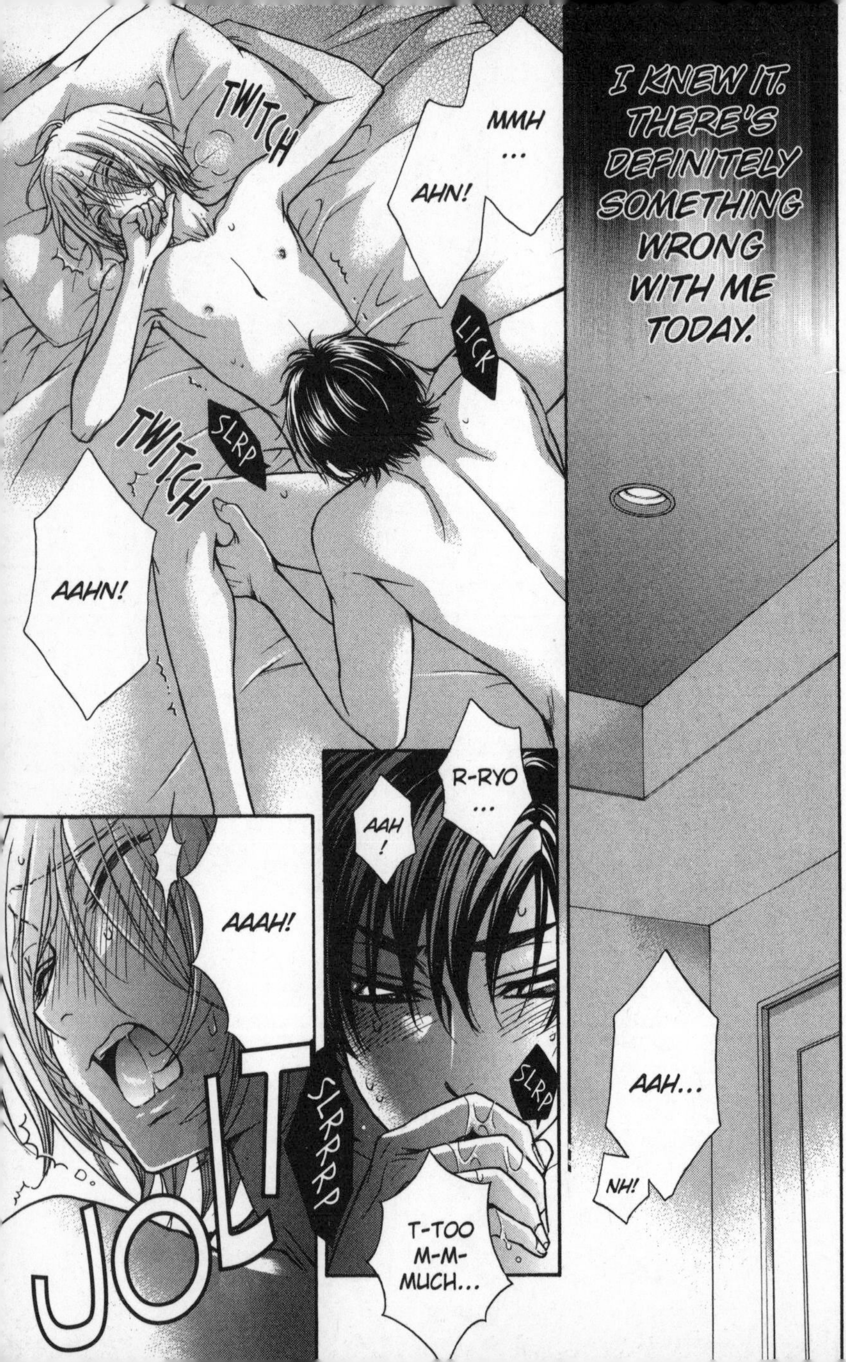
I KNEW IT. THERE'S DEFINITELY SOMETHING WRONG WITH ME TODAY.
AAH...
NH!
MMH ... AHN!
TWITCH
LICK
SLRP
TWITCH
AAHN!
R-RYO ...
AAH !
SLRP
SLRRRP
T-TOO M-M-MUCH...
AAAH!
JOLT

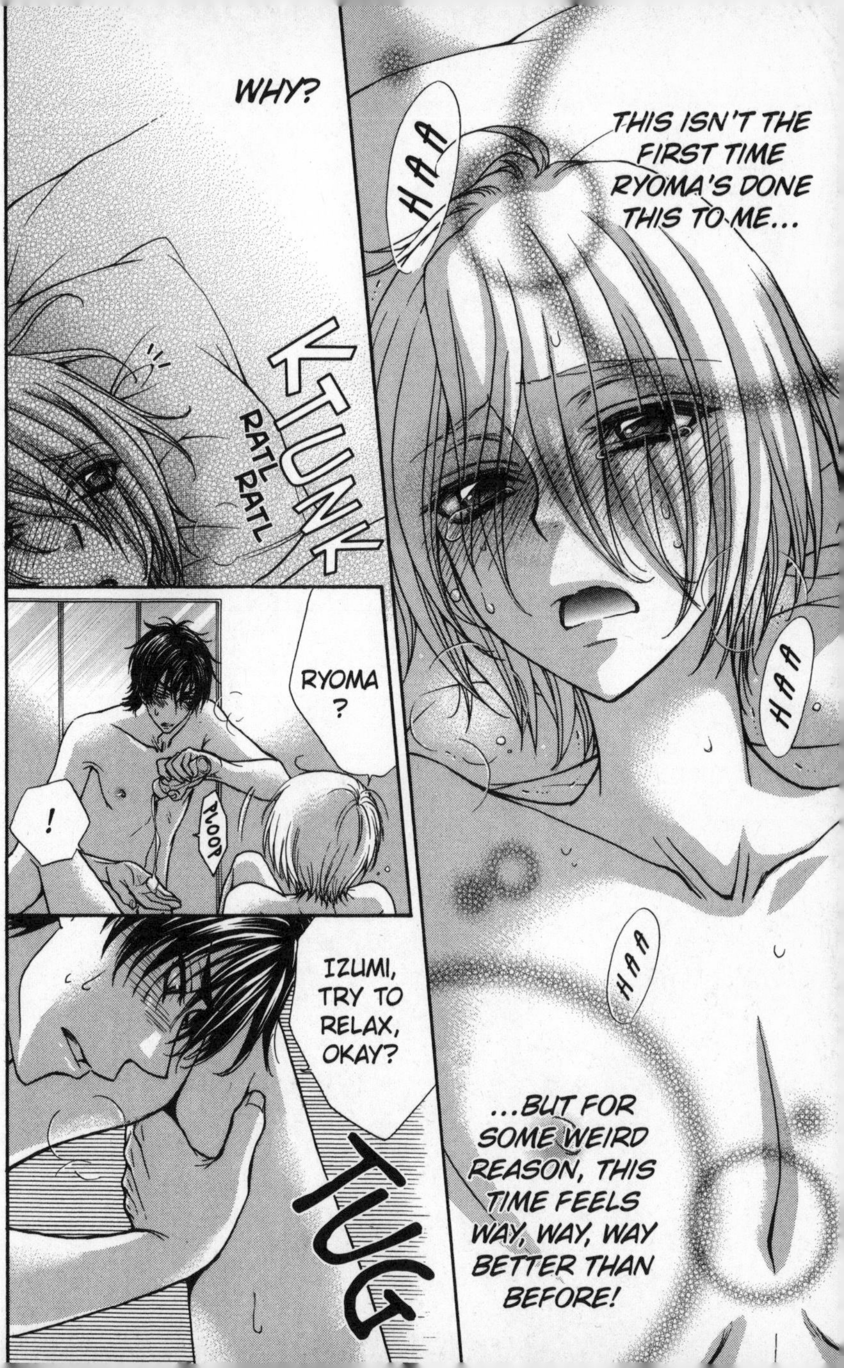
HAA
THIS ISN'T THE FIRST TIME RYOMA'S DONE THIS TO ME...
HAA
HAA
...BUT FOR SOME WEIRD REASON, THIS TIME FEELS WAY, WAY, WAY BETTER THAN BEFORE!
WHY?
KTUNK
RATL RATL
RYOMA?
!
PLOOP
IZUMI, TRY TO RELAX, OKAY?
TUG

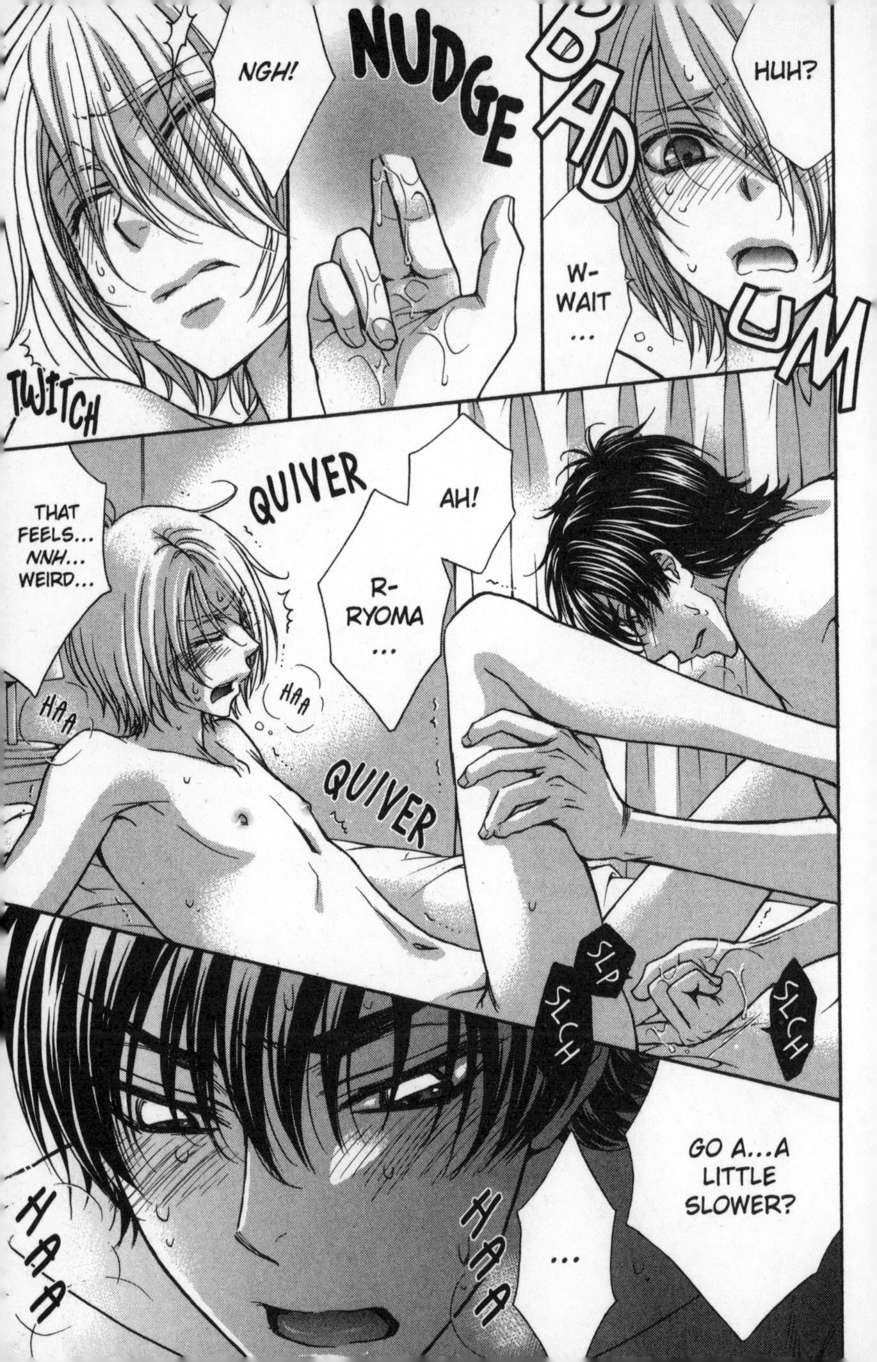
HUH?
BADUM
W-WAIT...
NUDGE
NGH!
TWITCH
AH!
R-RYOMA...
QUIVER
THAT FEELS... NNH... WEIRD...
HAA
HAA
QUIVER
SLCH
SLP
SLCH
GO A...A LITTLE SLOWER?
...
HAAA
HAAA

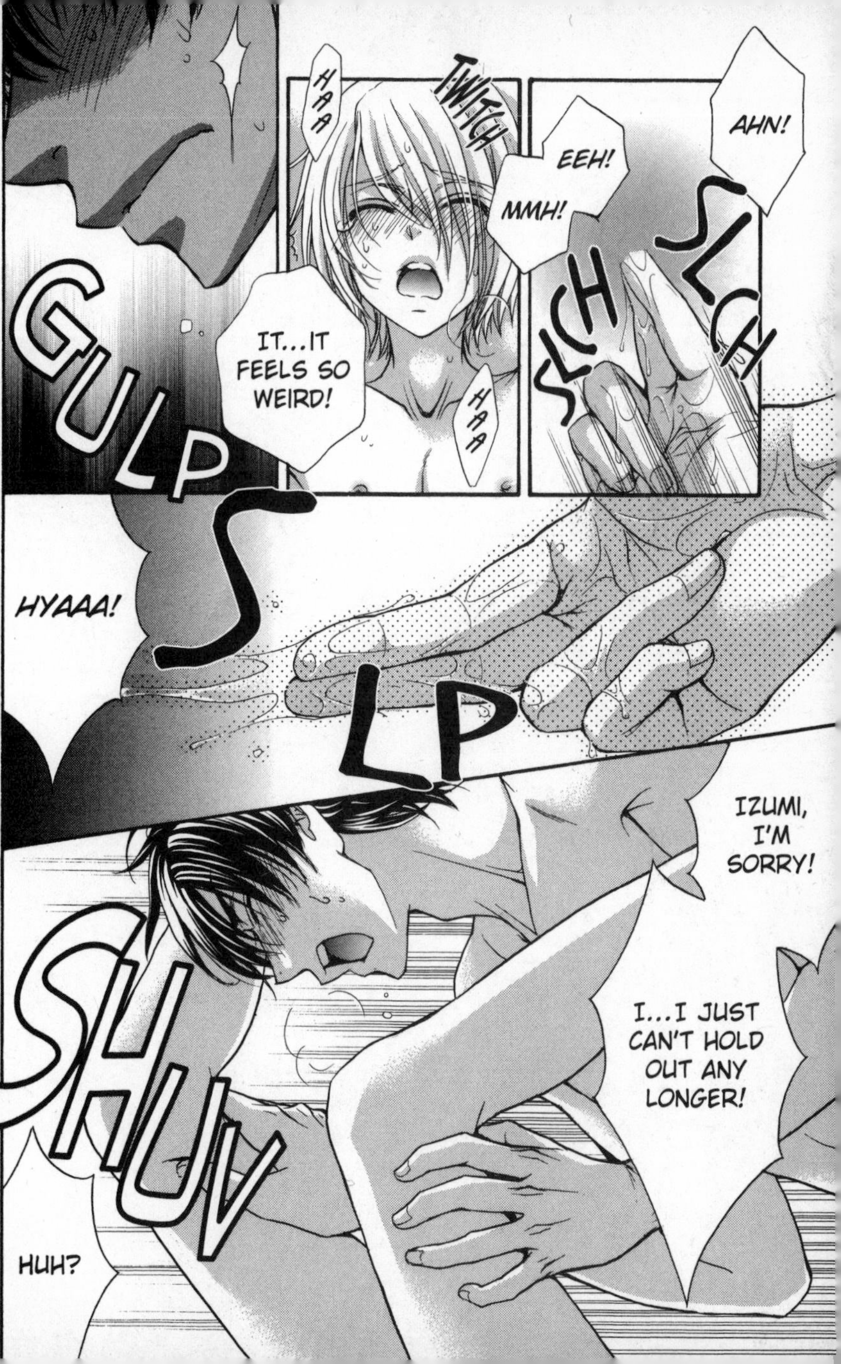
AHN!
EEH!
MMH!
SLCH
SLCH
TWITCH
HAAA
IT...IT FEELS SO WEIRD!
HAAA
GULP
SLP
HYAAA!
IZUMI, I'M SORRY!
I...I JUST CAN'T HOLD OUT ANY LONGER!
SHUV
HUH?

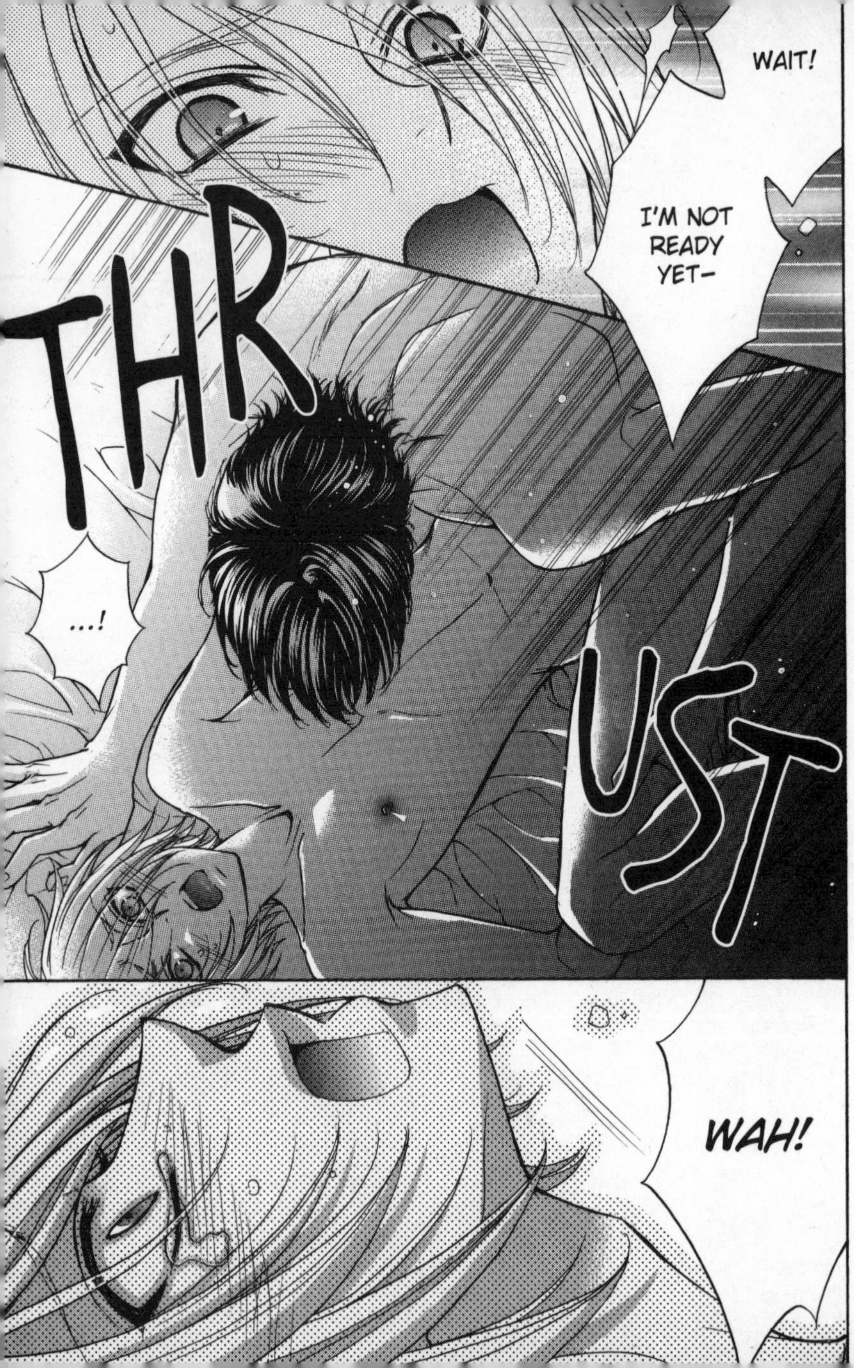
WAIT!
I'M NOT READY YET–
THRUST
...!
WAH!

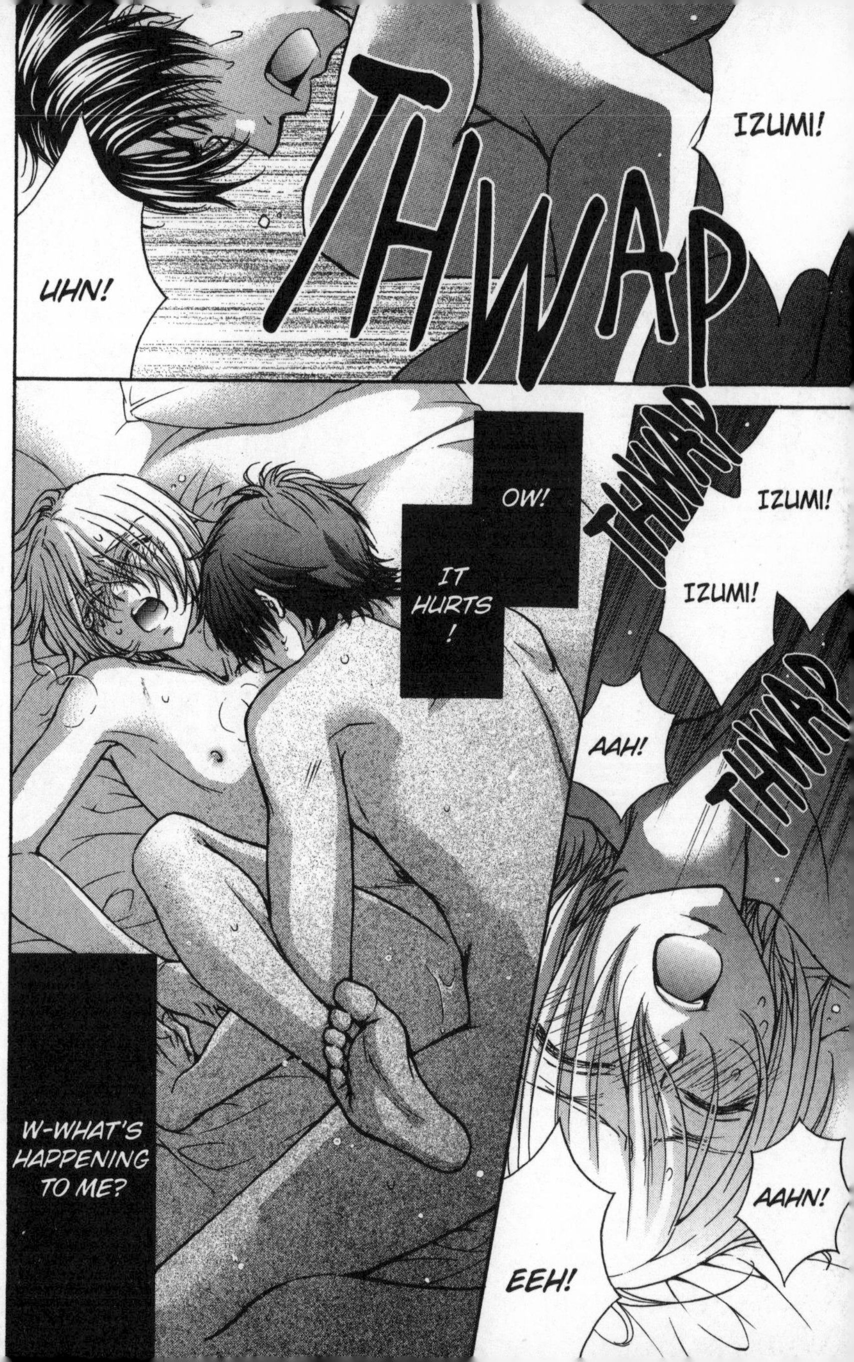
IZUMI!
THWAP
UHN!
THWAP
IZUMI!
IZUMI!
OW!
IT HURTS!
THWAP
AAH!
AAHN!
EEH!
W-WHAT'S HAPPENING TO ME?

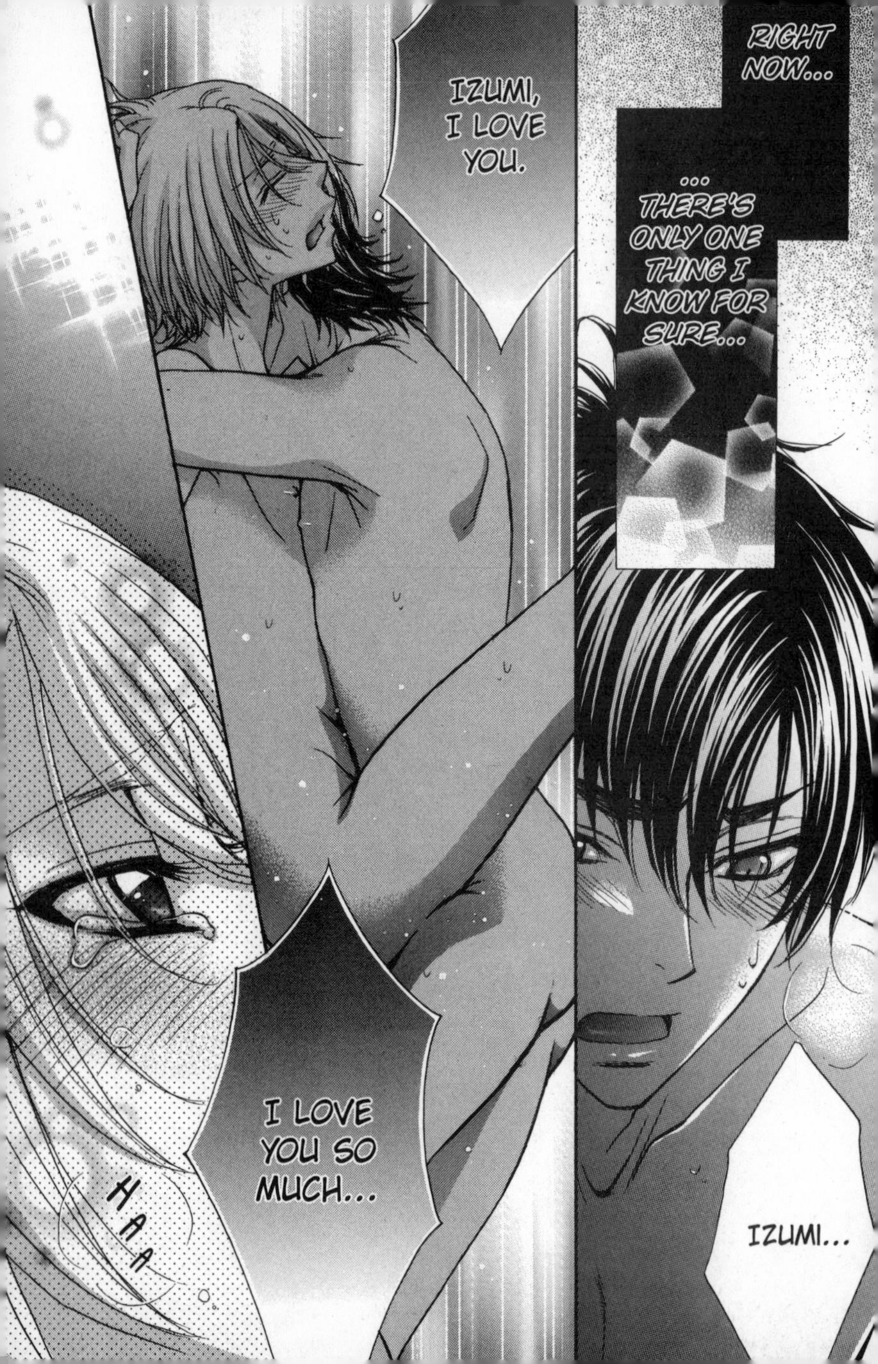
RIGHT NOW...
...THERE'S ONLY ONE THING I KNOW FOR SURE...
IZUMI...
IZUMI, I LOVE YOU.
I LOVE YOU SO MUCH...
HAA

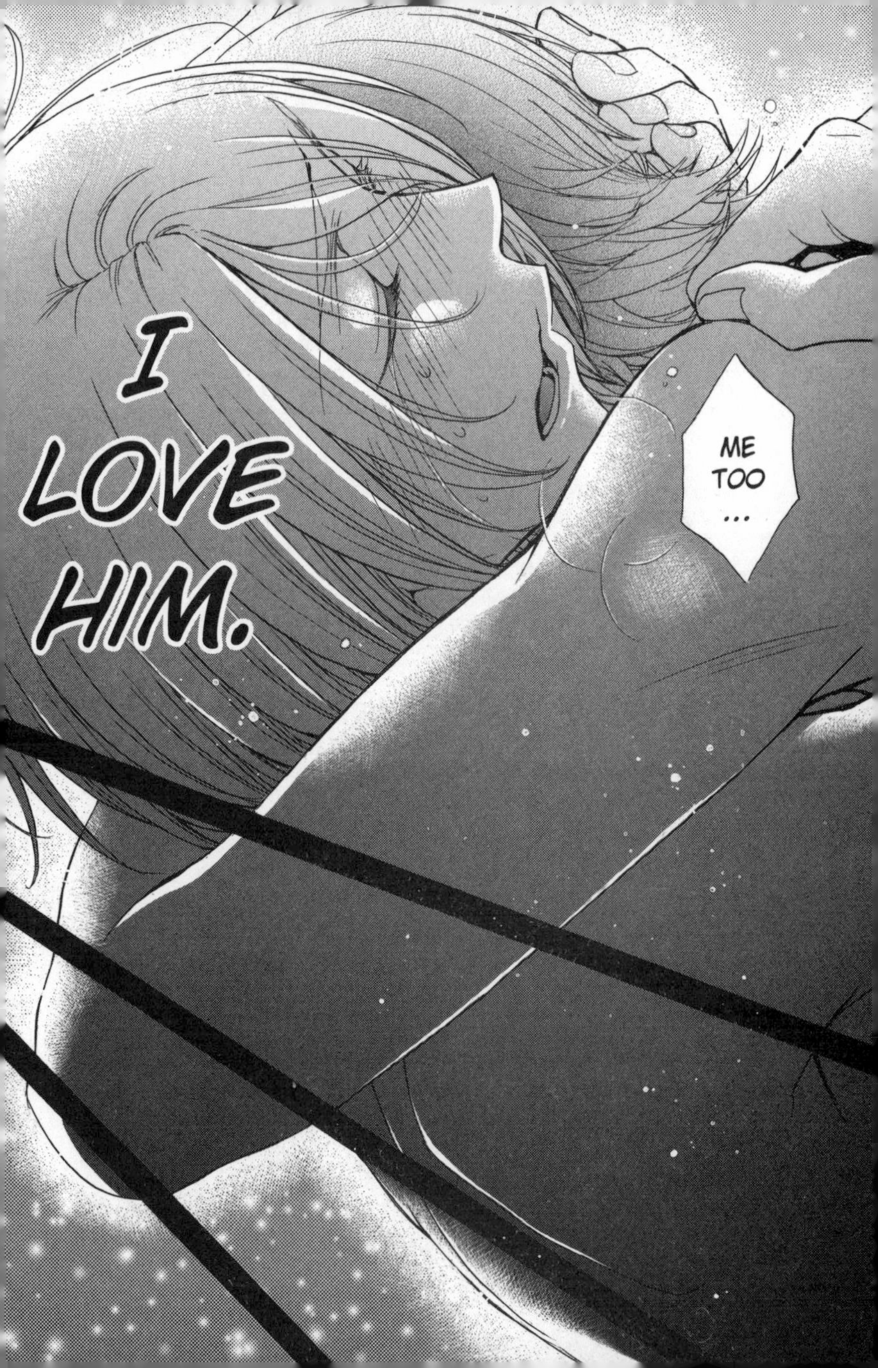
ME TOO ...
I LOVE HIM.

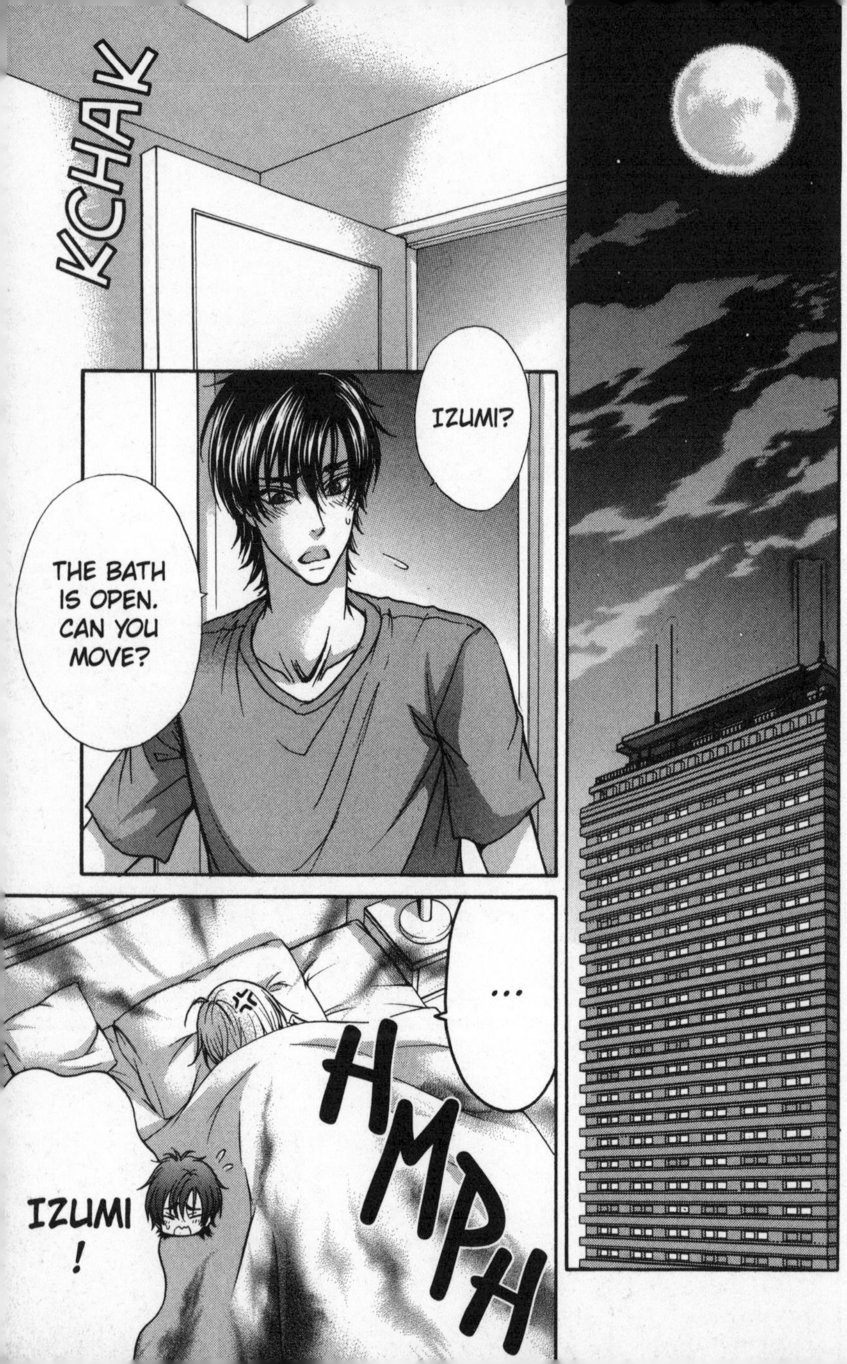
KCHAK
IZUMI?
THE BATH IS OPEN. CAN YOU MOVE?
...
HMPH
IZUMI!

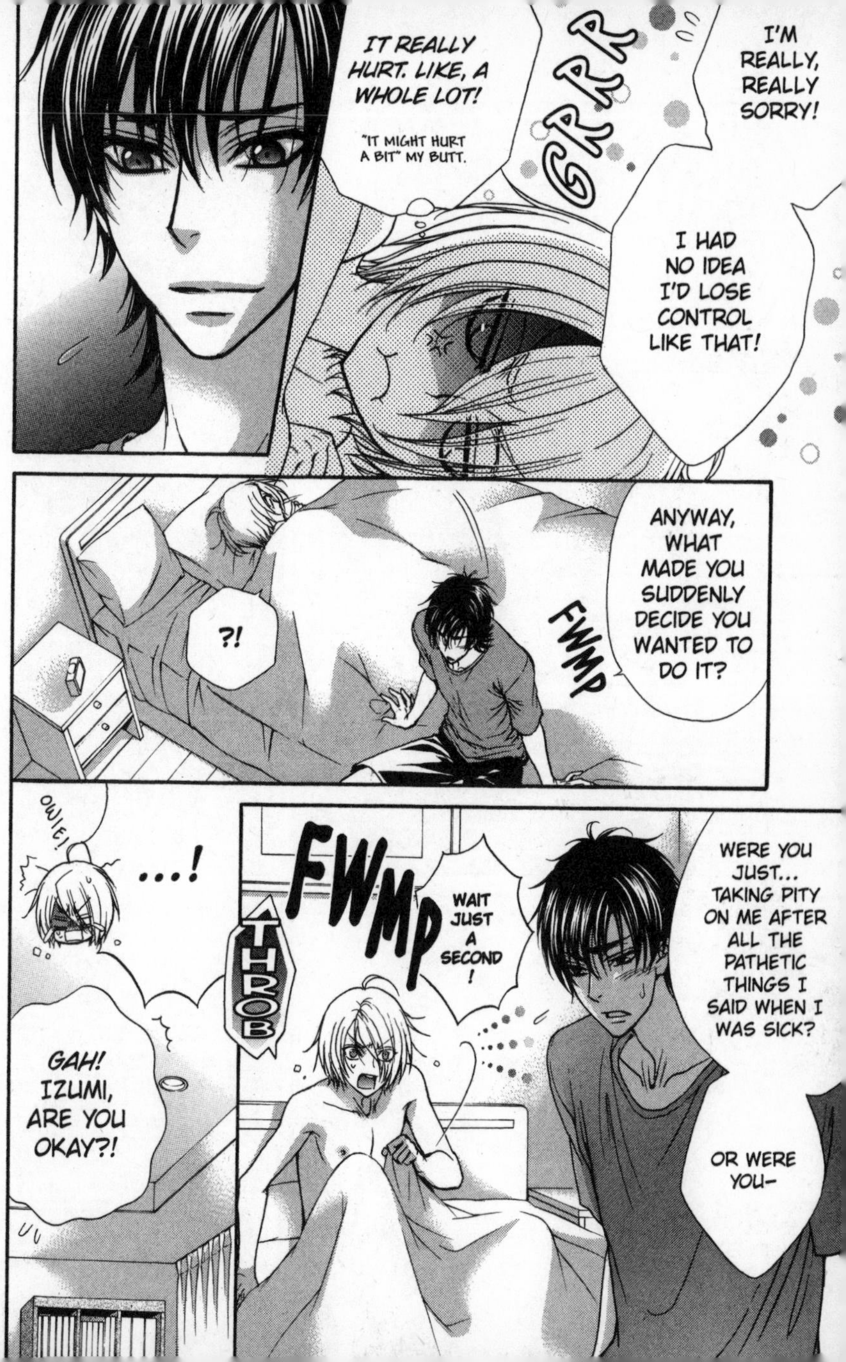
I'M REALLY, REALLY SORRY!
GRRR
I HAD NO IDEA I'D LOSE CONTROL LIKE THAT!
IT REALLY HURT. LIKE, A WHOLE LOT!
"IT MIGHT HURT A BIT" MY BUTT.
ANYWAY, WHAT MADE YOU SUDDENLY DECIDE YOU WANTED TO DO IT?
FWMP
?!
WERE YOU JUST... TAKING PITY ON ME AFTER ALL THE PATHETIC THINGS I SAID WHEN I WAS SICK?
OR WERE YOU-
WAIT JUST A SECOND!
FWMP
THROB
...!
OWIE!
GAH! IZUMI, ARE YOU OKAY?!

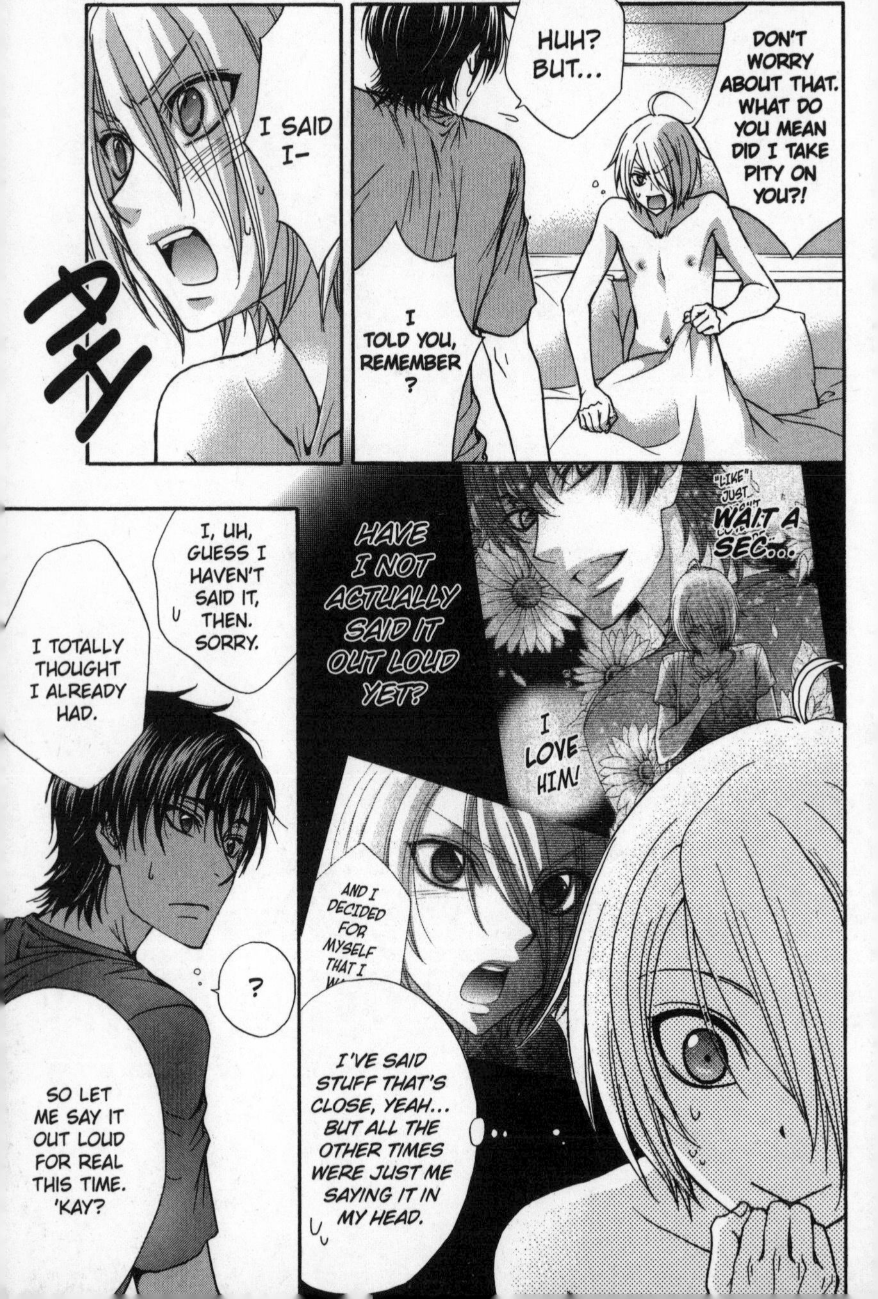
HUH? BUT...
DON'T WORRY ABOUT THAT. WHAT DO YOU MEAN DID I TAKE PITY ON YOU?!
I TOLD YOU, REMEMBER?
I SAID I–
HAVE I NOT ACTUALLY SAID IT OUT LOUD YET?
"LIKE" JUST
WAIT A SEC...
I LOVE HIM!
AND I DECIDED FOR MYSELF THAT I
I'VE SAID STUFF THAT'S CLOSE, YEAH... BUT ALL THE OTHER TIMES WERE JUST ME SAYING IT IN MY HEAD.
...
I, UH, GUESS I HAVEN'T SAID IT, THEN. SORRY.
I TOTALLY THOUGHT I ALREADY HAD.
?
SO LET ME SAY IT OUT LOUD FOR REAL THIS TIME. 'KAY?

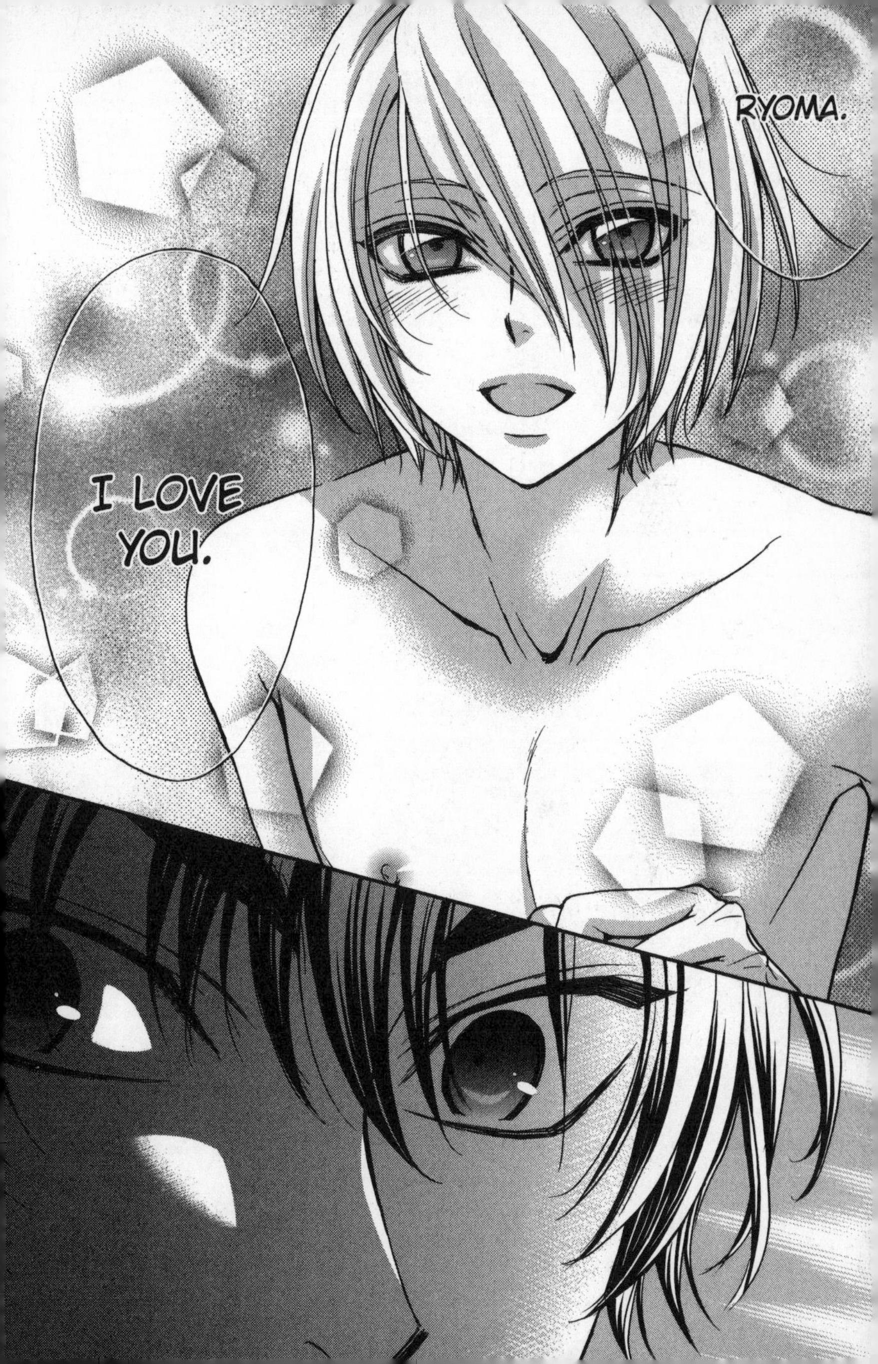
RYOMA.
I LOVE YOU.

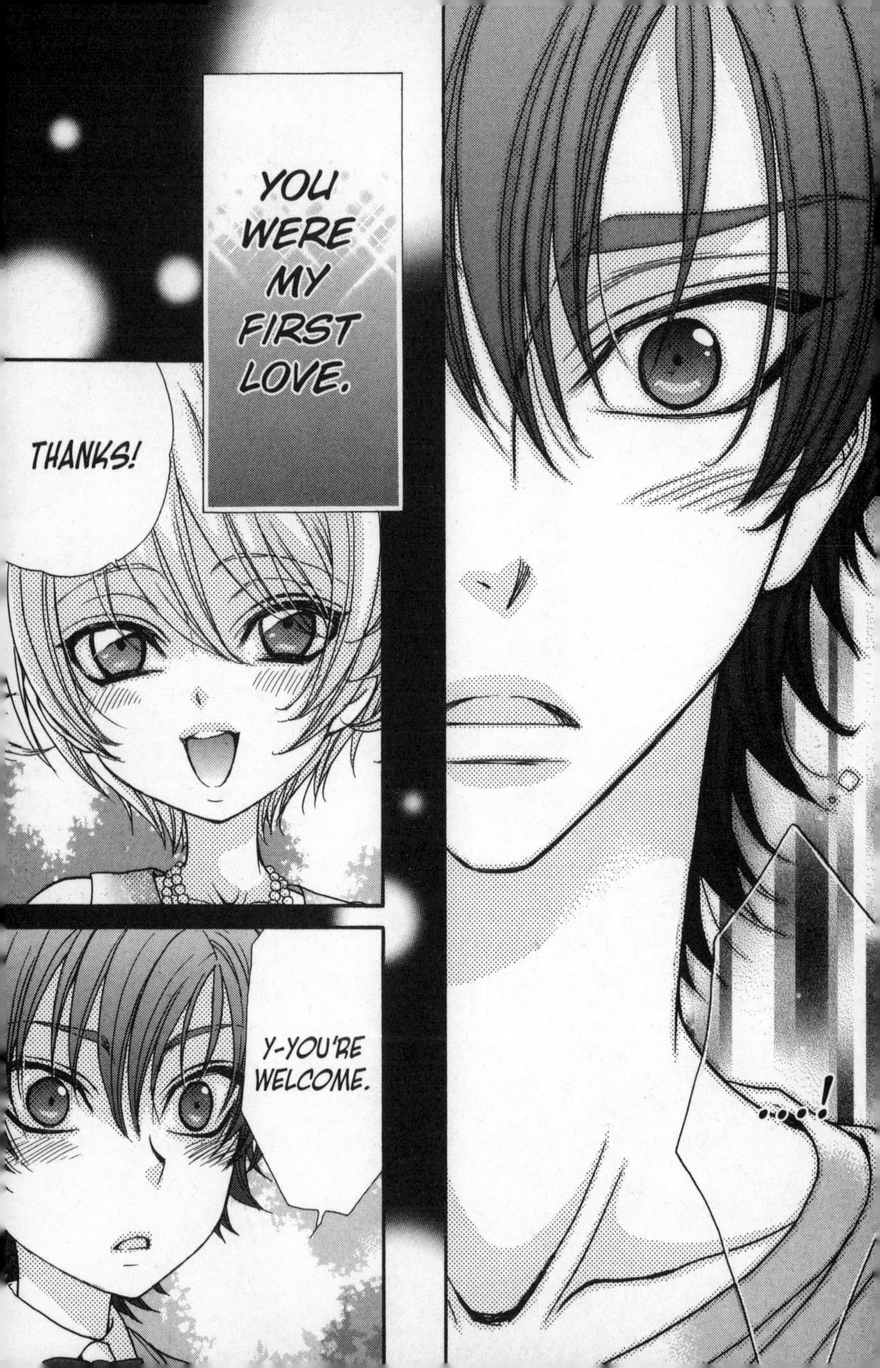
YOU WERE MY FIRST LOVE.
THANKS!
Y-YOU'RE WELCOME.
...!

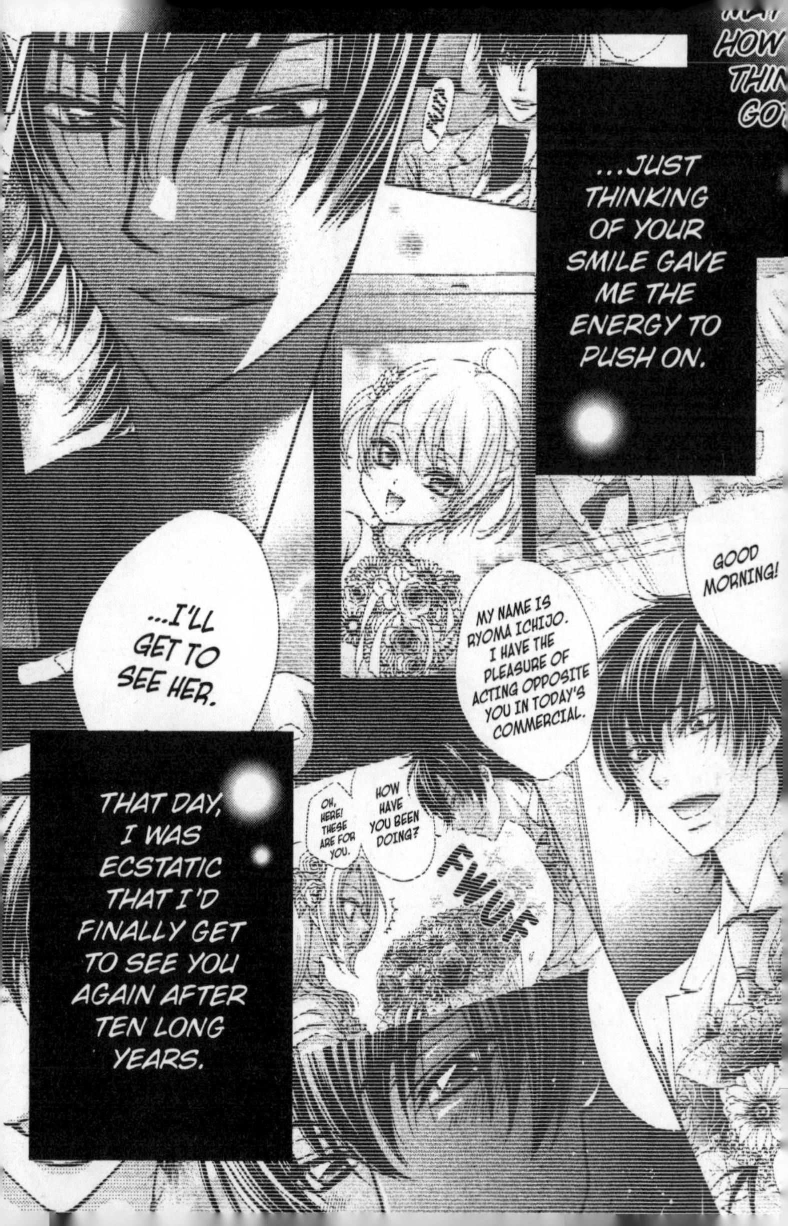
...JUST THINKING OF YOUR SMILE GAVE ME THE ENERGY TO PUSH ON.
...I'LL GET TO SEE HER.
GOOD MORNING!
MY NAME IS RYOMA ICHIJO. I HAVE THE PLEASURE OF ACTING OPPOSITE YOU IN TODAY'S COMMERCIAL.
HOW HAVE YOU BEEN DOING?
OH, HERE! THESE ARE FOR YOU.
FWUF
THAT DAY, I WAS ECSTATIC THAT I'D FINALLY GET TO SEE YOU AGAIN AFTER TEN LONG YEARS.

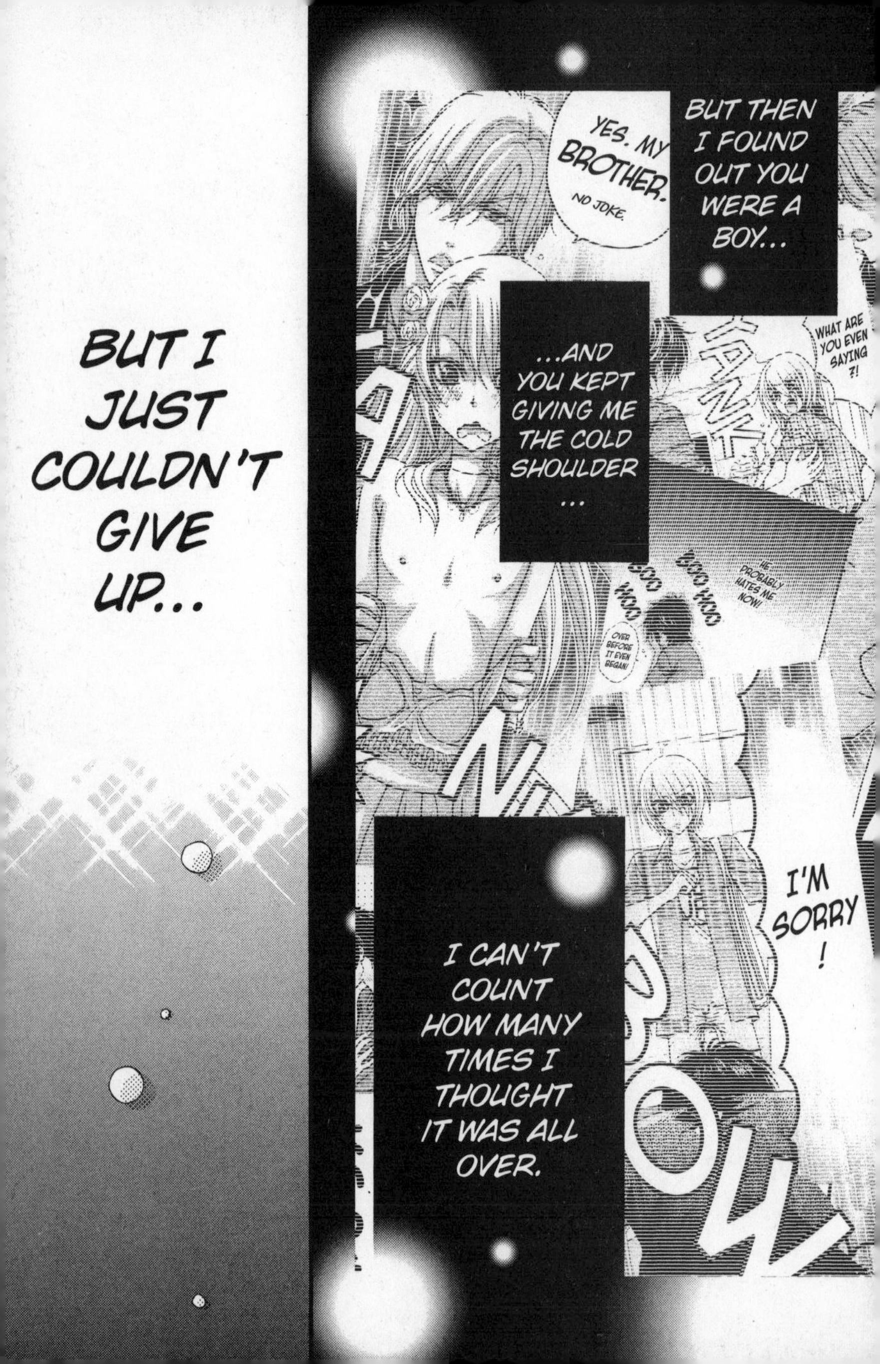
BUT THEN I FOUND OUT YOU WERE A BOY...
YES. MY BROTHER.
NO JOKE.
WHAT ARE YOU EVEN SAYING ?!
...AND YOU KEPT GIVING ME THE COLD SHOULDER ...
BOO HOO
BOO HOO
HE PROBABLY HATES ME NOW!
OVER BEFORE IT EVEN BEGAN!
I'M SORRY !
I CAN'T COUNT HOW MANY TIMES I THOUGHT IT WAS ALL OVER.
BUT I JUST COULDN'T GIVE UP...

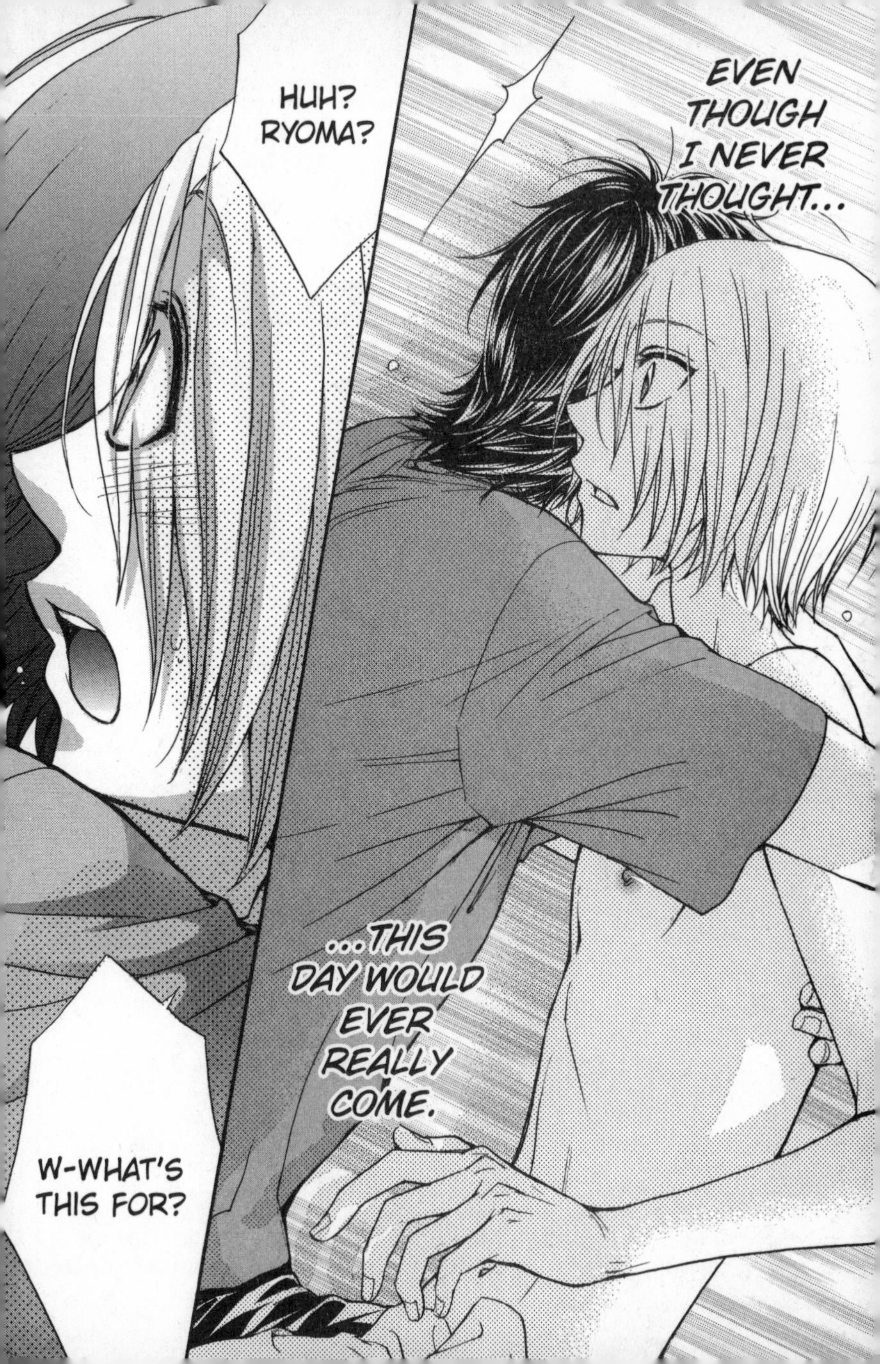
EVEN THOUGH I NEVER THOUGHT...
...THIS DAY WOULD EVER REALLY COME.
HUH? RYOMA?
W-WHAT'S THIS FOR?

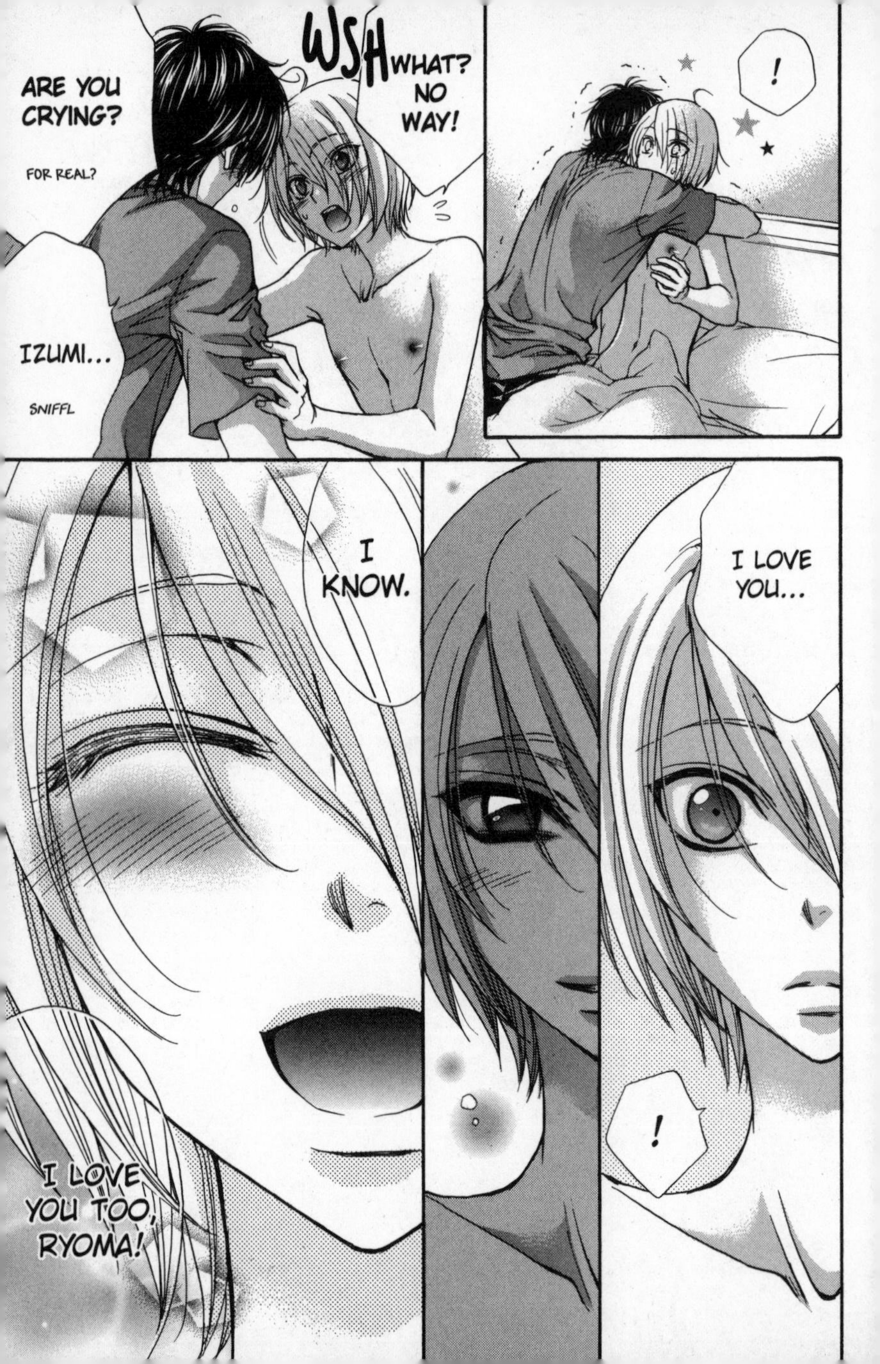
!
WSH
WHAT? NO WAY!
ARE YOU CRYING?
FOR REAL?
IZUMI...
SNIFFL
I LOVE YOU...
!
I KNOW.
I LOVE YOU TOO, RYOMA!

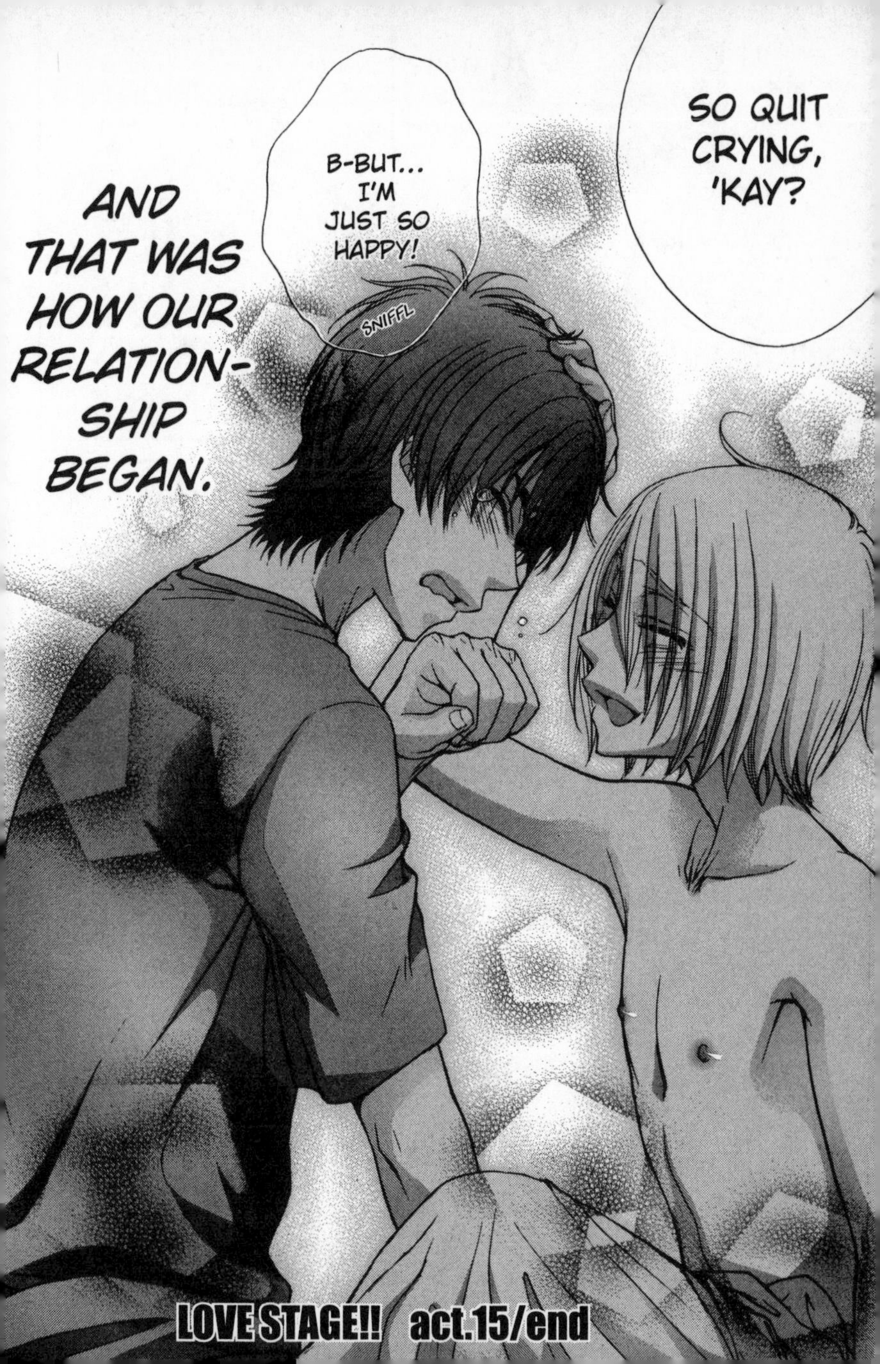
SO QUIT CRYING, 'KAY?
B-BUT... I'M JUST SO HAPPY!
SNIFFL
AND THAT WAS HOW OUR RELATION-SHIP BEGAN.
LOVE STAGE!! act.15/end

LOVE STAGE!!

LOVE STAGE!!

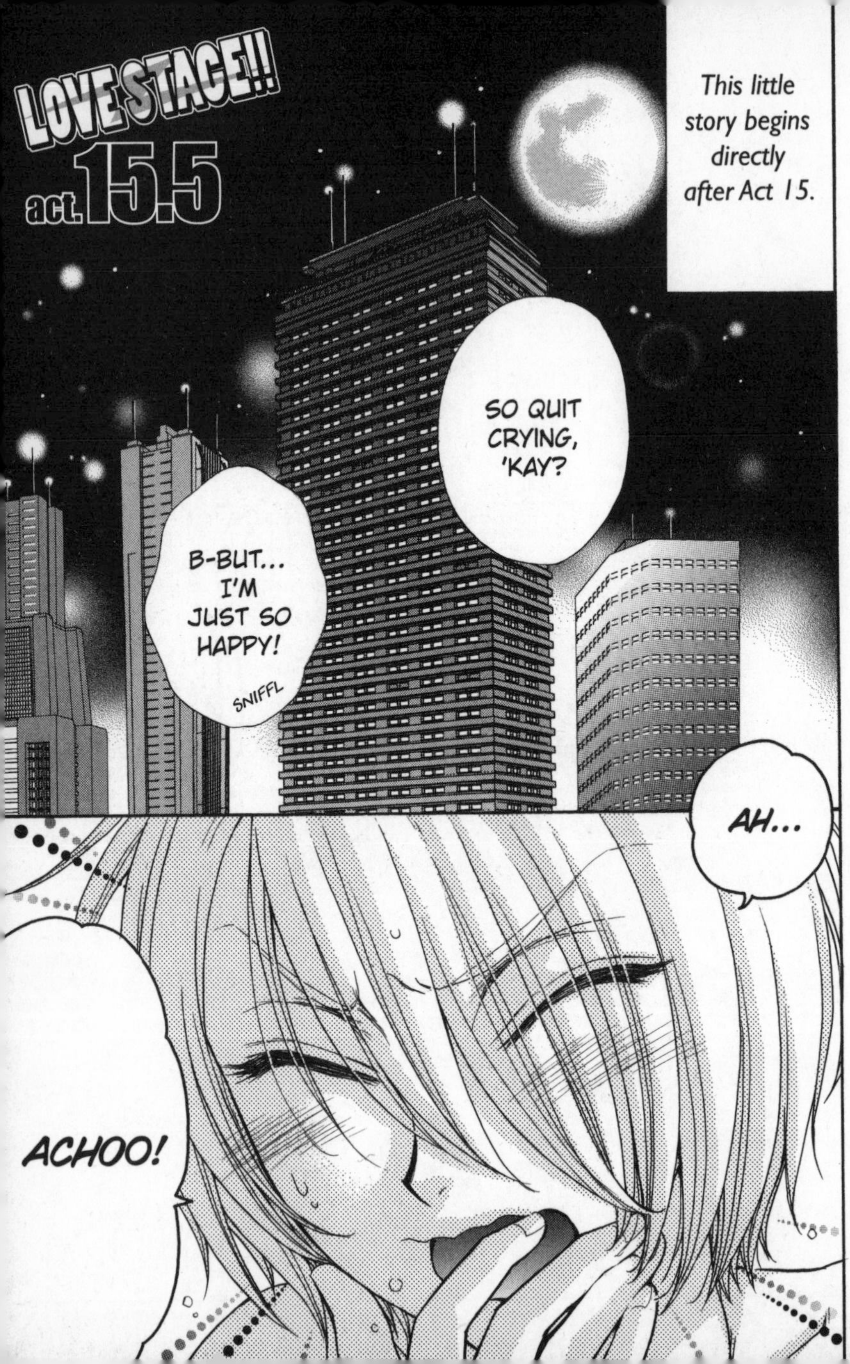
LOVE STAGE!!
act.15.5
This little story begins directly after Act 15.
SO QUIT CRYING, 'KAY?
B-BUT... I'M JUST SO HAPPY!
SNIFFL
AH...
ACHOO!

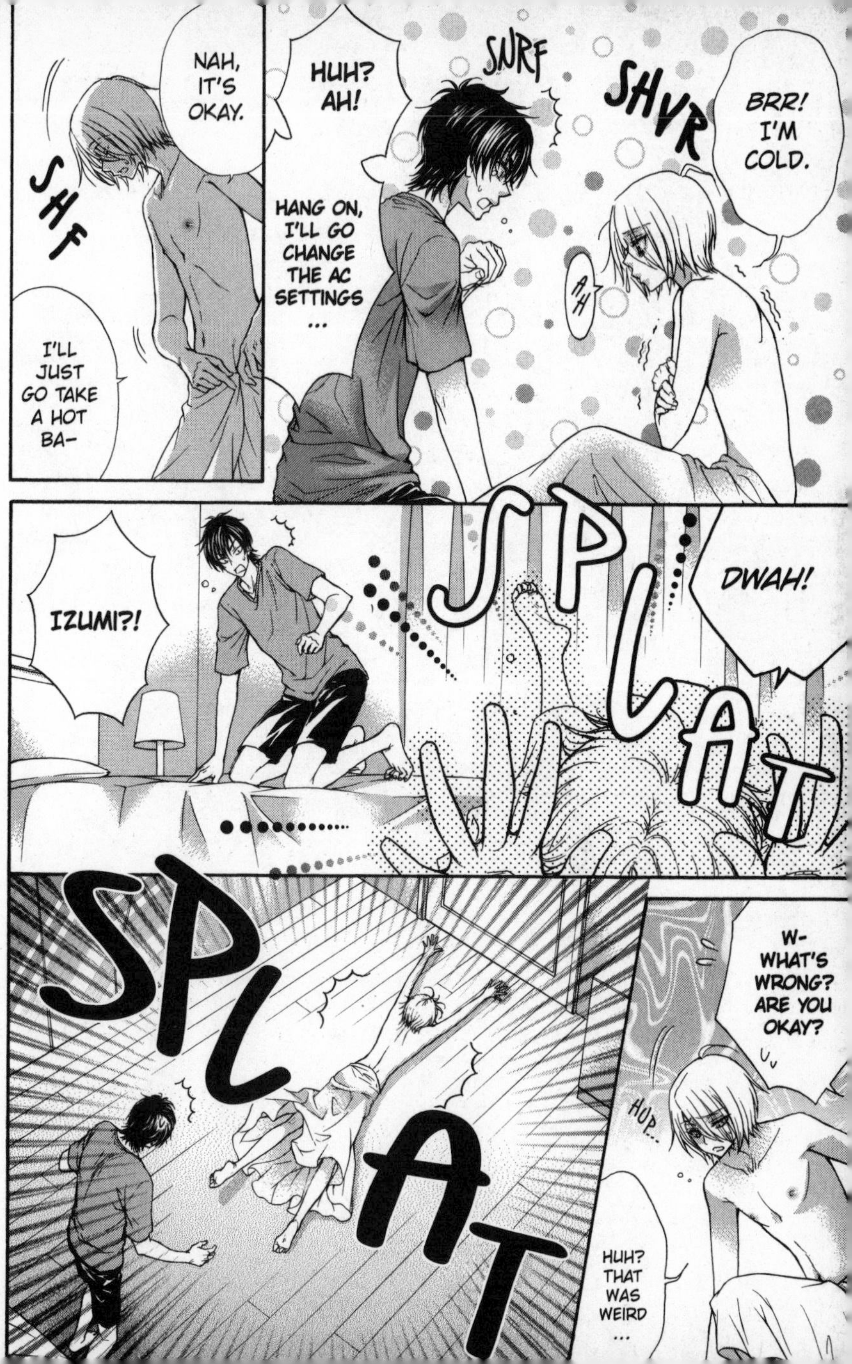
BRR! I'M COLD.
SHVR
SNRF
AH
HUH? AH!
HANG ON, I'LL GO CHANGE THE AC SETTINGS...
NAH, IT'S OKAY.
SHF
I'LL JUST GO TAKE A HOT BA-
DWAH!
SPLAT
IZUMI?!
....
W-WHAT'S WRONG? ARE YOU OKAY?
HUP...
HUH? THAT WAS WEIRD...
SPLAT

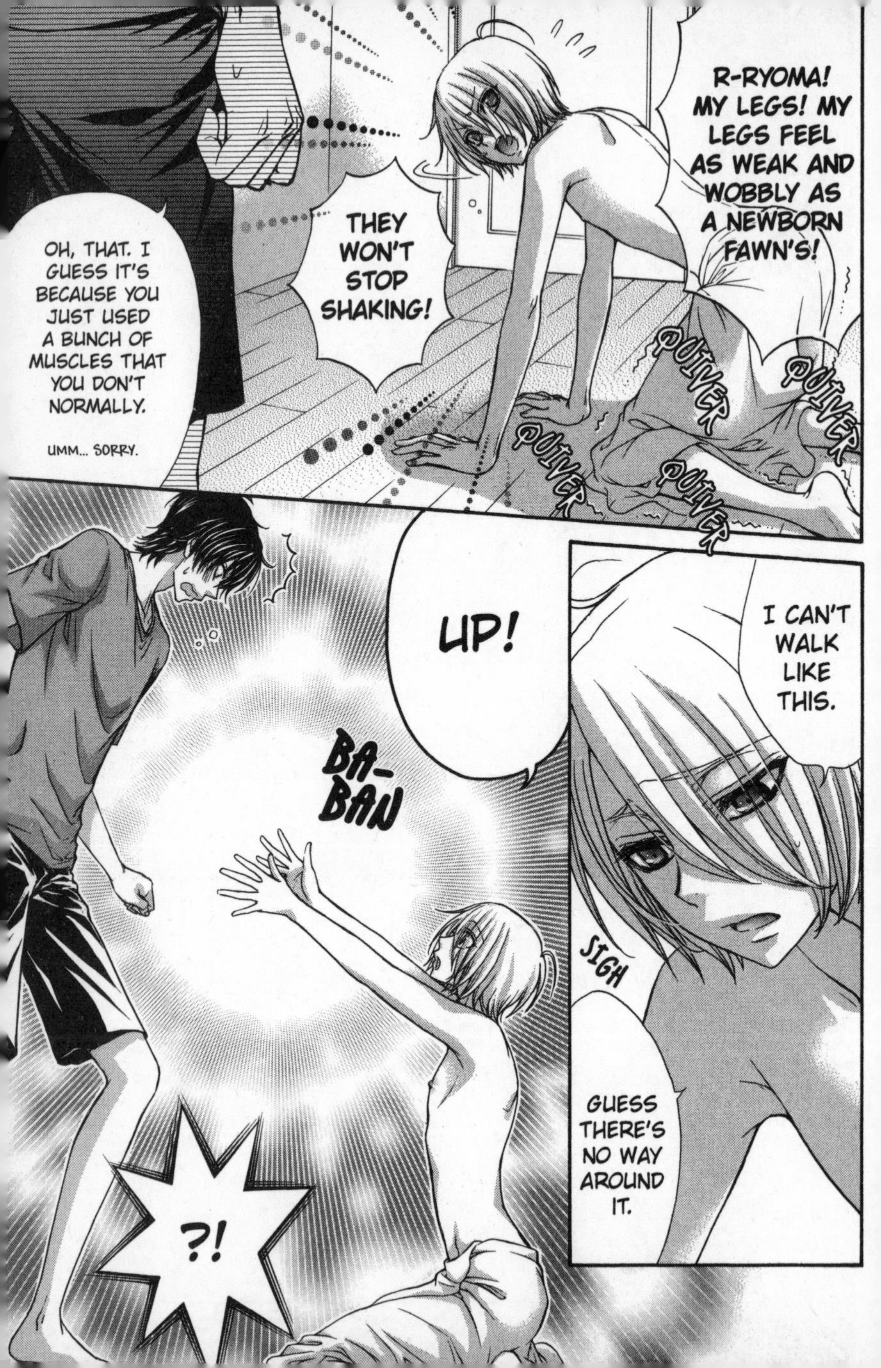
R-RYOMA! MY LEGS! MY LEGS FEEL AS WEAK AND WOBBLY AS A NEWBORN FAWN'S!
QUIVER QUIVER QUIVER QUIVER
THEY WON'T STOP SHAKING!
OH, THAT. I GUESS IT'S BECAUSE YOU JUST USED A BUNCH OF MUSCLES THAT YOU DON'T NORMALLY.
UMM... SORRY.
I CAN'T WALK LIKE THIS.
SIGH
GUESS THERE'S NO WAY AROUND IT.
UP!
BA-BAN
?!

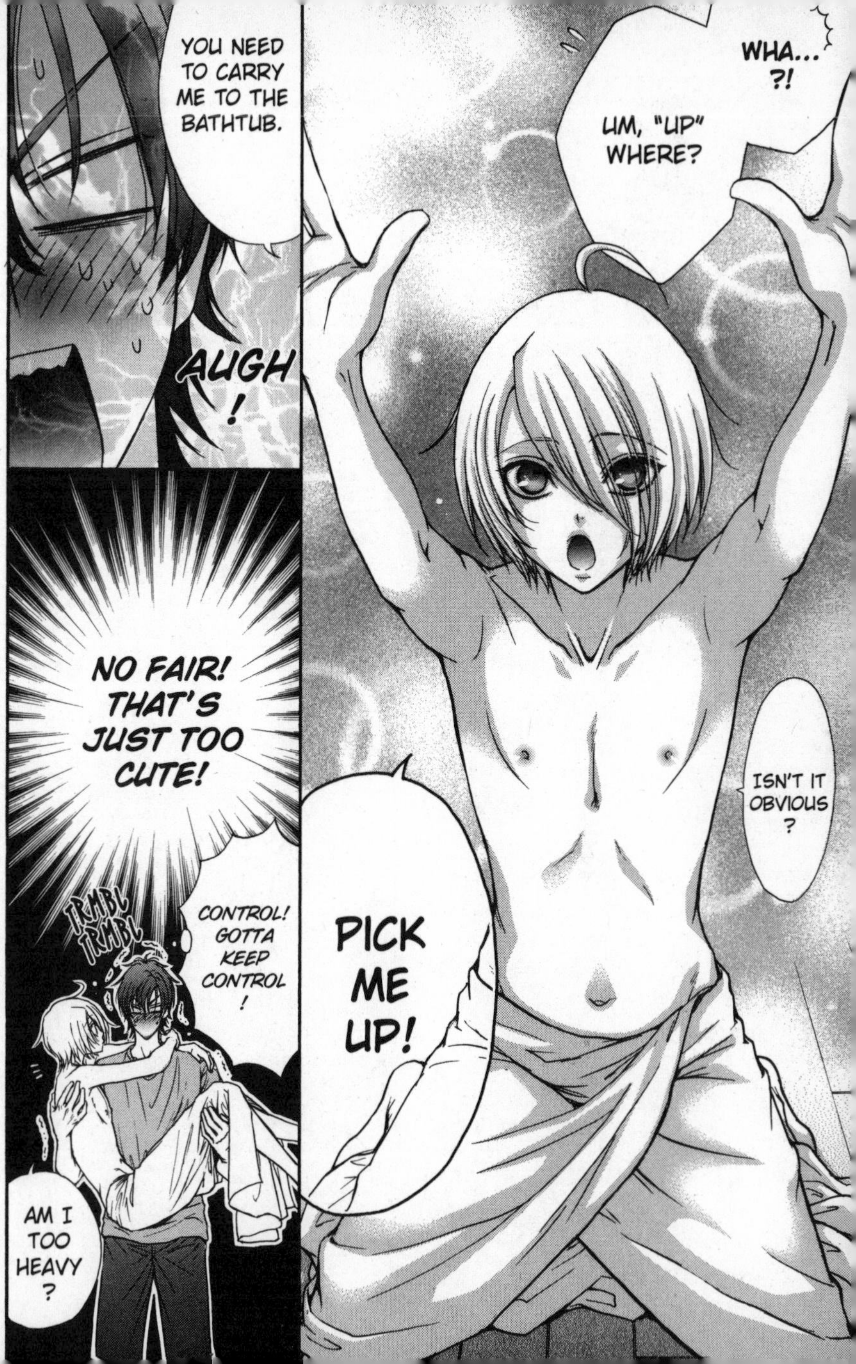
WHA...?!
UM, "UP" WHERE?
ISN'T IT OBVIOUS?
PICK ME UP!
YOU NEED TO CARRY ME TO THE BATHTUB.
AUGH!
NO FAIR! THAT'S JUST TOO CUTE!
TRMBL TRMBL
CONTROL! GOTTA KEEP CONTROL!
AM I TOO HEAVY?

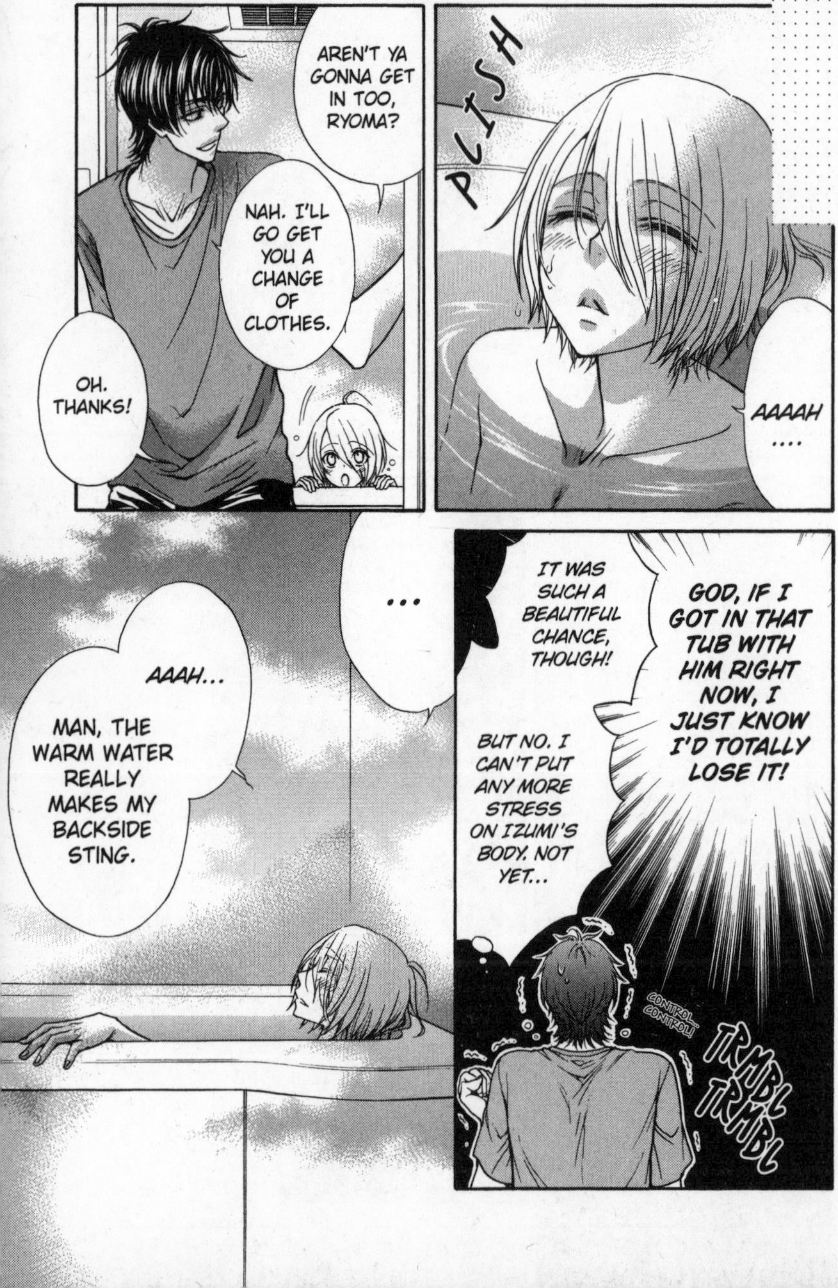
PLISH
AAAAH ....
AREN'T YA GONNA GET IN TOO, RYOMA?
NAH. I'LL GO GET YOU A CHANGE OF CLOTHES.
OH. THANKS!
GOD, IF I GOT IN THAT TUB WITH HIM RIGHT NOW, I JUST KNOW I'D TOTALLY LOSE IT!
IT WAS SUCH A BEAUTIFUL CHANCE, THOUGH!
BUT NO. I CAN'T PUT ANY MORE STRESS ON IZUMI'S BODY. NOT YET...
TRMBL TRMBL
CONTROL... CONTROL!
...
AAAH...
MAN, THE WARM WATER REALLY MAKES MY BACKSIDE STING.

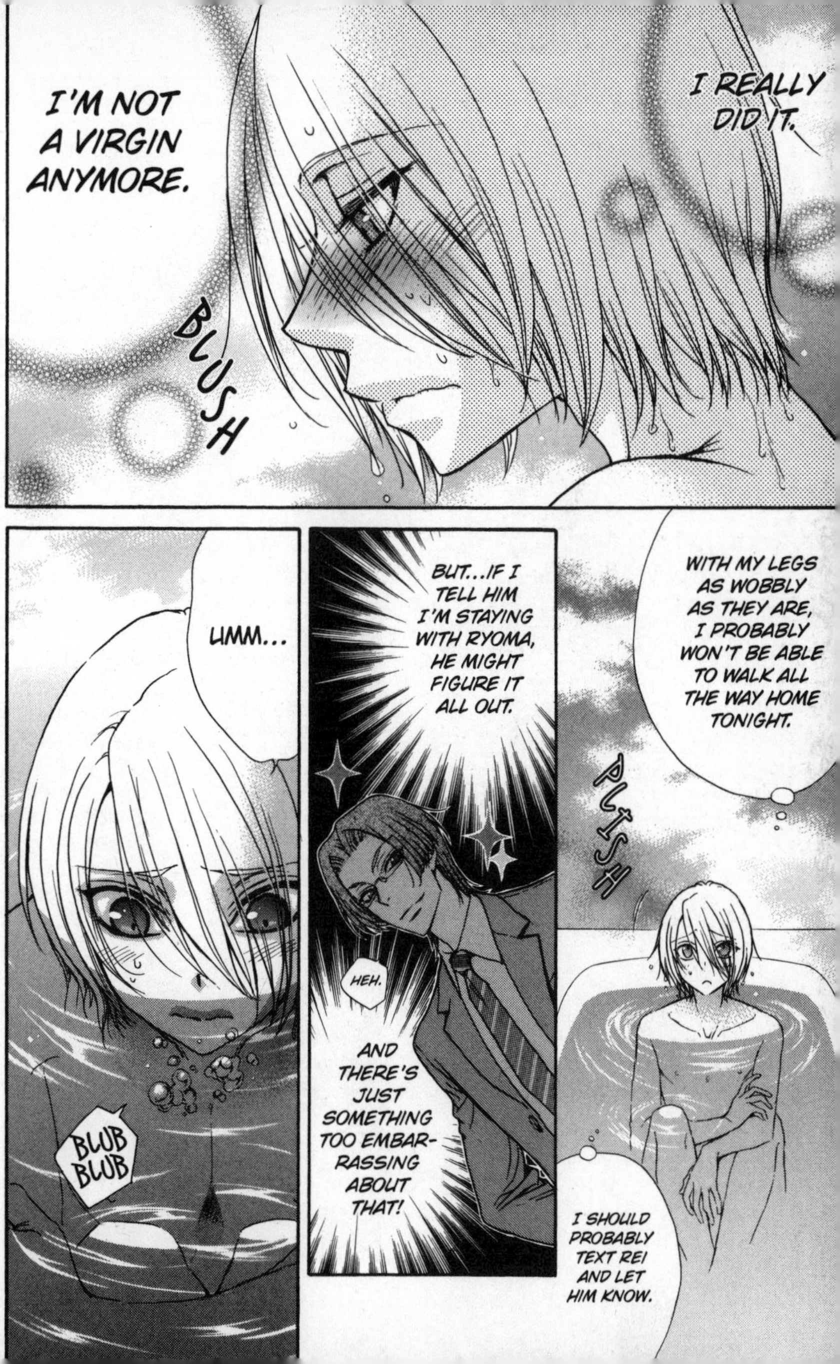
I REALLY DID IT.
I'M NOT A VIRGIN ANYMORE.
BLUSH
WITH MY LEGS AS WOBBLY AS THEY ARE, I PROBABLY WON'T BE ABLE TO WALK ALL THE WAY HOME TONIGHT.
PLISH
I SHOULD PROBABLY TEXT REI AND LET HIM KNOW.
BUT...IF I TELL HIM I'M STAYING WITH RYOMA, HE MIGHT FIGURE IT ALL OUT.
HEH.
AND THERE'S JUST SOMETHING TOO EMBAR-RASSING ABOUT THAT!
UMM...
BLUB BLUB

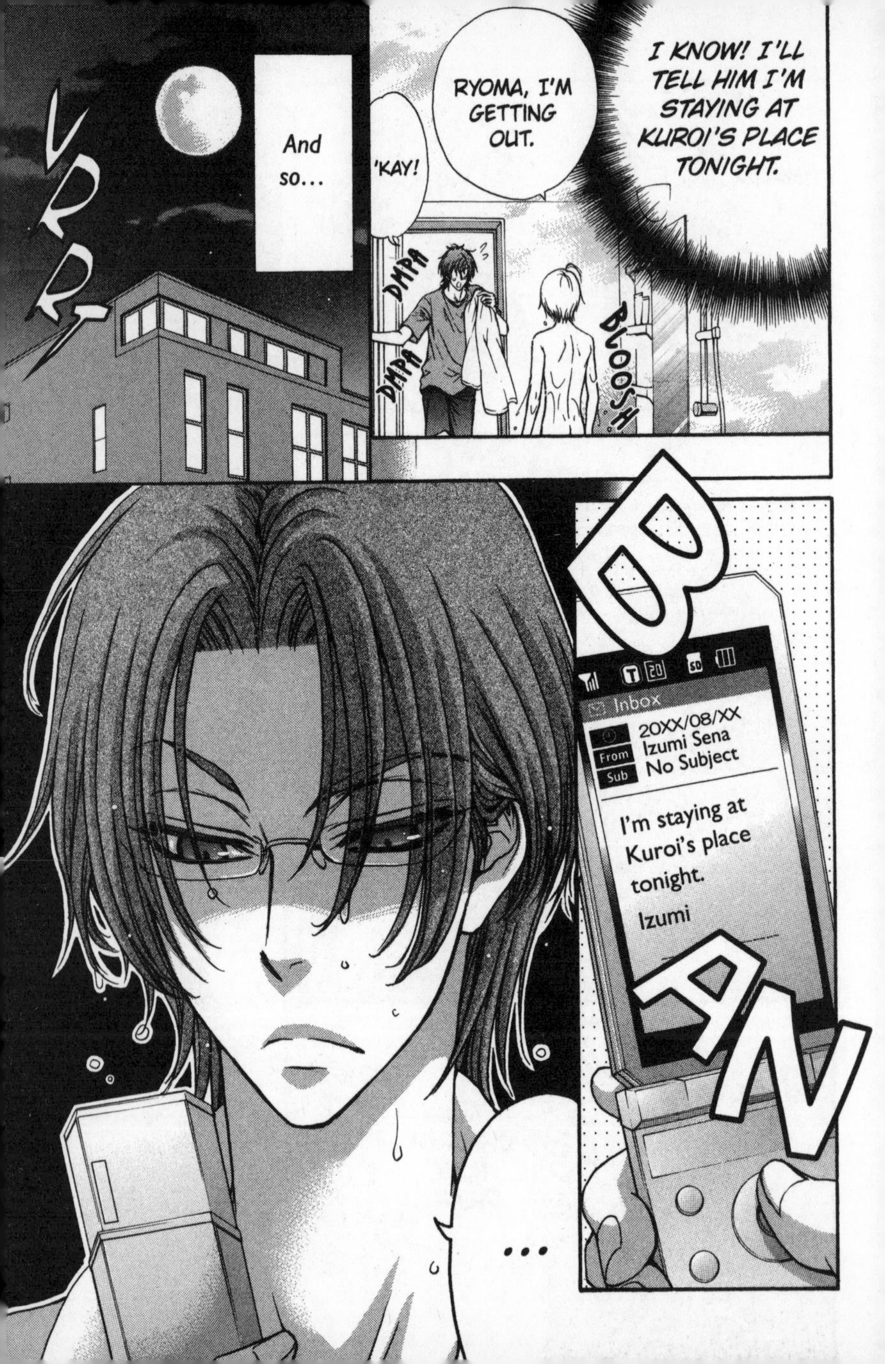
I KNOW! I'LL TELL HIM I'M STAYING AT KUROI'S PLACE TONIGHT.
RYOMA, I'M GETTING OUT.
'KAY!
DMPA
DMPA
BLOOSH
And so...
VRR
BAN
Inbox
20XX/08/XX
Izumi Sena
From
No Subject
Sub
I'm staying at Kuroi's place tonight.
Izumi
...

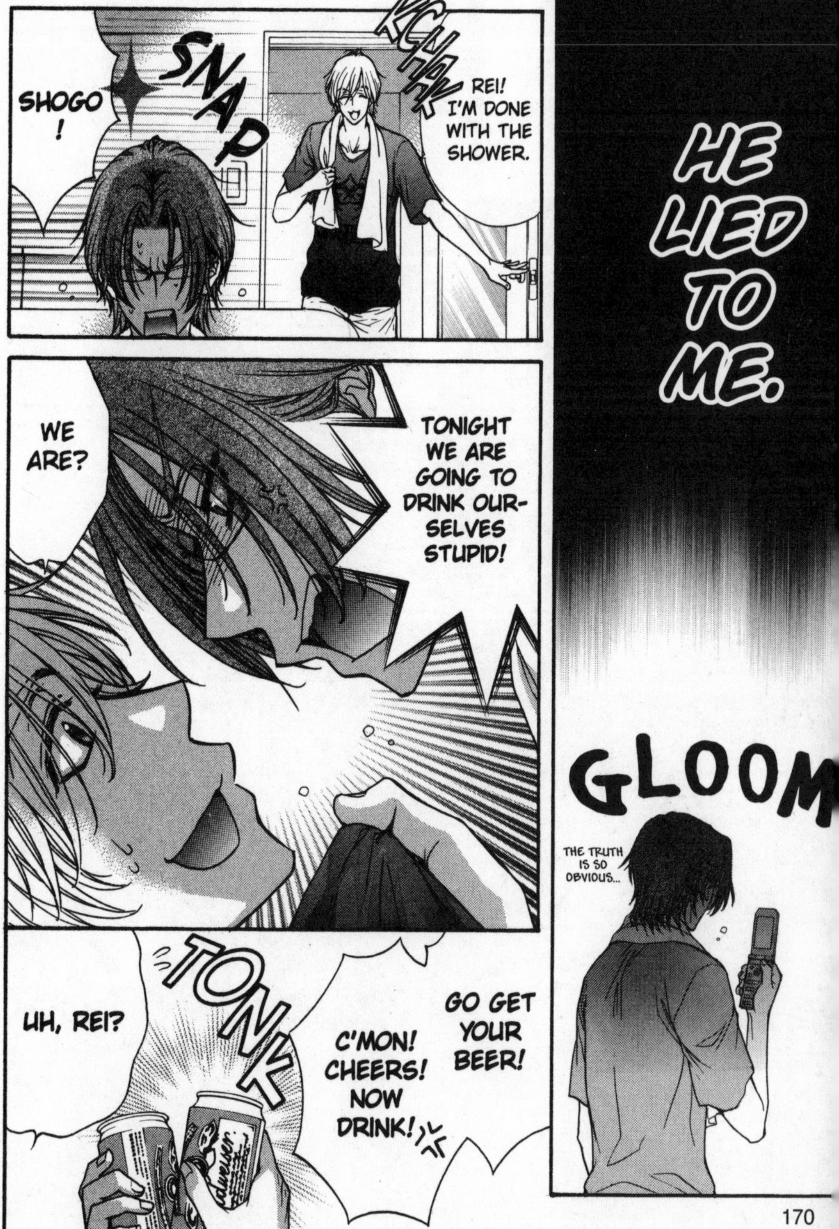
HE LIED TO ME.
GLOOM
THE TRUTH IS SO OBVIOUS...
KCHAK
REI! I'M DONE WITH THE SHOWER.
SNAP
SHOGO!
TONIGHT WE ARE GOING TO DRINK OUR-SELVES STUPID!
WE ARE?
GO GET YOUR BEER!
C'MON! CHEERS! NOW DRINK!
TONK
UH, REI?

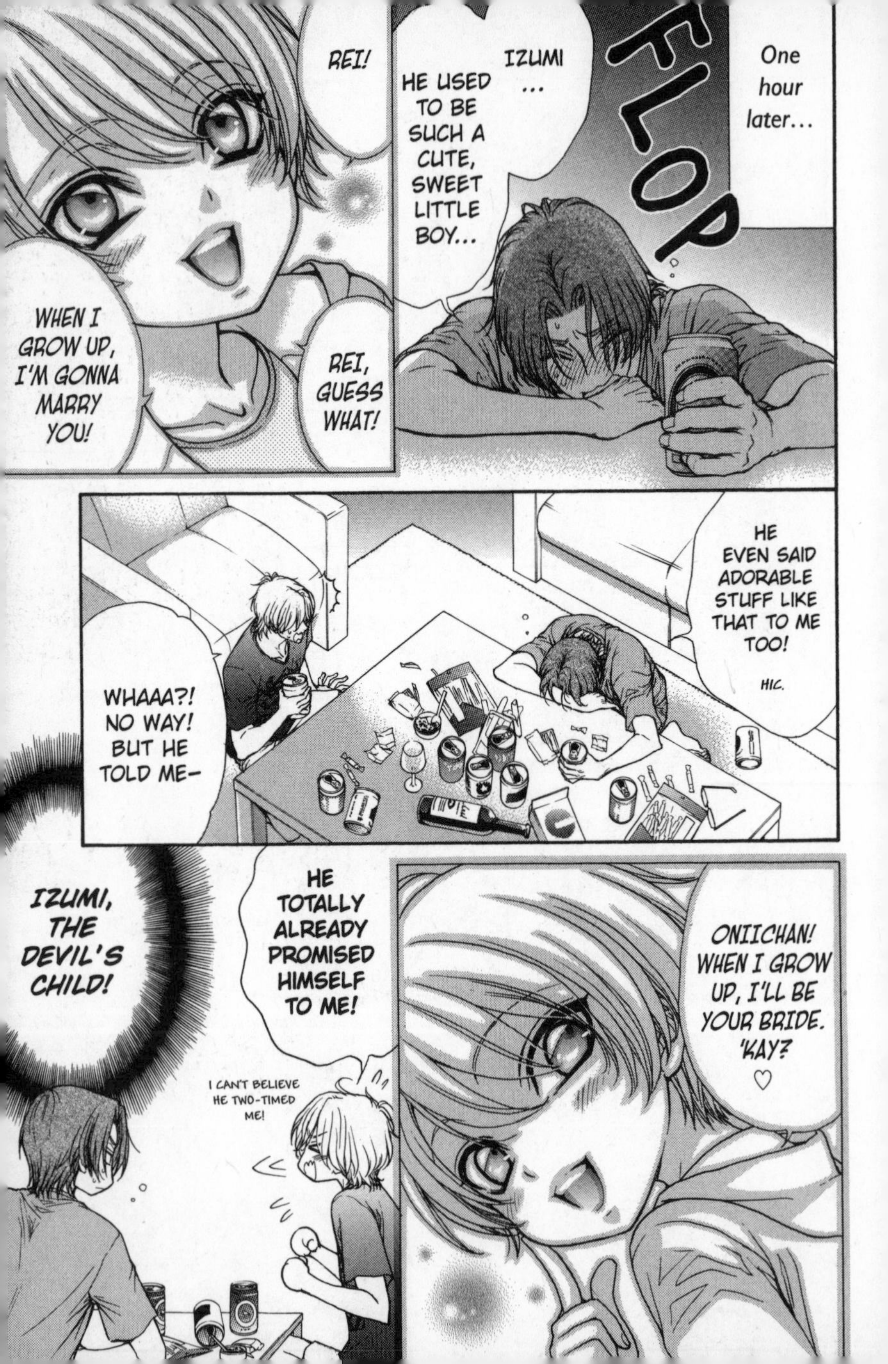
One hour later…
FLOP
IZUMI …
HE USED TO BE SUCH A CUTE, SWEET LITTLE BOY…
REI!
REI, GUESS WHAT!
WHEN I GROW UP, I'M GONNA MARRY YOU!
HE EVEN SAID ADORABLE STUFF LIKE THAT TO ME TOO!
HIC.
WHAAA?! NO WAY! BUT HE TOLD ME–
ONIICHAN! WHEN I GROW UP, I'LL BE YOUR BRIDE. 'KAY? ♡
HE TOTALLY ALREADY PROMISED HIMSELF TO ME!
I CAN'T BELIEVE HE TWO-TIMED ME!
IZUMI, THE DEVIL'S CHILD!

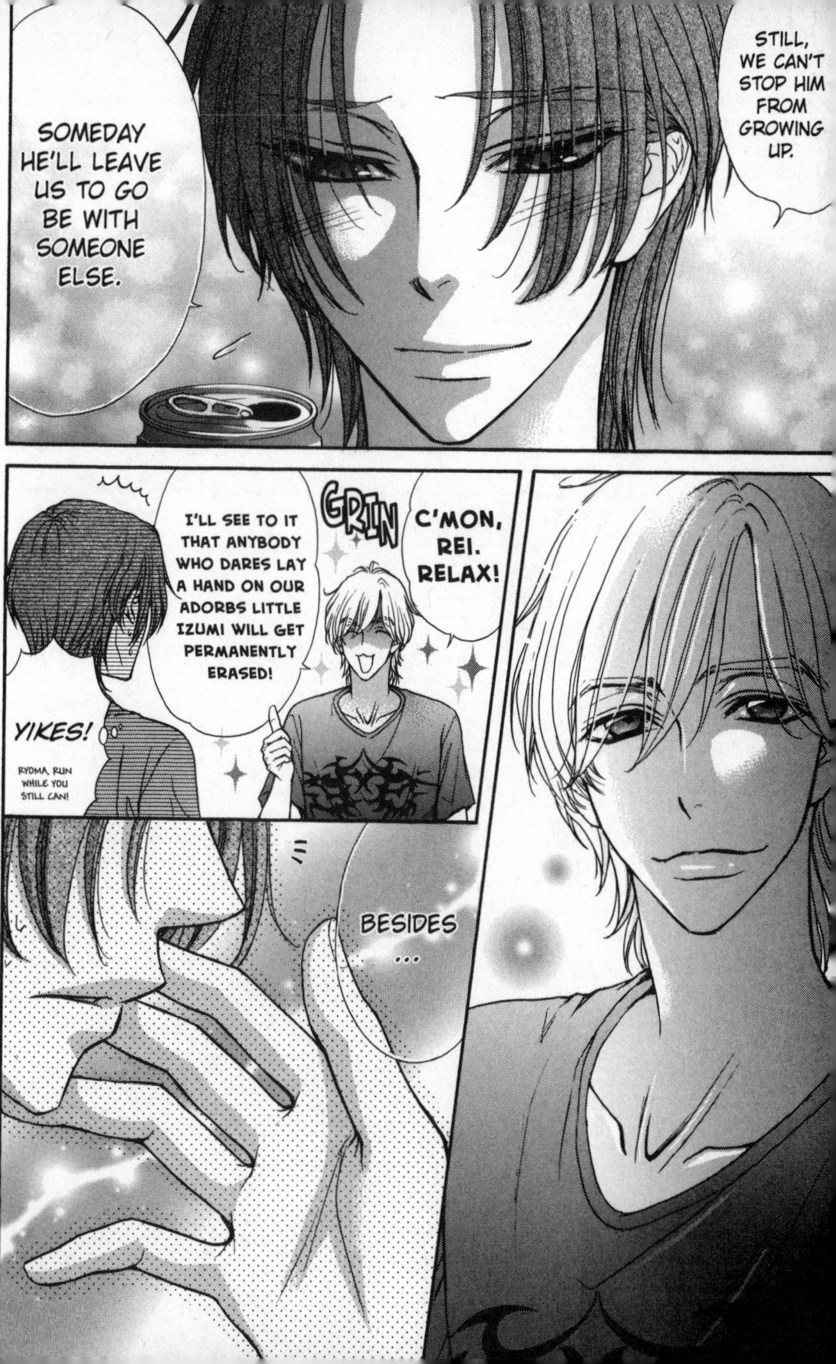

STILL, WE CAN'T STOP HIM FROM GROWING UP.
SOMEDAY HE'LL LEAVE US TO GO BE WITH SOMEONE ELSE.
C'MON, REI. RELAX!
GRIN
I'LL SEE TO IT THAT ANYBODY WHO DARES LAY A HAND ON OUR ADORBS LITTLE IZUMI WILL GET PERMANENTLY ERASED!
YIKES!
RYOMA, RUN WHILE YOU STILL CAN!
BESIDES ...

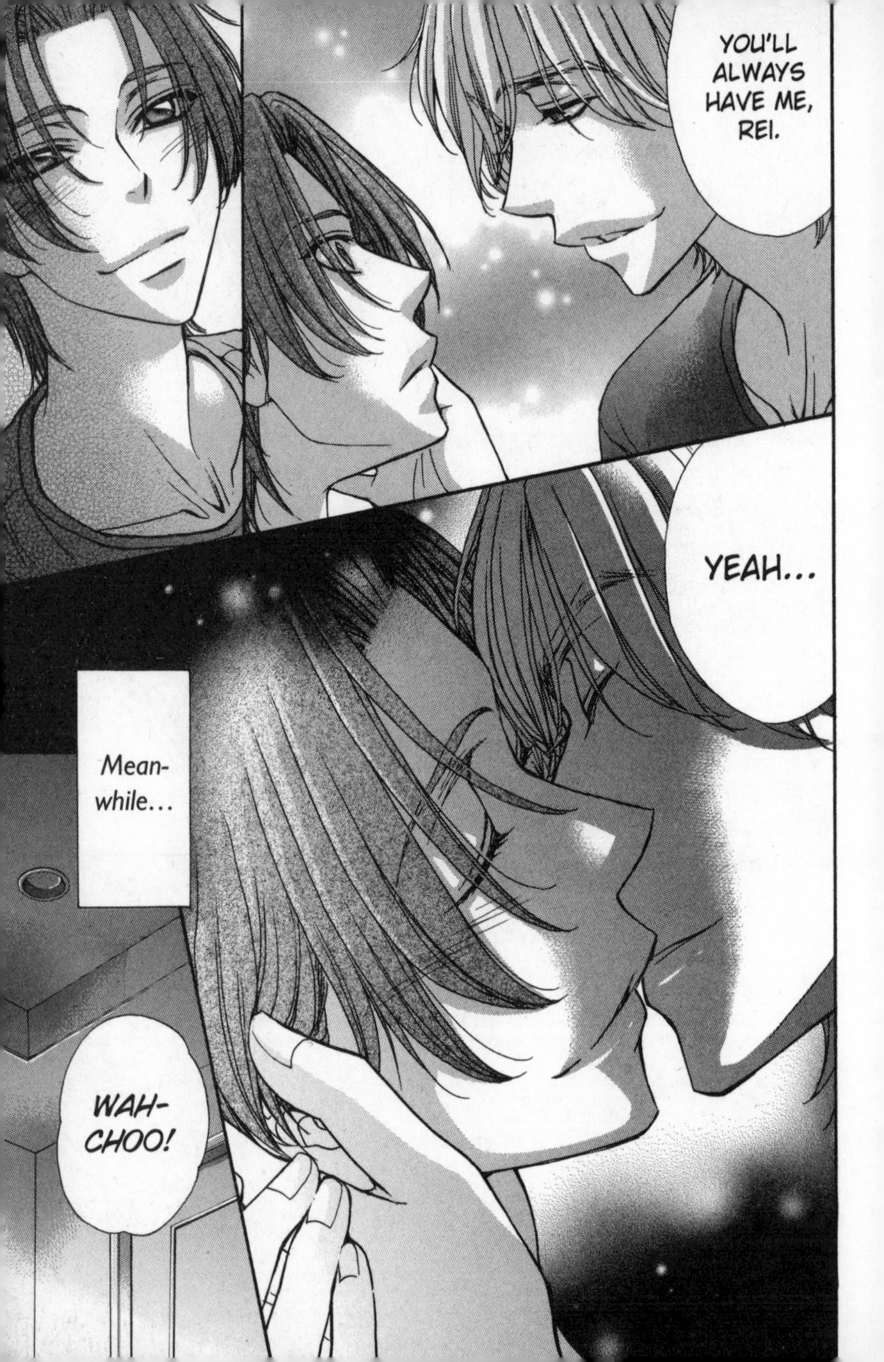
YOU'LL ALWAYS HAVE ME, REI.
YEAH...
Mean-while...
WAH-CHOO!

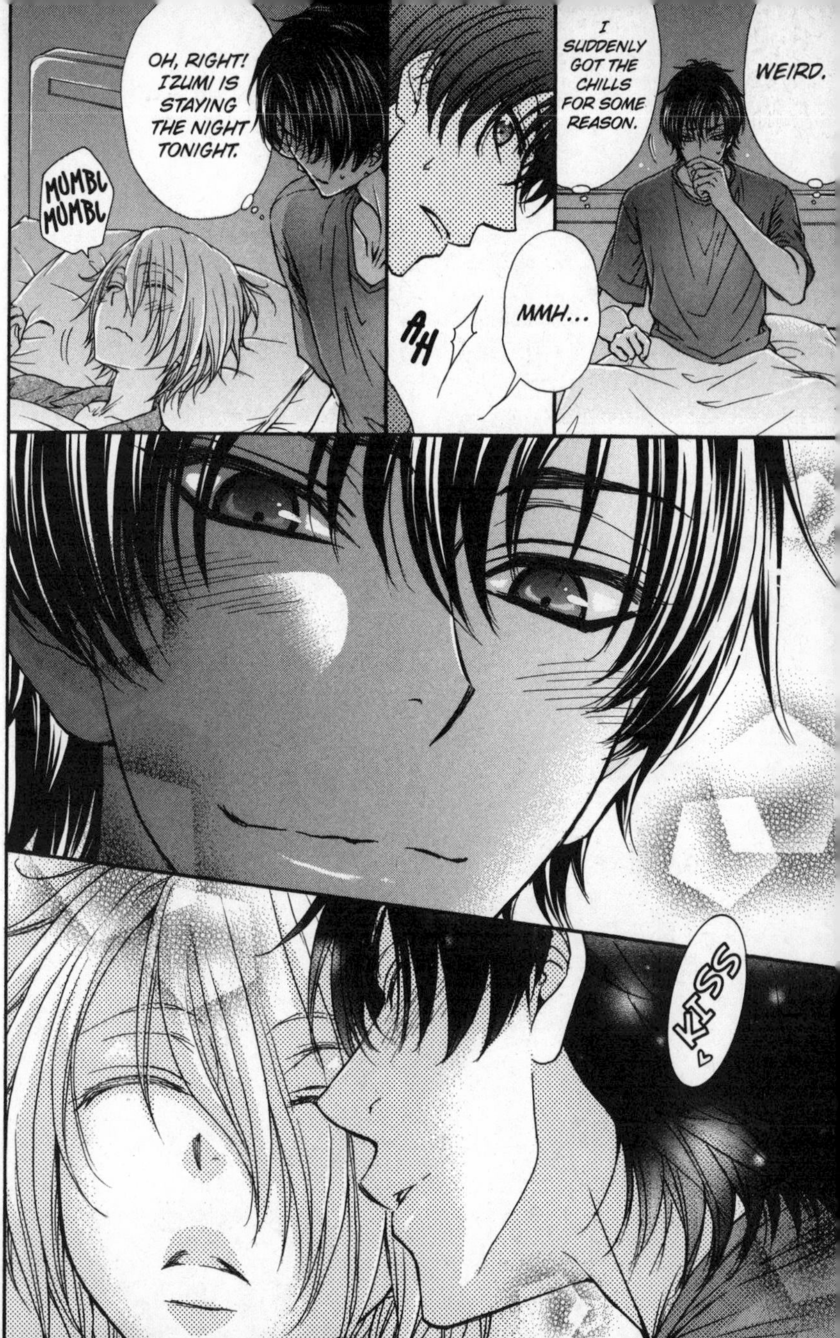
WEIRD.
I SUDDENLY GOT THE CHILLS FOR SOME REASON.
MMH...
AH
OH, RIGHT! IZUMI IS STAYING THE NIGHT TONIGHT.
MUMBL MUMBL
KISS

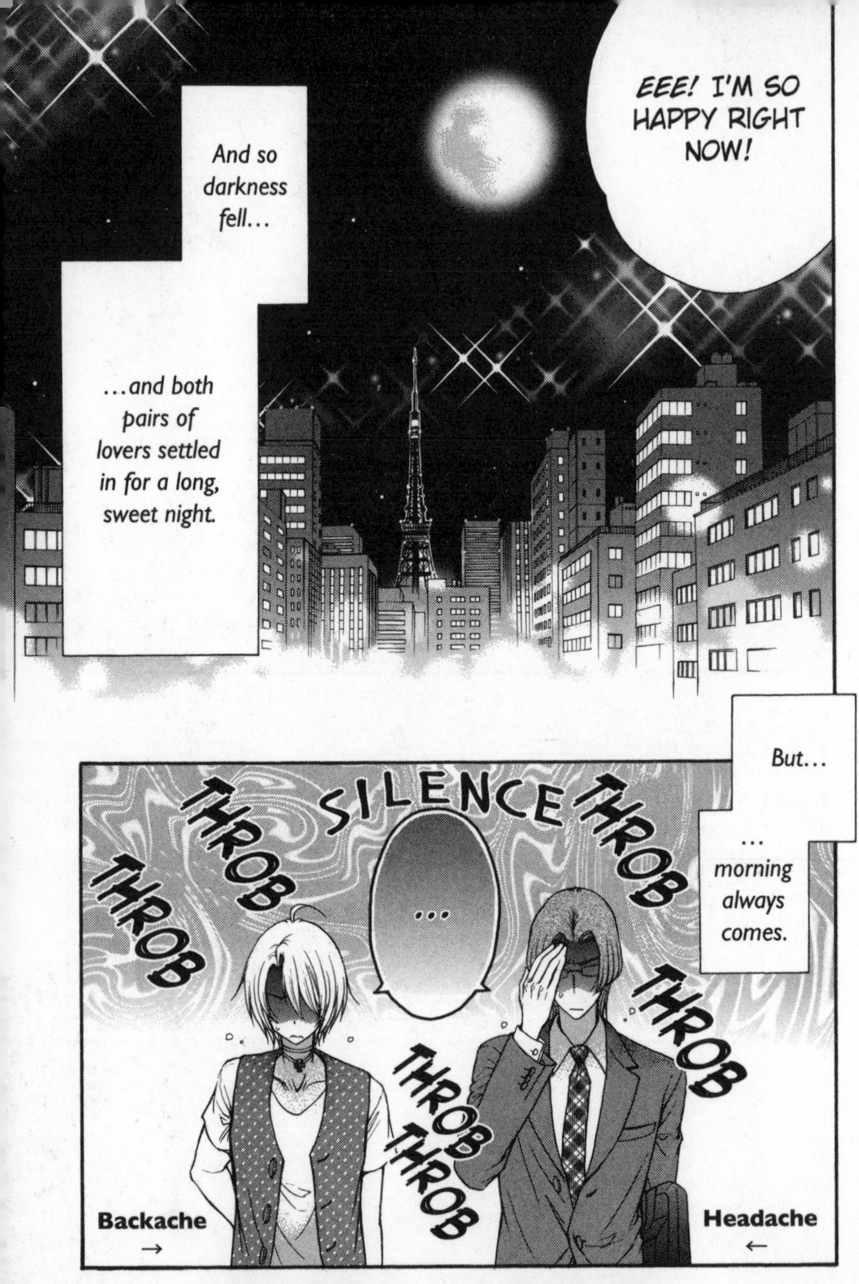
EEE! I'M SO HAPPY RIGHT NOW!
And so darkness fell...
...and both pairs of lovers settled in for a long, sweet night.
But...
...morning always comes.
THROB THROB
SILENCE
...
THROB THROB
THROB THROB
THROB THROB
Headache ←
Backache →

LOVE STAGE!! act.15.5/end

AFTERWORD

Hi! This is script writer Eiki Eiki! It's Volume 3, and Ryoma and Izumi have finally gotten together! It feels like this was the final chapter, but *Love Stage!!* will continue on for some time yet. I hope you will all stick around and keep reading!

For those of you surprised at Shogo and Rei suddenly acting all lovey-dovey in the bonus chapter, please see the *Back Stage!!* novels published by *Ruby Bunko* for all the juicy details. Thank you to everyone who helped us publish this volume and to everyone who has been so kind as to read it. See you next time! ♡

-Eiki Eiki 影木栄貴 LOVExxx

Hello! This is artist Taishi Zaou. Love Stage!! has finally reached Volume 3. Because of the release schedule of the anthology serializing it, we can only put out one volume a year, so I'm sure we must be making all of you wait. Sorry! By the way, the longer I work on something the more the character designs seem to change, don't they? Especially Ryoma. His face gets longer, his eyebrows get thicker... I'm trying to fix things as we go along, but if you look at him and think "has he changed?" I hope you will just smile and let it slide...please?

-Zaou Taishi 蔵王大志 PEACExxx

Eiki Eiki is the creator of numerous yaoi and shojo manga. Her previous English-language releases include *Train★Train*, *Millennium Prime Minister*, and *The Art of Loving*. Born on December 6th, she is a Sagittarius with an A blood type.

Taishi Zaou's works have been published in English, French, and German. Her previous English-language releases include *Green Light*, *Fevered Kiss*, *Living For Tomorrow*, *Mysterious Love*, and *Electric Hands*. She was born a Capricorn on January 10th and has an O blood type.

About the Creators

Their hit series *Love Stage!!* has been adapted into a drama CD and a television anime series. Eiki Eiki and Taishi Zaou also publish *doujinshi* (independent comics) under the name "Kozouya." You can find out more about them at their website, http://www.kozouya.com/.

Love Stage!!
Volume 3
SuBLime Manga Edition

Story by **Eiki Eiki**
Art by **Taishi Zaou**

Translation—**Adrienne Beck**
Touch-up Art and Lettering—**Wally**
Cover and Graphic Design—**Yukiko Whitley**
Editor—**Jennifer LeBlanc**

LOVE STAGE!! Volume 3
©Eiki EIKI 2013
©Taishi ZAOU 2013
Edited by KADOKAWA SHOTEN
First published in Japan in 2013
by KADOKAWA CORPORATION, Tokyo.
English translation rights arranged
with KADOKAWA CORPORATION, Tokyo.

ASUKA COMICS CL D X

Printed in the U.S.A.

Published by SuBLime Manga
P.O. Box 77010
San Francisco, CA 94107

10 9 8 7 6 5 4 3 2
First printing, September 2015
Second printing, January 2016

SUBLIME
www.SuBLimeManga.com